P9-DVT-255

TO

COSTA RICA

By
Karl Kahler

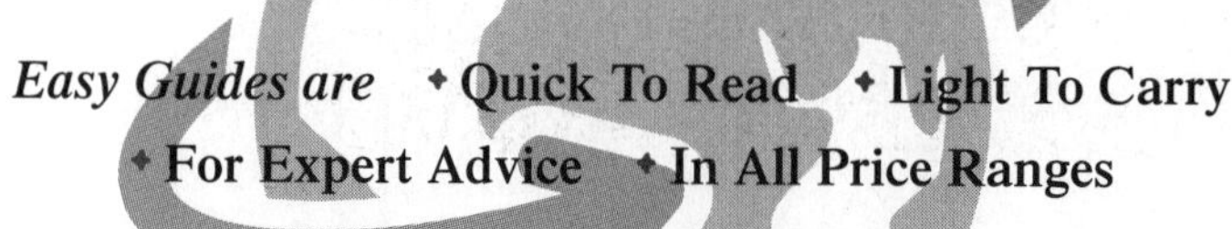

Easy Guides are • Quick To Read • Light To Carry
• For Expert Advice • In All Price Ranges

FrommerMedia LLC

CALGARY PUBLIC LIBRARY
NOV - 2016

Published by
FROMMER MEDIA LLC

Copyright © 2017 by Frommer Media LLC. All rights reserved. No part of this publication may be reproduced, stored in a retrieval system, or transmitted in any form or by any means, electronic, mechanical, photocopying, recording, scanning or otherwise, except as permitted under Sections 107 or 108 of the 1976 United States Copyright Act, without the prior written permission of the Publisher. Requests to the Publisher for permission should be addressed to customer_service@FrommerMedia.com.

Frommer's is a registered trademark of Arthur Frommer. Frommer Media LLC is not associated with any product or vendor mentioned in this book.

ISBN 978-1-62887-262-0 (paper), 978-1-62887-263-7 (e-book)

Editorial Director: Pauline Frommer
Developmental Editor: Shelley Bance
Production Editor: Lynn Northrup
Cartographer: Roberta Stockwell
Indexer: Maro Riofrancos

For information on our other products or services, see www.frommers.com.

Frommer Media LLC also publishes its books in a variety of electronic formats. Some content that appears in print may not be available in electronic formats.

Manufactured in the United States of America

5 4 3 2 1

FROMMER'S STAR RATINGS SYSTEM

Every hotel, restaurant and attraction listed in this guide has been ranked for quality and value. Here's what the stars mean:

★ Recommended
★★ Highly Recommended
★★★ A must! Don't miss!

AN IMPORTANT NOTE

The world is a dynamic place. Hotels change ownership, restaurants hike their prices, museums alter their opening hours, and buses and trains change their routings. And all of this can occur in the several months after our authors have visited, inspected, and written about these hotels, restaurants, museums, and transportation services. Though we have made valiant efforts to keep all our information fresh and up-to-date, some few changes can inevitably occur in the periods before a revised edition of this guidebook is published. So please bear with us if a tiny number of the details in this book have changed. Please also note that we have no responsibility or liability for any inaccuracy or errors or omissions, or for inconvenience, loss, damage, or expenses suffered by anyone as a result of assertions in this guide.

CONTENTS

ABOUT THE AUTHOR

Karl Kahler was born in Arkansas and grew up in California, Venezuela, Canada, Mexico, Alaska, and Bolivia with globe-trotting parents who worked in public and private schools. He has been visiting Costa Rica since 1994 and is currently the travel editor of the *Tico Times*. An honors graduate of the University of Southern California in history and journalism, he worked for the San Jose Mercury News in California for 25 years, starting as a copy editor and leaving as national editor. He has two grown sons, a lawyer and an actor.

Acknowledgments:

I am greatly indebted to Eliot Greenspan, the previous author of this book, for the rock-solid infrastructure he left me to build upon. His research, writing, and experience in Costa Rica are unparalleled, and they pervade every page.

ABOUT THE FROMMER'S TRAVEL GUIDES

For most of the past 50 years, Frommer's has been the leading series of travel guides in North America, accounting for as many as 24 percent of all guidebooks sold. I think I know why.

Though we hope our books are entertaining, we nevertheless deal with travel in a serious fashion. Our guidebooks have never looked on such journeys as a mere recreation, but as a far more important human function, a time of learning and introspection, an essential part of a civilized life. We stress the culture, lifestyle, history, and beliefs of the destinations we cover, and urge our readers to seek out people and new ideas as the chief rewards of travel.

We have never shied from controversy. We have, from the beginning, encouraged our authors to be intensely judgmental, critical—both pro and con—in their comments, and wholly independent. Our only clients are our readers, and we have triggered the ire of countless prominent sorts, from a tourist newspaper we called "practically worthless" (it unsuccessfully sued us) to the many rip-offs we've condemned.

And because we believe that travel should be available to everyone regardless of their incomes, we have always been cost-conscious at every level of expenditure. Though we have broadened our recommendations beyond the budget category, we insist that every lodging we include be sensibly priced. We use every form of media to assist our readers, and are particularly proud of our feisty daily website, the award-winning Frommers.com.

I have high hopes for the future of Frommer's. May these guidebooks, in all the years ahead, continue to reflect the joy of travel and the freedom that travel represents. May they always pursue a cost-conscious path, so that people of all incomes can enjoy the rewards of travel. And may they create, for both the traveler and the persons among whom we travel, a community of friends, where all human beings live in harmony and peace.

Arthur Frommer

THE BEST OF COSTA RICA

1

Costa Rica is one of the hottest vacation and adventure-travel destinations in Latin America, and for good reason. The country is rich in natural wonders and biodiversity, where you can still find yourself far from the madding crowds. Costa Rica boasts a wealth of unsullied beaches that stretch for miles, jungle rivers for rafting and kayaking, and spectacular cloud forests and rainforests with ample opportunities for bird-watching, wildlife viewing, and hiking. In addition to the trademark eco- and adventure-tourism offerings, you will find fetching resorts, plush spas, and spectacular boutique hotels and lodges. This chapter provides an overview of the highlights so you can plan your own adventure.

COSTA RICA'S best AUTHENTIC EXPERIENCES

- **Taking a Night Tour in a Tropical Forest:** Most Neotropical forest dwellers are nocturnal, so nighttime tours are offered at rainforest and cloud forest destinations throughout the country. Some of the better spots for night tours are **Monteverde** (p. 158), **Tortuguero** (p. 219), and **Drake Bay** (p. 198).
- **Soaking in a Volcanic Hot Spring:** Costa Rica's volcanoes have blessed the country with a host of natural hot spring spots. From the opulent grandeur of **Tabacón Grand Spa Thermal Resort** (p. 145) to the more humble options around **Rincón de la Vieja** (p. 102) to the remote hot river pools at **Río Perdido** (p. 109), mineral-rich, naturally heated waters are waiting to soothe what ails you.
- **Spotting a Resplendent Quetzal:** The iridescent colors and long, flowing tail feathers of this aptly named bird are breathtaking. This rare species can still be regularly sighted in the **Monteverde Cloud Forest Biological Reserve** (p. 165) and the **San Gerardo de Dota** region.
- **Meeting Monkeys:** Costa Rica's rainforests and cloud forests are home to four species of New World monkeys—howler, capuchin, squirrel, and spider. Your odds of seeing one or more are very good if you visit **Monteverde** (p. 158), **Tortuguero** (p. 219), **Manuel Antonio** (p. 182), or the **Osa Peninsula** (p. 200).

- **Zipping Through the Treetops:** All over the country, you'll find zipline canopy tours, in which you strap on a harness and zip from treetop to treetop while dangling from a cable, sometimes from hair-raising heights. Rarely has terror been so much fun. See chapter 12.
- **Pouring on the Salsa Lizano:** Whether you're eating at a *soda* (diner) or having breakfast at the Four Seasons, be sure to try some Salsa Lizano, a tangy, tamarind-based sauce that's used on everything from salad to rice and beans to grilled meats and poultry.
- **Touring a Coffee Plantation:** World-renowned and highly coveted, Costa Rican coffee can be enjoyed at its source all across the country. Peek inside the cup with a coffee tour—they're offered around the Central Valley, outside Monteverde, and elsewhere. See chapters 5 and 7.

COSTA RICA'S best FOR WILDLIFE VIEWING

- **Santa Rosa National Park** (northeast of Liberia, in Guanacaste): One of the largest and last remaining stands of tropical dry forest in Costa Rica, Santa Rosa National Park is a great place for all sorts of wildlife viewing. The sparse foliage, especially during the dry season, makes observation that much easier. See p. 107.
- **Monteverde Cloud Forest Biological Reserve** (in the mountains northwest of San José): There's something both eerie and majestic about walking around in the early-morning mist to the sound of birds calling and lizards skittering through the leaves, completely surrounded by towering trees heavy with bromeliads, orchids, moss, and vines. The reserve has a well-maintained network of trails, and the community is deeply involved in conservation. See p. 165.
- **Manuel Antonio** (on the central Pacific Coast): Here's a spectacular spot for monkeying around. The stunning park is the best place in the country to spot a variety of animals, especially monkeys, including the rare squirrel monkey. Keep your backpack snacks away from the nosy white-faced capuchins, who've been known to help themselves to treats. See "Manuel Antonio National Park" in chapter 8.
- **Osa Peninsula** (in southern Costa Rica): This is Costa Rica's most remote and biologically rich region. **Corcovado National Park,** the largest remaining patch of virgin lowland tropical rainforest in Central America, takes up much of the Osa Peninsula. Jaguars, crocodiles, tapirs, and scarlet macaws all call this place home. See chapter 9.
- **Tortuguero** (on the north Caribbean coast): Tortuguero has been called Costa Rica's Venice because it's laced with canals and transportation is by boat, but you'll feel more like you're floating down the wild, brown Amazon here. Exploring these narrow canals, you'll see a wide variety of aquatic birds, as well as caimans, sloths, and up to three types of monkeys. If you come between June and October, you could be treated to the

awe-inspiring spectacle of a green turtle laying her eggs—the beaches here are the largest nesting site in the Western Hemisphere for these endangered giants. See "Exploring Tortuguero National Park" in chapter 10.

COSTA RICA'S best ECOLODGES & WILDERNESS RESORTS

Ecolodges in Costa Rica range from tent camps with communal dining and no electricity or hot water to some of the most luxurious accommodations in the country.

- **Arenal Observatory Lodge** (near La Fortuna): Originally a research facility, this lodge now features exquisite gardens and comfortable rooms with impressive views of Arenal Volcano. Excellent trails lead to waterfalls and beautiful vistas, with a great hike to the summit of the dormant Cerro Chato volcano. Toucans frequent the trees near the lodge, raccoon-like coatis roam the grounds, and howler monkeys provide the wake-up calls. See p. 146.
- **Monteverde Lodge & Gardens** (Monteverde): One of the original ecolodges in Monteverde, this place has only improved over the years, with great guides, updated rooms, and lush gardens. See p. 162.
- **La Paloma Lodge** (Drake Bay): If your idea of the perfect nature lodge is one where your front porch provides prime-time viewing of flora and fauna, this place is for you. When you've logged enough porch time and are ready to venture out, the Osa Peninsula's lowland rainforests are just outside your door. See p. 203.
- **Bosque del Cabo Rainforest Lodge** (Osa Peninsula): Large, unique, and cozy private cabins perched on the edge of a cliff overlooking the Pacific Ocean and surrounded by lush rainforest make this a spectacular spot. See p. 210.
- **Lapa Ríos** (Osa Peninsula): This was one of Costa Rica's first luxury ecolodges to gain international acclaim, and it remains one of the best. The attention to detail, personalized service, and in-house tour guides are all top-notch. See p. 210.
- **Playa Nicuesa Rainforest Lodge** (Golfo Dulce): Accessible only by boat, this lodge is among the best options on the Golfo Dulce. Set in deep forest, it has individual bungalows with a perfect blend of rusticity and luxury, and the guides, service, and surrounding wildlife are all superb. See p. 215.
- **Tortuga Lodge** (Tortuguero): This lodge features a beautiful riverfront restaurant and swimming pool. The canals of Tortuguero snake through its maze of lowland primary rainforest. The beaches here are major sea-turtle nesting sites. See p. 223.
- **Selva Bananito Lodge** (in the Talamanca Mountains south of Limón): Providing direct access to the southern Caribbean lowland rainforest, this authentic ecolodge combines nature with adventure. You can hike along a riverbed, ride horses through the rainforest, climb 30m (100 ft.) up a ceiba tree, or rappel down a jungle waterfall here. See p. 239.

COSTA RICA'S best HOTELS

- **Hotel Grano de Oro** (San José): San José boasts dozens of colonial-era mansions that have been converted into hotels, but few do it like Grano de Oro, with its luxurious accommodations and professional service. All the guest rooms have attractive hardwood furniture, including antique armoires in some rooms. When it's time to relax, you can soak in a hot tub or have a drink in the rooftop lounge while taking in a commanding view of San José. See p. 57.
- **Finca Rosa Blanca Coffee Plantation Resort** (Heredia): If the cookie-cutter rooms of international resorts leave you cold, perhaps this unusual inn will be more your style. Square corners seem to have been prohibited here in favor of turrets and curving walls of glass, arched windows, and semicircular built-in couches. It's set into a lush hillside and surrounding organic coffee farm, just 20 minutes from San José. See p. 59.
- **Hotel Capitán Suizo** (Tamarindo): With a perfect beachfront setting, spacious rooms, lush gardens and grounds, and a wonderful pool, this is arguably the best option in Tamarindo. See p. 112.
- **Florblanca Resort** (Playa Santa Teresa): The individual luxury villas at this intimate resort feature massive living rooms and private balconies. The service, spa, and food are all outstanding, and the resort is spread over a lushly planted hillside, steps away from Playa Santa Teresa. See p. 136.
- **Hidden Canopy Treehouses** (Monteverde): The individual cabins are on high stilts and nestled into the surrounding cloud forest canopy. All abound in brightly varnished local hardwoods. The refined yet convivial vibe is palpable in the afternoon over tea or cocktails, when guests enjoy the main lodge's sunset view. See p. 161.
- **Arco Iris Lodge** (Monteverde): This small lodge is located on an expansive piece of property, but within easy walking distance of everything in Santa Elena. And it's the best deal in the Monteverde area to boot. The owners are extremely knowledgeable and helpful. See p. 163.
- **Arenas del Mar** (Manuel Antonio): The whole resort is surrounded by old-growth rainforest on a hilly piece of land abutting two pretty beaches. Try to snag one of the rooms featuring a wraparound balcony equipped with a sunken hot tub, then marvel at the panoramic coastal view while you soak. Arenas del Mar has a beautiful little spa and the best beach access in Manuel Antonio. See p. 187.
- **Playa Negra Guesthouse** (Cahuita): Located just across a dirt road from a long, isolated section of Playa Negra, this hotel has individual Caribbean-style bungalows that are cozy and beautifully designed, with full kitchens and gingerbread trim. The grounds are a riot of tropical flowers and tall palm trees, and the whole operation has an intimate and refined ambience. See p. 229.

COSTA RICA'S best RESTAURANTS

- **Grano de Oro Restaurant** (San José): This elegant boutique hotel has an equally fine restaurant serving contemporary fusion dishes and decadent desserts made with fresh local ingredients. The open-air seating in the central courtyard is delightful. See p. 63.
- **Abbocato** (Playa Panamá): The dynamic husband-wife chef team here serves up two unique nightly tasting menus—one Asian, one Mediterranean—executed with skill and creativity. See p. 90.
- **Ginger** (Playa Hermosa): Serving an eclectic mix of traditional and pan-Asian–influenced tapas, this sophisticated joint is taking this part of Guanacaste by storm. A list of creative cocktails complements the inventive dishes. See p. 90.
- **Papaya** (Brasilito): Housed in a simple, unassuming roadside hotel, this lively little restaurant serves fusion cuisine, using the region's freshest fish and seafood and other local ingredients, influenced by Asian and Latin American styles. See p. 100.
- **Pangas Beach Club** (Tamarindo): Executive chef Jean-Luc Taulere had a long, successful run in Playa Flamingo before moving to this relaxed, elegant restaurant. He combines his Catalan heritage with classical French training, fresh local ingredients, and a mix of local, fusion, and Asian influences. See p. 114.
- **Lola's** (Playa Avellanas): With a perfect setting on the sand and excellent hearty fare, Lola's is among the best casual beachfront restaurants in the country. The ocean-loving namesake mascot—a pet pig—adds to the restaurant's quirky charm. See p. 118.
- **Playa de los Artistas** (Montezuma): This place has the perfect blend of refined Mediterranean cuisine and beachside funkiness. There are only a few tables, so get here early. Fresh, grilled seafood is served in oversize ceramic bowls and on large wooden slabs lined with banana leaves. See p. 132.
- **Café Caburé** (Monteverde): In addition to the eclectic world cuisine served here, there's a delicious, wide-ranging, and very tempting selection of homemade chocolate treats. Enjoy the casual, open-air seating on the second-floor wooden balcony, and afterward take a chocolate tour (p. 168) or visit the Bat Jungle (p. 169). See p. 164.
- **Graffiti Resto Café & Wine Bar** (Jacó): From the small sushi bar in one corner to the graffiti-painted walls, this place is full of surprises. Pan-Asian cuisine blended with the chef's Alabama roots and New Orleans training results in culinary wonders utilizing local ingredients and spices. See p. 178.
- **Milagro** (Manuel Antonio): A casually elegant little place, Milagro has made a name for itself in the Manuel Antonio area. A humble coffee shop, breakfast joint, and lunch stop, it kicks up a notch at night with a creative Nuevo Latino menu that takes full advantage of the freshest local ingredients available. See p. 190.

- **La Pecora Nera** (Cocles, near Puerto Viejo): Surprisingly fine Italian cuisine in a tiny surfer town on the south Caribbean coast. Your best bet here is to allow yourself to be taken on a culinary roller-coaster ride with a mixed feast of the chef's nightly specials and suggestions. See p. 233.

COSTA RICA'S best FOR FAMILIES

- **La Paz Waterfall Gardens** (near Poás Volcano National Park): This multifaceted attraction features paths and suspended walkways alongside a series of impressive jungle waterfalls. Kids will love the hummingbird, wildcat, and reptile exhibits, and the impressive power of the waterfalls. See p. 68.
- **Playa Hermosa:** The protected waters of this Pacific beach make it a family favorite. Just because its waters are calm, however, doesn't mean it's boring. I recommend staying at the beachfront **Bosque del Mar** (p. 89) and checking in at **Aqua Sport** (p. 91), where you can rent sea kayaks, sailboards, paddleboats, beach umbrellas, and bicycles.
- **Tamarindo:** This surf town has a bit of something for everyone. It's a great spot for kids to learn how to surf or boogie-board, with a host of tours and activities to please the entire family. **Hotel Capitán Suizo** (p. 112) has an enviable location on a calm section of beach, plus spacious rooms and a great pool for kids and adults alike, with a long, sloping, shallow entrance. See chapter 6.
- **Arenal Volcano:** This adventure hot spot offers a nearly inexhaustible range of activities for all ages. From gentle safari floats and raging whitewater rafting to flat, easy hikes over hanging bridges or challenging scrambles over cooled lava flows, you're sure to find something that fits the interests and ability level of each member of the family. See chapter 7.
- **Monteverde:** This area not only has the country's most famous cloud forest, but also a wide variety of attractions and activities. After hiking through the reserve, you should be able to keep everyone happy and occupied riding horses; squirming at the serpentarium; or visiting the Monteverde Butterfly Garden, Frog Pond, Bat Jungle, or Orchid Garden. See chapter 7.
- **Jacó:** Jacó's streets are lined with souvenir shops, ice cream stands, and inexpensive eateries. Activity options range from surf lessons to a small-boat cruise among the crocodiles on the Tárcoles River. **Club del Mar Condominiums & Resort** (p. 176) is accommodating to families with small children. See chapter 8.
- **Manuel Antonio:** This national park has a bit of everything: miles of idyllic white sand beaches, myriad wildlife (with almost guaranteed monkey sightings), and plenty of tour options. Of the many lodging choices, **Hotel Sí Como No** (p. 187), with its spacious tropical suites, two pools, waterslide, and nightly movies, is a good bet. See chapter 8.

COSTA RICA'S best BEACHES

With more than 1,200km (750 miles) of shoreline on its Pacific and Caribbean coasts, Costa Rica offers beachgoers a wealth of options.

- **Playa Nacascolo:** With silky white sand, this is the best stretch of beach on the Papagayo Peninsula. The waters here are protected from ocean swells and are great for swimming. See "Exploring Playa Hermosa, Playa Panamá & Papagayo" in chapter 6.
- **Playa Avellanas:** Just south of Tamarindo, this white-sand beach has long been a favorite haunt for surfers, locals, and those in the know. Playa Avellanas stretches for miles, backed by protected mangrove forests. See p. 117.
- **Beaches Near Playa Sámara:** Playa Sámara is nice enough, but venturing slightly farther afield, you'll find two of the prettiest beaches along the entire Pacific Coast. **Playa Carrillo** is a long crescent of palm-backed white sand located just south of Sámara, while **Playa Barrigona** is a hidden gem tucked down a rugged dirt road to the north. See chapter 6.
- **Playa Montezuma:** This tiny beach town at the southern tip of the Nicoya Peninsula retains a funky sense of individuality, with plenty of isolated spots to lay down your towel. It's a favorite of backpackers and fire dancers, but you can also find upscale beachfront lodging and fine dining. Nearby, you'll find two impressive waterfalls, one of them emptying into an oceanfront pool, the other surrounded by thick forest. Farther afield, you can explore the biologically rich **Cabo Blanco** and **Curú** wildlife preserves. See p. 129.
- **Malpaís & Santa Teresa:** With its scattered luxury lodges, surf camps, and assorted hotels and hostels, this is the place to come if you're looking for miles of deserted beaches and great surf. See "Malpaís & Santa Teresa" in chapter 6.
- **Manuel Antonio:** Manuel Antonio National Park was the first beach destination to become popular in Costa Rica, and its beaches are still idyllic. The hills approaching the park offer captivating views over thick primary rainforest to the Pacific Ocean. See chapter 8.
- **Punta Uva & Manzanillo:** These beaches deliver true Caribbean splendor, with turquoise waters, coral reefs, and palm-lined stretches of nearly deserted white-sand beach. Tall coconut palms line the shore, providing shady respite, and the water is usually quite calm and good for swimming. See chapter 10.

COSTA RICA'S best ACTIVE ADVENTURES

- **Mountain Biking the Back Roads of Costa Rica:** The rustic back roads bemoaned by drivers are a huge boon for mountain bikers. The country has endless roads and trails to explore on two wheels. The area around La

Fortuna and Lake Arenal, with its widely varied terrain, is a top destination. See p. 140.

- **Rafting the Pacuare River** (near Turrialba): The best and most beautiful river for rafting in Costa Rica, the class III/IV Pacuare winds through primary and secondary forests, and it features one especially breathtaking section that passes through a narrow, steep gorge. For a real treat, take the 2-day Pacuare River trip, which includes an overnight at a lodge or tent camp on the side of the river. See p. 265.
- **Surfing & Four-Wheeling Guanacaste Province:** From Witch's Rock at Playa Naranjo near the Nicaraguan border to Playa Nosara, more than 100 km (60 miles) away, you'll find scores of world-class surf spots. In addition to the two mentioned, try a session at Playa Grande, Punta Langosta, and playas Negra, Avellanas, and Junquillal. Or find your own secret spot. See chapter 6.
- **Trying the Adventure Sport of Canyoning:** While every canyoning tour is unique, it usually involves hiking along and through the rivers and creeks of a steep mountain canyon, with periodic breaks to rappel down the face of a waterfall, jump off a rock into a jungle pool, or float down small rapids. See chapters 6, 7, and 9.
- **Diving off the Shores of Isla del Caño:** This uninhabited island is believed to have been used as a ceremonial burial site by the pre-Columbian residents of the area. Today, the underwater rocks and coral formations here provide arguably the best scuba diving and snorkeling opportunities in the country—aside from the far offshore Isla del Coco. See chapter 9.

COSTA RICA'S best WALKS

- **Lankester Gardens:** If you want a really pleasant but not overly challenging day hike, consider a walk among the hundreds of species of flora on display here. The trails meander from areas of well-tended open gardens to shady natural forests, plus there's a highly regarded orchid collection. See p. 80.
- **Rincón de la Vieja National Park:** Visit the geysers, mud pots, and fumaroles of "Costa Rica's Yellowstone," or hike down to the Blue Lake and Cangreja Falls, where you'll find a pristine turquoise pool fed by a rushing jungle waterfall. You can also hike up to two craters and a crater lake here, while the Las Pailas loop is ideal for those seeking a less strenuous hike. See p. 102.
- **Arenal National Park:** This park has several excellent trails that visit a variety of ecosystems, including primary and secondary rainforest, savanna, and old lava flows. Most of them are on the relatively flat flanks of the volcano, so there's not too much climbing involved. See "Exploring Arenal Volcano & La Fortuna" in chapter 7.
- **Monteverde Cloud Forest Biological Reserve:** Take a guided tour in the morning to familiarize yourself with the cloud forest, and then spend the

afternoon exploring the reserve on your own. Off the main thoroughfares, Monteverde reveals its rich mysteries with stunning regularity. Even without a guide, you should be able to enjoy sightings of a wide range of unique tropical flora and fauna, maybe even a resplendent quetzal. See p. 165.

- **Corcovado National Park:** The park has a well-designed network of trails, ranger stations, and camping facilities. Most of the lodges in Drake Bay and the Osa Peninsula offer day hikes into the park, but if you've come this far, you should hike in and camp at the Sirena ranger station. See "Puerto Jiménez: Gateway to Corcovado National Park" in chapter 9.
- **Cahuita National Park:** Fronted by the Caribbean and an idyllic beach, the park has flat, well-maintained trails through thick lowland forest. They are parallel to the beach, so you can hike out on the trail and back along the beach, or vice versa. White-faced and howler monkeys are common, as are brightly colored land crabs. See p. 234.

2 SUGGESTED ITINERARIES

Costa Rica is a compact yet immensely varied destination. On a trip to Costa Rica, you can visit rainforests, cloud forests, and active volcanoes, and walk along miles of beautiful beaches on both the Pacific and Caribbean coasts. Adventure hounds will have their fill choosing from an exciting array of activities, and those looking for some rest and relaxation can soak in hot springs or simply grab a lounge chair and a good book. Costa Rica's relatively small size makes visiting several destinations during a single vacation both easy and enjoyable.

Costa Rica is named after one coast, but has two: the Pacific and the Caribbean. These are as different from each other as are the Atlantic and Pacific coasts of North America.

Costa Rica's **Pacific coast** is the most extensive, and is characterized by a rugged though mostly accessible coastline where forested mountains often meet the sea. It can be divided into four regions—Guanacaste, the Nicoya Peninsula, the Central Coast, and the Southern Coast. Here are spectacular stretches of coastline and most of the country's top beaches. This coast varies from the dry, sunny climate of the northwest to the hot, humid rainforests of the south.

The **Caribbean coast** can be divided into two roughly equal stretches. The remote northeast coastline is a vast flat plain laced with rivers and covered with rainforest; it is accessible only by boat or small plane. Farther south, along the stretch of coast accessible by car, are uncrowded beaches and coral reef.

Bordered by Nicaragua in the north and Panama in the southeast, Costa Rica is only slightly larger than Vermont and New Hampshire combined. Much of the country is mountainous, with three major ranges running northwest to southeast. Among these mountains are several volcanic peaks, some of which are still active. Between the mountain ranges are fertile valleys, the largest and most populated of which is the Central Valley. With the exception of the dry Guanacaste region, much of Costa Rica's coastal area is hot and humid and covered with dense rainforests.

Costa Rica by Region

Costa Rica Regions in Brief

See the map on p. 11 for a visual reference of the regions detailed below.

San José San José is Costa Rica's capital and its primary business, cultural, and social center—and it sits close to the country's geographical center, in the heart of the Central Valley. It's a sprawling urban area, with a population of around one million. Its streets are narrow, in poor repair, poorly marked and often chock-full of speeding, honking traffic. However, a few notable parks, like the Parque La Sabana and Parque del Este, serve to lessen the urban blight. San José is home to the country's greatest collection of museums, fine restaurants and stores, galleries, and shopping centers.

The Central Valley The Central Valley is surrounded by rolling green hills and mountains that rise to heights between 900 and 1,200m (2,952–3,936 ft.) above sea level. The climate here is mild and springlike year-round. It's Costa Rica's primary agricultural region, with coffee farms making up the majority of landholdings. The rich volcanic soil of this region makes it ideal for farming. The country's earliest settlements were in this area, and today the Central Valley (which includes San José) is densely populated, crisscrossed by decent roads, and dotted with small towns. Surrounding the Central Valley are high mountains, among which are four volcanic peaks. Three of these, **Poás**, **Irazú** and **Turrialba,** are still active and have caused extensive damage during cycles of activity in the past 2 centuries. Many of the mountainous regions to the north and to the south of the capital of San José have been declared national parks (Tapantí, Juan Castro Blanco, and Braulio Carrillo) to protect their virgin rainforests against logging.

Guanacaste The northwestern corner of the country near the Nicaraguan border is the site of many of Costa Rica's sunniest and most popular **beaches,** including **Playa del Coco, Playa Hermosa, Playa Flamingo, Playa Conchal, Tamarindo,** and the **Papagayo Peninsula.** Scores of beach destinations, towns, and resorts are along this long string of coastline. Because many foreigners have chosen to build beach houses and retirement homes here, Guanacaste has experienced considerable development over the years. You won't find a glut of Cancún-style high-rise hotels, but condos, luxury resorts, and golf courses have sprung up along the coastline here. Still, you won't be towel-to-towel with thousands of strangers. On the contrary, you can still find long stretches of deserted sands. However, more and more travelers are using Liberia as their gateway to Costa Rica, bypassing San José and the central and southern parts of the country entirely.

With about 165cm (65 in.) of rain a year, this region is by far the driest in the country and has been likened to west Texas. Guanacaste province is named after the shady trees that still shelter the herds of cattle roaming the dusty savanna here. In addition to cattle ranches, Guanacaste has semiactive volcanoes, several lakes, and one of the last remnants of tropical dry forest left in Central America. (Dry forest once stretched all the way from Costa Rica up to the Mexican state of Chiapas.)

The Nicoya Peninsula Just south of Guanacaste lies the Nicoya Peninsula. Similar to Guanacaste in many ways, the Nicoya Peninsula is nonetheless somewhat more inaccessible, and less developed and crowded. However, this is changing. The beaches of **Santa Teresa** and **Malpaís** are perhaps the fastest-growing areas anywhere along the Costa Rican coast.

As you head south from Guanacaste, the region is similar in terms of geography, climate, and ecosystems, but begins to get more humid and moist, with taller and lusher forests. The Nicoya Peninsula itself juts out to form the Golfo de Nicoya (Nicoya Gulf), a large, protected body of water. Puntarenas, a small fishing city, is the main port found inside this gulf, and one of the main commercial ports in all of Costa Rica. Puntarenas is also the departure point for the regular car ferries that connect the Nicoya Peninsula to mainland Costa Rica.

The Northern Zone This inland region lies to the north of San José and includes rainforests, cloud forests, hot springs, the famous **Arenal Volcano**, the vast **Braulio Carrillo**

National Park, and numerous remote lodges. Because this is one of the few regions of Costa Rica without any beaches, it primarily attracts people interested in nature and active sports. **Lake Arenal** has some of the best windsurfing and kitesurfing in the world, as well as several good mountain-biking trails along its shores. The **Monteverde Cloud Forest,** perhaps Costa Rica's most internationally recognized attraction, is another top draw in this region.

The Central Pacific Coast Because it's the most easily accessible coastline in Costa Rica, the central Pacific coast has a vast variety of beach resorts and hotels. **Jacó,** a bustling beach town a little over an hour from San José, attracts sunbirds, charter groups, and a mad rush of Costa Rican tourists every weekend. It is also very popular with young surfers, and has a distinct party vibe. **Manuel Antonio,** one of the most emblematic destinations in Costa Rica, is built up around a popular coastal national park, and caters to people looking to blend beach time and fabulous panoramic views with some wildlife viewing and active adventures. South of Manuel Antonio, you'll encounter a wild coastal region where thick rainforests coat steep hillsides that lead down to the undeveloped beaches of Dominical, Matapalo, Uvita, and beyond. This region is also home to the highest peak in Costa Rica—**Mount Chirripó**—a beautiful summit, where frost is common.

The Southern Zone This hot, humid region is one of Costa Rica's most remote and undeveloped. It is characterized by dense rainforests, large national parks with protected areas, and rugged coastlines. Much of the area is uninhabited and protected in **Corcovado, Piedras Blancas,** and **La Amistad** national parks. A number of wonderful nature lodges are spread around the shores of the **Golfo Dulce** and along the **Osa Peninsula.** There's a lot of solitude to be found here, due in no small part to the fact that it's hard to get here and hard to get around. But if you like your ecotourism authentic and challenging, you'll find the Southern Zone to your liking.

The Caribbean Coast Most of the Caribbean coast is a wide, steamy lowland laced with rivers and blanketed with rainforests and banana plantations. The culture here is predominantly Afro-Caribbean, with many residents speaking an English or Caribbean patois. The northern section of this coast is accessible only by boat or small plane and is the site of **Tortuguero National Park,** which is known for its nesting sea turtles and riverboat trips. The towns of **Cahuita, Puerto Viejo,** and **Manzanillo,** on the southern half of the Caribbean coast, are increasingly popular destinations. The beautiful beaches and coastline here, as yet, have few large hotels. This area can be rainy, especially between December and April.

BLUEPRINTS FOR FABULOUS VACATIONS

The following itineraries were designed to help make the most of your time in Costa Rica—feel free to follow them to the letter. But if that's too structured, you might also use one or more of them as an outline and then fill in blanks with other destinations and attractions that strike your fancy.

COSTA RICA HIGHLIGHTS IN 1 WEEK

The timing is tight, but this itinerary packs a lot into a weeklong vacation. This route takes you to a trifecta of Costa Rica's primary tourist attractions: Arenal Volcano, Monteverde, and Manuel Antonio. You can explore and enjoy tropical nature, take in some beach time, and experience a few high-adrenaline adventures.

Day 1: Arrive & Settle into San José

If your flight gets in early enough and you have time, head downtown and tour the **Museos del Banco Central de Costa Rica (Gold Museum) ★★** (p. 67) and the nearby **Museo de Jade Marco Fidel Tristán (Jade Museum) ★★** (p. 66). But if you've enough time for only a little walk, stop at one of the roadside stands selling small bags of cut-up fruit. Depending on the season, you might find mango, pineapple, or papaya on offer. You might also find *mamón chino,* an odd-looking, golf ball–size fruit you might also know as rambutan or lychee.

While downtown, try to stop by the **Teatro Nacional (National Theater) ★★** (p. 74). If anything is playing that night, buy tickets for the show.

Day 2: Hot Stuff ★★

Rent a car and head to the Arenal National Park and the **Arenal Volcano ★★** area. Hike the **Sendero Coladas (Lava Flow Trail) ★★**, which will take you onto and over a cooled-off lava flow. Spend the evening in the natural hot springs at the **Tabacón Grand Spa Thermal Resort ★★★** (p. 145), working out the kinks from the road and hike. (The volcano may be dormant right now, but the natural hot springs are still working just fine.) You also might want to spring for a massage or spa treatment.

Day 3: Adventures Around Arenal, Ending in Monteverde ★★

Spend the morning doing something adventurous around Arenal National Park. Your options range from whitewater rafting or mountain biking to horseback riding and hiking to La Fortuna Waterfall. **Desafío Expeditions ★★** (p. 143) offers a great **canyoning** adventure. Allow at least 4 hours of daylight to drive around **Lake Arenal** to **Monteverde.** Stop for a break at the **Lucky Bug Gallery ★★** (p. 158), along the road between Tabacón and Nuevo Arenal, an excellent place to shop for gifts, artwork, and souvenirs. Once you get to Monteverde, settle into your hotel and head for a drink and dinner at **Trio ★★★**.

Day 4: Monteverde Cloud Forest Biological Reserve ★★★

Wake up early and take a guided tour of the **Monteverde Cloud Forest Biological Reserve ★★★** (p. 165). Spend the afternoon visiting any of the area's other attractions, which might include any combination of the following: the **Butterfly Garden ★** (p. 169), **Orchid Garden ★★** (p. 169), **Herpetarium Adventures ★** (p. 169), **Frog Pond of Monteverde,** and the **Bat Jungle ★★★** (p. 169).

Day 5: From the Treetops to the Coast ★★★

Use the morning to take one of the **zipline canopy tours** here. I recommend **Selvatura Park ★★** (p. 167), which has a wonderful canopy tour, as well as other interesting exhibits. Be sure to schedule the tour early enough so that you can hit the road by noon for your drive to **Manuel Antonio National Park.** Settle into your hotel and head for a **sunset drink** at **Agua Azul ★★** (p. 190), which offers up spectacular views over the rainforest to the sea.

Day 6: Manuel Antonio National Park ★★

In the morning, take a boat tour of the **Damas Island estuary** (p. 193), and then reward yourself for all the hard touring so far with an afternoon lazing on one of the beautiful beaches inside **Manuel Antonio National Park ★★** (p. 182). If you just can't lie still, hike the loop trail through the rainforest here and around **Cathedral Point ★★**. Make reservations at **Milagro ★★★** (p. 190) for an intimate and relaxed final dinner in Costa Rica.

Day 7: Saying Adiós

Drive back to **San José** in time to drop off your rental car and connect with your departing flight home.

UNDISCOVERED COSTA RICA

Despite Costa Rica's popularity and booming tourism industry, plenty of places are still off the beaten track. And believe me, you'll be richly rewarded for venturing down the road less traveled. Start off your trip with a rental car, which you can turn in after Montezuma. After that, fly to Golfito or Puerto Jiménez to explore Costa Rica's wild Southern Zone.

Day 1: Rincón de la Vieja National Park ★★

Not nearly as popular as the Arenal Volcano, the **Rincón de la Vieja Volcano,** along with its namesake **national park ★★** (p. 102), is an underexplored gem. The park features challenging and rewarding hikes, sulfur hot springs, volcanic mud deposits, and stunning jungle waterfalls. Try the vigorous 2-hour trek to **Blue Lake and La Cangreja Waterfall ★★** (p. 104), consisting of a beautiful forest waterfall emptying into a postcard-perfect turquoise lake. This is a great spot for a picnic lunch and a cool dip. If you have time and energy afterward, finish up with the relatively short and gentle **Las Pailas Loop ★**, which showcases the volcanic fumaroles and mud pots here.

Day 2: Horses, High Wires & Hot Springs

You did plenty of hiking yesterday, so start this day off with something a little different. **Hacienda Guachipelín ★★** (p. 104) offers a range of adventure activities, including horseback riding, river tubing, ziplining, and a waterfall rappel canyoning tour (see p. 261 for more about canyoning), in addition to a gorgeous set of natural hot mineral springs along the side of a jungle river.

Day 3: Going Deep Down Under

Sitting on top of a massive cave system, **Barra Honda National Park ★** (p. 122) is Costa Rica's top spot for spelunking. On a typical tour here, you'll descend into the depths of the **Terciopelo Cave** and visit the waterfalls and pools of **La Cascada.** After your visit here, drive to nearby **Playa Sámara,** about an hour away.

Gusto Beach ★★

With tables set in the sand and palm trees strung with rope lighting, this place serves up excellent Italian fare, as well as fresh grilled fish and meats. See p. 121.

Day 4: Beautiful Beaches

The Nicoya Peninsula has many of the same charms and nearly as many miles of beach as Guanacaste, but far fewer crowds. Although the beach at **Playa Sámara** is nice enough, I recommend heading to neighboring gems **Playa Barrigona** ★★ (p. 122) and **Playa Carrillo** ★★ (p. 121). If you like, sign up for an ultralight flight with the folks at the **Flying Crocodile** (p. 122).

Days 5 & 6: Montezuma

Montezuma is a great place to mix more beach time with wildlife sightings and visits to some impressive waterfalls. While you can certainly hike to the foot of the **Montezuma Waterfall** ★★ (p. 133), it's even better to visit as part of the **Waterfall Canopy Tour** ★ (p. 133). Take a horseback ride to **El Chorro Falls** ★ (p. 133), and if you time it right, you can ride home along the beach as the sun sets.

While in Montezuma, visit the **Cabo Blanco Absolute Nature Reserve** ★★ (p. 134), the country's first officially protected area. The main trail inside this park, **Sendero Sueco,** leads to the gorgeous and almost always deserted beach **Playa Balsita.** A trip to Cabo Blanco Nature Reserve can easily be combined with a **kayaking and snorkel tour** to the little cemetery island located just off the village of **Cabuya.**

Playa de los Artistas ★★★

Fresh grilled fish and other Mediterranean fare are the specialties here. If you're limber, slide onto a tatami mat set around one of the low tables closest to the water. See p. 132.

Days 7, 8 & 9: The Osa Peninsula & Golfo Dulce

The Southern Zone, including the Osa Peninsula and Golfo Dulce, is Costa Rica's most remote (and in many ways most rewarding) region. Here you'll find tiny towns and villages bordering vast tracts of lowland tropical forest that cascade down to the sea. This area is home to **Corcovado National Park** ★★★, the **Piedras Blancas National Park** ★★, and a host of other private reserves and protected areas. It is Costa Rica's prime area for wildlife-viewing and ecotourism. There are three main gateways to this region, **Drake Bay, Puerto Jiménez,** and **Golfito.** All can be reached by air or land, and all offer access to some of the top nature lodges in the country. Most of these remote lodges provide all meals and tours for their guests. See chapter 9.

THE BEST COSTA RICA ADVENTURES

Costa Rica is a major adventure-tourism destination. The following basic itinerary packs a lot of adventures into a single week; if you want to do some surfing, mountain biking, or kayaking, just schedule more time.

Day 1: Starting Out in San José

You'll probably have a little time to explore and enjoy **San José.** Head first to the **Plaza de la Democracia ★** (p. 73), where you'll find the **Museos del Banco Central de Costa Rica ★★** (p. 67) and the **Teatro Nacional** (p. 74). Take a break for an afternoon coffee at **Alma de Café ★** (p. 62) inside the Teatro Nacional. For a traditional Costa Rican dinner with a spectacular view of the city lights, head to **Tiquicia** (p. 65), which is in the hills above Escazú.

Days 2 & 3: Get Wet & Wild

Take a 2-day whitewater rafting expedition on the **Pacuare River** with **Ríos Tropicales ★★** (p. 266), and spend the night at their remote riverside lodge. When you finish running the Pacuare, they will transport you (as part of the trip package) to **La Fortuna ★★**.

Day 4: Waterfalls Two Ways

Go waterfall rappelling and canyoning with **Desafío Expeditions ★★** (p. 143) in the morning, and then hop on a horse or a mountain bike in the afternoon and stop at **La Fortuna Waterfall ★** (p. 151). Take the short hike down to the base of the falls and take a dip in the pool. In the evening, check out the hot springs at **Eco Termales ★★** (p. 153).

Day 5: Getting There Is Part of the Fun & Adventure

Arrange a **taxi-boat-horse** ride to **Monteverde** with **Desafío Expeditions ★★** (p. 143). Settle in quickly at your hotel and enjoy a zipline **canopy tour** in the afternoon. I recommend **Selvatura Park ★★**, which is located near the **Santa Elena Cloud Forest Reserve.** Finally, if you've got the energy, take a **night tour** through either the Santa Elena or Monteverde Cloud Forest Reserve.

Day 6: Monteverde Cloud Forest Biological Reserve ★★★

Wake up early and take a daytime guided tour of the **Monteverde Cloud Forest Biological Reserve ★★★**. Bring a lunch, and after the guided tour, spend the next few hours exploring the trails on your own. See if you can spot a **quetzal** (p. 165). Then transfer back to San José.

Day 7: Squeeze in a Soccer Game Before Departing

You'll most likely be on an early flight home from **San José,** but if you have a few hours to kill, head for a **hike** or **jog** around Parque La Sabana or, better yet, try to join a **pickup soccer game** (p. 69) here.

COSTA RICA FOR FAMILIES

Costa Rica is a terrific destination for families. If you're traveling with very small children, you might want to stick close to the beaches, or consider a large resort with a children's program and babysitting services. But for slightly older kids and teens, particularly those with an adventurous streak, Costa Rica is a lot of fun.

Day 1: Arrive in Guanacaste

Fly directly into **Liberia.** From here it's a drive of 30 to 45 minutes to any of the area's many beach resorts, especially around the **Papagayo Peninsula.** If you can afford them, the **Four Seasons Resort ★★★** (p. 89) and the **Andaz Peninsula Papagayo Resort ★★★** (p. 88) are standouts. Both have excellent children's programs and tons of activity and tour options. Alternatively, **Hotel Playa Hermosa Bosque del Mar ★★★** (p. 89) is a lovely beachfront boutique hotel on a quiet and calm section of Playa Hermosa.

Day 2: Get Your Bearings & Enjoy the Beach

Get to know and enjoy the facilities and activities offered up at your hotel or resort. Spend time on the beach or at the pool. Build some sand castles, or get involved in a pickup game of beach volleyball or soccer. In the afternoon, go on a **sail and snorkel cruise.** If you choose a large resort, check out the **children's program** and any scheduled **activities** or **tours** that appeal to anyone in the family. Feel free to adapt the following days' suggestions accordingly.

Day 3: Rafting on the Corobicí River

The whole family will enjoy a **rafting tour** on the gentle Corobicí River. **Rios Tropicales ★★** (p. 105) offers leisurely trips that are appropriate for all ages, except infants. In addition to the slow float and occasional mellow rapids, there'll be plenty of opportunities to watch birds and other wildlife along the way. If you're here between late September and late February, book a **turtle tour** (p. 115) at nearby **Playa Grande** for the evening. The whole family will be awestruck by the amazing spectacle of a giant turtle digging a nest and laying her eggs.

Day 4: El Viejo Wetlands ★★

About an hour's drive from the Guanacaste beaches, **El Viejo Wildlife Refuge & Wetlands ★★** (p. 101) makes a fabulous day trip. Set on a massive old farmstead bordering Palo Verde National Park, this private reserve offers up some of Guanacaste's best wildlife viewing. There are boat trips on the Tempisque River and safari-style open Jeep tours through surrounding wetlands, as well as a host of other cultural and adventure tour options. Lunch is served in a beautiful, century-old farm building.

Day 5: Hacienda Guachipelín ★★

Head for the hills and book a full-day Adventure Pass outing to **Hacienda Guachipelín** (p. 104), next to **Rincón de la Vieja National Park.**

Older and more adventurous children can go **river tubing**, do a **horseback ride,** or take one of the zipline **canopy tours.** Younger children should get a kick out of visiting the working farm and cattle ranch, butterfly garden, and serpentarium here.

Day 6: Learn to Surf

Head to **Tamarindo** ★ (p. 109) for the day and arrange for the whole family to take **surf** or **boogie-board lessons.** You can arrange classes and rent equipment at either **Kelly's Surf Shop** ★ (p. 116) or **Witch's Rock Surf Camp** ★ (p. 116).

Day 7: Leaving Liberia

Use any spare time before your flight out of **Liberia** to buy last-minute souvenirs and gifts, or just laze on the beach or by the pool.

THE BEST OF SAN JOSÉ & THE CENTRAL VALLEY

While most tourists opt to get out of San José quickly for greener pastures, Costa Rica's vibrant capital and the surrounding Central Valley offer plenty to see and do. If you have more time, take a whitewater rafting trip on the Pacuare River, tour a coffee farm, or head to Turrialba for a canyoning adventure and a visit to the Guayabo National Monument, Costa Rica's top archaeological site.

Day 1: Getting to Know the City

Start your day on the **Plaza de la Cultura.** Visit the **Museos del Banco Central de Costa Rica** ★★ (p. 67), and see if you can get tickets for a performance at the **Teatro Nacional** (p. 74). From the Plaza de la Cultura, stroll up Avenida Central to the **Museo Nacional de Costa Rica (National Museum)** ★★ (p. 67).

Restaurante Nuestra Tierra ★

It's a bit of a tourist trap, but this Costa Rican–themed restaurant is conveniently located and serves up dependable local cuisine. Order a *casado* (the local blue-plate special) for lunch. It will come served on a banana leaf spread over a large platter, presented by a waiter or waitress in traditional rural garb from a bygone era. See p. 62.

After lunch, head to the nearby **Museo de Jade Marco Fidel Tristán (Jade Museum)** ★★ (p. 66). As soon as you're finished taking in all this culture, some shopping at the open-air stalls at the **Plaza de la Democracia** (p. 73) is in order.

Café Mundo ★

Try dinner at the trendy local hangout **Café Mundo,** at Calle 15 and Avenida 9, 3 blocks east and 1 block north of the INS building. This busy and often bustling spot serves up a mix of bar food, local classics, and world cuisine in a rambling old converted home. See p. 63.

After dinner, head to the **Teatro Nacional** for the night's performance.

Day 2: Alajuela, Heredia & Environs

Rent a car for the next 2 days, and get an early start for the **Poás Volcano** ★★ (p. 79), before the clouds envelop the main crater. After visiting the volcano, head to **La Paz Waterfall Gardens** ★★ (p. 68). Take a walk on the waterfall trail, and enjoy the immense butterfly garden and lively hummingbird garden. This is a good place to have lunch. On your way back to San José, make a loop through the hills of **Heredia,** with a stop at **INBio Park** ★★ (p. 68). In addition to being a fascinating natural-history museum, INBio Park has a wonderful collection of intriguing animal sculptures by Costa Rican artist José Sancho.

Day 3: Cartago & the Orosi Valley

Start the day taking in the scenery from 3,378m (11,080 ft.) at the top of the **Irazú Volcano** ★★ (p. 79). After admiring the view and hiking the crater trail, head down into the country's first capital city, Cartago, visiting **Las Ruinas** ★ and the **Basílica de Nuestra Señora de los Angeles** ★★★ (p. 79), on your way to the Orosi Valley. As you drive the loop road around Lake Cachí, stop in **Ujarrás** to see the ruins of Costa Rica's oldest church, and to check out the sculpture collection at **La Casa del Soñador** (p. 81).

After Ujarrás, continue on to Orosi Valley, stopping at **Lankester Gardens** ★★ (p. 80), one of the top botanical gardens in the country. You'll want to spend at least 2 hours wandering around the gardens here. Upon returning to San José, you can return the rental car and rely on taxis in the city, as it's much easier and less stressful than dealing with downtown traffic.

Day 4: More City Sights & Shopping

Spend this day further exploring the capital. Start by heading out on Paseo Colón to the **Museo de Arte Costarricense (Costa Rican Art Museum)** ★★ (p. 67), and spend some time in its wonderful open-air sculpture garden. After visiting the museum, take a stroll around the expansive downtown **Parque La Sabana** (p. 69). Intrepid travelers can also do some shopping at the **Mercado Central** ★ (p. 73).

Grano de Oro Restaurant ★★★

For your final dinner, splurge a bit and head to the elegant **Grano de Oro Restaurant** ★★★, located inside the boutique hotel of the same name. See p. 63. Serving up sophisticated contemporary cuisine with the freshest local ingredients, this is arguably the best restaurant in the city.

After dinner, take a late-night turn on the dance floor at **Castro's** ★ (p. 75) or **Vértigo** ★★ (p. 75).

COSTA RICA IN CONTEXT

3

Pura Vida! (Pure Life!) is Costa Rica's unofficial national slogan, and in many ways it defines the country. You'll hear it exclaimed, proclaimed, and simply stated by *Ticos* (slang for Costa Ricans) from all walks of life, from children to octogenarians. It can be used as a cheer after your favorite soccer team scores a goal, or as a descriptive response when someone asks you, *"¿Cómo estás?"* ("How are you?"). It is symbolic of the easygoing nature of this country's people, politics, and personality.

Costa Rica itself is a mostly rural country with vast areas of protected tropical forests. It is one of the biologically richest places on earth, with a wealth of flora and fauna that attracts and captivates biologists, photographers, ecotourists, and casual visitors alike.

COSTA RICA TODAY

Costa Rica has a population of a little more than 5 million people, more than half of whom live in the urban Central Valley. Some 94 percent of the population is of Spanish or other European descent, and it is not unusual to see fair-skinned and blond Costa Ricans. This is largely because the small indigenous population here when the first Spaniards arrived was quickly reduced by war and disease. Some indigenous populations still remain, primarily on reservations around the country; the principal tribes include the Bribri, Cabécar, Boruca, and Guaymí. On the Caribbean coast, there is a substantial population of English-speaking black Creoles who came in the late–19th and early–20th centuries from Jamaica and other Caribbean islands as railroad builders and banana workers. Racial tension isn't palpable, but it exists, perhaps more out of historical ignorance rather than articulated prejudice.

Costa Ricans are a friendly and outgoing people. When interacting with visitors, Ticos are very open and helpful. But time has a relative meaning here, so don't expect punctuality as a rule.

In a region historically plagued by internal strife and civil wars, Costa Ricans are proud of their peaceful history, political stability, and relatively high level of development. However, this can also translate into arrogance and prejudice toward immigrants from neighboring countries, particularly Nicaraguans, who make up a large percentage of the workforce on many plantations.

Roman Catholicism is the official religion of Costa Rica, although freedom of religion is guaranteed by its constitution. More than 75 percent of the population identifies itself as Roman Catholic, while another 14 percent are part of evangelical Christian congregations. There is a small Jewish community as well. By and large, many Ticos are religiously observant, if not fervent, though just as many lead totally secular lives. *Pura vida.*

THE MAKING OF COSTA RICA

Early History

Little is known of Costa Rica's history before its colonization by Spanish settlers. The pre-Columbian Indians who made their home in this region of Central America never developed the large cities or advanced culture that appeared farther north in what would become Guatemala, Belize, and Mexico. There are no grand pyramids or large Mayan cities. However, ancient artifacts indicating a strong sense of aesthetics have been unearthed from scattered excavations around the country. Ornate gold and jade jewelry, intricately carved grinding stones, and artistically painted terra-cotta objects point to a small but highly skilled indigenous population.

Spain Settles Costa Rica

In 1502, on his fourth and last voyage to the New World, Christopher Columbus anchored just offshore from present-day Limón. Whether he actually gave the country its name—"Rich Coast"—is open to debate, but the Spaniards never did find many riches to exploit here.

The earliest Spanish settlers found that, unlike settlements to the north, the native population of Costa Rica was unwilling to submit to slavery. Despite their small numbers, scattered villages, and tribal differences, they fought back against the Spanish until they were overcome by superior firepower and European diseases. When the fighting ended, the European settlers in Costa Rica found that very few Indians were left to force into servitude. The settlers were thus forced to till their own lands, a situation unheard of in other parts of Central America. Few pioneers headed this way because they could settle in Guatemala, with its large native workforce. Costa Rica was nearly forgotten, as the Spanish crown looked elsewhere for riches to plunder and souls to convert.

It didn't take long for Costa Rica's few Spanish settlers to head for the hills, where they found rich volcanic soil and a climate that was less oppressive than in the lowlands. **Cartago,** the colony's first capital, was founded in 1563, but it was not until the 1700s that additional cities were established in this agriculturally rich region. In the late–18th century, the first coffee plants were introduced, and because these plants thrived in the highlands, Costa Rica began to develop its first cash crop. Unfortunately, it was a long and difficult journey transporting the coffee to the Caribbean coast and then onward to Europe, where the demand for coffee was growing.

From Independence to the Present Day

In 1821, Spain granted independence to its colonies in Central America. Costa Rica joined with its neighbors to form the Central American Federation; but in 1838, it withdrew to form a new nation and pursue its own interests. By the mid-1800s, coffee was the country's main export. Free land was given to anyone willing to plant coffee on it, and plantation owners soon grew wealthy and powerful, creating Costa Rica's first elite class.

The Little Drummer Boy

Costa Rica's national hero is Juan Santamaría. The legend goes that young Juan enlisted as a drummer boy in the campaign against William Walker. On April 11, 1856, when Costa Rican troops had a band of Walker's men cornered in an inn in Rivas, Nicaragua, Santamaría volunteered for a suicidal mission to set the building on fire. Although he was mortally wounded, Santamaría was successful in torching the building and driving Walker's men out. Today, April 11 is a national holiday.

This was a stormy period in Costa Rican history. In 1856, the country was invaded by mercenaries hired by **William Walker,** a soldier of fortune from Tennessee who was attempting to fulfill his grandiose dreams of presiding over a slave state in Central America (before his invasion of Costa Rica, he had invaded Nicaragua and Baja California). The people of Costa Rica, led by President Juan Rafael Mora, marched against Walker's men and chased them back to Nicaragua. Walker eventually surrendered to a U.S. warship in 1857, but, in 1860, he attacked Honduras, claiming to be its president. The Hondurans, who had had enough of Walker's shenanigans, executed him.

In 1889, Costa Rica held what is considered the first free election in Central American history. The opposition candidate won the election, and control of the government passed from one political party to another without bloodshed or hostilities. Thus, Costa Rica established itself as the region's only true democracy. In 1948, this democratic process was challenged by **Rafael Angel Calderón,** who served as the country's president from 1940 to 1944. After losing by a narrow margin, Calderón, who had the backing of the communist labor unions and Catholic Church, refused to concede the country's leadership to the rightfully elected president, **Otillio Ulate,** and a civil war ensued. Calderón was eventually defeated by **José "Pepe" Figueres.** In the wake of this crisis, a new constitution was drafted, which abolished Costa Rica's army.

An international star arose in Costa Rica when **Oscar Arias Sánchez** was elected president in 1986 and won the Nobel Peace Prize in 1987 for his successful mediation of the Sandinista-Contra war in Nicaragua and other regional conflicts. Costa Rica's best-known native son, he served from 1986 to 1990 and again from 2006 to 2010.

In 1994, history seemed to repeat itself—peacefully this time—when **José María Figueres** took the reins of government from the son of his father's adversary, Rafael Angel Calderón. In 2010, Costa Rica elected its first female president, **Laura Chinchilla.** On April 6, 2014, former university professor

Luis Guillermo Solís of the opposition Citizen's Action Party won a run-off election by a landslide over longtime San José mayor Johnny Araya. So far, Solis's presidency has been a mixed bag. He's had trouble moving legislation forward, and divisions within his own ruling coalition have been a large part of that problem. Longstanding structural issues have hampered attempts at addressing infrastructure and revenue problems.

RECOMMENDED READING

NATURAL HISTORY I think every visitor to Costa Rica should read *Tropical Nature* by Adrian Forsyth and Ken Miyata. It's a wonderfully written and lively collection of tales and adventures by two Neotropical biologists who spent quite some time in the forests of Costa Rica.

Mario A. Boza's beautiful *Costa Rica National Parks* has been reissued in an elegant coffee-table edition. Other worthwhile coffee-table books include *Rainforests: Costa Rica and Beyond* by Adrian Forsyth, with photographs by Michael and Patricia Fogden; and *Costa Rica: A Journey Through Nature* by Adrian Hepworth.

Two good choices for an introduction to Costa Rica's fauna are *The Wildlife of Costa Rica: A Field Guide* by Fiona Reid, Jim Zook, Twan Leenders, and Robert Dean; and *Costa Rica: Traveller's Wildlife Guides* by Les Beletsky. Both pack a lot of useful information into a concise package.

A Guide to the Birds of Costa Rica by F. Gary Stiles and Alexander Skutch is an invaluable guide for identifying the many birds you'll see during your stay. Most guides and nature lodges have a copy on hand. Bird-watchers might also consider *A Bird-Finding Guide to Costa Rica* by Barrett Lawson, which details the best birding sites throughout the country.

Other interesting natural-history books that survey the plants and animals of Costa Rica include *Costa Rica Natural History* by Daniel Janzen; *A Guide to Tropical Plants of Costa Rica* by Willow Zuchowsky; *The Natural History of Costa Rican Mammals* by Mark Wainwright; *A Guide to the Amphibians and Reptiles of Costa Rica* by Twan Leenders; and the classic *A Neotropical Companion* by John C. Kricher, in an expanded edition with color photos.

GENERAL INTEREST For a look into Costa Rican society, pick up *The Ticos: Culture and Social Change* by Richard, Karen, and Mavis Biesanz, an examination of the country's politics and culture. Also worth checking out is *The Costa Rica Reader: History, Culture, Politics,* a broad selection of stories and essays by Costa Ricans from all walks of life.

For more about the life and culture of Costa Rica's Talamanca coast, an area populated by Afro-Caribbean people whose forebears emigrated from Caribbean islands in the early–19th century, read Paula Palmer's *What Happen: A Folk-History of Costa Rica's Talamanca Coast,* a collection of oral histories.

FICTION & POETRY *Costa Rica: A Traveler's Literary Companion,* edited by Barbara Ras and with a foreword by Oscar Arias Sánchez, is a collection of short stories by Costa Rican writers, organized by regions of the country. Entries include works by many of the country's leading literary lights, and the geographical breakdown makes it a good companion as you travel from place to place around Costa Rica.

Young adults will enjoy Kristin Joy Pratt's *A Walk in the Rainforest,* while younger children will like the beautifully illustrated *The Forest in the Clouds* by Sneed Collard and Michael Rothman, and *The Umbrella* by Jan Brett. Pachanga Kids (www.pachangakids.com) has published several illustrated bilingual children's books with delightful illustrations by Ruth Angulo, including *Mar Azucarada/Sugar Sea* by Roberto Boccanera, and *El Coyote y la Luciérnaga/ The Coyote and the Firefly* by Yazmin Ross, which includes a musical CD.

One of the most important pieces in the Costa Rican canon, Carlos Luis Fallas's 1941 tome *Mamita Yunai* provides a stark look at the impact of the large banana giant United Fruit on the country. More recently, Fernando Contreras takes up where his predecessor left off in *Unico Mirando al Mar,* which describes the conditions of the poor, predominantly children, who scavenge Costa Rica's garbage dumps.

COSTA RICA IN POPULAR CULTURE

Music

Several musical traditions and styles meet and mingle in Costa Rica. The northern Guanacaste region is a hotbed of folk music that is strongly influenced by the *marimba* (wooden xylophone) traditions of Guatemala and Nicaragua, while also featuring guitars, maracas, and the occasional harp. On the Caribbean coast, you can hear traditional calypso sung by descendants of the original black workers brought here. Roving bands play a mix of guitar, banjo, washtub bass, and percussion in the bars and restaurants of Cahuita and Puerto Viejo.

Costa Rica also has a healthy contemporary music scene. The jazz-fusion trio **Editus** has won two Grammy awards for its work with Panamanian salsa giant (and movie star) **Rubén Blades. Malpaís,** the closest thing Costa Rica had to a super-group, suffered the sudden and tragic loss of its lead singer, but still has several excellent albums out.

Also look for music by **Cantoamérica,** which plays upbeat dance music ranging from salsa to calypso to merengue. Jazz pianist and former Minister of Culture **Manuel Obregón** (also a member of Malpaís) has several excellent solo albums out, including **Simbiosis** (2011)**,** on which he improvises along with the sounds of Costa Rica's wildlife, waterfalls, and weather.

Local label **Papaya Music ★★★** (www.papayamusic.com) has done an excellent job promoting and producing albums by Costa Rican musicians in a variety of styles and genres. They range from the Guanacasteca folk songs of **Max Goldemberg,** to the boleros of **Ray Tico,** to the original calypso of **Walter "Gavitt" Ferguson.** You can find their CDs at gift shops and record stores around the country.

Art

Unlike Guatemala, Mexico, or even Nicaragua, Costa Rica does not have a strong tradition of local or indigenous arts and crafts. The strong suit of Costa Rican art is European- and Western-influenced, ranging from neoclassical to modern in style.

Deceased and living legends of the art world include **Rafa Fernández, Lola Fernández,** and **Cesar Valverde.** Also be on the lookout for works by **Max Jiménez** (1900–74), **Francisco Amighetti** (1907–98), **Manuel de la Cruz** (1909–86), and **Teodorico Quiros** (1897–1977). These early-20th-century painters were responsible for the first semi-important local art movement.

Contemporary artists making waves and names for themselves include **Fernando Carballo, Rodolfo Stanley, Lionel González, Manuel Zumbado,** and **Karla Solano.**

Sculpture is perhaps one of the strongest aspects of the Costa Rican art scene, with the large bronze works of **Francisco "Paco" Zuñiga** among the best of the genre. Zuñiga's larger-than-life castings include exaggerated human proportions that recall Rodin and Botero. Meanwhile, the artists **José Sancho, Edgar Zuñiga,** and **Jiménez Deredia** are all producing internationally acclaimed pieces, many of monumental proportions. You can see examples by all these sculptors around the country, as well as at San José's downtown **Museo de Arte Costarricense ★★** (p. 67). Also enjoyable are the whimsical works of **Leda Astorga,** who sculpts and then paints a pantheon of plump and voluptuous figures in interesting and sometimes compromising poses.

You'll find the country's best and most impressive museums and galleries in San José (p. 66), and to a lesser extent in some of the country's larger and more popular tourist destinations, like Manuel Antonio and Monteverde.

Architecture

Costa Rica lacks the large-scale pre-Columbian ceremonial ruins found throughout much of the rest of Mesoamerica. The only notable early archaeological site is **Guayabo.** However, only the foundations of a few dwellings, a handful of carved petroglyphs, and some road and water infrastructure are still visible here.

Similarly, Costa Rica doesn't have the same large and well-preserved colonial-era cities found throughout much of the rest of Latin America. The original capital of **Cartago** (p. 78) has some old ruins and a few colonial-era buildings, as well as the country's grandest church, the **Basílica de Nuestra Señora de los Angeles (Basilica of Our Lady of the Angels) ★** (p. 79), which was built in honor of the country's patron saint, La Negrita, or the Virgin of Guadalupe. Although legend says the sculpture of the Virgin was discovered here in 1635, the church itself wasn't inaugurated until 1924.

A few modern architects are creating names for themselves. **Ronald Zurcher,** who designed the luxurious **Four Seasons Resort** (p. 89) and several other large hotel projects, is one of the shining lights of contemporary Costa Rican architecture.

TICO etiquette & CUSTOMS

In general, Costa Ricans are easygoing, friendly, and informal. That said, they tend to be somewhat conservative and treat everyone respectfully. In conversation, Ticos are relatively formal. When addressing someone, they use the formal *usted* in most instances, reserving the familiar *vos* or *tú* for friends, family, and children or teenagers.

Upon greeting or saying goodbye, both sexes shake hands, although across genders, a light kiss on one cheek is common.

Proud of their neutrality and lack of armed forces, everyday Costa Ricans are uncomfortable with confrontation. What may seem like playful banter or justified outrage to a foreign tourist may be taken very badly by a Tico. Avoid criticizing Costa Rica unless you know exactly to whom you're talking and what you're talking about.

In some cases, especially in the service industry, Ticos may tell you what they think you want to hear, just to avoid a confrontation—even if they know it might not turn out to be true. Sometimes Ticos will give you wrong directions instead of telling you they don't know the way.

Tico men tend to dress conservatively. In San José and other cities in the Central Valley, you will rarely see a Costa Rican man wearing short pants. In most towns and cities, tourists will stand out when wearing short pants, sandals, and other beach, golf, or vacation wear. Costa Rican women, on the other hand, especially young women, tend to show some skin in everyday, and even business, situations. Still, be respectful in your dress, especially if you plan on visiting churches, small towns, or local families.

Women, no matter how they dress, may find themselves on the receiving end of whistles, honks, hoots, hisses, and catcalls. For more information on this manifestation of Costa Rican machismo, see "Women Travelers" on p. 255.

Punctuality is not a Costa Rican strong suit. Ticos often show up anywhere from 15 minutes to an hour or more late to meetings and appointments—this is known as *la hora tica*, or "Tico time." That said, buses and local airlines, tour operators, movie theaters, and most businesses do tend to run on a relatively timely schedule.

EATING & DRINKING

Costa Rican food is not especially memorable, although some of the exotic fruits and vegetables served here certainly are. Creative chefs using fresh local ingredients have livened up the dining scene in San José and at most of the major tourist destinations, and a few are even turning out inventive takes on traditional Costa Rican classics. Outside of the capital and major tourist destinations, though, your options get very limited very fast; in fact, many destinations are so remote that you have no choice but to eat in the hotel's restaurant. At remote jungle lodges, the food is usually served buffet- or family-style; the quality can range from bland to inspired, depending on who's doing the cooking, and turnover in the kitchen is high.

Fortunately, eating in Costa Rica won't break your budget. At even the more expensive restaurants, it's hard to spend more than $50 a head unless you really splurge on drinks. It gets even cheaper outside the city and high-end hotels. But if you really want to save money, Costa Rican food, or *comida típica,* food is always the cheapest nourishment available. It's primarily served in *sodas,* Costa Rica's equivalent of diners.

Meals & Dining Customs

Rice and beans are the base of every Costa Rican meal—all three of them. At breakfast, they're called *gallo pinto* and come with everything from eggs to steak to seafood. At lunch or dinner, rice and beans are an integral part of the traditional *casado* (which means "married," and is derived from the days when a worker who brought one of these varied meals to work was thought to have a "married man's lunch"). A *casado* consists of rice 'n beans, a cabbage and tomato salad, fried plantains and chicken, fish, or beef. On the Caribbean coast, rice and beans are called "rice 'n' beans" and are cooked in coconut milk.

Dining hours in Costa Rica are flexible but generally follow North American customs. Some downtown restaurants in San José are open 24 hours; however, expensive restaurants tend to be open for lunch between 11am and 3pm and for dinner between 6 and 11pm.

APPETIZERS Known as *bocas* in Costa Rica, appetizers are served with drinks in most bars. Sometimes the *bocas* are free, but if not, they're usually inexpensive. Popular *bocas* include *gallos* (tortillas piled with meat, chicken, cheese, or beans), *ceviche* (a marinated seafood salad), tamales (stuffed cornmeal patties wrapped and steamed inside banana leaves), *patacones* (fried green plantain chips), and fried yuca.

SANDWICHES & SNACKS Ticos love to snack, and a large variety of tasty little sandwiches and snacks are available on the street, at snack bars, and in *sodas. Arreglados* are little meat-filled sandwiches, as are *tortas,* which are served on little rolls with a bit of salad tucked into them. Tacos, tamales, *gallos* (see above), and *empanadas* (turnovers) also are quite common.

MEAT Costa Rica is beef country, having long ago converted much of its rainforest to pastures for raising beef cattle. Consequently, beef is cheap and plentiful, although it might be a bit tougher—and cut and served thinner—than

Chifrijo: King of Costa Rican *Bocas*

Without a doubt, Costa Rica's most popular and famous *boca* is a bowl of *chifrijo.* The name is a phonetic abbreviation of its two most important ingredients: *chicharrones* (fried pork bellies) and *frijoles* (beans). A proper bowl of *chifrijo* will also have rice, *pico de gallo* (a tomato-based salsa) and a few slices of avocado, accompanied by some tortilla chips to scoop it all up.

The creation was the brainchild of Miguel Cordero, who began serving it in his family bar in Tibas in the early 1980s. The dish quickly spread like wildfire and can now be found in restaurants and bars around the country. Cordero had the foresight to trademark his dish, and in 2014 he began taking legal action against competitors for trademark infringement. Thanks to his trademark claims, restaurant and bar owners have had to scramble. You can still usually find *chifrijo* on the menu, only it might be called *frichijo,* or *hochifri,* or some other variation on the theme.

you are used to. One typical local dish is called *olla de carne,* a bowl of beef broth with large chunks of meat, local tubers, and corn. Spit-roasted chicken is also very popular and is meltingly tender. Lamb is used sparsely in Costa Rican cooking, although finer restaurants often serve a lamb dish or two.

SEAFOOD Costa Rica has two coasts, and plenty of seafood is available everywhere in the country. *Corvina* (sea bass) is the most commonly served fish and is prepared in numerable ways, including as *ceviche.* (But be careful: In many cheaper restaurants, particularly in San José, shark meat is often sold as *corvina.*) You should also come across *pargo* (red snapper), *dorado* (mahimahi), and tuna on some menus, especially along the coasts.

VEGETABLES On the whole, you'll find vegetables surprisingly lacking in the meals you're served in Costa Rica—usually nothing more than a little pile of shredded cabbage topped with a slice or two of tomato. For a more satisfying and filling salad, order *palmito* (hearts of palm salad). The heart (actually the stalk or trunk of these small palms) is boiled and then chopped into circular pieces and served with other fresh vegetables, with salad dressing on top. If you want something more than this, you'll have to order a side dish such as *picadillo,* a stew or purée of vegetables with a bit of meat in it.

One more vegetable worth mentioning is the *pejibaye,* a form of palm fruit that looks like a miniature orange coconut. Boiled *pejibayes* are frequently sold from carts on the streets of San José. When cut in half, a *pejibaye* reveals a large seed surrounded by soft, fibrous flesh. You can eat it plain, but it's usually topped with a dollop of mayonnaise.

FRUITS *Plátanos* (plantains) are giant relatives of bananas that are cooked and served with countless *casados* every day. Green plantains have a starchy flavor and consistency, but tbecome as sweet as candy as they ripen, especially when fried. Costa Rica has a wealth of delicious tropical fruits, including mangoes (the season begins in May), papayas, pineapples, melons, and bananas. Other fruits include *marañón,* which is the fruit of the cashew tree and has orange or yellow glossy skin; *granadilla* or *maracuyá* (passion fruit); *mamón chino,* which Asian travelers will immediately recognize as rambutan; and *carambola* (starfruit).

DESSERTS *Queque seco* (dry cake) is pound cake. *Tres leches* cake, on the other hand, is so moist that you almost need to eat it with a spoon. Flan is a typical custard dessert. It often comes as either *flan de caramelo* (caramel) or *flan de coco* (coconut). Numerous other sweets are available, many of which are made with condensed milk and raw sugar. *Cajetas* are popular handmade candies, made from sugar and various mixes of evaporated, condensed, and powdered milk. They are sold in differing-size bits and chunks at most *pulperías* (small stores) and streetside food stands.

BEVERAGES *Frescos, refrescos,* and *jugos naturales* are popular drinks in Costa Rica. They are usually made with fresh fruit and milk or water. Among the more common fruits used are mangoes, papayas, blackberries, and pineapples. You'll also come across *maracuyá* (passion fruit) and *carambola* (star fruit). Some of the more unusual frescos are *horchata* (made with rice flour and a lot of cinnamon) and *chan* (made with the seed of a plant found mostly in Guanacaste—definitely an acquired taste). The former is wonderful; the latter requires an open mind (it's reputed to be good for the digestive system). Order *un fresco con leche sin hielo* (a fresco with milk but without ice) if you want to avoid untreated water.

Costa Rica is a coffee mecca, but some coffee drinkers might be disappointed here. Most of the best coffee has traditionally been targeted for export, and Ticos tend to prefer theirs weak and sugary. Better hotels and restaurants, catering to foreign tastes, now serve up superior blends. If you want black coffee, ask for *café negro;* if you want it with milk, order *café con leche.*

For something different in the morning, ask for *agua dulce,* a warm drink made from melted sugar cane and served either with milk or lemon, or straight.

Costa Rica has seen an amazing boom in craft beers and places to drink them in the past few years. **Costa Rica's Craft Brewing Company** (www.beer.cr) has led the way. Its Libertas Golden Ale and Segua Red Ale are available at more and more restaurants and bars around the country, and can be purchased at larger supermarkets. These folks offer tours of their brewery and have a small brewpub at their main facility in Ciudad Colón, a western suburb of San Jose. Other brews and breweries to look for include Ambar by **Cervecera del Centro** (www.cerveceradelcentro.com); Majadera Pale Ale and Japiendin Tropical Ale from **Treinta y Cinco** (www.treintaycinco.com); and Witch's Rock Pale Ale and Gato Malo Dark Ale by the **Volcano Brewing Company** (www.volcanobrewingcompany.com) in Tamarindo.

Coconut, Straight Up

Throughout Costa Rica, keep your eye out for roadside stands selling fresh, green coconuts, or *pipas*. Green coconuts have very little meat, but are filled with copious amounts of a slightly sweet, clear liquid that is extremely refreshing. According to local legend, this liquid is pure enough to be used as plasma in an emergency situation. Armed with a machete, the *pipa* seller will grab a cold one, cut out the top, stick in a straw, and ask you for about C500.

SHOPPING

Costa Rica is not known as a shopping paradise, as most of what you'll find for sale is pretty run-of-the-mill, mass-produced souvenir fare. So scant are its handicraft offerings that most tourist shops sell Guatemalan clothing, Panamanian appliquéd textiles, Salvadoran painted wood souvenirs, and Nicaraguan rocking chairs. Still, Costa Rica does have a few locally produced arts and handicrafts to look out for, and a couple of towns and villages with well-deserved reputations for their unique works.

Perhaps the most famous of all towns for shopping is **Sarchí** ★ (p. 82), a Central Valley town filled with handicraft shops. Sarchí is best known as the citadel of the colorfully painted Costa Rican **oxcart,** reproductions of which are manufactured in various scaled-down sizes. These make excellent gifts.

(Larger oxcarts can be easily disassembled and shipped to your home.) A lot of furniture is also made in Sarchí.

In Guanacaste, the small town of **Guaitíl** (p. 117) is famous for its pottery. A host of small workshops, studios, and storefronts ring the town's central park (which is actually a soccer field). Many of the low-fired ceramic wares here carry ancient local indigenous motifs, while others get quirky modern treatments. You can find examples of this low-fired simple ceramic work in many gift shops around the country, and at roadside stands all across Guanacaste.

You might also run across **carved masks ★★★** made by the indigenous **Boruca** people of southern Costa Rica. The small Boruca villages where these masks are carved are off the beaten path, but you will find them for sale at some of the better gift shops around the country. These wooden masks come in a variety of sizes and styles, both painted and unpainted, and run anywhere from $20 to $150, depending on the quality of workmanship. But don't be fooled. You'll see scores of mass-produced wooden masks at souvenir and gift shops around Costa Rica. Many are imported from Mexico, Guatemala, and Indonesia. Real Boruca masks are unique indigenous art works, often signed by their carvers.

Much of the Costa Rican woodwork for sale is mass-produced. A couple of notable exceptions include the work of **Barry Biesanz ★★,** whose excellent hardwood creations are sold at better gift shops around the country, and the unique, large-scale sculptures created and sold at the **Original Grand Gallery** (p. 154) in La Fortuna.

Coffee remains a favorite gift item. It's a great deal, it's readily available, and Costa Rican coffee is some of the best in the world. See the "Joe to Go" box on p. 71 for tips on buying coffee in Costa Rica.

A few other items worth keeping an eye out for include reproductions of **pre-Columbian gold jewelry** and **carved-stone figurines.** The former are available as either solid gold, silver, or gold-plated. The latter, although interesting, can be extremely heavy.

Contemporary and **classic Costa Rican art** is another great option, both for discerning collectors and those looking for a unique reminder of their time in the country. San José has the most galleries and shops, but you will find good, well-stocked galleries in some of the more booming tourist destinations, including Liberia, Manuel Antonio, Jacó, and Monteverde.

Caveat Emptor

International laws prohibit trade in endangered wildlife, so don't buy any plants or animals, even if they're readily for sale. Do not buy any kind of sea-turtle products (including jewelry); wild birds; lizards, snakes, or cat skins; corals; or orchids (except those grown commercially). No matter how unique, beautiful, or insignificant it might seem, your purchase will directly contribute to the further hunting of animals and destruction of natural environments.

In addition, be careful when buying wood products, and try to buy sustainably harvested woods. Costa Rica's rainforest hardwoods are a finite and rapidly disappearing resource.

Finally, one item that you'll see at gift shops around the country is **Cuban cigars.** It's no longer illegal to bring them back to the United States.

WHEN TO GO

Costa Rica's high season for tourism runs from late November to late April, which coincides almost perfectly with the chill of winter in the United States, Canada, and Europe. The high season is also the dry season. If you want some unadulterated time on a tropical beach and a little less rain during your rainforest experience, this is the time to come. During this period (especially during the Christmas holiday and Holy Week before Easter), the tourism industry operates at full tilt—prices are higher, attractions are more crowded, and reservations need to be made in advance.

Local tourism operators often call the tropical rainy season (May through mid-Nov) the "green season," an apt euphemism. At this time of year, even brown and barren Guanacaste province becomes lush and verdant. Many locals will tell you the rainy season is their favorite time of year. It's easy to find or at least negotiate reduced rates, there are far fewer tourists, and the rain is often limited to a few hours each afternoon (although you can occasionally get socked in for a week at a time). One drawback: Some of the country's rugged roads become impassable without four-wheel-drive during the rainy season.

Weather

Costa Rica is a tropical country with distinct wet and dry seasons. However, some regions are rainy all year, and others are dry and sunny most of the year. Temperatures vary primarily with elevations, not with seasons: On the coasts, it's hot all year; in the mountains, it can be cool at night any time of year. Frost is common at the highest elevations (3,000–3,600m/9,840–11,808 ft.).

Average Daytime High Temperatures & Rainfall in San José

	JAN	FEB	MAR	APR	MAY	JUNE	JULY	AUG	SEPT	OCT	NOV	DEC
Temp (°F)	75	76	79	79	80	79	77	78	79	77	77	75
Temp (°C)	24	24	26	26	27	26	25	26	26	25	25	24
Days of rain	1.3	1.5	2.2	4.2	11.5	14.5	13.7	14.5	18.1	17.9	8.6	2.3

Generally, the **rainy season** (or "green season") is from May to mid-November in most of the country, with notable exceptions on the Caribbean coast. Costa Ricans call this wet time of year their winter. The **dry season,** considered summer by Costa Ricans, is from mid-November to April. In Guanacaste, the arid northwestern province, the dry season lasts several weeks longer than in other places. Even in the rainy season, days often start sunny, with rain falling in the afternoon and evening. On the Caribbean coast, especially south of Limón, you can count on rain year-round, although this area gets far less rain in September and October than the rest of the country, making this a great time to visit.

The most popular time of year to visit Costa Rica is in December and January, when everything is still green from the rains, but the sky is clear.

Holidays

Because Costa Rica is a Roman Catholic country, most of its holidays are church-related. The big ones are Christmas, New Year's, and Easter, which are all celebrated for several days. Holy Week (the week preceding Easter) is a huge holiday in Costa Rica, and many families head for the beach. (Controversially, many local governments allow no alcohol sales during Holy Week.) Also, there is no public transportation on Holy Thursday or Good Friday. Government offices and banks are closed on official holidays, transportation services are reduced, and stores and markets might also close.

Official holidays in Costa Rica include **January 1** (New Year's Day), **March 19** (St. Joseph's Day), Thursday and Friday of Holy Week, **April 11** (Juan Santamaría's Day), **May 1** (Labor Day), **June 29** (St. Peter and St. Paul Day), **July 25** (annexation of the province of Guanacaste), **August 2** (Virgin of Los Angeles's Day), **August 15** (Mother's Day), **September 15** (Independence Day), **October 12** (Discovery of America/Día de la Raza), **December 8** (Immaculate Conception of the Virgin Mary), **December 24** and **25** (Christmas), and **December 31** (New Year's Eve).

Calendar of Events

For information on events with no contact number listed, call the **Costa Rican Tourism Board (ICT)** at ✆ **866/COSTA RICA** in the U.S. and Canada, or 2223-1733 in Costa Rica, or visit **www.visitcostarica.com.**

JANUARY

Copa del Café (Coffee Cup), San José. Matches for this international event on the junior tennis tour are held at the Costa Rica Country Club (www.copacafe.com; ✆ **2228-9333**). First week in January.

Fiestas of Palmares, Palmares. Perhaps the largest and best organized of the traditional fiestas, it includes bullfights, a horseback parade (*tope*), concerts, carnival rides, and food booths (www.fiestaspalmares.com). First 2 weeks in January.

MARCH

Día del Boyero (Oxcart Drivers' Day), San Antonio de Escazú. Colorfully painted oxcarts parade through this suburb of San José, and local priests bless the oxen. Second Sunday in March.

National Orchid Show, San José. Orchid growers throughout the world gather to show their wares, trade tales and secrets, and admire the hundreds of species on display. Contact the Costa Rican Tourist Board for location and dates. Mid-March.

APRIL

Holy Week. Religious processions are held in cities and towns throughout the country. Week before Easter.

Juan Santamaría Day, Alajuela. Costa Rica's national hero is honored with parades, concerts, and dances. April 11.

JULY

Fiesta of the Virgin of the Sea, Puntarenas. A regatta of boats carrying a statue of the patron saint of Puntarenas marks this festival. A similar event is held at Playa del Coco. Saturday closest to July 16.

Annexation of Guanacaste Day, Liberia. Tico-style bullfights, folk dancing, horseback parades, rodeos, concerts, and other events celebrate the day when this region became part of Costa Rica. July 25.

AUGUST

Fiesta de la Virgen de Los Angeles, Cartago. This is the annual pilgrimage day of the patron saint of Costa Rica. Many people walk the 24km (15 miles) from San José to the basilica in Cartago. August 2.

SEPTEMBER

Costa Rica's Independence Day, nationwide. One of the most distinctive aspects of this festival is the nighttime marching-band parades of children in their school uniforms, who play the national anthem on steel xylophones. September 15.

International Beach Clean-Up Day. Chip in and help clean up the beleaguered shoreline of your favorite beach. Third Saturday in September.

OCTOBER

Limón Carnival/Día de la Raza, Limón. A smaller version of Mardi Gras, complete with floats and dancing in the streets, commemorates Columbus's discovery of Costa Rica. Week of October 12.

DECEMBER

El Tope and Carnival, San José. The streets of downtown belong to horses and their riders in a proud recognition of the country's important agricultural heritage. The next day, those same streets are taken over by carnival floats, marching bands, and street dancers. December 26 and 27.

Festejos Populares, San José. Bullfights, carnival rides, games of chance, and fast-food stands are set up at the fairgrounds in Zapote (www.festejospopulares.net). Last week of December.

COSTA RICA'S NATURAL WORLD

4

Costa Rica occupies a central spot in the isthmus that joins North and South America. For millennia, this land bridge served as a migratory thoroughfare and mating ground for species native to the once-separate continents. It was also where the Mesoamerican and Andean pre-Columbian indigenous cultures met.

In any one spot in Costa Rica, temperatures remain relatively constant year-round. However, they vary dramatically according to altitude, from tropically hot and steamy along the coasts to below freezing at the highest elevations. These variations in altitude, temperature, and precipitation give rise to a wide range of ecosystems and habitats, which are described in "Costa Rica's Ecosystems," below.

For its part, the countryside has a wide variety of ecosystems and habitats that have blessed it with a unique biological bounty. More than 10,000 identified species of plants, 880 species of birds, 9,000 species of butterflies and moths, and 500 species of mammals, reptiles, and amphibians are found here. For detailed information on some of the more common or evocative representatives of Costa Rica's flora and fauna, see p. 41.

Thankfully, for both visitors and the local flora and fauna alike, nearly one-quarter of Costa Rica's entire landmass is protected either as part of a national park or private nature reserve. This chapter includes descriptions of the most important national parks and bioreserves in the country.

THE LAY OF THE LAND

Costa Rica's Ecosystems

RAINFORESTS

Costa Rica's **rainforests** are classic tropical jungles. Some receive more than 7m (23 ft.) of rainfall a year, and their climate is typically hot and humid, especially in the lowland forests. Trees grow tall and fast, fighting for sunlight in the upper reaches. Life and foliage on the forest floor are surprisingly sparse. The main level of the rainforest is in the canopy, around 30m (98 ft.) high, where the vast majority of animals live, in towering trees festooned with vines and bromeliads.

IN SEARCH OF turtles

Few places in the world have as many sea-turtle nesting sites as Costa Rica. Along both coasts, five species come ashore at specific times of the year to dig nests in the sand and lay their eggs. Sea turtles are endangered throughout the world due to over-hunting, accidental deaths in fishing nets, development of beaches that once served as nesting areas, and the collection and sale (often illegally) of their eggs. International trade in sea-turtle products is already prohibited by most countries (including the U.S.), but sea-turtle numbers continue to dwindle.

The species of sea turtles that nest on Costa Rica's beaches are the **olive ridley** (known for mass egg-laying migrations, or *arribadas*), **leatherback, hawksbill, green,** and **Pacific green turtle.** Excursions to see nesting turtles have become common, and they are fascinating, but please make sure that you and/or your guide do not disturb the turtles. Any light source (other than red-tinted flashlights) can confuse female turtles and cause them to return to the sea without laying their eggs. In fact, as more development takes place on the Costa Rican coast, hotel lighting may cause the number of nesting turtles to drop. Luckily, many of the nesting beaches have been protected as national parks.

Here are the main places to see nesting sea turtles: **Santa Rosa National Park** (near Liberia, olive ridleys nest here July–Dec, and to a lesser extent Jan–June); **Las Baulas National Marine Park** (near Tamarindo, leatherbacks nest here early Oct through mid-Feb); **Ostional National Wildlife Refuge** (near Playa Nosara, olive ridleys nest here July–Dec, and to a lesser extent Jan–June); and **Tortuguero National Park** (on the northern Caribbean coast, green turtles nest here July through mid-Oct, with Aug–Sept the peak period; in lesser numbers, leatherback turtles nest here Feb–June, peaking Mar–Apr).

Among the most interesting of these trees is the parasitic strangler fig, the *matapalo* ("tree killer"), which grows on other trees until it envelops and suffocates them, then remains standing as a tree in its own right, with a hollow interior after the original tree rots away.

Mammals that call the Costa Rican rainforests home include the jaguar, three-toed sloth, two-toed sloth, four species of monkeys, and the Baird's tapir. Some of the prettiest birds you are likely to spot are the scarlet macaws and the many-colored toucans.

You can find these lowland rainforests along the southern Pacific coast and Osa Peninsula, as well as along the Caribbean coast. **Corcovado, Cahuita,** and **Manuel Antonio** national parks, as well as the **Gandoca–Manzanillo Wildlife Refuge,** are fine examples of lowland rainforests. Examples of mid-elevation rainforests include the **Braulio Carillo National Park** and the forests around **La Selva** and the **Puerto Viejo de Sarapiquí** region, and those around the **Arenal Volcano** and **Lake Arenal** area.

TROPICAL DRY FORESTS

In a few protected areas of Guanacaste, you will still find examples of the otherwise vanishing **tropical dry forest.** During the long and pronounced dry season (late Nov to late Apr), no rain relieves the unabated heat. In an effort

monkey BUSINESS

No trip to Costa Rica would be complete without at least one monkey sighting. Home to four distinct species of primates, Costa Rica offers the opportunity for one of the world's most gratifying wildlife-viewing experiences. Just listen for the deep guttural call of a howler or the rustling of leaves overhead—telltale signs monkeys are near.

Costa Rica's most commonly spotted monkey is the white-faced or **capuchin monkey** (*mono cara blanca* in Spanish), which you might recognize as the infamous culprit from the film *Outbreak* (though, in reality, they don't live in Africa). Capuchins are agile, medium-size monkeys that make good use of their long, prehensile tails. They inhabit a diverse collection of habitats, ranging from the high-altitude cloud forests of the central region to the lowland mangroves of the Osa Peninsula. It's almost impossible not to spot capuchins at Manuel Antonio, where they have become sadly dependent on feedings by tourists. Please do not feed wild monkeys (and try to keep your food away from them—they're notorious thieves), and boycott establishments that try to attract both monkeys and tourists with daily feedings.

Howler monkeys (*mono congo* in Spanish) are named for their distinct and eerie call. Large and mostly black, these monkeys can seem ferocious because of their physical appearance and deep, resonant howls that can carry for more than a mile. Biologists believe that male howlers mark the bounds of their territories with these sounds. In the presence of humans, however, howlers are actually timid and tend to stay higher up in the canopy than their white-faced cousins. Howlers are easy to spot in the dry tropical forests of coastal Guanacaste and the Nicoya Peninsula.

More elusive are **spider monkeys** (*mono araña* in Spanish). These long, slender monkeys are dark brown to black and prefer the high canopies of primary rainforests. Spiders are very adept with their prehensile tails, but actually travel through the canopy with a hand-over-hand motion frequently imitated by their less graceful human cousins on playground monkey bars around the world. I've had my best luck spotting spider monkeys along the edges of Tortuguero's jungle canals.

The rarest and most endangered of Costa Rica's monkeys is the tiny **squirrel monkey** (*mono titi* in Spanish). These small brown monkeys have dark eyes surrounded by large white rings, white ears, white chests, and very long tails. In Costa Rica, squirrel monkeys can be found only at Manuel Antonio and the Osa Peninsula. These seemingly hyperactive monkeys are predominantly fruit eaters and often feed on banana and other fruit trees near hotels. Squirrel monkeys usually travel in large bands, so if you do see them, you'll likely see quite a few.

to conserve precious water, the trees drop their leaves but bloom in a riot of color: Purple jacaranda, scarlet *poró,* and brilliant orange flame-of-the-forest are just a few examples. During the rainy season, this deciduous forest is transformed into a lush and verdant landscape.

Other common dry forest trees include the *guanacaste*, with its broad shade canopy, and distinctive *pochote*, its trunk covered in thick, broad thorns.

Because the foliage is less dense, dry forests are excellent places to view wildlife. Howler monkeys are often seen in trees, and coatis, pumas, and coyotes roam the ground. Some of the best dry forests are found in **Santa Rosa, Guanacaste, Rincón de la Vieja,** and **Palo Verde** national parks.

CLOUD FORESTS

At higher altitudes, you'll find Costa Rica's famed **cloud forests.** Here the steady flow of moist air meets the mountains and creates a nearly constant mist. Epiphytes—resourceful plants that live cooperatively on the branches and trunks of other trees—grow abundantly in the cloud forests, where they extract moisture and nutrients from the air. Because cloud forests are found in generally steep, mountainous terrain, the canopy here is lower and less uniform than in lowland rainforests, providing better chances for viewing elusive fauna.

The remarkable **resplendent quetzal** is perhaps the most famous and sought-after eye candy in Costa Rica's cloud forests, but there's an immense variety of flora and fauna here, including multiple hummingbird species, wildcats, monkeys, reptiles, amphibians and bats. **Orchids,** many of them epiphytic, thrive in cloud forests, as do mosses, ferns, and a host of other plants, many of which are exported as houseplants.

Costa Rica's most spectacular cloud forest is the **Monteverde Cloud Forest Biological Reserve,** followed closely by its neighbor the **Santa Elena Cloud Forest Reserve.** Much closer to San José, you can also visit the **Los Angeles Cloud Forest Reserve.**

MANGROVES & WETLANDS

Along the coasts, primarily where river mouths meet the ocean, you will find extensive **mangrove forests, wetlands,** and **swamps.** Mangroves, in particular, are an immensely important ecological phenomenon. Around the intricate tangle of mangrove roots exists one of the most diverse and rich ecosystems on the planet. All sorts of fish and crustaceans live in the brackish tidal waters. Many larger saltwater and open-ocean fish species begin life in the nutrient-rich and relatively safe environment of a mangrove swamp.

Mangrove swamps are havens for and home to scores of water birds: **cormorants, magnificent frigate birds, pelicans, kingfishers, egrets, ibises,** and **herons.** The larger birds tend to nest up high in the canopy, while the smaller ones nestle in the underbrush. And in the waters, **caimans** and **crocodiles** cruise the maze of rivers and canals.

Mangrove forests, swamps, and wetlands exist along both coastlines. Some of the prime areas that can be explored are around the **Sierpe river mouth** and **Diquís delta** near **Drake Bay,** the **Golfo Dulce** in the southern zone, **Palo Verde National Park** and the **Tempisque River** basin in Guanacaste, and the **Gandoca–Manzanillo Wildlife Refuge** on the Caribbean coast.

PARAMO

At the highest reaches, the cloud forests give way to **elfin forests** and ***páramos.*** More commonly associated with the South American Andes, a *páramo* is characterized by tundra-like shrubs and grasses, with a scattering of twisted, windblown trees. Reptiles, rodents, and raptors are the most common residents here, and since the vegetation is so sparse, they're often easier to spot. **Mount Chirripó, Chirripó National Park,** and the **Cerro de la Muerte (Mountain of Death)** are the principal areas to find *páramos* in Costa Rica.

VOLCANOES

Costa Rica is a land of high volcanic and seismic activity. The country has three major **volcanic mountain ranges,** and many of the volcanoes are still active, allowing visitors to experience the awe-inspiring sight of steaming **fumaroles,** if not sky-lighting **eruptions.** In ecological terms, cooled-off lava flows are fascinating laboratories, where you can watch pioneering lichen and mosses eventually give way to plants, shrubs, trees, and forests.

Arenal Volcano used to be a top spot for volcanic activity, but it went dark in 2010. One reliable place to view mud pots, fumaroles, and hot springs is **Rincón de la Vieja National Park.** Closer to San José, the **Poás** and **Irazú volcanoes** are both currently active, although relatively quiet. **Turrialba,** meanwhile, has been huffing and puffing so much that it shut down the international airport a few times and forced the closure of Turrialba Volcano National Park until it stops acting up.

Costa Rica's Top National Parks & Bioreserves

Costa Rica, which is smaller than West Virginia, has an astonishing 27 national parks, in addition to scores of public and private reserves dedicated to conservation, often funded in part by tourism. Some of these forests are totally inaccessible and even unexplored, notably the vast La Amistad International Park that straddles the Costa Rican-Panamanian border. Others are compact and easily walkable, including the two most popular parks in the country, Manuel Antonio and Poás Volcano.

Most of the national parks charge foreigners around $10 to $15 admission. Costa Ricans and legal residents pay much less. But some parks charge nothing, or they charge at one entrance but not at another.

This section is not a complete listing of all of Costa Rica's national parks and protected areas, but rather a selective list of those parks that are of greatest interest and accessibility. You'll find detailed information about food and lodging options near some of the individual parks in the regional chapters that follow.

If you're looking for a camping adventure or an extended stay in one of the national parks, I recommend **Corcovado, Santa Rosa, Rincón de la Vieja,** or **Chirripó.** Most of the others are better suited for day trips or guided hikes.

For more information, call the national parks information line at ✆ **1192,** or the main office at ✆ **2283-8004.**

THE CENTRAL VALLEY

Irazú Volcano National Park ★ Irazú Volcano is the highest (3,378m/11,080 ft.) of Costa Rica's active volcanoes and a popular day trip from San José. A paved road leads right up to the crater, and the lookout has a view of both the Pacific and the Caribbean on a clear day. The volcano last erupted in March 1963, on the same day U.S. President John F. Kennedy visited the country. The park has picnic tables, restrooms, an information center, and parking. **Location:** 55km (34 miles) east of San José.

Poás Volcano National Park ★★ Poás is another active volcano close to San José. The main crater is more than 1.6km (1 mile) wide, and it is constantly active with fumaroles and hot geysers. Poás is arguably a more inviting trip than Irazú because it's surrounded by dense cloud forest and has gentle trails to hike. The area around the volcano is lush, but much growth is stunted due to gases and acid rain. On January 8, 2009, a 6.1-magnitude earthquake struck Costa Rica, with its epicenter very close to Poás. The park was closed for several days, and an uptick in volcanic activity was noted. The park still sometimes closes when the gases get too feisty. The park has picnic tables, restrooms, and an information center. **Location:** 37km (23 miles) northwest of San José.

GUANACASTE & THE NICOYA PENINSULA

Palo Verde National Park ★ A must for bird-watchers, Palo Verde National Park is one of Costa Rica's best-kept secrets. This part of the Tempisque River lowlands supports a population of more than 50,000 waterfowl and forest bird species. Various ecosystems here include mangroves, savanna brush lands, and evergreen forests. The park has camping facilities, an information center, and some rustic, dorm-style accommodations at the Organization for Tropical Studies (OTS) research station here. **Location:** 200km (124 miles) northwest of San José. Be warned that the park entrance is 28km (17 miles) off the highway down a very rugged dirt road; it's another 9km (5½ miles) to the OTS station and campsites. For more information, call the OTS (www.threepaths.co.cr; ✆ **2524-0607**).

Rincón de la Vieja National Park ★★ This large tract of parkland experiences high volcanic activity, with numerous fumaroles and geysers, as well as hot springs, cold pools, and mud pots. You'll find excellent hikes to the upper craters and to several waterfalls. Camping is permitted at two sites, each with an information center, a picnic area, and restrooms. **Location:** 266km (165 miles) northwest of San José.

Santa Rosa National Park ★ Occupying a large section of Costa Rica's northwestern Guanacaste province, Santa Rosa has the country's largest area of tropical dry forest, important turtle-nesting sites, and the historically significant La Casona (p. 107) monument. The beaches are pristine with basic camping facilities, and the waves make them popular with surfers. An information center, picnic area, and restrooms are at the main campsite and entrance. Additional campsites are on the usually deserted and entirely undeveloped beaches here. **Location:** 258km (160 miles) northwest of San José. For more information, call the park office at ✆ **2666-5051.**

THE NORTHERN ZONE

Arenal National Park ★★ This park, created to protect the ecosystem that surrounds Arenal Volcano, has a couple of good trails and a prominent lookout point that is extremely close to the volcano. The main trail here takes you through a mix of transitional forest, rainforest, and open savanna, before an invigorating scramble over a massive rock field formed by a cooled-off lava flow. **Location:** 129km (80 miles) northwest of San José.

Caño Negro National Wildlife Refuge ★ A lowland swamp and drainage basin for several northern rivers, Caño Negro is excellent for bird-watching. A few basic *cabinas* and lodges are in this area, but the most popular way to visit is on a combined van and boat trip from the La Fortuna/Arenal area. **Location:** 20km (12 miles) south of Los Chiles, near the Nicaraguan border.

Monteverde Cloud Forest Biological Reserve ★★★ This private reserve might be the most famous forest in Costa Rica. It covers 10,520 hectares (26,000 acres) of primary forest, mostly mid-elevation cloud forest, with a rich variety of flora and fauna. Epiphytes thrive in the cool, misty climate. The most renowned resident is the spectacular resplendent quetzal. The park has a well-maintained trail system and some of the most experienced guides in the country. Nearby you can visit the Santa Elena or other reserves. **Location:** 167km (104 miles) northwest of San José.

CENTRAL PACIFIC COAST

Carara National Park ★★ Located just south of the famous bridge over the Río Tárcoles, where you always see crocodiles, Carara is a bird-watcher's dream, home to scarlet macaws, toucans, trogons, and hummingbirds. Several trails run through the park, including one that is wheelchair-accessible. The park's various ecosystems range from rainforests to mangroves, and this is a transitional zone where the dry forests of Guanacaste turn into the wet forests of the central Pacific. **Location:** 102km (63 miles) west of San José.

Manuel Antonio National Park ★★ Though physically small, Manuel Antonio is the most popular national park in Costa Rica with the largest number of hotels and resorts. This lowland rainforest has a healthy monkey population, including the endangered squirrel monkey, and the park is known for its splendid beaches. **Location:** 129km (80 miles) south of San José.

THE SOUTHERN ZONE

Corcovado National Park ★★★ The largest block of virgin lowland rainforest in Central America, Corcovado National Park receives more than 500cm (200 in.) of rain per year. It's remote, but easier to get to than you might think, and well worth it. Scarlet macaws are abundant, and it's home to two of the country's largest cats, the jaguar and the puma, and its largest land mammal, the Baird's tapir. There are camping facilities at the Sirena ranger station, but you'll have to hire a guide, get a permit, and plan ahead to square away all the logistics. **Location:** 335km (208 miles) south of San José, on the Osa Peninsula.

THE CARIBBEAN COAST

Cahuita National Park ★★ A combination land and marine park, Cahuita National Park protects one of the few remaining living coral reefs in the country. The topography here is lush lowland tropical rainforest. Monkeys, sloths, and birds are common. **Location:** On the Caribbean coast, 42km (26 miles) south of Limón.

Tortuguero National Park ★★ Tortuguero National Park has been called the Venice of Costa Rica because of its maze of jungle canals, which meander through a dense lowland rainforest. Small boats carry visitors through these waterways, where caimans, manatees, and numerous bird and mammal species are common. The extremely endangered great green macaw lives here. Green sea turtles nest on the beaches every year between June and October. The park has a small but helpful information office and some well-marked trails. **Location:** 258km (160 miles) northeast of San José.

COSTA RICAN WILDLIFE

For such a small country, Costa Rica is incredibly rich in biodiversity. With just .03 percent of the earth's landmass, the country is home to some 5 percent of its biodiversity. Whether you come to Costa Rica to check 100 or more species off your lifetime list, or just to escape from the rat race for a week or so, you'll be surrounded by a rich and varied tableau of flora and fauna.

In many instances, the prime viewing recommendations should be understood within the reality of actual wildlife viewing. Most casual visitors and even many dedicated naturalists will never see a wildcat or kinkajou. However, anyone working with a good guide should be able to see a broad selection of Costa Rica's impressive flora and fauna. The information that follows is a selective introduction to some of what you might see.

Scores of good field guides are available, including *Costa Rica: Traveller's Wildlife Guides* by Les Beletsky. Bird-watchers will want to pick up one or both of the following two books: *A Guide to the Birds of Costa Rica* by F. Gary Stiles and Alexander Skutch, and *Birds of Costa Rica* by Richard Garrigues and Robert Dean. Other specialized guides to mammals, reptiles, insects, flora, and more can be found at Zona Tropical (www.zonatropical.net), which is a Costa Rican-based publishing house that specializes in field guides and wildlife books.

Searching for Wildlife

The best way to see wildlife anywhere is to hire a local guide. Guides have an uncanny ability to spot, smell, hear or track animals that you would never see otherwise, including sloths, snakes, lizards, spiders, and birds. Guides are also useful for setting up telescopes and taking great pictures using your phone.

A few helpful hints:

- **Listen.** Pay attention to rustling in the leaves; whether it's monkeys up above or coati on the ground, you'll often hear an animal before seeing it.
- **Keep quiet.** Noise will scare off animals and prevent you from hearing their movements and calls.
- **Don't try too hard.** Soften your focus and allow your peripheral vision to take over, looking for glimpses of motion all around you.
- **Bring binoculars.** Some birding tours will provide good binoculars, but it's always nice to have your own.
- **Dress appropriately.** Light, long pants and long-sleeved shirts are the best way to protect against insects. Comfortable hiking boots or shoes are also essential, except where heavy rubber boots are necessary. Avoid loud colors; the better you blend in with your surroundings, the better your chances of spotting wildlife.
- **Be patient.** The jungle isn't on a schedule. However, your best shots at seeing forest fauna are in the very early morning and late afternoon hours.
- **Read up.** Familiarize yourself with what you're most likely to see. Most nature lodges have copies of wildlife field guides, though it's best to bring your own. A good all-around book to use is Carrol Henderson's *Mammals, Amphibians, and Reptiles of Costa Rica: A Field Guide.*

TIPS ON HEALTH, SAFETY & ETIQUETTE IN THE WILDERNESS

There's a certain amount of risk in any adventure activity, so know your limits. Be prepared for extremes in temperature and rainfall. A sunny morning hike can quickly become a cold and wet ordeal, so it's usually a good idea to carry along some kind of rain gear, or to have a dry change of clothing waiting at the end of the trail. And if you're planning a lot of beach time, don't forget sunscreen. Getting a bad sunburn is one of the easiest ways to ruin a vacation.

Remember that it's a jungle out there, and venomous snakes are abundant. Avoid touching vegetation as you walk, avoid walking on leafy or brushy ground, and don't put your hands or feet anywhere you can't see.

Avoid swimming in rivers unless a guide tells you it's safe. Most mangrove canals and river mouths in Costa Rica support healthy crocodile and caiman populations.

Bug bites will probably be your greatest health concern in the Costa Rican wilderness, but they aren't as big of a problem as you might expect. Coastal visitors will have trouble escaping the bites from the *purruja* sand fleas, especially below the knees. Long pants and sleeves are recommended. Mosquitoes can carry malaria or dengue (see "Staying Healthy" in chapter 11), but they feed at predictable hours and are easy to guard against with insect repellent. If you are bitten, some cortisone or Benadryl cream will help soothe the itching. ***And remember:*** Whenever you enter and enjoy nature, you should tread lightly and try not to disturb the natural environment. The popular slogan well known to most campers certainly applies here: "Leave nothing but footprints; take nothing but photos." Do not cut or uproot plants or flowers. Pack out everything you pack in, and please do not litter.

RESPONSIBLE TOURISM

Costa Rica is one of the planet's prime ecotourism destinations. Many of the hotels, isolated nature lodges, and tour operators around the country are pioneers and dedicated professionals in the sustainable tourism field. Many other hotels, lodges, and tour operators are earnestly jumping on the bandwagon and improving their practices, while still others are simply "green-washing," using the terms "eco," "green," and "sustainable" in their promo materials, but doing little real good in their daily operations.

In 2014, Costa Rica was ranked 54th globally in the Environmental Performance Index (EPI; http://epi.yale.edu). This is not a particularly impressive feat given the country's image and marketing strategy. Despite its reputation, the substantial amount of good work being done, and ongoing advances being made in the field, Costa Rica is by no means an ecological paradise free from environmental and social threats. Untreated sewage is dumped into rivers, bays, oceans, and watersheds at an alarming rate. Child labor and sexual exploitation are common, and certain sectors of the tourism trade only make these matters worse.

But over the last decade or so, Costa Rica has taken great strides toward protecting its rich biodiversity. Thirty years ago, it was difficult to find a protected area anywhere, but now more than 11 percent of the country is protected within the national park system. Another 10 to 15 percent of the land enjoys moderately effective preservation as part of private and public reserves, Indian reserves, and wildlife refuges and corridors. Still, Costa Rica's precious tropical hardwoods continue to be harvested at an alarming rate, often illegally, while other primary forests are clear-cut for short-term agricultural gain.

While you can find hotels and tour operators using sustainable practices all across Costa Rica—even in the San José metropolitan area—a few prime destinations are particular hot spots for sustainable tourism practices. Of note are the remote and wild Osa Peninsula and Golfo Dulce area of southern Costa Rica, the rural northern zone that includes both Monteverde and the Arenal Volcano and Lake Arenal attractions, and the underdeveloped Caribbean coast, with the rainforest canals of Tortuguero, Cahuita National Park, and the Manzanillo-Gandoca Wildlife Refuge.

In addition to focusing on wildlife viewing and adventure activities in the wild, ecolodges in these areas tend to be smaller, often lacking televisions, air-conditioning, and other typical luxury amenities. The more remote lodges usually depend on small solar and hydro plants for their power. That said, some of these hotels and lodges provide levels of comfort and service that are quite luxurious.

In Costa Rica, the government-run tourism institute (ICT) provides a sustainability rating of a host of hotels and tour agencies under its **Certific**

for Sustainable Tourism (CST) program. You can look up the ratings at the website www.turismo-sostenible.co.cr.

Bear in mind that this program is relatively new and the list is far from comprehensive. Many hotels and tour operators in the country haven't completed the extensive review and rating process. Moreover, die-hard ecologists find some of these listings and the criteria used suspect. Still, this list and rating system are a good start, and improving and evolving constantly.

A parallel program, **"The Blue Flag,"** is used to rate specific beaches and communities in terms of their environmental condition and practices. The Blue Flags are reviewed and handed out annually. Current listings of Blue Flag-approved beaches and communities can be found at www.visitcostarica.com.

SAN JOSÉ

Founded in 1737, San José was a forgotten backwater of the Spanish empire until the late–19th century, when it boomed with the coffee business. Sure, the city has its issues: gridlock traffic, poorly maintained sidewalks, and street crime. But, at 1,125m (3,690 ft.) above sea level, San José enjoys springlike temperatures year-round, and its location in the Central Valley—the lush Talamanca Mountains to the south, and the Poás, Barva, and Irazú volcanoes to the north—makes it a convenient base of exploration.

ESSENTIALS

Arriving

BY PLANE

Juan Santamaría International Airport (www.fly2sanjose.com; ✆ **2437-2626** for 24-hr. airport information; airport code SJO) is near the city of Alajuela, about 20 minutes from downtown San José. A taxi into town costs between C15,000 and C29,000, and a bus is only C555. The Alajuela–San José buses run frequently and will drop you off anywhere along Paseo Colón or at a station near the Parque de la Merced (downtown, btw. calles 12 and 14 and avs. 2 and 4). There are two lines: **Tuasa** (✆ **2442-6900**) buses are red; **Station Wagon** (✆ **2442-3226**) buses are yellow/orange. At the airport, the bus stop is directly in front of the main terminal, beyond the parking structure. Be sure to ask whether the bus is going to San José, or you'll end up in Alajuela. If you have a lot of luggage, you probably should take a cab.

Should I Stay, or Should I Go Now?

While most tourists enter Costa Rica through the international airport just outside this city, San José is not a place where most travelers linger. Costa Rica's bustling capital and population center is a good place to visit briefly, or to get things done that can't be done elsewhere, but it isn't a major tourist destination. Still, San José is the country's biggest urban center, with varied and active restaurant and nightlife scenes, several museums and galleries worth visiting, and a steady stream of theater, concerts, and other cultural events that you won't find elsewhere in the country.

San José

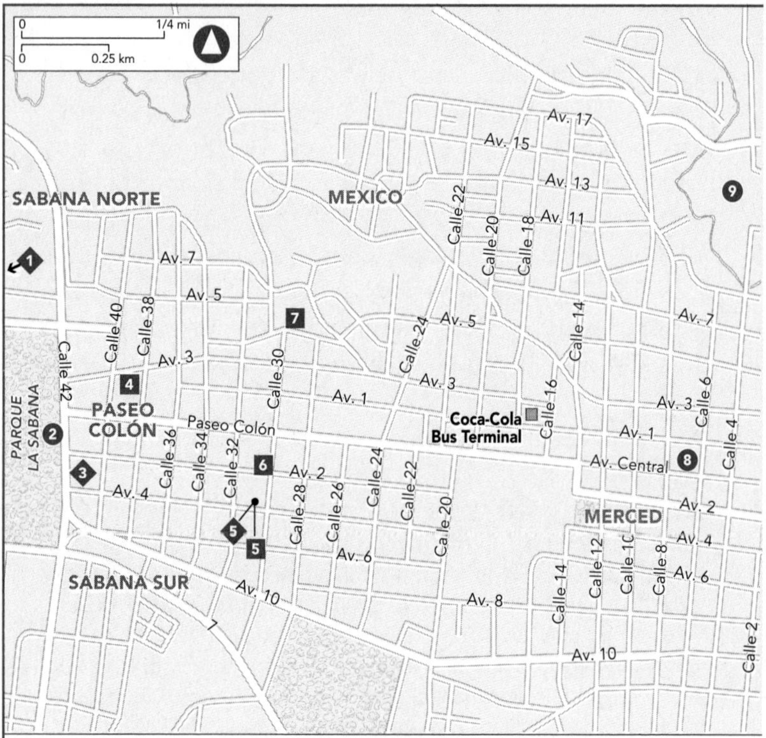

0 1/4 mi
0 0.25 km
SABANA NORTE
MEXICO
PARQUE LA SABANA
PASEO COLÓN
SABANA SUR
MERCED
Coca-Cola Bus Terminal
Paseo Colón
Av. 17
Av. 15
Av. 13
Av. 11
Av. 7
Av. 5
Av. 3
Av. 1
Av. Central
Av. 2
Av. 4
Av. 6
Av. 8
Av. 10
Calle 42
Calle 40
Calle 38
Calle 36
Calle 34
Calle 32
Calle 30
Calle 28
Calle 26
Calle 24
Calle 22
Calle 20
Calle 18
Calle 16
Calle 14
Calle 12
Calle 10
Calle 8
Calle 6
Calle 4
Calle 2

NICARAGUA
CARIBBEAN SEA
SAN JOSÉ
PACIFIC OCEAN
PANAMA

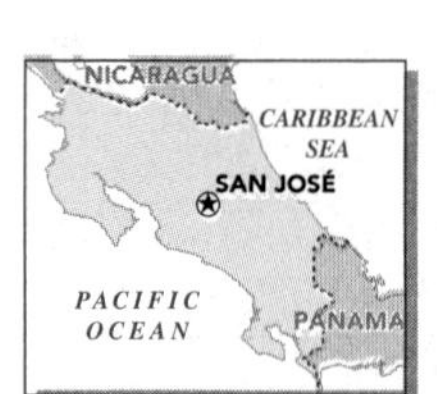

ATTRACTIONS ●

Mercado Central **8**
Museo de Arte Costarricense (Costa Rican Art Museum) **2**
Museo de Jade Marco Fidel Tristán (Jade Museum) **20**
Museo de Los Niños (Children's Museum) **9**
Museo Nacional de Costa Rica (National Museum) **19**
Museos del Banco Central de Costa Rica (Gold Museum) **14**
Parque La Sabana **2**

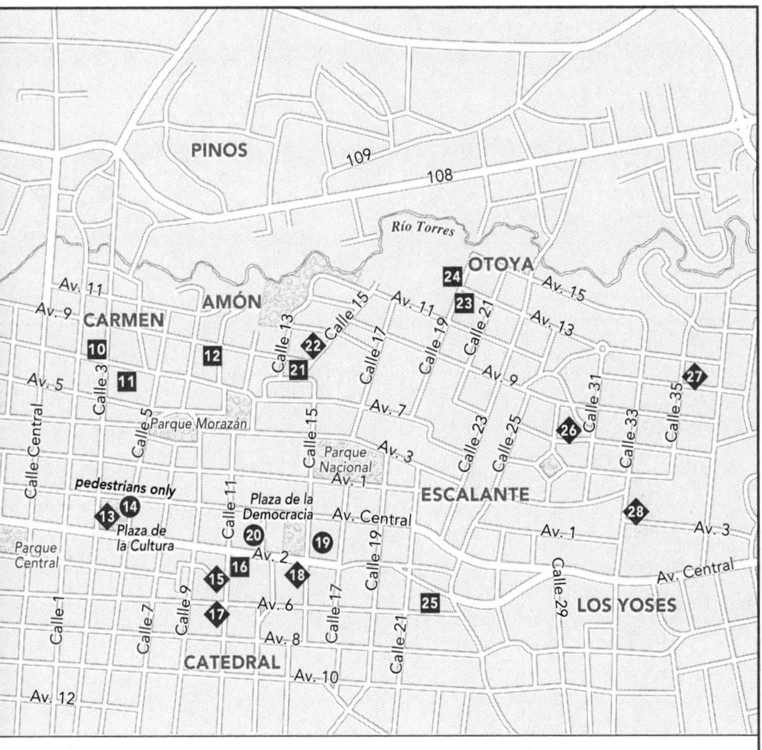

HOTELS ■

Aldea Hostel **6**
Costa Rica Backpackers **25**
Hostel Pangea **10**
Hotel Aranjuez **24**
Hotel Cacts **7**
Hotel Colonial **16**
Hotel Don Carlos **12**
Hotel Grano de Oro **5**
Hotel Rincón de San José **21**
Hotel Santo Tomás **11**
Kap's Place **23**
Tryp Sabana by Windham **4**

RESTAURANTS ◆

Alma de Café **13**
Café Mundo **22**
Grano de Oro Restaurant **5**
Kalú **26**
La Esquina de Buenos Aires **15**
Mantras Veggie Café and Tea House **27**
Olio **28**
Park Café **1**
Restaurante Nuestra Tierra **18**
Soda Tapia **3**
Tin Jo **17**

The Central Valley

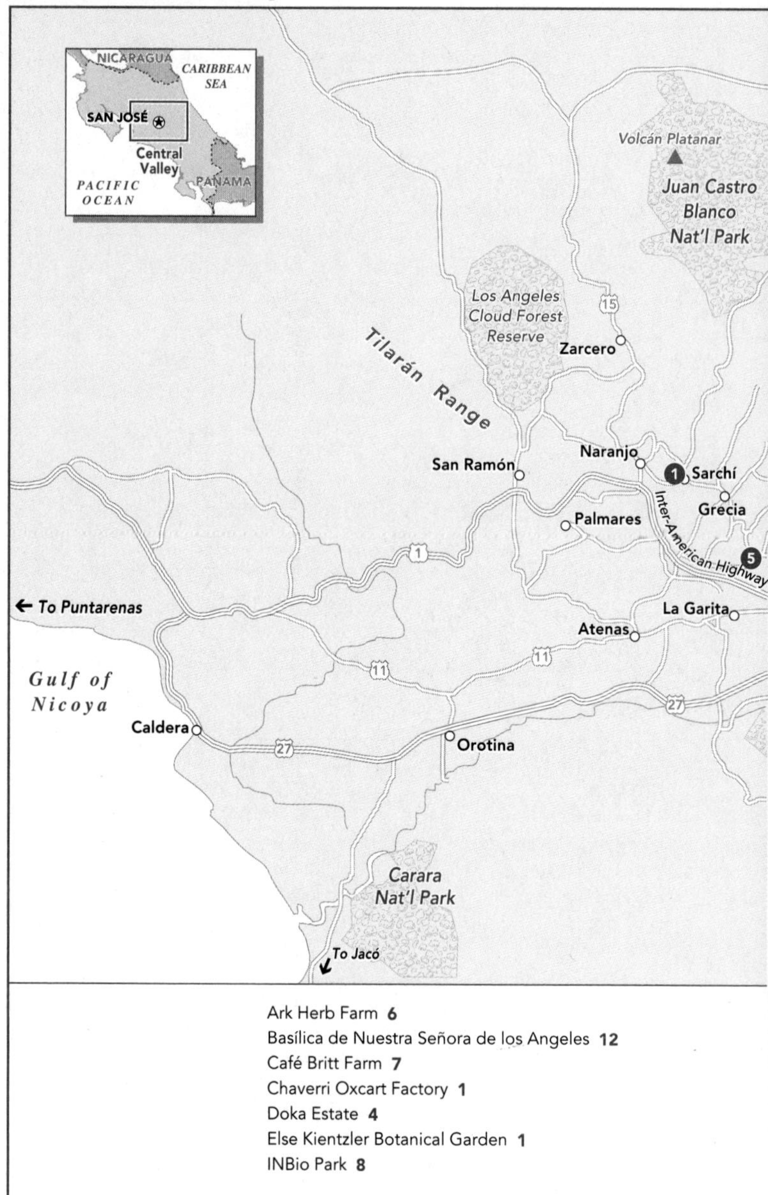

Ark Herb Farm **6**
Basílica de Nuestra Señora de los Angeles **12**
Café Britt Farm **7**
Chaverri Oxcart Factory **1**
Doka Estate **4**
Else Kientzler Botanical Garden **1**
INBio Park **8**

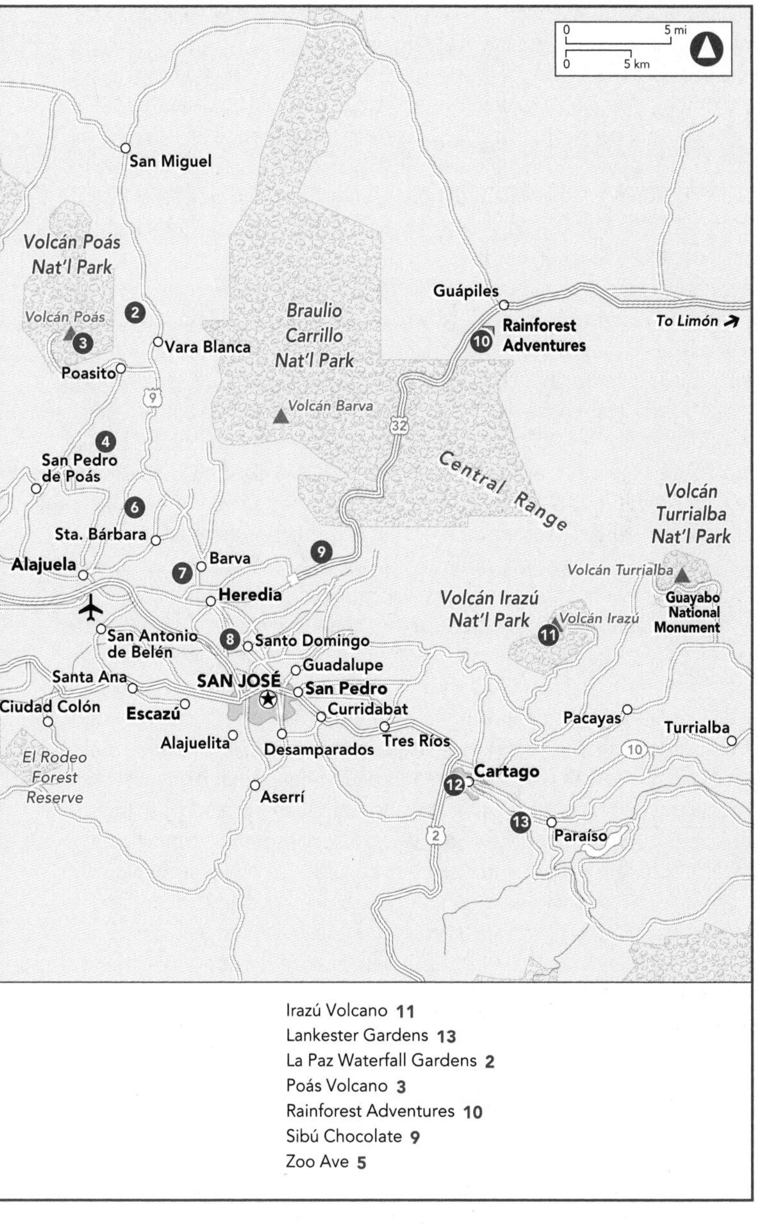
0 5 mi
0 5 km
San Miguel
Volcán Poás Nat'l Park
Volcán Poás
Vara Blanca
Poasito
Braulio Carrillo Nat'l Park
Volcán Barva
Guápiles
Rainforest Adventures
To Limón
San Pedro de Poás
Central Range
Volcán Turrialba Nat'l Park
Sta. Bárbara
Alajuela
Barva
Heredia
Volcán Turrialba
Guayabo National Monument
Volcán Irazú Nat'l Park
Volcán Irazú
San Antonio de Belén
Santo Domingo
Guadalupe
Santa Ana
SAN JOSÉ
San Pedro
Ciudad Colón
Escazú
Curridabat
Pacayas
Turrialba
Alajuelita
Desamparados
Tres Ríos
El Rodeo Forest Reserve
Cartago
Aserrí
Paraíso
Irazú Volcano 11
Lankester Gardens 13
La Paz Waterfall Gardens 2
Poás Volcano 3
Rainforest Adventures 10
Sibú Chocolate 9
Zoo Ave 5

Most car-rental agencies have desks and offices at the airport, but if you're planning to spend a few days in San José itself, I think a car is a liability. (If you're heading off immediately to the beach, though, it's much easier to pick up your car here than at a downtown office.)

Tip: Chaos and confusion greet arriving passengers the second they step out of the terminal. You face a gauntlet of aggressive taxi drivers, shuttle drivers waving signs, and people offering to carry your bags. Fortunately, the official airport taxi service (see below) has a booth inside the calm area just before the terminal exit. Keep a very watchful eye on your bags: Thieves have historically preyed on newly arrived passengers and their luggage. You should tip porters about C200 to C300 per bag.

In terms of taxis, you should stick with the official airport taxi service, **Taxis Unidos Aeropuerto** (www.taxiaeropuerto.com; ✆ **2221-6865**), which operates a fleet of orange vans and sedans. This service has a kiosk in the no man's land just outside the exit door for arriving passengers. Here they will assign you a cab. These taxis use meters, and fares to most downtown hotels should run between C14,000 and C28,000. Despite the fact that Taxis Unidos has an official monopoly at the airport, you will usually find a handful of regular cabs (in traditional red sedans) and "pirate" cabs, driven by freelancers using their own vehicles. You certainly could use either of these latter options ("pirate" cabs tend to charge a dollar or two less), but I highly recommend using the official service for safety and standardized prices.

You have several options for **exchanging money** when you arrive at the airport—but you'll get the best rate if you exchange your money at a bank, and until then you'll find that almost all businesses accept dollars. An ATM in the baggage claim area is connected to both the PLUS and Cirrus networks. A **Global Exchange** (www.globalexchange.co.cr; ✆ **2431-0686**) money exchange booth is just as you clear customs and immigration. It's open whenever flights arrive; however, it exchanges at more than 10 percent below the official rate. A branch of **Banco de San José** is inside the main terminal, on the second floor across from the airline check-in counters, as well as a couple more ATMs up there. Most taxis and all rental-car agencies accept U.S. dollars.

Tip: There's really no pressing need to exchange money the minute you arrive. Taxis Unidos accepts dollars. You can wait until after you settle into your hotel, and see if the hotel will give you a good rate of exchange, or use one of the many downtown banks or ATMs.

BY BUS

If you're coming to San José by bus, where you disembark depends on where you're coming from. (The different bus companies have their offices, and thus their dropoff points, all over downtown San José. When you buy your ticket, ask where you'll be let off.) Buses arriving from Panama pass first through Cartago and San Pedro before letting passengers off in downtown San José; buses arriving from Nicaragua generally enter the city on the west end of town, on Paseo Colón. If you're staying here, you can ask to be let off before the final stop.

SEARCHING FOR addresses

This is one of the most confusing aspects of visiting Costa Rica in general, and San José in particular. Although downtown San José often has street addresses and building numbers for locations, they are almost never used. Addresses are given as a set of coordinates such as "Calle 3 between avenidas Central and 1." It's then up to you to locate the building within that block, keeping in mind that the building could be on either side of the street. Many addresses include additional information, such as the number of meters from a specified intersection or some other well-known landmark. (These "meter measurements" are not precise but are a good way to give directions to a taxi driver. In basic terms, 100m = 1 block, 200m = 2 blocks, and so on.) These landmarks are what become truly confusing for visitors to the city because they are often simply restaurants, bars, and shops that would be familiar only to locals.

Things get even more confusing when the landmark in question no longer exists. The classic example of this is "the Coca-Cola," one of the most common landmarks used in addresses in the blocks surrounding San José's main market. The trouble is, the Coca-Cola bottling plant that it refers to is no longer there; the edifice is long gone, and one of the principal downtown bus depots stands in its place. Old habits die hard, though, and the address description remains. You might also try to find someplace near the *antiguo higuerón* ("old fig tree") in San Pedro. This tree was felled over a decade ago. In outlying neighborhoods, addresses can become long directions, such as "50m (½ block) south of the old church, then 100m (1 block) east, then 20m (two buildings) south."

Visitor Information

The **Costa Rican National Tourism Chamber** (**CANATUR;** www.canatur.org; ✆ **2440-1676**) has a desk at the Juan Santamaría International Airport, in the baggage claims area, just before customs. You can pick up maps and brochures, and they might even lend you a phone to make or confirm a reservation. It's usually open for all arriving flights.

City Layout

Downtown San José is laid out on a grid. *Avenidas* (avenues) run east and west, while *calles* (streets) run north and south. The center of the city is at **Avenida Central** and **Calle Central.** To the north of Avenida Central, the avenidas have odd numbers beginning with Avenida 1; to the south, they have even numbers beginning with Avenida 2. Likewise, calles to the east of Calle Central have odd numbers, and those to the west have even numbers. The main downtown artery is **Avenida 2,** which merges with Avenida Central on either side of downtown. West of downtown, Avenida Central becomes **Paseo Colón,** which ends at Parque La Sabana and feeds into the highway to Alajuela, the airport, Guanacaste, and the Pacific coast. East of downtown, Avenida Central leads to San Pedro and then to Cartago and the Inter-American Highway heading south. **Calle 3** takes you out of town to the north, onto the Guápiles Highway that leads to the Caribbean coast.

The Neighborhoods in Brief

San José is divided into dozens of neighborhoods, known as *barrios.* Most of the listings in this chapter fall within the main downtown area, but you'll need to know about a few outlying neighborhoods. In addition, the nearby suburbs of Escazú and Santa Ana are so close that they could almost be considered part of San José.

Downtown In San José's busy downtown, you'll find most of the city's museums, as well as a handful of small urban parks and open-air plazas, and the city's main cathedral. Many tour companies, restaurants, and hotels are located here. Unfortunately, traffic noise and exhaust fumes make this one of the least pleasant parts of the city. Streets and avenues are usually bustling and crowded with pedestrians and vehicular traffic, and street crime is most rampant here. Still, the sections of Avenida Central between calles 6 and 7, as well as Avenida 4 between calles 9 and 14, have been converted into pedestrian malls, greatly improving things on these stretches.

Barrio Amón/Barrio Otoya These two picturesque neighborhoods, just north and east of downtown, are the site of the greatest concentration of historic buildings in San José. Some of these have been renovated and turned into boutique hotels and atmospheric restaurants. If you're looking for character and don't mind the noise and exhaust fumes, this neighborhood makes a good base for exploring the city.

La Sabana/Paseo Colón Paseo Colón, a wide boulevard west of downtown, is an extension of Avenida Central and ends at Parque La Sabana. It has several good, small hotels and numerous restaurants. This is also where several of the city's car-rental agencies have their in-town offices. Once the site of the city's main airport, the Parque La Sabana (La Sabana Park) is San José's largest public park, with ample green areas, sports and recreation facilities, the National Stadium, and the Museo de Arte Costarricense (Costa Rican Art Museum). The neighborhoods north and south are Sabana Norte and Sabana Sur.

San Pedro/Los Yoses Located east of downtown San José, Los Yoses is an upper-middle-class neighborhood that is home to many diplomatic missions and embassies. San Pedro is a little farther east and is the site of the University of Costa Rica. Numerous college-type bars and restaurants are all around the edge of the campus, while more upscale and refined restaurants and boutique hotels can be found in the residential sections of both neighborhoods.

Escazú/Santa Ana Located in the hills west of San José, Escazú and Santa Ana are fast-growing suburbs. Although the area is only 15 minutes from San José by car, it feels much farther away because of its relaxed and suburban atmosphere. This area also has a large expat community with many bed-and-breakfast establishments and several of the area's best restaurants.

Heredia/Alajuela/Airport Area Heredia and Alajuela are two colonial-era cities that lie closer to the airport than San José. Alajuela is closest to the airport; Heredia is about midway between Alajuela and the capital. For more information on Heredia, see "Day Trips from San José" on p. 77. Several unique, high-end boutique hotels are in this area, and several large hotels are located on, or just off, the Inter-American Highway close to the airport.

GETTING AROUND

By Bus

Bus transportation around San José is cheap—the fare is usually somewhere around C195 to C475—although the Alajuela/San José buses that run in from the airport cost C555. The most important buses are those running east along Avenida 2 and west along Avenida 3. The **Sabana/Cementerio** bus runs from

Parque La Sabana to downtown and is one of the most convenient buses to use. You'll find a bus stop for the outbound Sabana/Cementerio bus near the main post office on Avenida 3 near the corner of Calle 2, and another one on Calle 11 between avenidas Central and 1. This bus also has stops all along Avenida 2. **San Pedro** buses leave from the end of the pedestrian walkway on Avenida Central between calles 9 and 11, and take you out of downtown heading east.

You pay as you board the bus. The city's bus drivers can make change, although they don't like to receive large bills. Be especially mindful of your wallet, purse, or other valuables, because pickpockets often work the crowded buses.

By Taxi

Although taxis in San José have meters (*marías*), the drivers sometimes refuse to use them, particularly with foreigners, so you'll occasionally have to negotiate the price. Always try to get them to use the meter first (say *"Ponga la maría, por favor"*). The official rate is C640 per kilometer (½ mile). If you have a rough idea of how far it is to your destination, you can estimate how much it should cost from this figure. Wait time is charged at C3,650 per hour, and is pro-rated for smaller increments.

Depending on your location, the time of day, and the weather (rain places taxis at a premium), it's relatively easy to hail a cab downtown. You'll always find taxis in front of the Teatro Nacional (albeit at high prices) and around the Parque Central at Avenida Central and Calle Central. Taxis in front of hotels and the El Pueblo tourist complex usually charge more than others, although this is technically illegal. Most hotels will gladly call you a cab, either for a downtown excursion or for a trip back out to the airport. You can also get a cab by calling **Coopetaxi** (**© 2235-9966**), **Coopeirazu** (**© 2254-3211**), **Coopetico** (**© 2224-7979**), or **Coopeguaria** (**© 2226-1366**). **Cinco Estrellas Taxi** (**© 2228-3159**) is based in Escazú but services the entire metropolitan area and airport, and claims to always have an English-speaking operator on call.

On Foot

Downtown San José is very compact. Nearly every place you might want to go is within a 15-by-4-block area. Because of traffic congestion, you'll often find it faster to walk than to take a bus or taxi. Be careful when walking the streets any time of day or night. Flashy jewelry, loosely held handbags or backpacks, and expensive camera equipment tend to attract thieves. **Avenida Central** is a pedestrian-only street from calles 6 to 7, and has been redone with interesting paving stones and the occasional fountain in an attempt to create a comfortable pedestrian mall. A similar pedestrian-only walkway runs along **Avenida 4,** between calles 9 and 14.

By Train

San José has sporadic and minimal urban commuter train service, and it is geared almost exclusively to commuters. There are three major lines. One line connecting the western neighborhood of Pavas with the eastern suburb of San Pedro passes right through downtown, with prominent stops at, or near, the

U.S. Embassy, Parque La Sabana, the downtown court area, and the Universidad de Costa Rica (University of Costa Rica) and Universidad Latina (Latin University). This train runs commuter hours roughly every hour between 5 and 8:30am and 4 and 7:30pm.

Another line runs between downtown San José and Heredia. This train runs roughly every 30 minutes between 5:30 and 8am, and 3:30 and 7:30pm.

And a third line runs between downtown San Jose and Cartago. This train runs roughly every 30 minutes between 6:30 and 8am, and between 3:30 and 7:30pm. This later route is potentially useful for tourists, but again, the train is predominantly for local commuters, and not geared toward tourists. You cannot purchase tickets in advance, and trains often fill up, leaving you waiting 30 minutes or more for the next train.

Fares range from C420 to C550, depending on the length of your ride.

By Car

It will cost you between $45 and $150 per day to rent a car in Costa Rica (the higher prices are for 4WD vehicles). Many car-rental agencies have offices at the airport. If not, they will usually either pick you up or deliver the car to any San José hotel. If you decide to pick up your rental car in downtown San José, be prepared for some very congested streets.

The following companies have desks at Juan Santamaría International Airport, as well as offices downtown: **Adobe Rent A Car** (www.adobecar.com; ✆ **2542-4800**); **Avis** (www.avis.com; ✆ **800/633-3469** in the U.S. and 800/879-2847 in Canada, or 2293-2222 central reservation number in Costa Rica); **Budget** (www.budget.com; ✆ **800/472-3325** in the U.S. and Canada, or 2255-4240 in San José); **Dollar** (www.dollar.com; ✆ **800/800-6000** in the U.S. and Canada, or 2257-1585 in San José); **Hertz** (www.hertz.com; ✆ **800/654-3131** in the U.S. and Canada, or 2221-1818 in San José); **National Car Rental** (www.nationalcar.com; ✆ **877/222-9058** in the U.S. and Canada, or 2221-4700 in San José); and **Payless Rent A Car** (www.paylesscar.com; ✆ **800/729-5377** in the U.S. and Canada, or 2432-4747 in Costa Rica).

Dozens of other smaller, local car-rental agencies are in San José, and most will arrange for airport or hotel pickup or delivery. Some of the more dependable local agencies are **Toyota Rent A Car** (www.toyotarent.com; ✆ **2256-5713**) and **Vamos Rent A Car ★★** (www.vamosrentacar.com; ✆ **800/950-8426** in the U.S. and Canada, or 2432-5258 in Costa Rica). Vamos gets especially high marks for customer service and transparency.

[FastFACTS] SAN JOSÉ

ATMs/Banks You'll find an extensive network of banks and ATMs around San José. Banks are usually open Monday through Friday from 9am to 4pm, although many have begun to offer extended hours. Post offices are generally open Monday through Friday from 8am to 5:30pm, and Saturday from 7:30am to noon. To protect against crime, some banks have taken to disabling their ATM networks at night.

Dentists Call your embassy, which will have a list of recommended dentists. Because treatments are so inexpensive in Costa Rica, dental tourism has become a popular option for people needing extensive work.

Doctors Contact your embassy for information on doctors in San José, or see "Hospitals," below.

Drugstores San José has countless pharmacies and drugstores. Many of them deliver at little or no extra cost. The pharmacy at the **Hospital Clínica Bíblica,** Avenida 14 between calles Central and 1 (✆ **2522-1000**), is open daily 24 hours, as is the **Hospital CIMA** pharmacy (✆ **2208-1080**) in Escazú. **Farmacia Fischel** (www.fischel.co.cr; ✆ **800/347-2435** toll-free in Costa Rica) has scores of branches around the metropolitan area.

Embassies & Consulates See chapter 11, "Planning Your Trip."

Emergencies In case of any emergency, dial ✆ **911** (which should have an English-speaking operator); for an ambulance, call ✆ **1028;** and to report a fire, call ✆ **1118.**

Hospitals **Clínica Bíblica,** Avenida 14 between calles Central and 1 (www.clinicabiblica.com; ✆ **2522-1000**), is conveniently close to downtown and has several English-speaking doctors. The **Hospital CIMA** (www.hospitalcima.com; ✆ **2208-1000**), located in Escazú on the Próspero Fernández Highway, which connects San José and the western suburb of Santa Ana, has the most modern facilities in the country.

Internet Access Internet cafes were once ubiquitous in San José but are now a rarity, with free Wi-Fi widely available in hotels and restaurants.

Police Dial ✆ **911** or 2295-3272 for the police. They should have someone available who speaks English.

Post Office The main post office *(correo)* is on Calle 2 between avenidas 1 and 3 (www.correos.go.cr; ✆ **2223-9766**). See "Mail & Postage" in chapter 11 for more information.

Restrooms Public restrooms are rare to nonexistent, but most big hotels and restaurants will let you use theirs. Downtown, you can find public restrooms at the entrance to the Museos del Banco Central de Costa Rica (p. 67).

Safety Pickpockets and purse snatchers are rife in San José, especially on public buses, in the markets, on crowded sidewalks, near hospitals, and lurking outside bank offices and ATMs. Leave most of your money and other valuables in your hotel safe, and carry only as much as you need when you go out. If you do carry anything valuable with you, keep it in a money belt or special passport bag around your neck. Day packs are a prime target of brazen pickpockets throughout the city. One common scam involves someone dousing you or your pack with mustard or ice cream. Another scamster (or two) will then quickly come to your aid, but they are usually much more interested in cleaning you out than cleaning you up.

Stay away from the red-light district northwest of the Central Market. Also be advised that the Parque Nacional is not a safe place for a late-night stroll. Other precautions include walking around corner vendors, not between the vendor and the building. The tight space between the vendor and the building is a favorite spot for pickpockets. Avoid parking your car on the street, and never leave anything of value in a car, even if it's in a guarded parking lot. Don't even leave your car unattended by the curb in front of a hotel while you dash in to check on your reservation. With these precautions in mind, you should have a safe visit to San José. Also, see "Safety" in chapter 11.

SAN JOSÉ HOTELS

San José offers up a wide range of hotel choices, from plush boutique hotels to budget *pensiones* and backpacker hangouts. Many downtown hotels and small inns are housed in beautifully converted and restored old mansions. The vast majority of accommodations—and the best deals—are in the moderate range, where you can find everything from elegant little inns to contemporary business class chains. Staying in San José puts you in the center of the action, and close to all of the city's museums, restaurants, and nightlife venues. However, it also exposes you to many urban pitfalls, including noise, traffic, pollution, and street crime.

Downtown San José/Barrio Amón

The urban center of San José is the city's heart and soul, with a wide range of hotels and restaurants and easy access to museums and attractions. It also has several popular public parks and plazas, and the atmospheric Barrio Amón, a charming neighborhood that is home to the city's greatest concentration of colonial-era architecture. The neighborhood's biggest drawbacks are the street noise, bus fumes, gridlocked traffic, and petty crime.

INEXPENSIVE

In addition to the hotels listed below, the **Hotel Colonial ★**, Calle 11, between avenidas 4 and 6 (www.hotelcolonialcr.com; ✆ **2223-0109**) and **Hotel Rincón de San José ★** (www.hotelrincondesanjose.com; ✆ **2221-9702),** on the corner of Avenida 9 and Calle 15, are solid boutique options.

For those on an even tighter budget, **Kap's Place** (wwwkapsplace.com; ✆ **2221-1169),** across from the Hotel Aranjuez on Calle 19 between avenidas 11 and 13, is another good choice, while real budget hounds might want to try **Hostel Pangea ★** (www.hostelpangea.com; ✆ **2221-1992)** on Avenida 7 and Calle 3, or **Costa Rica Backpackers** (www.costaricabackpackers.com; ✆ **2221-6191)** on Avenida 6 between calles 21 and 23.

Hotel Aranjuez ★★ On a quiet side street in the Barrio Amón neighborhood, five adjacent wooden homes have been joined in an intricate maze of hallways and courtyards to create one of the best budget hotels in the country. The courtyards and hallways overflow with mature trees, tropical flowers, and potted ferns. These lead to quiet nooks for reading and a half-dozen or so common areas where guests gather to trade travel tales and play board games. Rooms vary greatly in size but most feature high ceilings and handsome antique wood or tile floors. A massive breakfast buffet is served each morning and the staff couldn't be more accommodating and helpful. The only downside: Some of the nearly century-old walls in these homes are fairly thin, so noise can be a problem.

Calle 19, btw. avs. 11 and 13. www.hotelaranjuez.com. ✆ **2256-1825.** 35 units, 6 with shared bathroom. $58–$65 double. Rates include breakfast buffet. Free parking. **Amenities:** Free Wi-Fi.

Hotel Don Carlos ★★ Brimming with colonial-era charm and an unmistakably Costa Rican ambience, this converted downtown home once belonged to a former Costa Rican president. The rooms and hallways are decorated with a wealth of local Arts and Crafts—large stone sculptures, painted oxcart wheels, wall-mounted mosaics, antique oil paintings, and vivid stained-glass works, as well as lush potted plants and flowing fountains. Rooms can vary tremendously in size, so ask what you're getting before you book. The restaurant serves local cuisine and has a lovely covered patio. The hotel's Boutique Annemarie gift shop (p. 72) is one of the best stocked in Costa Rica.

779 Calle 9, btw. avs. 7 and 9, San José. www.doncarloshotel.com. ✆ **866/675-9259** in the U.S. and Canada, or 2221-6707 in Costa Rica. 30 units. $76 double, $95 family room for up to 5 guests. Rates include breakfast. Free parking. **Amenities:** Restaurant; bar; room service; free Wi-Fi.

Hotel Santo Tomás ★★ Built by a coffee baron more than 100 years ago, the house has been lovingly renovated by its owner, Thomas Douglas. Throughout the property you'll enjoy the deep, dark tones of well-aged wood, and various open-air terraces, interior courtyards, and garden nooks. Rooms vary in size, but most are spacious enough to have a small table and chairs. A newer annex adds even more spacious rooms with balconies. A small outdoor pool with a Jacuzzi is attached to the property; both are solar-heated and connected by a tiny water slide. The staff and management are wonderfully gracious, and the restaurant here is topnotch. ***Note:*** The neighborhood is a tad sketchy after dark, so take a taxi.

Av. 7, btw. calles 3 and 5. www.hotelsantotomas.com. ✆ **2255-0448.** 30 units. $59 double, $151 suite. Rates include breakfast. $12 parking nearby. **Amenities:** Restaurant; bar; lounge; exercise room; Jacuzzi; small outdoor pool; free Wi-Fi.

La Sabana/Paseo Colón

Located on the western edge of downtown, La Sabana Park is San José's largest city park, and Paseo Colón is a broad commercial avenue heading straight into the heart of the city. Stay in this neighborhood if you're looking for fast, easy access to the highways heading to Escazú, Santa Ana, the Pacific coast, and the airport and northern zone. Since it's on the edge of town, the area can be pretty dead at night.

EXPENSIVE

In addition to the hotel below, **Tryp Sabana by Windham ★** (www.tryphotels.com; ✆ **800/468 3261** in the U.S. and Canada, or 2547-2323 in Costa Rica), inside the Centro Colón building on Avenida 3, between calles 38 and 40, is a well-located business-class hotel, with a very good restaurant and excellent amenities.

Hotel Grano de Oro ★★★ This is the standard-bearer for luxury boutique hotels in San José. A combination of restoration and expansion has transformed this grand colonial-era mansion into a refined refuge in the center of a busy city. For those who can afford to splurge, the signature suite is elegantly decorated to evoke a bygone era, with wood-paneled walls, a carved antique bed, and a private Jacuzzi with views of the city skyline through massive picture windows. But if that's beyond your budget, there are appealing standard rooms too, with such niceties as wrought-iron bed frames, shiny wood floors, and plush bedding. The restaurant is one of the best in the city (p. 63) and the chic rooftop patio with its two large Jacuzzi spas will almost make you forget you are in bustling San José. A final reason to visit: Your money will do good. Owners Eldon and Lori Cook support a range of social and environmental causes.

Calle 30, no. 251, btw. avs. 2 and 4, 150m (1½ blocks) south of Paseo Colón. www.hotelgranodeoro.com. ✆ **2255-3322.** 40 units. $170–$328 double; $264–$372 suite. Free parking. **Amenities:** Restaurant; bar; lounge; 2 rooftop Jacuzzis; room service; spa services; free Wi-Fi.

INEXPENSIVE

In addition to the place mentioned below, **Aldea Hostal** (www.aldeahostelcostarica.com; ✆ **2233-6365**) is a popular hostel option, with a bustling little pizza restaurant attached.

Hotel Cacts ★ This budget hotel is housed in a converted family home on a side street about 2 blocks in from the busy Paseo Colón. There's a hostel-like vibe, a friendly staff, a small pool, and a Jacuzzi. The open-air rooftop patio has chairs and chaise lounges and offers a spectacular view of the city and surrounding mountains.

Av. 3 btw. calles 28 and 30, San José. www.hotelcacts.com. ✆ **2221-2928** or 2221-6546. 25 units. $66 double. Rates include taxes and breakfast buffet. Free parking. **Amenities:** Lounge; Jacuzzi; small outdoor pool; free Wi-Fi.

San Pedro/Los Yoses

Located just east of downtown, Los Yoses is home to numerous foreign embassies and consulates, and was one of the city's early upper-class outposts, while San Pedro is home to the University of Costa Rica and offers up a distinct college town vibe. Staying here, you'll be close to much of the city's action but still enjoy some peace and quiet. If you've rented a car, be sure your hotel provides secure parking or you'll have to find (and pay for) a nearby lot.

MODERATE

Hotel Milvia ★ Housed in a converted old wooden plantation home, this boutique hotel is the handiwork of Steve Longrigg and Florencia Urbina. Steve has decades in the hospitality industry in Costa Rica, and Florencia is one of the country's more prominent artists and the former director of the Costa Rican Art Museum (p. 67). Rooms, hallways, and common areas feature a varied and striking collection of contemporary Costa Rican art by Florencia and her friends. Guest rooms are also blessed with plenty of natural light, and most lead out onto a veranda or common courtyard sitting area. All of these common areas overflow with tropical plants and flowers and striking artworks. This hotel is close to the Universidad Latina and one of the city's few train lines, so street noise can be a problem at times.

1 block north and 2 blocks east of the Muñoz y Nanne Supermarket, San Pedro. www.hotelmilvia.com. ✆ **2225-4543.** 9 units. $69 double. Rates include continental breakfast. **Amenities:** Free Wi-Fi.

Escazú & Santa Ana

Located just west of San José, these affluent suburbs, which were once almost entirely farmlands and vacation estates, have boomed as the metropolitan area continues to grow and expand. The two largest cities in this area, Escazú and Santa Ana, are popular with the Costa Rican professional class, as well as North American retirees and expatriates. Quite a few hotels have sprung up to cater to their needs. Both have large modern malls, endless little strip malls, and important business parks. It's easy to commute between Escazú or Santa Ana and downtown San José via car, bus, or taxi. And the area is about the same distance from the airport as downtown San José.

MODERATE

In addition to the hotel below, the **Courtyard San José** ★ (www.marriott.com; ✆ **888/236-2427** in the U.S. and Canada, or 2208-3000), **Residence Inn San José Escazú** ★ (www.marriott.com; ✆ **888/236-2427** in the U.S. and Canada, or 2588-4300), and **Holiday Inn Express** ★ (www.hiexpress.com; ✆ **800/315-2621** in the U.S. and Canada, or 2506-5000 in Costa Rica) are all modern business-class hotels a few miles from each other, right on the western Próspero Fernández Highway connecting Santa Ana and Escazú with San José.

For a great boutique option in Escazu, try **Casa de las Tias** (www.casadelastias.com; ✆ **2289-5517**), which is owned and run by Xavier and Pilar, a very personable husband-wife team.

Alta Hotel ★★ This boutique hotel is blessed with old-world charm. High arches and curves abound. The top touch is the winding interior alleyway that snakes down from the reception through the hotel. Most of the rooms have superb views of the Central Valley from private balconies; the others have pleasant garden patios. Guestrooms are all up to modern resort standards (although some have cramped bathrooms), and are minimalist in style, with white-washed walls and black-and-white photos from the 1920s. The suites are far larger, each with a separate sitting room and big Jacuzzi-style tubs in spacious bathrooms. The hotel's La Luz restaurant is a winner, serving up organic Mediterranean fare.

Alto de las Palomas, old road to Santa Ana. www.thealtahotel.com. ✆ **888/388-2582** in the U.S. and Canada, or 2282-4160. 23 units. $119–$136 double; $279 suite, taxes included. Rates include continental breakfast. Free parking. **Amenities:** Restaurant; bar; concierge; small exercise room; Jacuzzi; midsize outdoor pool; room service; sauna; free Wi-Fi.

Heredia & Alajuela (Airport Area)

Alajuela and Heredia, two colonial-era cities that lie much closer to the airport than San José, are great places to find small, distinct, and charming hotels. To learn more about Heredia, see "Day Trips from San José," later in this chapter. If you plan to get yourself to a remote beach or rainforest lodge as quickly as possible, using San José and the Central Valley purely as a transportation hub, or if you just detest urban clutter, noise, and pollution, you might do well to choose one of the hotels listed below.

EXPENSIVE

Finca Rosa Blanca Coffee Plantation & Inn ★★★ This fanciful boutique hotel is the loving creation of its amiable owners Glen and Teri Jampol. All rooms here are either junior suites, suites, or villas, and no two are alike. The large Rosa Blanca Suite with its master bedroom in a tall turret is one of the highlights, but more intimate options include the second-floor El Guarumo with its free-form tile tub in a corner nook, with great evening views. Set on a high hillside on the flank of the Barva volcano, the inn maintains 14 hectares (35 acres) of prize-winning organic coffee under cultivation, and it offers an excellent coffee tour. Organic gardens and greenhouses supply the produce for the wonderful organic farm-to-table restaurant, **El Tigre**

Vestido. The owners here are committed environmentalists and leaders in the local sustainable tourism field.

Santa Bárbara de Heredia. www.fincarosablanca.com. ✆ **305/395-3042** in the U.S., or 2269-9392 in Costa Rica. 15 units. $320–$565 double. Rates include breakfast. Free parking. **Amenities:** Restaurant; bar; lounge; outdoor pool; spa; concierge; room service; free Wi-Fi.

Marriott Costa Rica Hotel ★★★ Designed to resemble a colonial-era mansion, the Marriott is close enough to the airport to be considered an "airport hotel," yet feels like an isolated country retreat. The entryway opens onto a massive central courtyard meant to mimic Havana's Plaza de Armas. The elegant, traditional-style rooms are large and have views of the surrounding hillsides, suburbs, and coffee fields. There are several distinct dining choices, and the Casa de Café coffee house and restaurant actually fronts a small working coffee field. With tennis courts, a golf driving range, pools, and a top spa, guests rarely run out of amusements here.

San Antonio de Belén. www.marriott.com. ✆ **2298-0000.** 299 units. $180–$293 double; suites $248–$451. Valet parking. **Amenities:** 3 restaurants; 2 bars; concierge; golf driving range; spa; Jacuzzi; 2 outdoor pools; room service; sauna; 2 tennis courts; free Wi-Fi.

Peace Lodge ★★★ Part of the popular **La Paz Waterfall Gardens** (p. 68), Peace Lodge is about 45 minutes from the airport, near the Poás Volcano. The rooms and villas are huge and feature faux rustic decor, including massive four-poster log beds and river stone fireplaces. All come with a Jacuzzi on their private balconies, while the deluxe rooms also feature an immense bathroom with a second indoor Jacuzzi backed by a full wall of orchids, flowers, and bromeliads, with a working waterfall. Guests enjoy hiking trails, butterfly exhibits, and Frisbee golf. Nightly rates can be steep, but remember: They get you not only these fanciful rooms but also unlimited access to the Waterfall Gardens.

6km (3¾ miles) north of Varablanca on the road to San Miguel. www.waterfallgardens.com. ✆ **954/727-3997** in the U.S., or 2482-2720 in Costa Rica. 17 units. $257–$530 double; $597–$684 villa. **Amenities:** Restaurant; bar; Jacuzzi; 2 outdoor pools; free Wi-Fi.

MODERATE

If you want a classic airport hotel, with regular shuttle service, both the **Courtyard by Marriott ★** (www.marriott.com; ✆ **888/236-2427** in the U.S. and Canada, or 2429-2700 in Costa Rica) and **Holiday Inn Express ★** (www.hiexpress.com; ✆ **800/439-4745** in the U.S. and Canada, or 2443-0043 in Costa Rica) are solid U.S.-chain hotels located right across from the airport.

Hotel Bougainvillea ★ Tennis courts, a large pool, a bar and business center—for those hankering for a real resort experience, this three-story property is the ticket. It's not fancy by any means, with endless corridors and spacious but faceless rooms. But the lovely landscaping of the grounds, the unusually attentive service, and the fact that there's a very good restaurant here make up for a lot. Each of the rooms has a balcony; ask for one overlooking the gardens, as they're much quieter and have nicer views.

In Santo Tomás de Santo Domingo de Heredia, 100m (1 block) west of the Escuela de Santo Tomás, San José. www.hb.co.cr. ✆ **866/880-5441** in the U.S. and Canada, or 2244-1414 in Costa Rica. 81 units. $117 double; $147 suites. Rates include breakfast buffet. **Amenities:** Restaurant; bar; pool; 2 lighted tennis courts; free Wi-Fi.

Pura Vida Hotel ★★ Located just 10 minutes from the airport, this homey little inn is run by the genial couple Bernie Jubb and Nhi Chu. Rooms and private *casitas* (little houses) are spread around a spacious compound and lush gardens of vine-covered arbors, fruit trees, and exotic flowers. The two-bedroom *casitas* are perfect for families. Nhi is an expert chef specializing in Asian cuisine. Three-course fixed-menu meals are served around long communal tables and need to be booked in advance. The hotel is located just a kilometer or two north of downtown Alajuela.

Tuetal de Alajuela. www.puravidahotel.com. ✆ **2430-2929** or 8878-3899. 6 units. $89–$112 double. Rates include breakfast and one-way airport transfer. **Amenities:** Restaurant; free Wi-Fi.

INEXPENSIVE

Villa San Ignacio ★★ Formerly the Orquideas Inn, this boutique hotel is only 10 minutes or so from the airport, on the road that leads to the summit of the Poás Volcano. After a major remodeling, it has emerged as a quietly elegant lodging, with soft colors, plush appointments, and minimalistic decor, all at an amazing price. The hotel sits on 22 acres of land with tall native trees on a sloping hillside and is great for bird-watching. There's a refreshing mid-size rectangular pool off the main lobby and restaurant area, with low-lying Balinese-style chaise lounges. The Pandora restaurant serves excellent creative concoctions rooted in locally grown ingredients, and sometimes has live music on weekends. There are actually several routes to the top of Poás, and this hotel can be a bit hard to find, so be sure you're armed with good directions or a GPS. ***Note:*** Street noise can be a problem in some rooms.

Poás de Alajuela. www.villasanignacio.com. ✆ **8492-1133.** 12 units. $95 double. Rates include breakfast. Free parking. **Amenities:** Restaurant; bar; pool; free Wi-Fi.

WHERE TO EAT

San José has a variety of restaurants serving cuisines from all over the world. You can find superb French, Italian, and contemporary fusion restaurants around the city, as well as Peruvian, Japanese, Swiss, and Spanish spots. The greatest concentration and variety of restaurants is in the downtown area, as well as in the nearby suburbs of Escazú and Santa Ana. If you're looking for cheap eats, you'll find them all across the city in little restaurants known as *sodas,* which are the equivalent of diners in the United States.

Fruit vendors stake out spots on almost every street corner in downtown San José. If you're in town between April and June, you can sample more varieties of mangoes than you ever knew existed. Be sure to try a green mango with salt and chili peppers—it's guaranteed to wake up your taste buds. Another common street food is *pejibaye,* a bright orange palm nut about the size of a plum. They're boiled in big pots on carts; you eat them in much the same way you eat an avocado, and they taste a bit like squash.

Downtown San José

EXPENSIVE

La Esquina de Buenos Aires ★★ ARGENTINE/STEAKHOUSE Frankly, the Argentines do steak much better than the Ticos, and this Argentine-themed steakhouse is one of the best restaurants in the city. The decor and ambience are pure Porteño, and the extensive menu features a long list of grilled meats, some very good pastas, and various seafood and poultry offerings. The place is festive and almost always filled to brimming, so you'll need reservations.

Calle 11 and Av. 4. ✆ **2223-1909** or 2257-9741. Main courses C5,300–C13,800. Mon–Fri 11:30am–3pm and 6–10:30pm; Sat 12:30pm–11pm; Sun noon–10pm.

MODERATE

Restaurante Nuestra Tierra ★ COSTA RICAN Designed to recreate the feel of an old Costa Rican homestead kitchen, Nuestra Tierra has wait staff in traditional garb serving traditional Costa Rica fare. Customers sit at heavy wooden tables on bench seating. Bunches of bananas and onions and scores of painted enamel coffee mugs hang from wooden columns and beams. Hefty portions are served on banana leaves draped over large plates. The prices are a bit high for what you get, but service is prompt and pleasant.

Av. 2 and Calle 15. ✆ **2258-6500.** Main courses C6,000–C15,000. Daily 24 hrs.

Tin Jo ★★★ CHINESE/PAN-ASIAN This has long been one of the best and most popular restaurants in the city. Costa Rica has a long history of Chinese immigration, and this family restaurant is on its second generation. The menu here, however, wanders far and wide, with more traditional Szechuan and Cantonese plates sharing the menu with a mix of Thai, Japanese, Indian, and even Malay dishes. There are several dining rooms here, featuring decor from each of the countries or regions. The multiple vegetarian options are all clearly marked as to whether they are vegan and/or gluten-free.

Calle 11, btw. avs. 6 and 8. www.tinjo.com. ✆ **2221-7605** or 2257-3622. Reservations recommended. Main courses C6,000–C14,000. Mon–Fri 11:30am–2:30pm and 6–10pm (Fri until 11pm); Sat noon–3pm and 6–11pm; Sun noon–9pm.

INEXPENSIVE

Alma de Café ★ CAFE/COFFEEHOUSE Housed in an anteroom off the main lobby of the neo-baroque National Theater (Teatro Nacional), what should be just a simple coffee shop and restaurant is elevated by its setting—marble tables and floors, as well as elaborate painted ceiling murals, and regularly rotating exhibits of contemporary local artists. The menu features healthful salads, a selection of crepes, sandwiches, and lasagnas. Alma de Café often stays open late on theater performance nights.

In the Teatro Nacional, Av. 2, btw. calles 3 and 5. ✆ **2010-1119.** Sandwiches C3,000–C6,200; main courses C4,000–C6,500. Mon–Sat 9am–7pm; Sun 9am–6pm.

Barrio Amón/Barrio Otoya

MODERATE

Café Mundo ★ INTERNATIONAL A popular spot with a lively atmosphere and artsy ambience, this restaurant is housed in a remodeled old mansion, with tables and chairs spread through several rooms, hallways, outdoor patios, and terraces. The largest dining room here features floor-to-ceiling flowers painted by Costa Rican artist Miguel Casafont. Other rooms feature antique wallpaper and painted tile floors. Serving what I'd call bar-food-plus, the menu features a solid selection of salads, thick-crust pizzas, pastas, and a range of main dishes running the gamut from seafood-stuffed tenderloin to chicken in a honey-mustard sauce.

Calle 15 and Av. 9, 200m (2 blocks) east and 100m (1 block) north of the INS Building. ✆ **2222-6190.** Main courses C4,500–C20,000. Mon–Thurs 11am–10:30pm; Fri 11am–11:30pm; Sat 5–11:30pm.

Kalú ★★ CAFE/BISTRO Costa Rican–born chef Camille Ratton trained at Le Cordon Bleu and has created a wonderfully casual little bistro restaurant and gallery in a converted 1950s-era Art Deco home in a quiet neighborhood. The menu features a range of light and healthy options like salads and lettuce wraps, as well as tacos, panini, burgers, and more. But there are also more sophisticated options like fresh mahimahi in a Romesco sauce or risotto with three types of mushrooms. Don't miss out on the desserts, Camille's specialty—especially the Tarta Cahuita, an individual tartlette with a caramelized banana filling, grated lime peel, and chocolate ganache. Kalú serves brunch on the weekends and is renowned for its coffee, serving 34 different preparations of java. The attached **Kiosco** (p. 73) is one of San Jose's more creative gift shops.

Calle 31 and Av. 5. www.kalu.co.cr. ✆ **2253-8426.** Main courses C4,850–C10,500. Tues–Fri noon–10pm; Sat 9am–10pm; Sun 9am–4pm.

La Sabana/Paseo Colón

EXPENSIVE

Grano de Oro Restaurant ★★★ INTERNATIONAL It's no accident that the city's most elegant boutique hotel (p. 57) also has one of its most revered fine dining restaurants. The owners wooed and won French-born Francis Canal, a classically trained chef who has never stopped evolving, combining classic techniques from his homeland with local ingredients, tropical flavors, and contemporary fusion elements. That means a meal here might include an appetizer of Costa Rican snails in puff pastry, followed by local pork with tamarind sauce or sea bass crusted with macadamia nuts. The 200-plus bottle wine list features offerings from four continents, and nearly a dozen choices daily by the glass. Be sure to leave room for dessert. The namesake pie is a silky layering of coffee and mocha mousse on a rich cookie crust. The main dining room, a white linen and fine china affair, rings an open-air central courtyard, with a flowing fountain, tall potted trees, and large stained-glass features.

Calle 30, no. 251, btw. avs. 2 and 4, 150m (1½ blocks) south of Paseo Colón. www.hotelgranodeoro.com. ✆ **2255-3322.** Reservations recommended. Main courses C10,000–30,000. Daily 7am–10pm.

MODERATE

Park Café ★★ FUSION While the Grano de Oro thrives on elegance and consistency, this place has a more "off the cuff" vibe. But the payoff from British chef Richard Neat, who ran a two-star Michelin restaurant in London before moving to Costa Rica, can also be substantial. The menu changes seasonally, but always features creative, contemporary dishes with sometimes dazzling presentations, often in tapa-sized portions to encourage broad samplings. Recent options include prosciutto-wrapped scallops topped with fried onion rings in a Malbec reduction, and a rabbit breast served with confit of rabbit-stuffed ravioli and grilled artichokes. The restaurant is spread throughout the interior courtyard and garden of a stately old home that functions as an antiques and decorative arts shop by day.

Sabana Norte, 1 block north of Rostipollos. www.parkcafecostarica.blogspot.com. ✆ **2290-6324.** Reservations recommended. Main courses C3,900–C7,000. Tues–Sat 5:30pm–9pm.

INEXPENSIVE

Soda Tapia ★ COSTA RICAN Dine with the locals at this prototypical Tico *soda* in a retro 1950s-style American diner, complete with bright lights and Formica tables. The food is solid and the service speedy. Its extended hours make it a good choice for a late-night bite. The main branch is just across from the popular La Sabana Park and Museo de Arte Costarricense (p. 67). Other branches are around the Central Valley, including ones in Santa Ana (Centro Comercial Vistana Oeste, across from MATRA; ✆ **2203-7175**) and Alajuela (Centro Comercial Plaza Real Alajuela; ✆ **2441-6033**).

Calle 42 and Av. 2, across from the Museo de Arte Costarricense. www.facebook.com/sodatapia.com. ✆ **2222-6734.** Sandwiches C4,000–C4,400; main dishes C3,000–C5,000. Mon–Thurs 6am–2am; Fri–Sun 24 hrs.

San Pedro/Los Yoses

MODERATE

Olio ★★ MEDITERRANEAN This dimly lit, intimate restaurant has a romantic vibe, with several small rooms and quiet nooks located off the main dining area. A laundry list of classic Greek, Italian, and Spanish dishes is served in tapas-size portions, alongside more hearty pasta and main-course options. The wine list ventures far and wide to include offerings from Chile, Argentina, and even Bulgaria.

Barrio Escalante, 400m (4 blocks) east of Antigua Aduana. www.oliorestaurante.com. ✆ **2281-0541.** Reservations recommended. Main courses C4,950–C13,750. Mon–Wed 11:45am–11pm; Thurs–Fri 11:45am–midnight; Sat 5:30pm–midnight.

INEXPENSIVE

Mantras Veggie Café and Tea House ★★ VEGETARIAN This is among the best vegetarian restaurants in the city, with garden seating under bright red canvas umbrellas. The menu features a broad mix of soups, salads, wraps, sandwiches, and main dishes in both vegan and raw states. Signature dishes here include the raw zucchini "pasta" with pesto and the pad Thai. A

DINING UNDER THE stars

One of the best Costa Rican experiences is dining on the side of a volcano with the lights of San José shimmering below. These hanging restaurants, called *miradores,* are a resourceful response to the city's topography. Because San José is in a broad valley surrounded on all sides by volcanic mountains, people who live in these mountainous areas have no place to go but up—so they do, building roadside cafes up the sides of the volcanoes.

The food at most of these establishments is not spectacular, but the views often are, particularly at night, when the wide valley sparkles in a wash of lights. The town of **Aserrí,** 10km (6¼ miles) south of downtown San José, is the king of *miradores,* and **Mirador Ram Luna ★** (www.restauranteramluna.com; ✆ **2230-3022**) is the king of Aserrí. Grab a window seat and, if you've got the fortitude, order a plate of *chicharrones* (fried pork rinds). There's often live music. You can hire a cab for around C15,000 or take the Aserrí bus at Avenida 6 between calles Central and 2. Just ask the driver where to get off.

Miradores are also in the hills above Escazú and in San Ramón de Tres Ríos and Heredia. The most popular is **Le Monestère ★** (www.monastere-restaurant.com; ✆ **2289-4404;** closed Sun), an elegant converted church serving somewhat overrated French and Belgian cuisine in a spectacular setting above the hills of Escazú. I recommend coming here just for the less formal **La Cava Lounge ★**. I also like **Mirador Tiquicia ★** (✆ **2289-7330**), which occupies several rooms in a sprawling old Costa Rican home and has live folkloric dance shows on Thursdays.

broad selection of herbal teas are sold here, many grown on-site or purchased at local organic markets.

2 blocks east and ¼ block west of El Farolito, in Barrio Escalante. ✆ **2253-6715.** Main courses C3,850–C3,800. Mon–Sat 8:30am–5pm.

Escazú & Santa Ana

These two suburbs have the most vibrant restaurant scenes in the Central Valley, and much of the action takes place, oddly, in modern strip malls.

Two great one-stop options to consider are **Plaza Itskatzú,** just off the highway and sharing a parking lot with the Courtyard San José, and **Avenida Escazú,** which is anchored by the Marriott Residence Inn and is located next to the CIMA Hospital. Good options at Plaza Itskatzú include **Chancay ★** (www.chancay.info; ✆ **2588-2327**), which serves Peruvian and Peruvian/Chinese cuisine; and **Samurai Fusion ★** (✆ **2288-2240**), a fine sushi and teppanyaki joint.

Over on Avenida Escazú, you'll find **Saga ★** (www.sagarestaurant.com; ✆ **2289-6615**) with a contemporary-casual bistro menu; **Terraza Toscana ★★** (www.terrazzatoscanacr.com; ✆ **4000-2220**), an excellent and elegant Italian restaurant; and **L'Ile de France ★★** (✆ **2289-7533**), a top-notch, high-end French restaurant.

EXPENSIVE

Bacchus ★★ ITALIAN This elegant restaurant, inside an adobe home built in 1870, is one of the best Italian options in the city. Thin-crust pizzas come out of the wood-burning oven from the open kitchen. The pastas and raviolis are homemade and all are scrumptious, particularly the pappardelle with white wine, arugula, carrots, and crabmeat. From the selection of creative desserts, the banana and apple croquettes (in phyllo dough and topped with a Grand Marnier sauce) reigns supreme. Regularly rotating art exhibits adorn the walls and there's an ample open-air covered patio.

Downtown Santa Ana. www.bacchus.cr. ✆ **4001-5418.** Reservations required. Main courses C6,500–C14,700. Mon–Fri noon–3pm and 6–11pm; Sat noon–11pm; Sun noon–9pm.

MODERATE

Product-C ★★ SEAFOOD Although San José is inland, this fish market and restaurant prides itself on daily predawn runs to Puntarenas and other coastal supply points to get the freshest catch possible. It even set up the first oyster farm in Costa Rica, producing small yet very tasty oysters. The daily chalkboard menu features a range of specials that complements the simple menu here. Feel free to check out the display case and choose whatever fish or seafood strikes your fancy, and have it cooked to order in any number of styles.

Av. Escazú. www.product-c.com. ✆ **2288-5570.** Reservations recommended. Main courses C6,500–C13,000. Mon–Sat noon–11pm; Sun noon–6pm.

EXPLORING SAN JOSÉ

San José has some of the best and most modern museums in Central America, with a wealth of fascinating pre-Columbian artifacts. Standouts include the Museo de Jade (Jade Museum) and the Museo de Arte Costarricense (Costa Rican Art Museum), featuring a fine collection of Costa Rican art, and a large and varied, open-air sculpture garden.

Just outside San José in the Central Valley are also several great things to see and do. With day trips out of the city, you can spend quite a few days in this region.

The Top Attractions

DOWNTOWN

Museo de Jade Marco Fidel Tristán (Jade Museum) ★★ MUSEUM No commodity was more valuable among the pre-Columbian cultures of Central America and Mexico than jade; it was worth more than gold. Set on the western edge of the Plaza de la Democracia, this new five-story building has more than 7,000 sq. m (75,347 sq. ft.) of exhibition space, which for the first time ever is enough to display the museum's impressive 7,000-piece collection. The museum also houses an extensive collection of pre-Columbian polychrome terra-cotta bowls, vases, and figurines, some of which are startlingly modern in design (and exhibit a surprisingly advanced technique). Particularly intriguing is a vase that incorporates actual human teeth, and a display that shows how jade was embedded in human teeth merely for decorative purposes. All of the wall text is translated into English. Allot at least an hour or two to tour this museum.

Calle 13, btw. avenidas 2 and Central. ✆ **2521-6610.** Admission $15 adults, $5 students with valid ID, free for children 10 and under. Daily 10am–5pm.

Museos del Banco Central de Costa Rica (Gold Museum) ★★ MUSEUM A trove of some 1,600 gold pieces dating from 500 B.C. to A.D. 1500 is the primary lure here; visitors are usually bowled over by the intricate workmanship on the small gold items. Interestingly, gold was used in many forms, from cast animal figurines to jewelry to functional pieces. But the museum goes beyond the shiny, yellow stuff with a smartly curated survey of pre-Columbian culture, including exhibits on history, metalworking, and customs. The Gold Museum is directly underneath the downtown Plaza de la Cultura, and the same complex contains the Museo Numismático, a coin museum. Admission is free every Wednesday. Allow 2 hours for a visit here.

Calle 5, btw. avs. Central and 2, underneath the Plaza de la Cultura. www.museosdelbancocentral.org. ✆ **2243-4202.** Admission C5,500 adults, C4,000 students, free for children 11 and under. Free admission Wed. Daily 9:15am–5pm. Closed Jan 1, May 1, Holy Thurs, Good Fri, Easter, and Dec 25.

Museo Nacional de Costa Rica (National Museum) ★★ MUSEUM An excellent overview of the archaeological, historical, and natural wonders of Costa Rica from pre-Columbian times to the present, awaits visitors at this beautiful yellow building. Exhibits include pre-Columbian gold, jade, stone, and ceramic artifacts, including some of Costa Rica's striking stone spheres. Interpretive signs in both English and Spanish provide insight into the colonial period and the early republic, and there's a big atrium featuring multiple species of butterflies. The museum is housed in the Bellavista Fortress, a former army barracks, where the turrets still bear the bullet marks from fighting in the 1948 civil war. It takes a good 2 hours to see everything here.

Calle 17, btw. avs. Central and 2, on the Plaza de la Democracia. www.museocostarica.go.cr. ✆ **2257-1433.** Admission $9 adults, $4 students, free for children under 12. Tues–Sat 8:30am–4:30pm; Sun 9am–4:30pm. Closed Jan 1, May 1, Holy Thurs, Good Fri, Easter, and Dec 25.

LA SABANA/PASEO COLON

Museo de Arte Costarricense (Costa Rican Art Museum) ★★ ART MUSEUM Originally the main terminal and control tower of San José's first international airport, this museum houses the largest and most important collection of works by Costa Rican artists from the colonial time to the present. The museum's permanent collection has over 6,000 pieces, including works by big names like Juan Manuel Sánchez, Max Jiménez, Francisco Amighetti, Lola Fernández, and more. There's a sizable collection of Amighetti's stark and minimalistic lithographs, and 19th-century oil paintings of classic rural country scene's like "El Portón Rojo" ("The Red Door") by Teodorico Quiros. On the back patio—which used to lead to the tarmac—is a sculpture garden. This museum is free, and anchors the eastern edge of La Sabana city park, making it easy to combine a visit with a stroll through the park. Allot 2 hours for a museum visit.

Calle 42 and Paseo Colón, Parque La Sabana Este. www.musarco.go.cr. ✆ **2256-1281.** Free admission. Tues–Sun 9am–4pm.

Outlying Attractions

Café Britt Farm ★ COFFEE FARM Café Britt is one of the largest coffee producers in Costa Rica, and the company has put together an interesting and professional tour and stage production at its farm, which is 20 minutes outside of San José. Here you'll see how coffee is grown, and you'll visit the roasting and processing plant to learn how a coffee "cherry" is turned into a delicious roasted bean. Tasting sessions are offered for visitors to experience the different qualities of coffee. The farm also has a restaurant and a store where you can buy coffee and coffee-related gift items. The entire tour, including transportation, takes about 3 to 4 hours. Allow some extra time and an extra $10 for a visit to the nearby working plantation and mill. You can even strap on a basket and go out coffee picking during harvest time.

North of Heredia on the road to Barva. www.coffeetour.com. ✆ **2277-1600.** Admission $22 adults, $17 children 6–11; $39 adults and $34 children, including transportation from downtown San José. Add $15 for lunch buffet. Tours daily at 9:30 and 11am; 1:15 and 3:15pm. Store and restaurant daily 8am–5pm.

Doka Estate ★ COFFEE FARM This large and long-standing coffee estate/farm in Alajuela offers a tour that takes you from "seed to cup." Along the way, you'll get a full rundown of the processes involved in the growing, harvesting, curing, packing, and brewing of award-winning coffee. This coffee tour is similar to that offered at **Café Britt** (see above), but has a more down-home feel. Also on-site: a butterfly garden, Bonsai tree, and orchid exhibit. Allow about 2½ hours.

Sabanilla de Alajuela. www.dokaestate.com. ✆ **888/946-3652** in the U.S. and Canada, or 2449-5152 in Costa Rica. Admission $20 adults, $16 students with valid ID, $10 children 6–12, free for children 5 and under. Packages including transportation and breakfast or lunch available. Tours daily at 9, 10, and 11am; 1:30 and 2:30pm. Reservations required.

INBio Park ★★ MUSEUM/NATURE PARK Founded by the National Biodiversity Institute (Instituto Nacional de Biodiversidad, or INBio), this place is part museum, part educational center, and part nature park. In addition to watching a 15-minute informational video, visitors can tour two large pavilions explaining Costa Rica's biodiversity and natural wonders, and hike on trails that recreate the ecosystems of a tropical rainforest, dry forest, and premontane forest. A 2-hour guided hike is included in the entrance fee, and self-guided-tour booklets are also available. There's a good-size butterfly garden, as well as a Plexiglas viewing window into the small lagoon. One of the attractions is the series of animal sculptures donated by one of Costa Rica's premier artists, José Sancho. A simple cafeteria-style restaurant serves lunch, and there's a coffee shop and gift shop. You can easily spend 2 to 3 hours here.

400m (4 blocks) north and 250m (2½ blocks) west of the Shell station in Santo Domingo de Heredia. www.inbioparque.com. ✆ **2507-8107.** Admission $25 adults, $19 students, $15 children 12 and under. Fri 9am–3pm (admission closes at 2pm); Sat–Sun 9am–4pm.

La Paz Waterfall Gardens ★★ NATURAL ATTRACTION The original attraction here consists of a series of trails through primary and secondary forests alongside La Paz River, with lookouts over a series of powerful falls, including the namesake La Paz Fall. In addition to the orchid garden and a hummingbird garden, you must visit the huge butterfly garden. A small serpentarium, featuring a mix of venomous and nonvenomous native snakes, several terrariums containing frogs and lizards, and a section of wildcats and local monkey species in large enclosures are added attractions. While the admission fee is a little steep, everything is well done, especially the trails and waterfalls. That said, some find the whole operation a little artificial in feel. Yet it's a good place to get a broad experience in one compact package, especially for families with young children. This is also a nice stop after a morning visit to the Poás Volcano. Plan to spend 3 to 4 hours here. The hotel rooms here at **Peace Lodge** (p. 60) are some of the nicest in the country.

6km (3¾ miles) north of Varablanca on the road to San Miguel. www.waterfallgardens.com. ✆ **2482-2720.** Admission $40 adults, $24 children 3–12, free for children 2 and under. Daily 8am–5pm. No easy or regular bus service here; come in rental car or taxi, or arrange transport with La Paz.

Sibú Chocolate ★★★ CAFE/CHOCOLATE FACTORY Chocolate lovers will definitely want to visit this gourmet organic chocolate maker, which features a small cafe, gift shop, and tours of its production facility. Tasting tours are offered at 10:30am and last about an hour. The tour includes an informative presentation about the history and techniques of chocolate making, as well as several tempting tastings.

San Isidro de Heredia. www.sibuchocolate.com. ✆ **2268-1335.** Tasting tours $24 (Tues–Sat 10:30am; reservations essential). Gift shop and production facility Tues–Sat 8am–5pm.

Zoo Ave ★ ZOO Dozens of scarlet macaws, reclusive owls, majestic raptors, several different species of toucans, and a host of brilliantly colored birds from Costa Rica and around the world make this one exciting place to visit. In total, over 115 species of birds are on display, including some 80 species found in Costa Rica. Bird-watching enthusiasts will be able to get a closer look at birds they might have seen in the wild. Other critters to observe include iguana, deer, tapir, ocelot, puma, and monkey—and look out for the 3.6m (12-ft.) crocodile. Zoo Ave houses only injured, donated, or confiscated animals. It takes about 2 hours to walk the paths and visit all the exhibits here.

La Garita, Alajuela. www.rescateanimalzooave.org. ✆ **2433-8989.** Admission $20 adults, $15 students with valid ID. Daily 9am–5pm.

Outdoor Activities & Spectator Sports

Because of the chaos and pollution, you'll probably want to get out of the city before undertaking anything too strenuous. But if you want to brave the elements, San José does have a few outdoor activities to enjoy. For information on horseback riding, hiking, and whitewater rafting trips from San José, see "Day Trips from San José," later in this chapter.

Parque La Sabana ★★ (La Sabana Park, at the western end of Paseo Colón), formerly San José's international airport, is the city's center for active sports and recreation. Here you'll find jogging trails, a banked bicycle track, soccer fields, a roller-rink, a few public tennis courts, and the huge National Stadium. Aside from events at the stadium, all the facilities are free and open to the public. On weekends, you'll usually find free aerobics, yoga, or dancercise classes taking place. Families gather for picnics, people fly kites, pony rides are available for the kids, and everyone strolls through the outdoor sculpture garden. If you really want to experience the local culture, try getting into a pickup soccer game. However, be careful in this park, especially at dusk or after dark, when it becomes a favorite haunt for youth gangs and muggers.

SOCCER (FUTBOL) ★ Ticos take their *fútbol* seriously. Costa Rican professional soccer is some of the best in Central America, and the national team, or *Sele (selección nacional),* qualified for the World Cup in 2002 and 2006. Although they failed to qualify for the 2010 World Cup in South Africa, they did qualify for the 2014 in Brazil—and did quite well, considering the odds, losing to the Netherlands on penalty kicks in the quarterfinals.

The local professional soccer season runs from August through June, with a break for Christmas and New Year's, and separate championship playoffs every December and July. The main San José team is Saprissa (affectionately called *El Monstruo,* or "The Monster"). **Saprissa's stadium** is in Tibás (www.saprissa.com; ✆ **2240-4034;** take any Tibás bus from Calle 2 and Av. 5). Games are often held on Sunday at 11am, but occasionally are scheduled for Saturday afternoon or Wednesday evening. Check the local newspapers for game times and locations.

International and other important matches are held in the **National Stadium** on the northeastern corner of Parque La Sabana.

Aside from major international matches at the National Stadium, you don't need to buy tickets in advance. Tickets generally run between C1,500 and C8,000. It's worth paying a little extra for *sombra numerado* (reserved seats in the shade). This will protect you from both the sun and the more rowdy aficionados. Periodic outbursts of violence, both inside and outside the stadiums, have marred the sport here, so be careful. Other options include *sombra* (general admission in the shade), *palco* and *palco numerado* (general admission and reserved mezzanine), and *sol general* (general admission in full sun).

It is possible to buy tickets to most sporting events in advance from **E-Ticket** (www.eticket.cr), but the site is entirely in Spanish.

Especially for Kids

Museo de Los Niños (Children's Museum) ★ MUSEUM A massive attraction that's both fun and informative, the Museo del Los Niños features interactive exhibits and educational displays describing everything from the rainforest to pre-Columbian village life to the interior of a spaceship (in honor of Costa Rican astronaut Franklin Chang). The simulated earthquake exhibit is always a favorite. It's housed in a former prison, so if anyone in your family is acting out, you can actually lock them in an old prison cell to set them straight. The museum is also home to the National Auditorium, and often features temporary exhibitions of contemporary art. You can easily spend 2 to 3 hours here, but you'll want to take a taxi for transportation, as the museum borders a rather seedy section of the city's red-light district.

Calle 4 and Av. 9. www.museocr.org. ✆ **2258-4929.** Admission C2,200 adults, free for children 15 and under. Tues–Fri 8am–4:30pm; Sat–Sun 9:30am–5pm.

SHOPPING

Serious shoppers may be disappointed in San José, as aside from oxcarts and indigenous masks, there isn't much that's distinctly Costa Rican. To compensate for its relative lack of goods, Costa Rica does a brisk business in selling crafts and clothes imported from Guatemala, Panama, and Ecuador.

San José's central shopping corridor is bounded by avenidas 1 and 2, from about Calle 14 in the west to Calle 13 in the east. For several blocks west of the Plaza de la Cultura, **Avenida Central** is a pedestrian-only street mall where you'll find store after store of inexpensive clothes for men, women, and children. Depending on the mood of the police that day, you might find a lot of street vendors as well. Most shops in the downtown district are open Monday through Saturday from about 8am to 6pm. Some shops close for lunch, while others remain open. You'll be happy to find that sales and import taxes have already been figured into display prices.

With globalization taking hold in Costa Rica, much of the local shopping scene has shifted to large megamalls, modern multilevel affairs with

joe TO GO

Two words of advice: Buy coffee.

Coffee is the best shopping deal in all of Costa Rica. Although the best Costa Rican coffee is allegedly shipped off to North American and European markets, it's hard to beat the coffee that's roasted right in front of you here. Best of all is the price: 1 pound of coffee sells for around $4 to $7. It makes a great gift and truly is a local product.

Café Britt is the big name in Costa Rican coffee. It has the largest export business in the country, and, although high-priced, its blends are very dependable. Café Britt is widely available at gift shops around the country, and at the souvenir concessions at both international airports. Also good are the coffees roasted and packaged in Manuel Antonio and Monteverde, by **Café Milagro** and **Café Monteverde,** respectively. If you visit either of these places, definitely pick up their beans.

In general, the best place to buy coffee is in any supermarket. Why pay more at a gift or specialty shop? If you buy prepackaged coffee in a supermarket in Costa Rica, the whole beans will be marked either *grano* (grain) or *grano entero* (whole bean). If you opt for ground varieties (*molido*), be sure the package is marked *puro;* otherwise, it may be mixed with a good amount of sugar, the way Ticos like it.

One good coffee-related gift to bring home is a coffee sock and stand. This is the most common mechanism for brewing coffee beans in Costa Rica. It consists of a simple circular stand, made out of wood or wire, which holds a "sock." Put the ground beans in the sock, place a pot or cup below it, and pour boiling water through. You can find the socks and stands at most supermarkets and in the Mercado Central. In fancier crafts shops, you'll find them made out of ceramic. Depending on its construction, a stand will cost you between $1.50 and $15; socks run around 30¢, so buy a few spares.

cineplexes, food courts, and international brand-name stores. The biggest and most modern of these malls include the **Mall San Pedro, Multiplaza** (one each in Escazú and the eastern suburb of Zapote), and **Terra Mall** (on the outskirts of downtown on the road to Cartago). Although they lack the charm of small shops found around San José, they are a reasonable option for one-stop shopping; most contain at least one or two local galleries and crafts shops, along with a large supermarket, which is always the best place to stock up on local coffee, hot sauces, liquors, and other nonperishable foodstuffs.

Shopping A to Z

ART GALLERIES

Galería Kandinsky ★ Owned by the daughter of one of Costa Rica's most prominent modern painters, Rafa Fernández, this small gallery usually has a good selection of high-end contemporary Costa Rican paintings, be it the house collection or a specific temporary exhibit. Centro Comercial Calle Real, San Pedro. ✆ **2234-0478.**

Galería Valanti ★★ This is a well-lit and expertly curated gallery. The collection here is ever-evolving, but always includes a good mix of contemporary and classic Costa Rican and Latin American artists. Av. 11, no. 3395, btw. calles 33 and 35, Barrio Escalante. www.galeriavalanti.com. ✆ **2253-1659.**

CHOCOLATE

Sibú Chocolate ★★★ Building on the success of their organic chocolate production and tour operation in the hills of Heredia (p. 82), the folks at Sibú Chocolate now have a store in Escazú also. This is a great place to pick up a mix of their wonderful truffles and bonbons, as well as cacao powder, chocolate bars, and cacao nibs. This is also a great place to grab a cup of hot chocolate and a pastry. San Isidro de Heredia. www.sibuchocolate.com. ✆ **2268-1335.**

HANDICRAFTS

The range and quality of craftworks for sale here has improved greatly in recent years. In addition to the places listed below, you might want to check out the works of Lil Mena, a local artist who specializes in working with and painting on handmade papers and rough fibers, and **Cecilia "Pefi" Figueres ★★**, who specializes in brightly colored abstract and figurative ceramic bowls, pitchers, coffee mugs, and more. Both Mena and Figueres are sold at some of the better gift shops around the city.

Biesanz Woodworks ★★ Biesanz makes a wide range of high-quality wood items, including bowls, jewelry boxes, humidors, and some nifty sets of chopsticks. The company is actively involved in local reforestation, too. Bello Horizonte, Escazú. www.biesanz.com. ✆ **2289-4337.** Call for directions and off-hour appointments.

Boutique Annemarie ★ Occupying two floors at the Hotel Don Carlos (p. 56), this shop has an amazing array of wood products, leather goods, papier-mâché figurines, paintings, books, cards, posters, and jewelry. You'll see most of this merchandise at the city's other shops, but not in such quantities or in such a relaxed and pressure-free environment. At the Hotel Don Carlos, Calle 9, btw. avs. 7 and 9. ✆ **2233-5343.**

Chietón Morén ★★★ *Chietón Morén* means "fair deal" in the Boruca language. This place features Arts and Crafts from a dozen or so different Costa Rican indigenous communities displayed in a space that is part museum and part showroom and market. It operates as a nonprofit and is certified "fair trade," and all profits are given directly back to the artisans and their communities. Offerings include a wide range of textiles, carved masks, prints, and jewelry. Calle 1, btw. avs. 10 and 12. www.chietonmoren.org. ✆ **2221-0145.**

Galería Namu ★★★ Galería Namu has some very high-quality Arts and Crafts, specializing in truly high-end indigenous works, including excellent Boruca and Huetar carved masks and "primitive" paintings. It also carries a good selection of more modern Arts and Crafts, including the ceramic work of Cecilia "Pefi" Figueres. This place organizes tours to visit various indigenous tribes and artisans as well. Av. 7, btw. calles 5 and 7. www.galerianamu.com. ✆ **2256-3412.**

Kiosco ★★★ Attached to the restaurant Kalú (p. 63), this place features a range of original and one-off pieces of functional, wearable, and practical jewelry made by contemporary Costa Rican and regional artists and designers. While the offerings are regularly changing, you'll usually find a selection of jewelry, handbags, shoes, dolls, furniture, and knickknacks. Often the pieces are made with recycled or sustainable materials. Calle 31 and Av. 5, Barrio Escalante. www. kalu.co.cr/boutique-kiosco-sjo. ✆ **2253-8426.**

Mercado Central ★ Although this tight maze of stalls is primarily a food market, vendors also sell souvenirs, leather goods, musical instruments, and many other items. Be especially careful with your wallet, purse, and prominent jewelry, as skilled pickpockets frequent the area. All the streets surrounding the Mercado Central are jammed with produce vendors selling from small carts or loading and unloading trucks. It's always a hive of activity, with crowds of people jostling for space on the streets. Your best bet is to visit on Sunday or a weekday; Saturday is particularly busy. Btw. avs. Central and 1 and calles 6 and 8, San José. No phone.

Plaza de la Democracia ★★ Two long rows of outdoor stalls sell T-shirts, Guatemalan and Ecuadorian handicrafts and clothing, small ceramic *ocarinas* (a small musical wind instrument), and handmade jewelry. The atmosphere here is much more open than at the Mercado Central, which can be a bit claustrophobic. You might be able to bargain prices down a bit, but bargaining is not a traditional part of the vendor culture here, so you'll have to work hard to save a few bucks. On the west side of the Plaza de la Democracia, Calle 13, btw. avs. Central and 2. No phone.

NIGHTLIFE

Catering to a mix of tourists, college students, and party-loving Ticos, San José has a host of options to meet the nocturnal needs of visitors and residents alike. You'll find plenty of interesting clubs and bars, a wide range of theaters, and some very lively discos and dance salons.

To find out what's going on in San José while you're in town, go to **www. ticotimes.net,** or pick up ***La Nación*** (Spanish; www.nacion.com). The former is a good place to find out where local expats are hanging out; the latter's "Viva" and "Tiempo Libre" sections have extensive listings of discos, movie theaters, and live music.

The Performing Arts

Visiting artists stop in Costa Rica on a regular basis. Recent concerts have featured hard rockers Aerosmith, Red Hot Chili Peppers, and Metallica, Mexican crooner Lila Downs, pop legend Elton John, Colombian sensation Shakira, and Latin heartthrob Marc Anthony. These performances take place at one of San José's performing arts theaters or one of the city's large sporting stadiums.

The **National Symphony Orchestra** (✆ **2240-0333**) is respectable by regional standards, although its repertoire tends to be rather conservative. Symphony season runs March through November, with concerts roughly every other weekend at the Teatro Nacional. Tickets cost between C4,000 and C7,000 and can be purchased at the box office.

Costa Rica's cultural panorama changes drastically every March when the country hosts large arts festivals. One of these is El Festival Nacional de las Artes, featuring purely local talent. **El Festival Internacional de las Artes** (FIA) is a major month-long party with a nightly smorgasbord of dance, theater, and music from around the world—although it became known as FIASCO in 2015 when it was canceled because of poor planning and miscommunication with artists. For dates and details, contact the **Ministry of Youth and Culture** (www.mcj.go.cr; ✆ **2221-2022**), although information is in Spanish.

It is possible to buy tickets to many cultural events and concerts in advance from **E-Ticket** (www.eticket.cr), though the site is entirely in Spanish.

Teatro Nacional (National Theater) ★★ Costa Rica's most elegant and elaborate theater, the Teatro Nacional opened in 1897. Funded with a special tax on coffee, and modeled on the Paris Opera House, this neo-baroque theater features marble floors and columns, numerous sculptures including busts of Beethoven and Chopin, and a painted fresco on the main auditorium's ceiling meant to suggest the majesty of the Sistine chapel. It is home base for the National Symphony Orchestra, and site of numerous other cultural events. Av. 2, btw. calles 3 and 5. www.teatronacional.go.cr. ✆ **2010-1110.**

The Club, Music & Dance Scene

You'll find plenty of places to hit the dance floor in San José. Salsa and merengue are the main beats that move people here, and many of the city's dance clubs, discos, and salons feature live music on the weekends. You'll find a pretty limited selection, though, if you're looking to catch some small-club jazz, rock, or blues performances.

The daily "Viva" and Friday's "Tiempo Libre" sections of *La Nación* newspaper have weekly performance schedules. Some dance bands to watch for are Gaviota,

Chocolate, Son de Tikizia, Taboga Band, and La Orquestra Son Mayor. While Ghandi, Foffo Goddy, Kadeho, Evolucion, and Akasha are popular local rock and pop groups, Marfil is a good cover band, and the Blues Devils, Chepe Blues, and the Las Tortugas are outfits that play American-style hard rock and blues. If you're looking for jazz, check out Editus, El Sexteto de Jazz Latino, or pianist and former Minister of Culture Manuel Obregón. Finally, for a taste of something eclectic, look for Santos y Zurdo, Sonámbulo Psicotrópical, or Cocofunka.

Most of the places listed below charge a nominal cover charge; sometimes it includes a drink or two.

Castro's ★ This is a classic Costa Rican dance club. The music varies throughout the night, from salsa and merengue to reggaeton and occasionally electronic trance. It's open daily from noon to anytime between 3 and 6am. Av. 13 and Calle 22, Barrio México. ✆ **2256-8789.**

Vértigo ★★ Tucked inside a nondescript office building and commercial center on Paseo Colón, this club remains one of the more popular places for rave-style late-night dancing and partying. The dance floor is huge, the ceilings are high, and electronic music rules the roost. It's open Friday and Saturday till 6am. Edificio Colón, Paseo Colón. www.vertigocr.com. ✆ **2257-8424.**

The Bar Scene

San José has something for every taste. Lounge lizards will be happy in most hotel bars downtown, while students and the young at heart will have no problem mixing in at the livelier spots around town. Sports fans have plenty of places to catch the most important games of the day, and a couple of brewpubs are drastically improving the quality and selection of the local suds.

The best part of the varied bar scene in San José is something called *bocas,* the equivalent of tapas in Spain: a little dish of snacks that arrives at your table when you order a drink. Although this is a somewhat dying tradition, especially in the younger, hipper bars, you will still find *bocas* alive and well in the older, more traditional San José drinking establishments. The most traditional of these are known locally as *cantinas.* In most, the *bocas* are free, but in some, where the dishes are more sophisticated, you'll have to pay for the treats. You'll find drinks reasonably priced, with beer costing around $3 to $4 a bottle, and mixed drinks costing $4 to $10.

El Cuartel de la Boca del Monte ★★ This popular bar, one of San José's best, began life as an artist-and-bohemian hangout, and has evolved into a massive melting pot, attracting everyone from the city's young hipsters to foreign exchange students. Live music is usually Monday, Wednesday, and Friday nights, when the place is packed shoulder to shoulder. From Monday to Friday it's open for lunch and again in the evenings; on weekends it opens at 6pm. On most nights it's open till about 1am, although the revelry might continue till about 3am on Friday or Saturday. Av. 1, btw. calles 21 and 23 (50m/½ block west of the Cine Magaly). ✆ **2221-0327.**

El Sótano ★★ "El Sótano" means "the basement," and that's just where you'll find this tiny bar and performance space. Most nights, some of the city's best jazz and blues players hold down the scene, and on Tuesdays they host an open jam session. There's a small menu of bar food and sandwiches. When there's no live band, the house music is entirely played from vinyl. Upstairs from El Sótano is a separate bar and lounge space, El Solar. It's open until 2am daily. Calle 3, btw. avs. 9 and 11. ✆ **2221-2302.**

HANGING OUT IN SAN PEDRO

The funky 2-block stretch of **San Pedro** ★★ just south of the University of Costa Rica has been dubbed La Calle de Amargura, or the "Street of Bitterness," and it's the heart and soul of this eastern suburb and college town. Bars and cafes are mixed in with bookstores and copy shops. After dark the streets are packed with teens, students, and professors barhopping and just hanging around. You can walk the strip until someplace strikes your fancy—or you can try one of the places listed below. ***Note:*** La Calle de Amargura attracts a certain unsavory element. Use caution here. Try to visit with a group, and avoid carrying large amounts of cash or wearing flashy jewelry.

Jazz Café ★ The intimate Jazz Café is one of the more happening spots in San Pedro. Jazz buffs will want to test their knowledge by trying to identify the various artists depicted in large sculpted busts behind the main stage. Most nights feature live music. It's open daily till about 2am. Sister club **Jazz Café Escazú** (**✆ 2288-4740**) is on the western end of town. Next to the Banco Popular on Av. Central. www.jazzcafecostarica.com. ✆ **2253-8933.**

Mundoloco El Chante ★★ This club is the brainchild of DJ, radio host, and musician Bernal Monestel. The performance space in the back hosts live music or DJs most nights—usually with a slight cover charge. Bands tend to be eclectic, with a tendency toward electronic and world music, in addition to the homegrown rock and reggae outfits that are popular with the university crowd this place tends to attract. Southeast corner of the Banco Popular on Av. Central. www.facebook.com/MundolocoElChante. ✆ **2253-4125.**

Casinos

Gambling is legal in Costa Rica, and there are casinos at many major hotels. However, as with Tico bullfighting, some idiosyncrasies are involved in gambling here. If blackjack is your game, you'll want to play "rummy." The rules are almost identical, except that the house doesn't pay 1½ times on blackjack—instead, it pays double on any three of a kind or three-card straight flush. If you're looking for roulette, what you'll find here is a bingo-like spinning cage of numbered balls. The betting is the same, but some of the glamour is lost.

You'll also find a version of five-card-draw poker, but the rule differences are so complex that I advise you to sit down and watch for a while and then ask questions before joining in. That's about all you'll find. There are no craps tables or baccarat.

There's some controversy over slot machines, but you will be able to play electronic slots and poker games. Most casinos here are casual and small by international standards. You may have to dress up slightly at some of the fancier hotels, but most are accustomed to tropical vacation attire.

DAY TRIPS FROM SAN JOSÉ

San José makes an excellent base for exploring the lovely Central Valley. For first-time visitors, the best way to make the most of these excursions is usually to take a guided tour, but if you rent a car, you'll have greater independence. Some day trips also can be done by public bus.

Organized Tours

A number of companies offer a wide variety of primarily nature-related day tours out of San José. The most reputable include **Costa Rica Sun Tours ★** (www.crsuntours.com; ✆ **866/271-6263** in the U.S. and Canada, or 2296-7757 in Costa Rica); **Horizontes Nature Tours ★★** (www.horizontes.com; ✆ **888/786-8748** in the U.S. and Canada, or 2222-2022); and **Swiss Travel Service** (www.swisstravelcr.com; ✆ **2282-4898**). Prices range from around $35 to $70 for a half-day trip, and from $70 to $160 for a full-day trip.

Before signing on for a tour of any sort, find out how many fellow travelers will be accompanying you, how much time will be spent in transit and eating lunch, and how much time will actually be spent doing the primary activity. I've had complaints about tours that were rushed, that spent too much time in a bus or on secondary activities, or that had a cattle-car, assembly-line feel to them. You'll find many tours that combine two or three different activities or destinations.

The most popular day trip destination from San José is **Rainforest Adventures ★** (www.rainforestadventure.com; ✆ **866/759-8726** in the U.S. and Canada, or 2257-5961 in Costa Rica), built on a private reserve bordering Braulio Carrillo National Park. It boasts a pioneering aerial tram built by rainforest researcher Donald Perry, whose cable-car system through the forest canopy at Rara Avis helped establish him as an early expert on rainforest canopies. On the **90-minute tram ride** through the treetops, visitors have the chance to glimpse the complex web of life that makes these forests unique. Additional attractions include a butterfly garden, serpentarium, and frog collection. There's also a zipline tour, and the grounds feature well-groomed trails through the rainforest and a restaurant. With all this on offer, a trip here can easily take up a full day. If you want to spend the night, 10 simple but clean and comfortable bungalows cost $125 per person per day (double occupancy), including three meals, a guided hike, taxes, the tram ride, and use of the rest of the facilities.

The cost for a full-day tour, including both the **aerial tram and canopy tour,** as well as all the park's other attractions, is $99 for adults; students and anyone under 18 pay $65. Packages, including round-trip transportation and lunch, are also available. Alternatively, you can drive or take one of the frequent Guápiles buses—they leave every half-hour throughout the day and cost C1,405—from the Caribbean bus terminal (Gran Terminal del Caribe) on Calle Central and Avenida 15. Ask the driver to let you off in front of the *teleférico* (cable car). If you're driving, head out on the Guápiles Highway as if driving to the Caribbean coast. Watch for the tram's roadside welcome center—it's hard to miss. This is a popular tour for groups, so get an advance reservation in the high season and, if possible, a ticket; otherwise you could wait a long time for your tram ride or even be shut out. The tram handles about 80 passengers per hour, so scheduling is tight.

Several companies offer cruises to the white sand beaches of the remote and uninhabited **Tortuga Island in the Gulf of Nicoya.** These full-day tours generally entail an early departure for the 1½-hour chartered bus ride to Puntarenas, where you board your vessel for a 1½-hour cruise to Tortuga Island. Then you get several hours on the uninhabited island, where you can swim, lie on the beach, play volleyball, or try a canopy tour, followed by the return journey.

The original and most dependable company running these trips is **Calypso Tours** ★ (www.calypsocruises.com; ✆ **855/855-1975** in the U.S. and Canada, or 2256-2727 in Costa Rica). The tour costs $145 per person and includes round-trip transportation from San José, Jacó, Manuel Antonio or Monteverde, a buffet breakfast before embarking on the boat, all drinks on the cruise, and a buffet lunch on the beach at the island. The Calypso Tours main vessel is a huge motor-powered catamaran. The company also runs a tour to a private nature reserve at **Punta Coral** ★. The beach is much nicer at Tortuga Island, but the tour to Punta Coral is more intimate, and the restaurant, hiking, and kayaking are all superior. Daily pickups are from San José, Manuel Antonio, Jacó, and Monteverde, and you can use the day trip on the boat as your transfer or transportation option between any of these towns and destinations.

Cascading down Costa Rica's mountain ranges are dozens of tumultuous rivers, several of which are very popular for **whitewater rafting and kayaking.** If I had to choose just one day trip out of San José, it would be whitewater rafting. For $100 or less, you can spend a day rafting a beautiful river through lush tropical forests, and multi-day trips are also available. Some of the most reliable rafting companies are **Aventuras Naturales** ★★ (www.adventurecostarica.com; ✆ **888/680-9031** in the U.S., or 2225-3939 in Costa Rica); **Exploradores Outdoors** ★ (www.exploradoresoutdoors.com; ✆ **646/205-0828** in the U.S. and Canada, or 2222-6262 in Costa Rica); and **Ríos Tropicales** ★★ (www.riostropicales.com; ✆ **866/722-8273** in the U.S. and Canada, or 2233-6455 in Costa Rica). These companies all ply a number of rivers of varying difficulties, including the popular Pacuare River. For details, see "Whitewater Rafting & Kayaking" in chapter 12.

Cartago & the Orosi Valley

These two regions southeast of San José can easily be combined into a day trip. You might also squeeze in a visit to the Irazú Volcano (see above for details).

CARTAGO

Cartago is the original capital of Costa Rica. Founded in 1563, it was Costa Rica's first city—and was, in fact, the *only* city for almost 150 years. Irazú Volcano rises up from the edge of town, and although it's quiet these days, it has not always been so peaceful. Earthquakes have damaged Cartago repeatedly over the years, so today few of the old colonial buildings are left standing. In

HOLY SMOKE! FINDING THE RIGHT volcano TRIP

Poás, Irazú, and Arenal volcanoes are three of Costa Rica's most popular destinations, and the first two are easy day trips from San José (see below). Although numerous companies offer day trips to Arenal, I don't recommend them because travel time is at least 3½ hours in each direction.

Most tour companies in the city and hotel tour desks can arrange a day trip to any of these volcanoes. Prices range from $30 to $50 for a half-day trip, and from $50 to $120 for a full-day trip.

The 3,432m (11,256-ft.) **Irazú Volcano** ★ (✆ **2200-4422**) is historically one of Costa Rica's more active volcanoes, although it's relatively quiet these days. It last erupted on March 19, 1963, the day that President John F. Kennedy arrived in Costa Rica. There's a good paved road right to the rim of the crater, where a desolate expanse of gray sand nurtures few plants and the air smells of sulfur. The landscape here is often compared to that of the moon. There are magnificent views of the fertile Meseta Central and Orosi Valley as you drive up from Cartago, and if you're very lucky, you might be able to see both the Pacific Ocean and the Caribbean Sea. Clouds usually descend by noon, so get here as early in the day as possible.

The visitor center has info on the volcano and natural history. A short trail leads to the rim of the volcano's two craters, their walls a maze of eroded gullies feeding onto the flat floor far below. This is a national park, with an admission fee of $15 adults, $5 children, charged at the gate. Dress in layers; this might be the tropics, but it can be cold up top if the sun's not out. The park restaurant, at an elevation of 3,022m (9,912 ft.), with walls of windows looking out over the valley far below, claims to be the highest restaurant in Central America.

Poás Volcano ★★ (✆ **2482-1228**) is 37km (23 miles) from San José on narrow roads that wind through a landscape of fertile farms and dark forests. As at Irazú, there's a paved road right to the top, although you'll have to hike in about 1km (½ mile) to reach the crater. The volcano stands 2,708m (8,882 ft.) tall and is located within a national park, which preserves not only the volcano but also dense stands of virgin forest. Poás's crater, said to be the second largest in the world, is more than a mile across. Geysers in the crater sometimes spew steam and muddy water 180m (590 ft.) into the air, making this the largest geyser in the world. There's an information center where you can see a slideshow about the volcano, and there are well-groomed and well-marked hiking trails through the cloud forest that rings the crater. About 15 minutes from the parking area, along a forest trail, is an overlook onto beautiful Botos Lake, which has formed in one of the volcano's extinct craters.

Be prepared when you come to Poás: This volcano is often enveloped in dense clouds. If you want to see the crater, it's best to come early and during the dry season. Moreover, it can get cool up here, especially when the sun isn't shining, so dress appropriately. Admission to Poás Volcano National Park is $15.

the center of the city, a public park winds through the ruins of a large church that was destroyed in a 1910 earthquake before it could be finished.

Cartago's most famous building is the **Basílica de Nuestra Señora de los Ángeles (Basilica of Our Lady of the Angels)** ★★★, which is dedicated to the patron saint of Costa Rica and stands on the east side of town. Within the walls of this Byzantine-style church is a shrine containing the tiny carved figure of **La Negrita,** the Black Virgin, which is nearly lost amid its ornate

La Negrita

Legend has it that while gathering wood, a girl named Juana Pereira stumbled upon the statue of La Negrita sitting atop a rock. Juana took it home, but the next morning it was gone. She went back to the rock, and there it was again. This was repeated three times, until Juana took her find to a local priest. The priest took the statue to his church for safekeeping, but the next morning it was gone, only to be found sitting upon the same rock later that day. The priest eventually decided that the strange occurrences were a sign that the Virgin wanted a temple or shrine built to her upon the spot. And so work was begun on what would eventually become today's impressive basilica.

Miraculous healing powers have been attributed to La Negrita, and, over the years, parades of pilgrims have come to the shrine seeking cures for their illnesses and difficulties. August 2 is her patron saint's day. Each year, on this date, tens of thousands of Costa Ricans and foreign pilgrims spend hours walking to Cartago from San José and elsewhere in the country out of devotion to La Negrita.

altar. Legend has it that La Negrita first revealed herself on this site to a peasant girl in 1635. The walls of the shrine are covered with a fascinating array of tiny silver images left as thanks for cures affected by La Negrita. Amid the plethora of diminutive silver arms and legs, there are also hands, feet, hearts, lungs, kidneys, eyes, torsos, breasts, and—peculiarly—guns, trucks, beds, and planes. Outside the church, vendors sell a wide selection of these trinkets, as well as little candle replicas of La Negrita.

GETTING THERE **Lumaca** buses (✆ **2537-2320**) depart San José for Cartago every 3 to 5 minutes between 4:30am and 9pm, with slightly less frequent service until midnight, from Calle 5 and Avenida 10. You can also pick up one en route at any of the little covered bus stops along Avenida Central in Los Yoses and San Pedro. The length of the trip is 45 minutes; the fare is about $1.10. The Paraíso bus stop is 1 block south and ¾ block west of the Catholic church ruins in Cartago (the ride takes 30–40 min., and the fare is around 65¢).

Lankester Gardens ★★ GARDEN Costa Rica has more than 1,400 varieties of orchids, and almost 800 species are cultivated and on display at this botanical garden. Created in the 1940s by English naturalist Charles Lankester, the gardens are now administered by the University of Costa Rica. The primary goal is to preserve the local flora, with an emphasis on orchids and bromeliads. Paved, well-marked trails meander from open, sunny gardens into shady forests. In each environment, different species of orchids are in bloom. An information center and a gift shop are also on-site. Plan to spend between 1 and 3 hours here if you're interested in flowers and gardening. You can easily combine a visit here with a tour at Cartago and/or the Orosi Valley and Irazú Volcano.

1km (½ mile) east of Cartago, on road to Paraíso de Cartago. www.jbl.ucr.ac.cr. ✆ **2511-7939.** Admission $10 adults, $7.50 students and children 6–16. Daily 8:30am–4:30pm.

OROSI VALLEY

The Orosi Valley, southeast of Cartago, is generally considered one of the most beautiful valleys in Costa Rica. The Reventazón River meanders through this steep-sided valley until it collects in the lake formed by the Cachí Dam. A well-paved road winds a near-perfect loop around the lake, allowing for easy access to all the attractions listed below. Scenic overlooks are near the town of Orosi, at the head of the valley, and above Ujarrás. This is primarily an agricultural area, but the valley comes alive on weekends as picnickers and bicyclists fill the roads and restaurants.

Near the town of Cachí, you'll find **La Casa del Soñador (House of the Dreamer)** ★ (✆ **8955-7779**), the home and gallery of the late sculptor Macedonio Quesada and his sons, who carry on the family tradition. Quesada earned fame with his primitive sculptures of La Negrita (see above) and other religious and secular characters carved on coffee tree roots and trunks. You can see some of Macedonio's original work here, including his version of "The Last Supper" carved onto one of the walls of the main building. You can also shop its current collection of small sculptures, carved religious icons, and ornate walking sticks.

From the Orosi Valley, it's a quick shot to the entrance to the **Tapantí National Park** ★ (✆ **2571-1781** or 2206-5615), where you can find both gentle and strenuous hiking trails, as well as riverside picnic areas. The park is open daily from 8am to 4pm; admission is $10.

If you're interested in staying here, consider the splendid **Hotel Rio Perlas** ★★ (www.hotelrioperlascr.com; ✆ **2533-3341**), the valley's only luxury resort, spa, and casino. It's 2km (1.2 miles) west of Puente Negro in Orosi, on the road following the river. Another good option is the charming **Orosi Lodge** ★ (www.orosilodge.com; ✆ **2533-3578**), on the south side of Orosi next to some simple hot-spring pools.

GETTING THERE If you're driving, take the road to Paraíso from Cartago, head toward Orosi, and continue around the lake counterclockwise, passing through Cachí and Ujarrás and back to Paraíso. It is difficult to explore this whole area by public bus because this is not a densely populated region and connections are often infrequent or unreliable. Regular buses do run from Cartago to Orosi, Cachí, and Ujarrás, but they do not go around the entire loop. These buses run roughly every half-hour and leave the main bus terminal in Cartago. The trip takes 30 minutes, and the fare runs between C250 and C500, depending on where you get off the bus.

Heredia, Sarchí ★ & Zarcero

In the volcanic hillsides northwest of San José, the scenery is rich and verdant, and the small towns and scattered farming communities are truly representative of Costa Rica's agricultural heartland and *campesino* (small farmer) tradition.

All of these cities and towns are northwest of San José and can be combined into a long day trip (if you have a car), perhaps in conjunction with a visit to Poás Volcano and/or the La Paz Waterfall Gardens. Sarchí and Zarcero can also be convenient stopping points on the way to La Fortuna and the Arenal Volcano area. This is a great area to explore on your own in a rental car, if you don't mind getting lost a bit (roads are narrow, winding, and poorly marked). The road to Heredia turns north off the highway from San José to the airport. If you're going to Sarchí, take the highway west toward Puntarenas. Turn north to Grecia and then west to Sarchí. There'll be plenty of signs.

HEREDIA

Founded in 1706 on the flanks of the impressive Barva Volcano, Heredia is known as "Ciudad de las Flores," City of Flowers, though that's reportedly because of the large number of people here with the name Flores. It's also said to represent the beauty of women from Heredia. Of all the cities in the Central Valley, Heredia has the most colonial feel—you'll still see adobe buildings with Spanish tile roofs along narrow streets. Heredia is also the site of the **National University,** and you'll find some nice coffee shops and bookstores near the school.

Surrounding Heredia is an intricate maze of picturesque villages and towns, including Santa Bárbara, Santo Domingo, Barva, and San Joaquín de Flores. San Isidro de Heredia has a lovely, large church with an ornate facade. However, the biggest attraction up here is **INBio Park ★★** (p. 68). Located on 5 hectares (12 acres) in Santo Domingo de Heredia, this place is part museum, part educational center, and part nature park. This is also where you'll find the **Café Britt Farm ★** (p. 68). Anyone with an interest in medicinal herbs should plan a visit to the **Ark Herb Farm ★** (www.arkherbfarm.com; ✆ **8922-7599** or 2269-4847). These folks offer guided tours of their gardens, which feature more than 300 types of medicinal plants. The tour costs $12 per person, and includes light refreshments. Reservations are required.

Buses (✆ **2233-8392**) leave for Heredia every 10 minutes between 5am and 11pm from Calle 1, between avenidas 7 and 9, or from Avenida 2, between calles 12 and 14. Bus fare is C445.

SARCHÍ ★

Sarchí is Costa Rica's main artisan town. The colorfully painted miniature **oxcarts** that you see all over the country are made here. Oxcarts such as these were once used to haul coffee beans to market. Today, although you might occasionally see oxcarts in use, most are purely decorative. However, they remain a well-known symbol of Costa Rica. In addition to miniature oxcarts, many carved wooden souvenirs are made here with rare hardwoods from the nation's forests. The town has dozens of shops, and all have similar prices. Perhaps your best one-stop shop in Sarchí is the large and long-standing **Chaverri Oxcart Factory ★★** (✆ **2454-4411**), which is right in the center of things, but it never hurts to shop around and visit several of the stores.

While there are no noteworthy accommodations in Sarchí itself, the plush **El Silencio Lodge & Spa** (www.elsilenciolodge.com; ✆ **2231-6122**) is about a 35-minute drive away in a beautiful mountain setting.

GETTING THERE **Tuan** (✆ **2494-2139**) buses leave San José for Grecia, with connections to Sarchí from Calle 18 between avenidas 3 and 5. The fare is C985. Alternatively, you can take one of the Alajuela-Sarchí buses, leaving every 30 minutes from Calle 8 between avenidas Central and 1 in Alajuela.

Else Kientzler Botanical Garden ★★ GARDEN Located on the grounds of an ornamental flower farm on the outskirts of Sarchí, these are extensive, impressive, and lovingly laid-out botanical gardens. Over 2.5km (1.5 miles) of trails run through a collection of more than 2,000 species of flora. All the plants are labeled with their Latin names, with some further explanations around the grounds in both English and Spanish. On the grounds are a topiary labyrinth, as well as a variety of lookouts, gazebos, and shady benches. A children's play area features some water games, jungle gym set-ups, and a child-friendly little zipline tour. Over 40 percent of the gardens are wheelchair-accessible.

About 6 blocks north of the central soccer stadium in the town of Sarchí, Alajuela. ✆ **2454-2070.** Admission $12 adults, $9 students with valid ID and children 5–12. Entrance includes a 1-hr. guided tour. Reservations recommended. Daily 8am–4pm.

ZARCERO

Beyond Sarchí, on picturesque roads lined with cedar trees, is the town of Zarcero. In a small park in the middle of town is a **menagerie of sculpted shrubs** that includes a monkey on a motorcycle, people and animals dancing, an ox pulling a cart, a man wearing a top hat, and an elephant. Behind all the topiary is a wonderful rural **church.** It's not worth the drive just to see this park, but it's a good idea to take a break in Zarcero to walk the gardens if you're on the way to La Fortuna and Arenal.

Daily **buses** (✆ **2255-0567**) for Zarcero leave from San José hourly from the Atlántico del Norte bus station at Calle 12, avenidas 14 and 18. This is actually the Ciudad Quesada–San Carlos bus. Just tell the driver that you want to get off in Zarcero, and keep an eye out for the topiary. The ride takes around 1½ hours, and the fare is around C1,870.

6 GUANACASTE & THE NICOYA PENINSULA

Guanacaste and the Nicoya Peninsula are Costa Rica's "Gold Coast"—and not because this is where Spanish conquistadors found vast quantities of the precious metal ore. Instead, it's because more and more visitors to Costa Rica are choosing this region as their first—and often only—stop. Beautiful beaches abound along this coastline. Several are packed with a mix of hotels and resorts, some are still pristine and deserted, and others are backed by small fishing villages. Beaches range from long, broad sections of sand stretching on for miles, to tiny pocket coves bordered by rocky headlands.

This is Costa Rica's most coveted vacation destination and the site of its greatest tourism development. The international airport in Liberia receives daily direct flights from several major U.S. and Canadian hub cities, allowing tourists to visit some of the prime destinations without having to go through San José.

This is also Costa Rica's driest region. The rainy season starts later and ends earlier, and overall it's more dependably sunny here than in other parts of the country. Combine this climate with a coastline that stretches south for hundreds of miles, from the Nicaraguan border all the way to the Nicoya Peninsula, and you have an equation that yields beach bliss.

One caveat: During the dry season (mid-Nov to Apr), when sunshine is most reliable, the hillsides in Guanacaste turn browner than the Texas plains. Dust from dirt roads blankets the trees in many areas, and the vistas are far from tropical. Driving these dirt roads without air-conditioning and with the windows rolled up tight can be extremely unpleasant.

On the other hand, if you happen to visit this area in the rainy season (particularly May–Aug), the hillsides are a beautiful, rich green, and the sun usually shines all morning, with an afternoon shower—in time for a nice siesta.

Inland from the beaches, Guanacaste remains Costa Rica's "Wild West," a land of dry plains populated with cattle ranches and

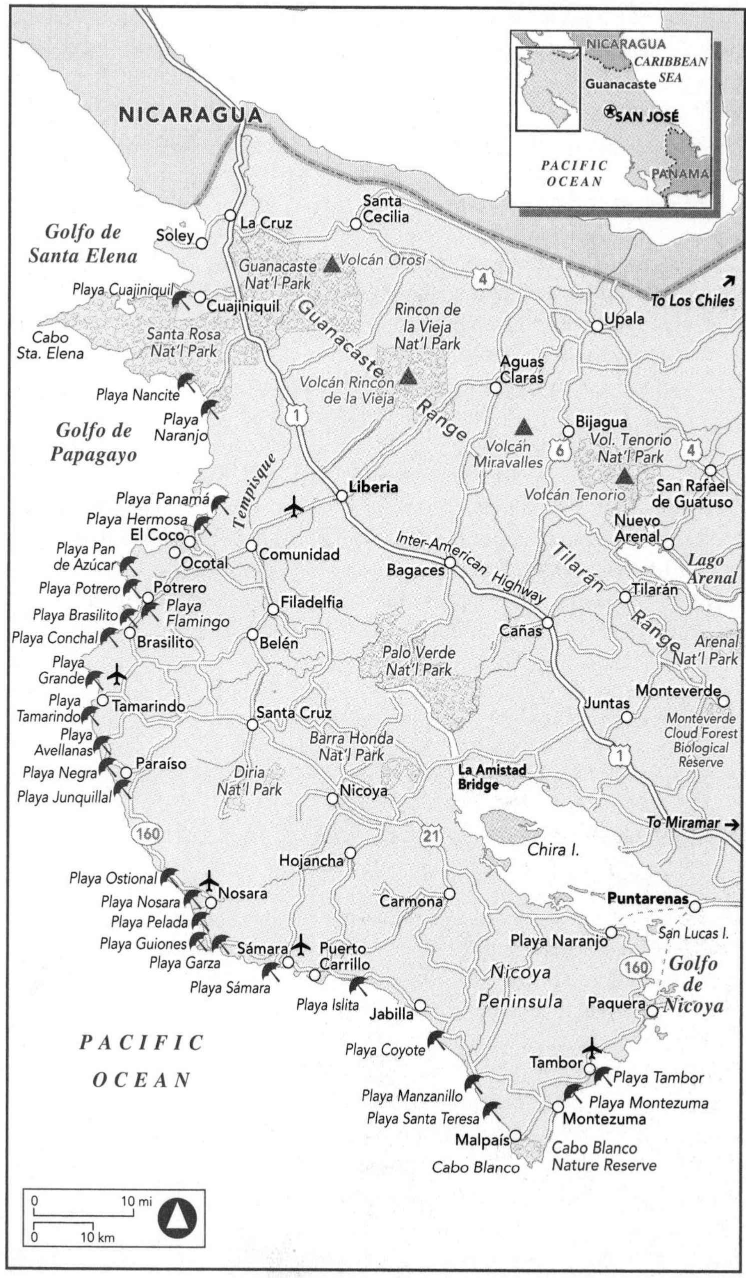

GUANACASTE & THE NICOYA PENINSULA | Introduction

cowboys, known here as *sabaneros,* derived from the Spanish word for "savanna" or "grassland."

Guanacaste is home to several active volcanoes and some beautiful national parks, including **Santa Rosa National Park ★**, the site of massive sea-turtle nestings and of a major battle to maintain independence; **Rincón de la Vieja National Park ★★**, which features hot springs and bubbling mud pots, pristine waterfalls, and an active volcanic crater; and **Palo Verde National Park ★**, a beautiful expanse of mangroves, wetlands, and savanna.

Heading south from Guanacaste takes you to the Nicoya Peninsula, where you'll find the beach towns of **Sámara, Nosara, Montezuma, Malpaís,** and **Santa Teresa.** The beaches of the Nicoya Peninsula don't get nearly as much attention or traffic as those to the north in Guanacaste. However, they are just as stunning, varied, and rewarding.

With easy access via paved roads and the time-saving La Amistad Bridge, Playa Sámara is one of the coastline's more popular destinations, especially with Ticos looking for a quick and easy weekend getaway. Just north of Sámara, Nosara and its neighboring beaches remain remote and sparsely visited, thanks in large part to the horrendous dirt road that separates these distinctly different destinations. However, Nosara is widely known and coveted as one of the country's top **surf spots,** with a host of different beach and point breaks from which to choose.

Down on the tip of the peninsula sit Montezuma, Malpaís, and Santa Teresa. Montezuma, with its jungle waterfalls and gentle surf, is the original beach destination out this way. However, it has been eclipsed by the up-and-coming hot spots of Malpaís and Santa Teresa, two adjacent beach areas popular with surfers, sun seekers, and a host of A-list celebrities.

PLAYA HERMOSA ★, PLAYA PANAMA ★ & PAPAGAYO ★

258km (160 miles) NW of San José; 40km (25 miles) SW of Liberia

This area is one of Costa Rica's standouts, with the Papagayo Peninsula sheltering a large gulf, small bays, and beautiful beaches. While much of the coast in this vicinity is coveted by surfers, the waters here tend to be protected and calm, making them good destinations for families. **Playa Hermosa ★** means "beautiful beach," an apt moniker for this pretty crescent of sand. Surrounded by steep, forested hills, this curving gray beach is long and wide and the surf is usually quite gentle. Fringing the beach is a swath of trees that stay surprisingly green even during the dry season. The shade provided by these trees, along with the calm waters, make this site very appealing. Rocky headlands jut out into the surf at both ends of the beach, and at the base of these rocks are fun tide pools to explore.

Beyond Playa Hermosa lies **Playa Panamá ★** and the calm **Bahía Culebra ★**, a large, protected bay dotted with small, private patches of beach and ringed with mostly intact dry forest. On the northwestern reaches of Bahía Culebra is the **Papagayo Peninsula ★**, home to two large resorts and a championship golf course. This peninsula has a half-dozen or so small to midsize beaches, the nicest of which might be **Playa Nacascolo ★★★**, inside the domain of the Four Seasons Resort here—but all beaches in Costa Rica are public, so you can still visit, albeit after passing through security and parking at the public parking lot.

Essentials

ARRIVING **By Plane:** The **Daniel Oduber International Airport** (**© 2668-1010;** airport code LIR) in Liberia receives a steady stream of scheduled commercial and charter flights throughout the year. Major North American airlines have direct links to Liberia. In addition, numerous commercial charter flights from various North American cities fly in throughout the high season. Check with your travel agent.

Sansa (www.flysansa.com; **© 877/767-2672** in the U.S. and Canada, or 2290-4100 in Costa Rica) and **Nature Air** (www.natureair.com; **© 800/235-9272** in the U.S. and Canada, or 2299-6000 in Costa Rica) both have several flights daily to Liberia. Fares run between $105 and $155 each way.

From the airport, you can hire a taxi to bring you to any beach destination in this area. The ride should take between 25 and 30 minutes and cost $40 to $60.

The following car rental companies all have local agencies: **Adobe** (**© 2667-0608**), **Alamo** (**© 2668-1115**), **Avis** (**© 2668-1196**), **Budget** (**© 2668-1118**), **Dollar** (**© 2668-1001**), **Hertz** (**© 2668-1179**), **Thrifty** (**© 2665-0787**), and **Toyota** (**© 2668-1212**). You can also reserve with these and most major international car-rental companies via their San José and international offices.

By Car: From San José, you can either take the Inter-American Highway (CR1) north all the way to Liberia from downtown San José, or first head west out of the city on the San José–Caldera Highway (CR27). When you reach Caldera, follow the signs to Puntarenas, Liberia, and the Inter-American Highway (CR1). This latter route is a faster and flatter drive.

Once you reach the main intersection of CR1 at the crossroads of Liberia, turn left onto CR21 toward Santa Cruz and the beaches of Guanacaste. The turnoff for the Papagayo Peninsula is prominently marked 8km (5 miles) south of the Liberia airport. At the corner here, you'll see a massive Do It Center hardware store and lumberyard.

If you are going to a hotel along the Papagayo Peninsula, turn at the Do It Center and follow the paved road out and around the peninsula. If you are going to Playa Panamá or Playa Hermosa, you should also turn here and take the access road shortcut that leads from a turnoff on the Papagayo Peninsula road, just beyond the Do It Center, directly to Playa Panamá. When you reach Playa Panamá, turn left for Playa Hermosa.

To get to Playa Hermosa, you can also continue on a little farther west on CR21 and, just past the village of Comunidad, turn right. In about 11km (6¾ miles), you'll come to a fork in the road; take the right leg.

These roads are all relatively well marked, and a host of prominent hotel billboards should make it easy enough to find the beach or resort you are looking for. The drive takes about 4 to 4½ hours from San José.

By Bus: A **Tralapa** express bus (✆ **2221-7202**) leaves San José daily at 3:30pm from Calle 20 and Avenida 3, stopping at Playa Hermosa and Playa Panamá, 3km (1¾ miles) farther north. The one-way fare for the 5-hour trip is around C5,500.

Gray Line (www.graylinecostarica.com; ✆ **800/719-3105** in the U.S. and Canada, or 2220-2126 in Costa Rica) and **Interbus** (www.interbusonline.com; ✆ **4100-0888**) both have two daily buses leaving San José for all beaches in this area, one in the morning and one in the afternoon. The fare is around $50. Both companies will pick you up at most San José–area hotels, and they make connections to most other major tourist destinations.

You can take a bus from San José to Liberia and then take a bus from Liberia to Playa Hermosa and Playa Panamá. **Transportes La Pampa** buses (✆ **2665-7530**) leave Liberia for Playa Hermosa and Playa Panamá at least a half-dozen times daily between 4:30am and 5:30pm. The trip lasts 40 minutes because the bus stops frequently to drop off and pick up passengers. The one-way fare costs C750. These bus schedules change from time to time, so it's best to check in advance. During the high season and on weekends, extra buses from Liberia are sometimes added. You can also take a bus to Playa del Coco, from which playas Hermosa and Panamá are a relatively quick taxi ride away. Taxi fare should run C8,000 to C10,000.

Playas Hotels

EXPENSIVE

In addition to the Four Seasons, the **Andaz Peninsula Papagayo Resort ★★★** (http://papagayo.andaz.hyatt.com; ✆ **800/233-1234** in the U.S. and Canada, or 2690-1234 in Costa Rica) is another excellent, large-scale luxury resort on the Papagayo Peninsula.

El Mangroove ★★★ In your room at El Mangroove, you may forget you're in Costa Rica and feel like a Wall Street executive in a penthouse suite in Manhattan—except for the hammock in the living room. The king-size bed is plush, the TV is huge, and the minibar is stocked. Along with modern furniture and chic art, it has high-speed Internet and everything is new. This luxury hotel, established in 2014, has a 24-hour gym, a fully equipped spa, an adventure center, a kids' clubhouse, and a long, narrow pool perfect for swimming laps. Next to the pool are cabanas with comfy couches, TVs, and minibars, and just beyond is an immaculate beach with waves gentle enough for a toddler and a stunning view of the serene Papagayo Gulf. The Makoko Restaurant, overseen by Sebastian La Rocca, a culinary director with world-class credentials, is outstanding.

Playa Panamá, Papagayo Gulf. www.elmangroove.net. ✆ **855/219-9371** from the U.S. and Canada, 2105-7575 in Costa Rica. 85 suites. Standard rooms $249–$373, master suites $600–$800, plus tax and $20 resort fee. Free valet parking. **Amenities:** 2 restaurants; 2 bars; gift shop; spa; gym; kids zone; tour operator; car rental; large outdoor swimming pool; Wi-Fi covered by $20 resort fee.

Four Seasons Resort Costa Rica ★★★ Ideally located on the neck of a stunning peninsula with pristine, white-sand beaches on either side, the Four Seasons is hands-down the premier luxury resort hotel in Costa Rica, if not in all of Central America. Its unique look, designed by the celebrated architect Ronald Zurcher, features roof lines and building shapes meant to evoke turtles and armadillos. Rooms are large, plush, and graced with colorful patterned throw pillows and rattan and fine wood furnishings. Suites and villas are dazzling, with multiple rooms, full kitchens, and private infinity pools. Four restaurants offer up the top-notch dining experience you'd expect from the Four Seasons—and the hotel's famed service remains peerless. The Arnold Palmer-designed golf course has ocean views from the tees, greens, and fairways of 15 of its 18 holes.

Papagayo Peninsula. www.fourseasons.com/costarica. ✆ **800/332-3442** in the U.S., or 2696-0000 in Costa Rica. 182 units. $475–$900 double; suites and villas $800 and up. Children stay free in parent's room. **Amenities:** 4 restaurants; 2 bars; babysitting; children's programs; championship 18-hole golf course; 3 outdoor pools; room service; spa; 5 tennis courts; watersports equipment; free Wi-Fi.

MODERATE

Bosque del Mar ★★★ One of the prettiest hotels in the area, Bosque del Mar is distinguished by beautiful wooden lattice work throughout the rooms and their exteriors, and by tall, V-shaped roofs. Suites are spread around a free-form pool amid the shade of tall, lovingly preserved old-growth trees (which are inhabited by iguanas and troops of monkeys). These gorgeous trees are everywhere, popping up through decks and roofs in the main lobby and even jutting through the balcony of one of the junior suites. Steps away from the sand on the quiet southern end of Playa Hermosa, this is among the best beachfront boutique hotels in the area. All rooms have two queen beds, as well as air-conditioning, TV, a mini-fridge, and a safe. The oceanfront suites are colorful, comfortable, and practical, with hot tubs on private balconies.

Playa Hermosa. www.bosquedelmar.com. ✆ **2672-0046.** 35 units. $141–$250 double, tax included. **Amenities:** Restaurant; bar; outdoor pool; spa services; free Wi-Fi.

INEXPENSIVE

Villa del Sueño Hotel ★★ Tall trees and mature gardens give this sprawling complex of hotel rooms and condo units a cool and refreshing feel, even on the hottest of Guanacaste's summer days. A thatched-roof tiki bar just off the main pool also helps beat the heat. The eye-pleasing Mediterranean architecture features lots of big arches and red-tile roofs. Of the two swimming pools, one has a little island sporting three palm trees, and the beach is just a 3-minute walk away. Red tile floors, bright tropical paintings, and wall hangings give the rooms a cheery feel, and those on the second floor enjoy higher ceilings. Standard hotel rooms and privately owned suites are divided by a little road, and there is Wi-Fi on the side closest to the beach. The in-house restaurant is one of the best in town, with live music three times a week in the high season.

Playa Hermosa, Guanacaste. www.villadelsueno.com. ✆ **800/378-8599** in the U.S., or 2672-0026 in Costa Rica. 46 units. $79–$155 double; $119–$299 suites; plus tax. **Amenities:** Restaurant; bar; room service; 2 outdoor pools; free Wi-Fi.

Where to Eat

In addition to the places listed below, the restaurant at **Villa del Sueño Hotel** (see above) is a real standout.

Abbocato ★★★ FUSION/BISTRO Husband-wife chefs Andrea and Paola create two distinct nightly tasting menus. One typically features Asian-inspired flavors and preparations, and the other is Mediterranean in style. It's anybody's guess which of the two is behind any one dish, but no matter, everything is sublime. On the Asian side, you might get home-smoked fresh tuna in a light ginger dressing with homemade pickles; on the Mediterranean side, it could be mushroom sausage in a phyllo quiche shell with pesto and Fontina cheese. As for the ambience: The dining room features travertine tile floors, heavy wooden tables, walls of glass, and high peaked ceilings with exposed wood beams. It opens onto a broad patio that overlooks the Pacific Ocean and provides great sunset views. An excellent wine list and cellar complete the experience. Abbocato is also open for lunch and tapas.

Inside Hacienda del Mar, 1km (½ mile) inland from Playa Panamá. www.abbocatocr.com. ✆ **2672-0073** or 8820-2576. Reservations necessary for dinner. Main courses $10–$35. 4-course prix-fixe dinner $45. Tues–Sat noon–9pm.

Ginger ★★ INTERNATIONAL/TAPAS With a design by famed Costa Rican architect Víctor Cañas, creative cocktails, and a wide-ranging tapas menu, this is easily the hippest place to drink and dine in the Papagayo area. The entire restaurant is open air, on a raised deck under tall trees, with angled steel supports and slanted rooflines. The menu spans the globe from Thailand to Spain to Italy. The firecracker shrimp and the shredded-pork lettuce wraps in a mango-tamarind sauce are especially good. And there are more than a dozen options among the specialty martinis, margaritas, and mojitos. Friday night is "Martini Night," featuring $3 martinis.

On the main road, Playa Hermosa. www.gingercostarica.com. ✆ **2672-0041.** Tapas $5–$13. Tues–Sun 5–10pm.

Exploring Playa Hermosa, Playa Panamá & Papagayo

Most of the beaches here are usually quite calm and good for swimming. If you want to do some diving, check any of the dive operations listed in the Playa del Coco & Playa Ocotal section (see below).

Charlie Don't Surf, but Ollie Does

Ollie's Point is named after Oliver North, the former lieutenant colonel at the center of the Iran-Contra scandal. A secret airstrip near the point was used covertly by the CIA to fly in supplies for the Nicaraguan Contra rebels during the guerrilla war in the 1980s. One of the biggest surf breaks in Costa Rica, Ollie's Point can be reached by boat from Playa del Coco or Tamarindo.

In the middle of Playa Hermosa, **Aqua Sport** (✆ **2672-0051**) is the place to go for watersports equipment rentals. Kayaks, sailboards, canoes, bicycles, beach umbrellas, snorkel gear, and parasails are available at reasonable rates. You'll also find a small supermarket, public phones, and a restaurant.

Because the beaches in this area are relatively protected and generally flat, surfers should look into boat trips to nearby **Witch's Rock ★★** and **Ollie's Point ★** (p. 96).

The waters here are prime sportfishing grounds, and there's a nice marina near the Four Seasons and Andaz resorts. Aside from that, there is a host of boats anchored off both Playa Hermosa and nearby Playa del Coco. Try http://getmyboat.com for discounted charters.

Most of these companies mentioned above also have fishing trips for two to four anglers for $400 to $1,200. **Dream On Sportfishing ★★** (www.dreamonsportfishing.com; ✆ **8735-3121**) or **North Pacific Tours ★** (www.northpacifictours.com; ✆ **2670-1564**) are excellent fishing operators.

If you're interested in sailing, check in with any of the sailboat charter outfits listed in the Playa del Coco section below. All have a range of full- and half-day tours, with snorkel stops as well as sunset cruises.

Both **Charlie's Adventures ★** (www.charliesadventure.com; ✆ **2672-0317**) and **Swiss Travel Service** (www.swisstravelcr.com; ✆ **2668-1020**) have a wide range of activities and tours, including trips to Santa Rosa or Rincón de la Vieja national parks, and rafting on the Corobicí River. These operations have desks at several of the hotels around here and will pick you up at any hotel in the area.

The best zipline canopy tour in this area is the **Witch's Rock Canopy Tour ★★** (www.witchsrockcanopytour.com; ✆ **2696-7101**), a bit before the main entrance to the Four Seasons Resort. For $75, the 1½-hour tour covers 3km (1¾ miles) of cables touching down on 24 platforms and crossing three suspension bridges.

PLAYA DEL COCO & PLAYA OCOTAL ★

253km (157 miles) NW of San José; 35km (22 miles) W of Liberia

Playa del Coco is one of Costa Rica's busiest and most developed beach destinations. A large modern mall and shopping center anchor the eastern edge of town. You'll pass through a tight jumble of restaurants, hotels, and souvenir shops for several blocks before you hit the sand and sea; homes, condos, and hotels are strung along the access roads that parallel the beach in either direction. This has long been a popular destination for middle-class Ticos and weekend revelers from San José. It's also a prime base for some of Costa Rica's best scuba diving. The beach, which has grayish-brown sand and gentle surf, is quite wide at low tide and almost nonexistent at high tide. The crowds that come here like their music loud and late, so if you're in search of a quiet retreat, stay away from the center of town. Still, if you're looking for a beach with a wide range of hotels, lively nightlife, and plenty of cheap food and beer, you'll enjoy Playa del Coco. (And by the way, it's often called Playas del Coco, presumably because there's more than one beach in the area.)

Also worth checking out is **Playa Ocotal ★**, a few miles to the south. This tiny pocket cove features a small salt-and-pepper beach bordered by high bluffs that's quite beautiful. When it's calm, there's good snorkeling around rocky islands close to shore.

Essentials

ARRIVING **By Plane:** The nearest airport with regularly scheduled flights is in Liberia. From there, you can hire a taxi to take you to Playa del Coco or Playa Ocotal, about a 25-minute drive, for $35 to $60.

By Car: From Liberia, head west on CR21 toward Santa Cruz. Just past the village of Comunidad, turn right. In about 11km (6¾ miles), you'll come to a fork in the road. Take the left fork. The right fork goes to Playa Hermosa. The drive takes about 4 hours from San José.

By Bus: Pulmitan express buses (✆ **2222-1650** in San José, or 2670-0095 in Playa del Coco) leave San José for Playa del Coco at 8am and 2 and 4pm daily from Calle 24 between avenidas 5 and 7. Allow 5 hours for the trip. A one-way ticket is C4,350. From Liberia, buses (✆ **2666-0458**) to Playa del Coco leave regularly throughout the day between 5am and 7pm. A one-way ticket for the 40-minute trip costs around C850. These bus schedules change frequently, so it's always best to check in advance. During the high season and on weekends, extra buses from Liberia are sometimes added. The direct bus for San José leaves Playa del Coco daily at 4 and 8am and 2pm. Local buses for Liberia leave daily between 5am and 7pm.

Depending on demand, the Playa del Coco buses sometimes go as far as Playa Ocotal; it's worth checking beforehand. Otherwise, a taxi should cost around C3,000 to C5,000.

Gray Line (www.graylinecostarica.com; ✆ **800/719-3105** in the U.S. and Canada, or 2220-2126 in Costa Rica) and **Interbus** (www.interbusonline.com; ✆ **4031-0888**) both have two daily buses leaving San José for the beaches in this area, one in the morning and one in the afternoon. The fare is $50. Both companies will pick you up at most San José-area hotels, and have connections to most other tourist destinations around Costa Rica.

VILLAGE LAYOUT Playa del Coco is a compact and busy beach town. At the center of town, running for a few hundred meters in either direction is a seafront walkway, or *malecón*. You'll find benches spread along this walkway, as well as patches of grass and a basketball court. Most hotels and restaurants are either on the water, on the road leading into town, or on the road that heads north, about 100m (328 ft.) inland from and parallel to the beach.

Playa Ocotal is south of Playa del Coco on a paved road that leaves the main road about 183m (600 ft.) before the beach. It's a small collection of vacation condos and hotels with one bar and a restaurant on the beach.

GETTING AROUND You can rent cars from any number of rental companies. Most are based in Liberia, or at the airport. See p. 87.

If you can't flag down a **taxi** on the street, call ✆ **2670-0408.**

FAST FACTS The nearest major hospital is in Liberia (✆ **2690-2300**). For the local **health clinic,** call ✆ **2670-1717;** for the local **pharmacy,** call ✆ **2670-2050.** For local **police,** dial ✆ **2670-0258.** You'll find several banks and ATMs.

Playas Hotels

MODERATE

Coco Beach Hotel & Casino ★ If you want to be in the center of the action, this is the place for you. Set right in the heart of Playa del Coco's busiest restaurant, bar, and commercial strip, the hotel offers clean if fairly plain rooms that get a shot of life from bright, multicolor paintings based on local indigenous designs. The staff is friendly and helpful. Thatched-roof structures ring the pool area and separate the rooms from the street, helping to block the blazing Guanacaste sun and street noise. The beach is 2 blocks away.

Playa del Coco, Guanacaste. www.cocobeachcr.com. ✆ **2670-0494.** 32 units. $145–$186 double. Rates include full breakfast. **Amenities:** Restaurant; bar; small casino; small outdoor pool; free Wi-Fi.

El Ocotal Beach Resort ★ This small resort has an enviable location, perched on a steep hillside overlooking the Pacific Ocean. Most rooms enjoy these wonderful views, which is their biggest selling point. The rooms and facilities themselves are a mixed bag (some just fine, some showing their age), and service and upkeep can be lax at times. El Ocotal operates one of the best dive operations in the area.

Playa del Coco, Guanacaste. www.ocotalresort.com. ✆ **2670-0321.** 42 units. 12 bungalows, 3 suites. $99–$220 double; $110–$265 bungalow and suite. Rates include full breakfast. Free for kids under 12. **Amenities:** Restaurant; Jacuzzi; 3 outdoor pools and 3 plunge pools; lighted tennis court; free Wi-Fi.

INEXPENSIVE

Hotel M&M Beach House ★ With a perfect location on the beach, the M&M also comes with a price that's nice. The two-story building is rectangular and open to the air in the middle, with nice lounging areas upstairs and downstairs facing the beach. There's no restaurant or bar, but breakfast is included, and there's a shared kitchen. Rooms have TVs and fans but no A/C or hot water—though you may find that in this heat you prefer a cold shower anyway. Pets are welcome for $10 extra, and guests can use the swimming pool at the newly acquired M&M Garden House, a 5-minute walk away.

150m west of the police station on the beach, Playa del Coco. www.hotelmym.com. ✆ **2670-1212.** 17 units. $47–$54 double, including tax and breakfast. **Amenities:** Shared kitchen; free Wi-Fi.

EN ROUTE: BETWEEN PLAYA DEL COCO & PLAYA FLAMINGO

Hotel Sugar Beach ★★ Spread over a gently curved, forested hillside that cradles Playa Pan de Azúcar, this isolated hotel's lovely grounds are rich in wildlife. It's not uncommon to find troops of howler monkeys in the trees here, so be prepared for some unrequested early wake-up calls. While there are no private beaches in Costa Rica, for all intents and purposes the beach here is the exclusive playground of the hotel guests. (Playa Pan de Azúcar means "Sugar Bread Beach," but the bread was dropped in translation, and it's known in English simply as "Sugar Beach.") The rocky outcroppings just off and around this beach are very good for snorkeling. Rooms are all spacious, spotless, and comfortable, some with romantic four-poster beds.

Playa Pan de Azúcar. www.sugar-beach.com. ✆ **2654-4242.** 32 units. $158–$198 double; $277–$280 suite; $575–$667 3-bedroom villa. Rates include breakfast and taxes. **Amenities:** Restaurant; bar; small pool; free Wi-Fi.

Where to Eat

A clutch of basic open-air *sodas* is at the traffic circle in the center of El Coco village, serving Tico standards, with an emphasis on fried fish. Prices are quite low—and so is the quality, for the most part.

You can get excellent Italian food, however, at **Soda Mediterránea** ★ (✆ **8742-6553**), in the little El Pueblito strip mall on the road running north and parallel to the beach, and a good mix of Mediterranean and Peruvian cuisine at the beachfront **Donde Claudio & Gloria** ★ (✆ **2670-1514**). For a quick or light meal, try **Le Coq** (✆ **2670-0608**), an open-air Lebanese restaurant on the main drag in the center of town.

Right on the main strip, you'll also find members of the Papagayo restaurant group: **Papagayo Seafood** ★ (✆ **2670-0298**), **Papagayo Steak House** ★ (✆ **2670-0605**), and **Papagayo Sushi Boat** ★ (✆ **2670-0298**).

MODERATE

Citron ★★★ FUSION/INTERNATIONAL Even though it's in a small strip mall, this is easily the town's most elegant and creative restaurant. The service is top-notch, the setting romantic (local cane ceiling, soft lighting, neutral colors) and the food is leaps and bounds better than what you'll get elsewhere in the area. Citron does particularly well by sea bass, usually served with orzo and a Catalan sauce. Other star dishes include the tenderloin and portobello risotto in red-wine reduction, and the vanilla crème brûlée, which is made with local organic vanilla. There's outdoor seating on a broad, open deck, but the daytime heat and nighttime bugs often make this a less than ideal option.

In the Pacífico mall, on the main road into town. Playa del Coco. www.citroncoco.com. ✆ **2670-0942.** Main courses $12–$19. Mon–Sat 5:30–10pm.

Father Rooster ★ SEAFOOD/BAR A casual, open-air beachfront bar, Father Rooster is just steps from the water on tiny Playa Ocotal. Burgers, tacos, beer-battered fish or shrimp, nachos, and other bar fare are served. The building itself is a rustic wood affair painted in haphazard primary colors, with a pool table in one room. Most people try to get seats at the tables on the sand; all are shaded by canvas umbrellas and a tall mango tree. On the weekends, you'll sometimes catch a live band here.

On the beach, Playa Ocotal. www.fatherrooster.com. ✆ **2670-1246.** Main courses C6,500–C9,000. Daily 11:30am–10pm.

The Lookout ★ SEAFOOD/BAR It's worth the short drive or taxi ride to this rooftop bar restaurant on the outskirts of Playa del Coco, for the outstanding sunsets and upscale pub food. Menu standouts include the tuna poke nachos and the lobster grilled cheese, both created from locally sourced seafood. A wide-ranging selection of Costa Rican craft beers is available, as well as fresh, locally farmed oysters.

On the outskirts of Playa del Coco, inside the Hotel Chantel. www.thelookoutcoco.com. ✆ **8755-7246.** Main courses C3,000–C8,500. Tues–Sun 3pm–10pm.

Exploring Playa del Coco & Playa Ocotal

Plenty of boats are anchored at Playa del Coco, and that means plenty of opportunities to go fishing, diving, or sailing. Still, the most popular activities, especially among the hordes of Ticos who come here, are lounging on the beach, walking along the *malecón*, hanging out in the *sodas,* cruising the bars and discos at night, and playing pick-up soccer. (The soccer field is in the middle of town.) You can also arrange horseback rides; ask at your hotel.

If you're staying at a hotel without a pool, or just want a sense of exclusivity on the beach, you might check out **Café de Playa Beach & Dining Club** (www.cafedeplaya.com; ✆ **2670-1621**). In addition to having an excellent restaurant, it offers day passes for $15 allowing access to the pool and a private lawn fronting the beach, which is filled with comfortable teak chaise longues. There's also watersports equipment rental and tour options, and a small spa.

Organized Tours

The **Congo Trail Canopy Tour ★** (✆ **2666-4422** or 2697-1801) is set in a stand of thick, tropical dry forest on the outskirts of Playa del Coco, along a dirt road that leads to Playa Pan de Azúcar. In addition to a zipline, there's a small butterfly farm and a few zoo enclosures, with monkeys and reptiles. The tour runs every day from 8am to 5pm, and costs $35 for the canopy tour, plus $5 to see the animals.

Several cruising sailboats and longtime local salts offer daily sailing excursions. The 47-foot ketch-rigged ***Kuna Vela*** (www.kunavela.com; ✆ **8301-3030**) and the 45-foot ketch ***Seabird*** (www.seabirdsailingexcursions.com; ✆ **8880-6393**) both ply the waters off Playa del Coco. They also offer half- and full-day and sunset sailing options, with snorkel stops and an open bar.

Scuba diving is the most popular watersport in the area, and dive shops abound. **Sirenas Diving Costa Rica ★★** (www.sirenasdivingcostarica.com; ✆ **2670-0603**), **Summer Salt ★** (www.summer-salt.com; ✆ **2670-0308**), and **Rich Coast Diving ★★** (www.richcoastdiving.com; ✆ **2670-0176**) are the most established and offer equipment rentals and dive trips. A two-tank dive, with equipment, should cost between $85 and $150 per person, depending on the distance to the dive site. The more distant dive sites visited include the Catalina Islands and Bat Island. All shops also offer PADI certification courses.

Full- and half-day sportfishing excursions can be arranged through any of the hotel tour desks, or with **Dream On Sportfishing ★★** (www.dreamonsportfishing.com; ✆ **8735-3121**) or **North Pacific Tours ★** (www.northpacifictours.com; ✆ **2670-1564**). A half-day of fishing, including the boat, captain, food, and tackle, should cost $800 to $1150 for two to four passengers; a full day, $700 to $1,200.

Playa del Coco has no surfing to speak of, but is a popular jumping-off point for **daily boat trips** to Witch's Rock and Ollie's Point in Santa Rosa National Park (p. 107). Most of the above-mentioned sportfishing and dive operations also ferry surfers to these isolated surf breaks. A boat that carries five surfers for a full day, including lunch and beer, should run $350 to $600. ***Note:*** Both Witch's Rock and Ollie's Point are technically within Santa Rosa National Park. Permits are required, and boats without permits are sometimes turned away. If you decide to go, be sure your boat captain is licensed and has cleared access to the park. You will also have to pay the park's $15 fee. **Single Fin Surf Charters** (www.singlefinsurfcharters.com; ✆ **8935-2583**) offers a plush trip out to these surf spots at $235 per person for a full-day trip. But if you ask around town, you should be able to find one of the local skippers, who tend to offer trips for up to six surfers for much less. Alternatively, check the website www.getmyboat.com.

Pacific Coast Stand Up Paddle & Surf Trips (www.pacificcoastsuptours.com; ✆ **8359-8115**) offer lessons and guided outings for both traditional surfing and for those looking to try out stand-up paddling (a sport that can be done without traveling to another beach area).

Nightlife

Playa del Coco is one of Costa Rica's liveliest beach towns after dark. Most of the action is centered along a 2-block section of the main road into town, just before you hit the beach. Here you'll find the **Lizard Lounge ★** (✆ **2670-0307**), which has a raucous party vibe. Just across the street is the large, open-air **Zi Lounge ★★** (www.zilounge.com; ✆ **2670-1978**). For a gringo-influenced sports bar, try **Coconutz ★** (www.coconutz-costarica.com; ✆ **2670-1982**). Just off the beach, at the center of town you'll find **Beach Bums Bar & Grill ★** (✆ **2671-0110**). This is a very popular spot, with frequent live bands and DJs. On the south end of the beach, reached via a rickety footbridge over the estuary, you'll find **La Vida Loca ★** (✆ **2670-0181**), a beachfront bar with tables for pool, Ping-Pong, and foosball, and live bands.

PLAYAS CONCHAL ★★, BRASILITO, FLAMINGO ★★ & POTRERO

280km (174 miles) NW of San José; 67km (42 miles) SW of Liberia

Playa Conchal ★★ is the first in a string of beaches stretching north along this coast. It's almost entirely backed by the massive Westin Playa Conchal resort and Reserva Conchal condominium complex. The unique beach here was once made up primarily of soft crushed shells—a shell-collectors'

heaven. Unfortunately, as Conchal's popularity spread, unscrupulous builders brought in dump trucks to haul away the namesake seashells for landscaping and construction, and the impact is, sadly, quite noticeable. The beach is still primarily comprised of crushed bits of polished sea shells, but it's become increasingly hard to find larger pieces or complete shells.

Just beyond Playa Conchal to the north, you'll come to **Playa Brasilito,** a tiny beach town and one of the few real villages in the area. The soccer field is in the center, and around its edges are a couple of little *pulperías* (general stores). The long stretch of gray sand beach has a quiet, undiscovered feel to it.

Playa Flamingo ★★ is one of the prettiest beaches in the region. A long, broad stretch of pinkish white sand, it is on a long spit of land that forms part of Potrero Bay. At the northern end of the beach is a high rock outcropping upon which most of Playa Flamingo's hotels and vacation homes are built. This rocky hill has great views.

If you continue along the road from Brasilito without taking the turn for Playa Flamingo, you'll come to **Playa Potrero,** located in a broadly curving bay, protected by the Flamingo headlands. The sand here is a brownish gray, but the beach is long, clean, deserted, and very calm for swimming. You can see the hotels of Playa Flamingo across the bay. Drive a little farther north and you'll find the still-underdeveloped beaches of **Playa Prieta ★**, **Playa La Penca ★** and **Playa Pan de Azúcar ★★**.

Essentials

ARRIVING **By Plane:** The nearest airport with regularly scheduled flights is in Tamarindo (p. 109) although it is also possible to fly into Liberia (p. 87). From either of these places, you can arrange for a taxi to drive you to any of these beaches. Playas Brasilito and Conchal are about 25 minutes from Tamarindo and 40 minutes from Liberia. A taxi from Tamarindo should cost around $35 to $50, and between $50 and $70 from Liberia.

By Car: Two major routes head to these beaches from San José. The most direct is by way of the La Amistad Bridge over the Tempisque River. Take the Inter-American Highway west from San José. Just 47km (29 miles) past the turnoff for Puntarenas, you'll see signs for the turnoff to the bridge. After crossing the Tempisque River, follow the signs for Nicoya, continuing north to Santa Cruz. About 16km (10 miles) north of Santa Cruz, just before the village of Belén, take the turnoff for playas Conchal, Brasilito, Flamingo, and Potrero. After another 20km (12 miles), at the town of Huacas, take the right fork to reach these beaches. The drive takes about 4½ hours.

Alternatively, you can drive here via Liberia. When you reach Liberia, turn west and follow the signs for Santa Cruz and the various beaches. Just beyond the town of Belén, take the turnoff for playas Flamingo, Brasilito, and Potrero, and continue following the directions given above. This route takes around 5 hours.

By Bus: Tralapa express buses (✆ **2221-7202** in San José, or 2654-4203 in Flamingo) leave San José daily at 8 and 10:30am and 3pm from Calle 20, between avenidas 3 and 5, stopping at playas Brasilito, Flamingo, and Potrero, in that order. The ride takes around 5 hours. A one-way ticket costs C6,290.

The same company's buses to Santa Cruz (✆ **2680-0392**) connect with one of the several buses from Santa Cruz to Playa Potrero. Buses depart San José for Santa Cruz roughly every 2 hours daily between 7:15am and 6pm from Calle 20 between avenidas 3 and 5. The trip duration is around 4 hours; the fare is C5,425. From Santa Cruz, the ride is about 90 minutes; the fare is C1,500.

Gray Line (www.graylinecostarica.com; ✆ **800/719-3105** in the U.S. and Canada, or 2220-2126 in Costa Rica) and **Interbus** (www.interbusonline.com; ✆ **4031-0888**) both have two daily buses leaving San José for the beaches in this area, one in the morning and one in the afternoon. The fare is $50. Both companies will pick you up at most San José–area hotels, and offer connections to most other tourist destinations in the country.

Express buses depart **Playa Potrero** for San José at 3 and 9am and 2pm, stopping a few minutes later in playas Flamingo and Brasilito. Ask at your hotel where to catch the bus. Buses to **Santa Cruz** leave Potrero at regular intervals throughout the day and take about 90 minutes. If you're heading north toward Liberia, get off the bus at Belén and wait for a bus going north. Buses leave Santa Cruz for San José roughly every other hour between 6am and 6pm.

Playas Hotels

EXPENSIVE

Westin Playa Conchal Resort & Spa ★★★ This is among the most appealing large-scale, all-inclusive resorts anywhere in Costa Rica. Not only does it sit on one of the country's prettiest beaches, but its massive, amoeba-like free-form swimming pool is a marvel, meant to mimic a tropical lagoon. (Parents might want to tag their kids with GPS chips in order not to lose them in one of the many interconnected sections of water.) Guests are treated to numerous restaurants, all first-rate. Every one of the handsome rooms here is rightly considered a suite and comes with either one king-size or two double beds. All have either a private patio or balcony in front of the sliding-door entrance. For golfers there's a wide, open resort-style course with trees and water features that attract a range of local wildlife. One of the lakes is even home to a resident caiman. Guests enjoy a wide range of complimentary activities and use of nonmotorized watersports equipment.

Playa Conchal. www.westinplayaconchal.com. ✆ **800/937-8461** in the U.S., or 2654-3442 in Costa Rica. 406 units. $415 and up double; $850 and up suite double; children 3–12 add $160–$185 per child per day; kids 13 and up charged as adults; kids under 3 free. Rates include all meals, drinks, and taxes. **Amenities:** 6 restaurants; 5 bars; casino; babysitting; bike rental; children's programs; golf course and pro shop; exercise facilities and spa; 2 large outdoor pools w/Jacuzzis; room service; 4 lighted tennis courts; watersports equipment rental; free Wi-Fi.

MODERATE

Bahía del Sol Beachfront & Boutique Hotel ★★ Mother Nature rules at this small resort, a place beloved by both humans and other critters for its handsome, lush landscaping, in particular the flowering ginger that overflows in the tropical gardens. The hotel is located on a grassy patch of land just in from the center of Playa Potrero, a calm and protected beach with hard-packed, dark gray sand. The interior isn't quite as spectacular: Rooms are simple and plain, with high ceilings and beds that can be too hard. That said, the housekeeping staff is diligent and rooms are fairly priced, particularly the studio apartments with kitchenettes, which are good for families or for longer stays. A very good restaurant is also on the property, as is a small spa. Daily yoga and Pilates classes are included in the rate.

Playa Potrero. www.bahiadelsolhotel.com. ✆ **866/223-2463** in the U.S. and Canada, or 2654-4671 in Costa Rica. 28 units. $120–$225 double; $240–$410 suite. Rates include breakfast. **Amenities:** Restaurant; bar; Jacuzzi; pool; room service; spa; free Wi-Fi.

INEXPENSIVE

A string of inexpensive *cabinas* line the main road leading into Brasilito, just before you hit the beach. It's also possible to camp on playas Potrero and Brasilito. At the former, contact **Mayra Camping** (✆ **2654-4213**); at the latter, try **Camping Brasilito** (✆ **2654-4452**). Both of these places offer some budget rooms as well. Each charges around C4,000 per person to make camp and use the basic restroom facilities, or around C15,000 to C30,000 per person to stay in a rustic room.

Conchal Hotel ★★ Burned to the ground in early 2013, the Conchal was quickly rebuilt and is better than ever. Rooms are spacious and feature sturdy steel bed frames, white linens and whitewashed walls offset with bright primary accents. Superior rooms come with large, flat-screen televisions and more space. Most rooms open onto a private or shared balcony or veranda fronting the small central pool and gardens. Despite its name, this hotel really should be considered part of Playa Brasilito, which is about 2 blocks away. Owners Simon and Hilda are delightful and very hands-on. The hotel's tropical fusion Papaya restaurant (p. 100) is one of the best in the area.

Playa Brasilito. www.conchalcr.com. ✆ **2654-9125.** 13 units. $96 double; $238 family suite. Rates include continental breakfast and taxes. Reduced rates available in off-season. **Amenities:** Restaurant; bar; pool; free Wi-Fi.

Hotel Brasilito This longstanding budget hotel has clean, well-kept rooms in a pair of two-story wood buildings just a stone's throw from the water. Snag a room with a balcony and you'll be in budget heaven. The owners offer excellent in-house tour operation and the open-air restaurant, El Oasis, is equally recommendable.

Playa Brasilito. www.hotelbrasilito.com. ✆ **2654-4237.** 15 units. $44–$84 double. **Amenities:** Restaurant; free Wi-Fi.

Where to Eat

You can't go wrong at **El Coconut Beach Club ★★** (www.elcoconuttamarindo.com; ✆ **2654-4300;** see "Organized Tours & Activities," below.

EXPENSIVE

Camarón Dorado ★ SEAFOOD The quintessential beach restaurant, complete with plastic lawn furniture and Tiki torches set in the sand, Camarón Dorado offers a seafood-centric menu featuring a half-dozen preparations of fresh local fish, lobster, shrimp, and shellfish (with fried chicken, steaks, and burgers for carnivores). Everything is very well prepared, although the success this place enjoys has led it to jack up the prices a bit above what you should be paying in what is really a simple, beachfront fish shack.

Playa Brasilito. www.hotelbrasilito.com. ✆ **2654-4237.** 15 units. $44–$84 double. Daily 11am–10pm.

MODERATE

Marie's ★★ COSTA RICAN/SEAFOOD Marie has been serving fresh, fairly priced food here for decades, and her restaurant is justifiably popular. She's still running the show, which means the menu thankfully hasn't changed from burritos and quesadillas, plus simply grilled fish or chicken. The large, open-air restaurant features extremely high thatched roofs with slow-turning ceiling fans.

Playa Flamingo. www.mariesrestaurantincostarica.com. ✆ **2654-4136.** Main courses C3,800–C13,000. Daily 6:30am–9:30pm.

Papaya ★★★ INTERNATIONAL/SEAFOOD Easily the finest restaurant in the Brasilito/Conchal area, Papaya specializes in Pacific Rim fusion and Nuevo Latino fare. Occupying a large, open-air second-floor space overlooking the pool and gardens of the Conchal Hotel, it's also date-night central, thanks to its dim lighting and tabletop candles. Either go with a special from the chalkboard or try the fresh mahimahi in a coconut crust or local lobster tails with Chinese five-spice seasoning. A winner!

Playa Brasilito. ✆ **2654-9125.** Main courses C8,750–C11,400. Thurs–Tues 7am–8:30pm.

INEXPENSIVE

Coco Loco ★★★ COSTA RICAN/SEAFOOD While many still bemoan the closing of Mar y Sol restaurant, there's plenty of reason to rejoice, now that its former owner, chef Jean-Luc Taulere, has opened up this casual beachfront bar and restaurant. It has a lovely setting, with teak tables under white canvas umbrellas spread out on the sand at the far southern end of Playa Flamingo. The menu features such items as blackened swordfish wraps, fresh yellowfin tuna tacos, and slow-cooked pork ribs in a pineapple barbecue sauce. Some dishes are served inside a hollowed-out half-coconut, including the fresh ceviche, homemade coconut ice cream, and house specialty Loco Coco, a coconut rice dish featuring mussels, octopus, and fresh-caught snapper, with a Thai-inspired basil, ginger, and lime sauce. Come for a drink at sunset (there's an extensive cocktail menu) and stay longer, as there's often live music after sundown.

South end of Playa Flamingo. www.cocolococostarica.com. ✆ **2654-6242.** Main courses C3,400–C5,700. Daily 11am–9pm.

Exploring Playas Conchal, Brasilito, Flamingo & Potrero

Playa Conchal ★★, which is most famous for its crushed seashells, is also stunningly beautiful, but the dropoff is quite steep, making it notorious for strong riptides. The water at **Playa Brasilito** is often fairly calm, which makes it a good swimming choice. This is also a great base for visiting other nearby and less popular beaches, like **Playa La Penca ★★** and **Playa Pan de Azúcar ★★**, both of which are north of here.

Playa Flamingo is a long and beautiful stretch of soft white sand, although the surf can sometimes get a bit rough. The beach doesn't have much shade, so be sure to use plenty of sunscreen and bring an umbrella if you can. If you're not staying here, parking spots are available all along the beach road—just don't leave anything of value in the car. **Playa Potrero** has much gentler surf and is the better swimming beach. However, the beach is made up of hard-packed dark sand that is much less appealing than that of Playa Flamingo.

Tip: All beaches in Costa Rica are public property. But the land behind the beaches is not, and the Westin hotel owns almost all of it in Playa Conchal, so the only public access is along the soft-sand road that follows the beach south from Brasilito. Before the road reaches Conchal, you'll have to ford a small river and then climb a steep, rocky hill, so four-wheel-drive is recommended.

Organized Tours & Activities

You can rent jet skis and Wave Runners on the beach in Playa Conchal from **Dorado Jet Ski Tours** (✆ **8824-4293**). This operation also offers guided snorkel tours to the Catalina Islands, as well as wet and wild "Banana Boat" rides, where a group of friends and family get pulled behind a speedboat on a giant, inflatable, banana-shaped boat.

You can rent jet skis, boogie boards, skim boards, and stand-up paddle boards on Playa Flamingo from **Playa Vida** (✆ **2654-4444**). This company is on the south side of the Flamingo Beach resort and offers guided snorkel tours to the Catalina Islands.

If your hotel doesn't have a pool or beach access, you can always head to **El Coconut Beach Club** (www.elcoconut-tamarindo.com; ✆ **2654-4300**), which has both. It's located right on Playa Potrero. You can enjoy the facilities, as long as you eat and drink at the excellent **Buena Vista Beach Restaurant.**

Scuba diving is quite popular here. **Costa Rica Diving** (www.costarica-diving.com; ✆ **2654-4148**) has a shop in Flamingo and offers trips to the Catalina Island for around $85.

A Day Trip to El Viejo Wetlands

Located a bit inland from the Guanacaste agricultural town of Filadelfia and bordering the Palo Verde National Park, **El Viejo Wildlife Refuge & Wetlands ★★** (www.elviejowetlands.com; ✆ **2296-0966**) is a unique and intriguing option for a day tour. The principal attraction here is the wildlife, which is abundant, and can be viewed from both open-air safari-style vehicles and small boats on the Tempisque River. You'll see scores of water birds and probably a crocodile or two. The main hacienda-style building at the heart of this operation dates to 1870, and is where excellent Costa Rican lunches are served. Additional tour options here include a zipline canopy tour, and a tour of the on-site organic farm and sugar cane processing mill, or *trapiche*. Rates run from $60 to $130, depending on how many activities or tours you take and whether or not you want lunch.

Although the Flamingo Marina is currently closed, you still have plenty of sportfishing and sailboat charter options here. Jim McKee, the former force behind the Flamingo Marina, manages a fleet of boats. Contact him via his company, **Oso Viejo** (www.flamingobeachcr.com; ✆ **8827-5533** or 2653-8437). A full-day fishing excursion costs between $700 and $2,200, depending on the size and quality of the boat, and distance traveled to the fishing grounds. Half-day trips cost between $500 and $700.

If you're looking for a full- or half-day sail or sunset cruise, check in with Oso Viejo to see what boats are available, or ask about the 52-foot cutter ***Shannon.*** Prices range from around $50 to $120 per person, depending on the length of the cruise. Multiday trips are also available.

Another option is to head down the beach at Playa Potrero to the **Costa Rica Sailing Center** (www.costaricasailing.com; ✆ **8699-7289**), which offers sailing lessons and rentals, with a wide range of small sailcraft. The center also rents out stand-up paddle boards, kayaks, fishing gear, and snorkel equipment.

Nightlife

Pretty much all the nightlife in Playa Conchal happens at the large Westin resort (p. 98), which has a range of bars, nightly entertainment, and a casino. In Brasilito, there might be live music or sporting events on the TVs at **Tiki's Seaside Grille** (✆ **2654-9028**). With both a disco and casino, **Amberes** (✆ **2654-4001**), up the hill at the north end of town, is the undisputed hot spot.

In Potrero, the rooftop bar at **La Terraza de los Mariscos** (✆ **2654-4379**) sometimes has live music. But even better is **Bar La Perla ★** (✆ **2654-4500**), a simple concrete slab building with a corrugated zinc roof and mostly open walls using chain link fencing for window screens. Located on a dusty corner, this is a very typical Costa Rican-style cantina, but it draws a good mixed crowd of locals, expats and tourists alike.

Learn the Language

The **Centro Panamericano de Idiomas** (www.cpi-edu.com; ✆ **2265-6306**), which has schools in San José and Monteverde, has a branch in Flamingo, across from the Flamingo Marina, facing Potrero Bay. A 1-week program with 4 hours of class per day and a home stay with a Costa Rican family costs $730.

RINCÓN DE LA VIEJA NATIONAL PARK ★★

242km (150 miles) NW of San José; 25km (16 miles) NW of Liberia

This sprawling national park begins on the flanks of the Rincón de la Vieja Volcano and includes this volcano's namesake active crater. Down lower is an area of geothermal activity similar to that of Yellowstone National Park in the United States. Fumaroles, geysers, and hot pools cover this small area, creating a bizarre, otherworldly landscape. In addition to hot springs and mud pots, you can explore waterfalls, a lake, and volcanic craters. Bird-watching here is rewarding, as the sparse foliage of the dry forest makes spotting easier, and from the high volcanic slopes you enjoy sweeping views out to the ocean.

Essentials

ARRIVING **By Car:** You'll first need to get to Liberia, the largest city in northern Guanacaste. It sits at the intersection of the Inter-American Highway (CR1) and the CR21, which connects Liberia to the Guanacaste beaches. From Liberia, head north on CR1 toward Peñas Blancas and the Nicaraguan border.

To reach the **Las Pailas (Las Espuelas) entrance,** drive about 5km (3 miles) north of Liberia and turn right on the dirt road to the park. The turnoff is well marked. In about 12km (7½ miles), you'll pass through the small village of Curubandé. Continue on this road for another 6km (3¾ miles) until you reach Hacienda Guachipelín. The lodge is private property, and the owners charge vehicles a small toll to pass through their gate and continue on to the park. Pass through the gate and continue for another 4km (2½ miles) until you reach the park entrance.

What's in a Name?

Rincón de la Vieja literally means "the old lady's corner." In this case, "la vieja" has the connotation of a witch or hag, while "rincón" is better interpreted as "lair." The name is derived from a legend that a woman's father threw her lover into the smoking, belching volcanic crater, and she moved onto the mountain and became a hermit, said to have healing powers.

Two routes lead to the **Santa María entrance.** The principal route heads out of the northeastern end of Liberia toward the small village of San Jorge. This route is about 25km (16 miles) long and takes about 45 minutes. A four-wheel-drive vehicle is required. Alternatively, you can reach the entrance on a turnoff from the Inter-American Highway at Bagaces. From here, head north through Guayabo, Aguas Claras, and Colonia Blanca. Though the road is paved up to Colonia Blanca, a four-wheel-drive vehicle is required for the final, very rough 10km (6¼ miles) of gravel road.

Rincón de la Vieja Hotels

In addition to the hotel listed below, a couple of other good choices are near the park. On the Cañas Dulces road, **Buena Vista Lodge** ★ (www.buenavistalodgecr.com; ✆ **2690-1414**) is set on the edge of the national park and offers a wide range of activities and attractions, including its own waterslide and canopy tour.

If you're looking for a little luxury in this area, check out the **Hotel Borinquen Mountain Resort** ★★ (www.borinquenresort.com; ✆ **2690-1900**).

Around Aguas Claras, **Finca La Anita** ★★ (www.laanitarainforestranch.com; ✆ **8388-1775** or 2466-0228) is a remote and rustic, yet very cozy lodge, with a series of wooden cabins set on a working farm, on the edge of lush rain and cloud forests. The area around the lodge is home to several hot springs, and this area also provides easy access to the seldom-used Santa María sector of Rincón de la Vieja National Park.

Hacienda Guachipelín ★★ A first-rate hotel, working horse and cattle ranch, and huge adventure center: What's not to like? If you're coming here anyway for one or more of the many activities, save yourself the drive back and spend the night in a well-appointed room on immaculate grounds for a surprising price. With some 60 to 80 horses available at any time, overseen by 20 *sabanero* cowboys, horseback riding here is almost a must. ("Don't worry," says the head cowboy, "the horses all speak English!") The whitewater tubing is superb, as are the ziplining, the canyoning, and the mud bath at the hot springs. Rooms are laid out in a large horseshoe around an ample garden area a short walk from the main lodge and restaurants. Rooms are spacious, airy and pretty, with heavy wood and iron-framed beds and lots of natural light. The hotel operates a free shuttle several times a day to the national park entrance, as well as to its own riverside hot springs in the middle of a pristine forest.

Rincón de la Vieja (23km/14 miles northeast of Liberia). www.guachipelin.com. ✆ **888/730-3840** in the U.S. and Canada, or 2690-2900 for reservations in Costa Rica, or 2666-8075 at the lodge. 54 units. $102 double; $121 superior double; $189 suite. Rates include taxes and breakfast. Rates higher during peak periods. **Amenities:** Restaurant; outdoor pool; small spa; free Wi-Fi.

Exploring Rincón de la Vieja National Park

Rincón de la Vieja National Park has several excellent trails. The easiest hiking is the gentle **Las Pailas loop ★**. This 3km (1.75-mile) trail is just off the Las Espuelas park entrance and passes by several bubbling mud pots and steaming fumaroles. Don't get too close, or you could get scalded. Happily, the strong sulfur smell given off by these formations works well as a natural deterrent. This gentle trail crosses a river, so you'll have to either take off your shoes or get them wet. The whole loop takes around 2 hours at a leisurely pace.

A more grueling hike here is to the **Blue Lake** and **La Cangreja Waterfall ★★**. Along this well-marked 9.6km (6-mile) round-trip trail, you'll pass through several ecosystems, including tropical dry forest, transitional moist forest, and open savanna. You are likely to spot a variety of birds and mammals and have a good chance of coming across a group of the raccoon-like coati. While not requiring any great climbs or descents, the hike is nonetheless long and arduous (some say too arduous for what you see). At the end of your 2-hour hike in, you'll come to the aptly named Blue Lake, where a 30m (98-ft.) waterfall empties into a small, crystal-blue pond. This is a great spot for a swim. Pack a lunch and have a picnic before hiking back out.

Because of volcanic activity and the extreme nature of the hike, the summit trail has been closed to visitors since late 2013. If it's reopened, energetic hikers can tackle the **summit ★** and explore the several craters and beautiful lakes up here. On a clear day, you'll be rewarded with a fabulous view of the plains of Guanacaste and the Pacific Ocean below. The trail is 16.6km (10.3 miles) round-trip and should take about 7 hours (the trailhead is at the ranger station). It heads pretty much straight up the volcano and is pretty steep in places. Along the way, you pass through several different ecosystems, including sections of tropical moist and tropical cloud forests, while climbing some 1,000m (3,280 ft.) in altitude. After about 6km (3.7 miles), the trail splits. Take the right-hand fork to the Cráter Activo ("Active Crater"). Filled with rainwater, this crater is some 700m (2,296 ft.) in diameter and still active. Off to the side is the massive Laguna Jigueros. Because this crater emits large amounts of sulfur and acid gases, it's not recommended that you linger here long. If you have the energy, a side trail leads to the Von Seebach Crater.

The park entrance fee is $15 per person per day, and the park is open Tuesday to Sunday from 8am to 4pm.

Camping will cost you an extra $2 per person per day. There are actually two entrances and camping areas here: **Santa María** and **Las Pailas** (also called Las Espuelas; ✆ **2666-5051**) ranger stations. Las Pailas is by far the more popular and accessible, and it's closer to the action. These small camping areas are near each other. For those seeking a less rugged tour of the park, there are several lodges around the park that offer guided hikes and horseback rides into it.

Organized Tours

Hacienda Guachipelín (see above) offers up a range of adventure tour options, including horseback riding, whitewater tubing, ziplining, canyoning, rappelling, hot springs, and mud baths. If all of this sounds good to you, buy the **1-Day Adventure pass ★★**, so you can do all of the above any day (except the canyoning and rappelling, which are offered only a couple of times a week) at a published price of $90, including lunch. For a daylong multi-adventure package, this is one of the best bargains anywhere in Costa Rica. Almost all Guanacaste beach hotels and resorts offer day trips here, or you can book directly with the lodge. ***Be forewarned:*** During high season, the operation has a cattle-car feel, with busloads of day-trippers coming in from the beach.

The **Río Tempisque Basin ★**, southwest of town, is one of the best places in the country to spot marsh and stream birds by the hundreds. This area is an important breeding ground for gallinules, jacanas, and limpkins, as well as numerous heron and kingfisher species and the roseate spoonbill. Several tour operators offer excursions in the region. **Swiss Travel Services** (www.swisstravelcr.com; ✆ **2282-4898**) is the largest and most reliable of the major operators here.

One of the most popular tours is a boat tour down the Bebedero River to **Palo Verde National Park ★**, which is south of Cañas and is best known for its migratory bird populations. Some of the best bird-watching requires little more than walking around the park's biological station.

You can get a similar taste of these waterways and bird-watching opportunities at **El Viejo Wetlands** (p. 101) and **Rancho Humo** (p. 122).

Leisurely raft trips (with little whitewater) are offered by **Ríos Tropicales ★★** (www.riostropicales.com; ✆ **2233-6455**), about 40km (25 miles) south of Liberia. Its 2-hour ($110) float trips are great for families and bird-watchers. Along the way, you may see many of the area's more exotic fauna: howler monkeys, iguanas, caimans, coatis, otters, toucans, parrots, motmots, trogons, and many other species of birds. Aside from your binoculars and camera, a swimsuit and sunscreen are the only things you'll need. Ríos Tropicales is based out of the Restaurant Rincón Corobicí, right on the Inter-American Highway (CR1).

For a much wetter and wilder ride, **Hacienda Guachipelín** (see above) offers exhilarating whitewater tubing trips on the narrow Río Colorado.

Outdoor Activities

The active Rincón de la Vieja Volcano has blessed this area with several fine hot springs and mud baths. Even if you're not staying at the **Hacienda Guachipelín** (see above) or the **Hotel Borinquen Mountain Resort** (see above), you can take advantage of their hot spring pools and hot mud baths. Both have on-site spas offering massages, facials, and other treatments.

Up the road from its lodge, Hacienda Guachipelín has opened the **Río Negro Hot Springs ★★** (**© 2666-8075**). A $15 entrance fee gets you access to the pools and an application of the hot volcanic mud. For $62 you can do a horseback ride from the main lodge to the springs. A wide range of massages, mud wraps, facials, and other treatments are available at reasonable prices.

At the **Hotel Borinquen Mountain Resort,** a $25 entrance fee allows you access to a range of **hot spring–fed pools ★**, which vary from tepid to very hot, as well as the fresh volcanic mud bath area and large freshwater pool.

Finally, **Vandara Hotsprings ★★** (www.vandarahotsprings.com; **© 4000-0660**) is an excellent spa and adventure center run by the staff of Buena Vista Lodge, with a pretty artificial pool fed by natural hot springs. Unlike many of the pools mentioned above, this one has no sulfuric smell. Admission runs $30, but various packages, with a canopy tour, horseback ride, waterslide, hanging bridges, and other activities, are also available. Meals and spa treatments are also offered.

Located about 25km (16 miles) south of Liberia, the **Llanos de Cortés Waterfall ★★** is one of the most beautiful falls in Costa Rica, with an excellent pool at the base for cooling off and swimming. At roughly 12m (39 ft.) wide, the falls are actually slightly wider than they are tall. This is a good spot for a picnic. Because of construction on the highway, the turnoff for the dirt road to the falls is poorly marked, but it's about 3km (1¾ miles) north of the crossroads for Bagaces. From the turnoff, you must drive a rough dirt road to the parking area and then hike down a short, steep trail to the falls. A donation of C1,000 is suggested to support the local school. Even though guards are on duty, be careful about leaving anything of value in your car.

Shady Business

This province gets its name from the abundant guanacaste (*Enterolobium cyclocarpum*), Costa Rica's national tree. This distinctive tree is known for its broad, full crown, which provides welcome shade on the Guanacaste's hot plains and savannas. The guanacaste is also known as the elephant-ear tree because of the distinctive shape of its large seedpods. Its fragrant white flowers bloom between February and April.

Especially for Kids

Believe it or not, antelopes, zebras, giraffes, and elands roam the grassy plains of Guanacaste. **Africa Safari Adventure Park** (www.africasafaricostarica.com; ✆ **2288-1000**) offers safari-style open-jeep tours through its 100-hectare (247-acre) private reserve, populated with a wide range of non-native (predominantly African) species. All the animals are herbivores, so don't expect to see any lions, hyenas, or cheetahs. While many biologists frown on the idea of bringing African animals to Costa Rica for the entertainment of tourists, a visit can make you feel like you're in the Serengeti instead, and the animals have plenty of room to roam. The tours here visit two local waterfalls, so bring a swimsuit, as you'll want to take a quick dip. Admission, which is $100 for adults, and $50 for children 11 and under, includes a 90-minute guided tour and safari-style tractor ride through the park. The company also offers a separate ATV tour, and full-day passes are available. Africa Safari Adventure Park is located just off the Inter-American Highway, 8km (5 miles) south of Liberia. The park is open daily from 9am to 5pm.

Santa Rosa National Park ★

Known for its remote, pristine beaches (reached by several kilometers of hiking trails or 4WD vehicle), **Santa Rosa National Park ★** (www.acguanacaste.ac.cr; ✆ **2666-5051;** entrance $15; day visits 8am–3:30pm) is an isolated place to camp on the beach, surf, bird-watch, or maybe even see sea turtles. Located 30km (19 miles) north of Liberia and 21km (13 miles) south of La Cruz on the Inter-American Highway, Costa Rica's first national park blankets the Santa Elena Peninsula. Unlike other national parks, it was founded not to preserve the land but to protect a building, **La Casona ★★**, where Costa Rica fought its most important battle on its own soil. In March 1856, days after the mercenary army of U.S. adventurer William Walker invaded Costa Rica on foot, Costa Rican forces surprised, shocked, and routed the foreigners in this very place, killing 26 and capturing 19. Costa Rican-led forces went on to defeat Walker's men on Nicaraguan soil in the Second Battle of Rivas, setting the stage for Walker's removal from office and eventual execution. La Casona was destroyed by arson in 2001, but it has been completely rebuilt with exquisite attention to period detail, and it's among the best museums dedicated to a single historical event that you'll find anywhere.

If all this learning has put you in the mood for hiking, try the **Indio Desnudo (Naked Indian) trail,** a 2.6km (1.5-mile) loop that might take you about 45 minutes. It cuts through a small patch of tropical dry forest and into overgrown former pastureland that is a habitat for white-tailed deer, coatis, and howler and white-faced monkeys.

Camping is allowed at several sites in the park for $19 per person per day. Camping is near the entrance, the principal ranger station, La Casona, and by playas Naranjo and Nancite.

THE BEACHES ★★

About 8km (5 miles) west of La Casona, down a rugged road that's impassable during the rainy season and rough on 4WD vehicles even in the dry season, is **Playa Naranjo.** Then 4km (2½ miles) north of Naranjo, along a hiking trail that follows the beach, you'll find **Playa Nancite. Playa Blanca** is 21km (13 miles) down a dirt road from Cuajiniquil, which is 20km (12 miles) north of the park entrance. None of these three beaches has shower or restroom facilities except Playa Nancite, where the facilities are in a reservation-only camping area. Bring your own water, food, and anything else you'll need, and expect to find things relatively quiet and deserted.

Playa Nancite is known for its *arribadas* ("arrivals," or mass egg-layings) of olive ridley sea turtles, which come ashore to nest by the tens of thousands each year in October. Playa Naranjo is legendary for its perfect surfing waves. This spot is legendary among surfers who have come by boat from Playa del Coco or Tamarindo to ride the towering waves at **Witch's Rock.**

On the northern side of the peninsula is **Playa Blanca,** a remote, calm, white-sand beach. It's accessible during the dry season by way of the small village of Cuajiniquil.

If you head north from Cuajiniquil on a rugged dirt road for a few kilometers, you'll come to a small annex to the national park system at **Playa Junquillal** ★ (✆ **2666-5051**), not to be confused with the more-developed beach of the same name farther south in Guanacaste. This is a handsome little beach that is often good for swimming. You'll have to pay the park entrance fee ($10) to use the beach, and $2 more to camp. There are basic restroom and shower facilities.

Río Celeste ★★ & Tenorio Volcano

One of Costa Rica's best-kept secrets is the **Río Celeste ★★**, the stunning, sky-blue river that is the centerpiece of Tenorio Volcano National Park. The unique color of the Celeste is caused by aluminosilicate particles suspended in the water that reflect sunlight only in the blue spectrum, and the effect is glorious. The Río Celeste Waterfall, with its cool blue pool at the bottom, is arguably the most beautiful in the country. Río Celeste ("sky-blue river") is inside the **Parque Nacional Volcán Tenorio** (Tenorio Volcano National Park; ✆ **2206-5369;** daily 8am to 4pm; admission $12). An easy trail follows the river and its prime attractions—the Blue Lagoon, the Borbollones where the water bubbles because of venting gas, and the Teñidores ("dyer's shop"), where you can see two colorless rivers collide and turn blue. The hike is one-way in, one-way out, and could be jogged in an hour or strolled for three or four. Be aware that rainstorms can turn the water muddy and brown, so check with the rangers at the entrance on the current state of the water and weather outlook. ***Tip:*** Once you've seen Río Celeste, you've seen the best of Tenorio Volcano National Park, so this makes a great day trip from Arenal, Monteverde, and elsewhere.

GETTING THERE Tenorio National Park is located near the small town of Bijagua. The road to Bijagua (CR6) heads north off of the Inter-American Highway about 5km (3 miles) northwest of Cañas. From here, it's another 30km (18½ miles) to Bijagua, and another 12km (7½ miles) to the park entrance. The last part of this is on rough dirt roads, and even though it's a short distance as the crow flies, it can often take 30 to 40 minutes. There are also other ways to access the area if coming from La Fortuna.

HOTELS

If you do want to overnight here, look up the humble yet delightful **La Carolina Lodge** ★ (www.lacarolinalodge.com; ✆ **843/343-4201** in the U.S. and Canada, or 2466-6393), which is on a working farm, next to a clear flowing river. Another solid option is the **Celeste Mountain Lodge** ★ (www.celestemountainlodge.com; ✆ **2278-6628**), a handsome property boasting swell views of the surrounding volcanoes.

Near Miravalles Volcano

Part of a string of active volcanoes running down the spine of the country, the **Miravalles Volcano** is a major energy supplier for the country's electric grid, but a rather undiscovered area for tourism. **Río Perdido** ★★ (www.rioperdido.com; ✆ **888/326-5070** in the U.S. and Canada, or 2673-3600) aims to change all that. With a setting among rolling hills and striking rock formations, this **hotel, spa, and adventure center** features lovely rooms and a gorgeous hot spring complex. The hot springs here range from a modern pool structure fed by warm mineral waters up near the main lodge, to a natural river with pools of clear water and varied temperatures. The lodge also has a zipline canyon tour, an extensive mountain bike park, and whitewater tubing.

PLAYA TAMARINDO ★ & PLAYA LANGOSTA ★★

295km (183 miles) NW of San José; 73km (45 miles) SW of Liberia

Tamarindo is the biggest boomtown in Guanacaste, and many say the boom has gone too far, too fast. The main road into Tamarindo, sometimes featuring bumper-to-bumper traffic, is a helter-skelter jumble of strip malls, surf shops, hotels, and restaurants. Ongoing development is spreading up the hills inland from the beach and south to Playa Langosta. None of it is regulated or particularly well planned out.

Still, the wide range of accommodations, abundant restaurants, and active nightlife, along with very dependable surf, have established Tamarindo as one of the most popular beaches on this coast. The beautiful beach here is a long, wide swath of white sand that curves gently from one rocky headland to another. Fishing boats bob at their moorings and brown pelicans skim the water's surface just beyond the breakers. Tamarindo is very popular with surfers, who ply the break right here or use the town as a jumping-off place for beach and point breaks at playas Grande, Langosta, Avellanas, and Negra.

Essentials

ARRIVING **By Plane:** Both **Nature Air** (www.natureair.com; ✆ **800/235-9272** in the U.S. and Canada, or 2299-6000 in Costa Rica) and **Sansa**

6 Playa Tamarindo & Playa Langosta

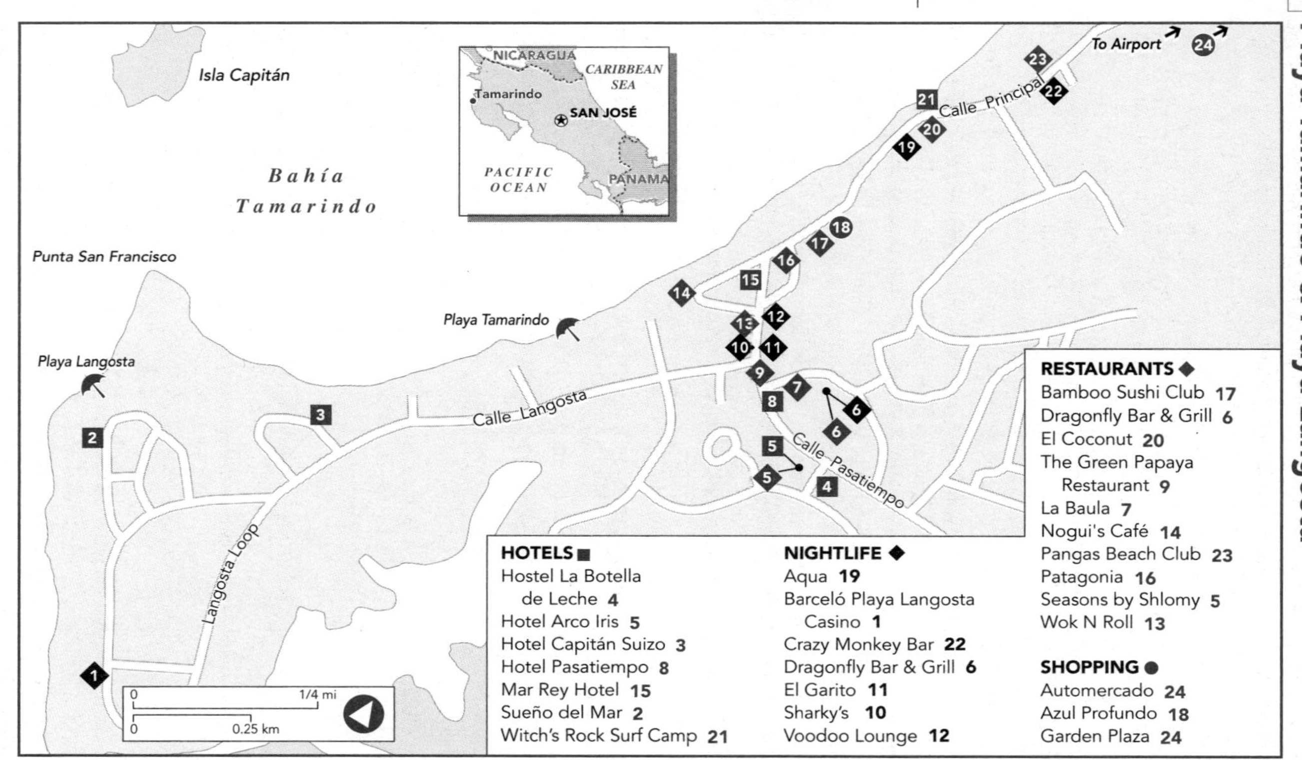

(www.flysansa.com; ✆ **877/767-2672** in the U.S. and Canada, or 2290-4100 in Costa Rica) have several daily direct flights throughout the day to the small airstrip on the outskirts of Tamarindo. Fares run $141 to $158. During the high season, additional flights are sometimes added. Nature Air also connects Tamarindo and Arenal, Liberia, and Quepos.

Whether you arrive on Sansa or Nature Air, a couple of cabs or minivans are always waiting for arriving flights. It costs C8,000 to C10,000 to ride into town.

If you're flying into Liberia, a taxi should cost around $120. Alternatively, you can use **Tamarindo Transfers & Tours** (www.tamarindoshuttle.com; ✆ **929/800-4621** in the U.S., or 2653-4444 in Costa Rica), which charges $20 per person, one-way for a shared shuttle, with a three-person minimum.

By Car: The most direct route from San José is by way of the La Amistad bridge. From San José, you can either take the Inter-American Highway (CR1) north from downtown San José, or first head west out of the city on the San José–Caldera Highway (CR27). This latter route is a faster and flatter drive. When you reach Caldera on this route, follow the signs to Puntarenas, Liberia, and the Inter-American Highway (CR1). This will lead you to the unmarked entrance to CR1. You'll want to pass under the bridge and follow the on-ramp, which will put you on the highway heading north. Just 47km (29 miles) north of the Puntarenas exit on the Inter-American Highway, you'll see signs for the turnoff to the bridge. After crossing the river, follow the signs for Nicoya and Santa Cruz. Continue north out of Santa Cruz, until just before the village of Belén, where you will find the turnoff for Tamarindo. In another 20km (12 miles), take the left fork for Playa Tamarindo at Huacas and continue on until the village of Villareal, where you make your final turn into Tamarindo. The trip should take around 4 hours.

You can also drive here via Liberia. When you reach Liberia, turn west and follow the signs for Santa Cruz and the various beaches. Just beyond the town of Belén, take the turnoff for playas Flamingo, Brasilito, and Tamarindo, and follow the signs. This route takes around 5 hours.

By Bus: Alfaro express buses (www.empresaalfaro.com; ✆ **2222-2666** in San José, or 2653-0268 in Tamarindo) leave San José daily for Tamarindo at 11:30am and 3:30pm, departing from Calle 14 between avenidas 3 and 5. **Tralapa** (✆ **2221-7202**) also has two daily direct buses to Tamarindo leaving at 7:15am and 4pm from their main terminal at Calle 20 between avenidas 3 and 5. The trip takes around 5 hours, and the one-way fare is around C5,7300.

You can also catch a bus to Santa Cruz from either of the above bus companies. Buses leave both stations for Santa Cruz roughly every 2 hours between 6am and 6pm. The 4-hour, one-way trip is around C5,650. Buses leave Santa Cruz for Tamarindo roughly every 1½ hours between 5:45am and 10pm; the one-way fare is C685.

Gray Line (www.graylinecostarica.com; ✆ **800/719-3105** in the U.S. and Canada, or 2220-2126 in Costa Rica) and **Interbus** (www.interbusonline.com; ✆ **4031-0888**) both have two daily buses leaving San José for Tamarindo (one in the morning, one in the afternoon); the fare is $50. Both companies will pick you up at most San José-area hotels, and offer connections to other major tourist destinations in Costa Rica.

Direct buses leave Tamarindo for San José daily at 3:30 and 5:30am (except on Sun) and 2 and 4pm. Buses to Santa Cruz leave roughly every 2 hours between 4:30am and 8:30pm. In Santa Cruz, you can transfer to one of the frequent San José buses.

VILLAGE LAYOUT The road leading into town runs parallel to the beach and ends in a small cul-de-sac just past the Mar Rey Hotel. A major side road, a left turn just before the Mar Rey, leads farther on, to Playa Langosta. To reach playas Avellanas, Negra, and Junquillal, you have to first head out of town and take the road toward Santa Cruz.

GETTING AROUND **Adobe** (✆ **2542-4800**), **Alamo** (✆ **2653-0727**), **Budget** (✆ **2436-2000**), **Economy** (✆ **2653-0752**), **Hertz** (✆ **2653-1358**), and **Thrifty** (✆ **2653-0829**) have rental car offices in Tamarindo.

The town itself is very compact and you should be able to walk most places. Still, a large fleet of taxis are usually cruising around town, or hanging out at principal intersections and meeting points. If you need to, you can contact **Taxi Tamarindo** (✆ **8918-3710**).

FAST FACTS The local **police** can be reached at ✆ **2653-0283.** A large **Banco Nacional** branch is located on the road southeast of the large, white Pacific Park condos, and a branch of the **Banco de Costa Rica** is in the Plaza Conchal mall. Several pharmacies are also in town.

Playas Hotels

In addition to the hotels listed below, Tamarindo, Playa Langosta, and Playa Grande have a wide range of beach houses and condos for rent by the night, the week, or the month. For more information on this option, check out **RE/MAX Tamarindo** (www.remax-oceansurf-cr.com; ✆ **866/976-8898** in the U.S. and Canada, or 2653-0073 in Costa Rica) or **RPM Vacation Rentals ★** (www.rpmvacationrentals.com; ✆ **2653-0738**). You'll also find many options on VRBO.com and FlipKey.com.

EXPENSIVE

Hotel Capitán Suizo ★★★ It doesn't get much better than this. Built in 1995 and owned by Ursula Schmid of Switzerland, this luxury hotel on the quieter southern end of Tamarindo Beach has top-notch service, and the rooms are large, well-kept, and thoroughly inviting. Most feature colonial-style terra- cotta floors and four-poster canopy beds. Private balconies and patios open onto exuberant tropical gardens, where monkeys are common visitors. The hotel's free-form pool is one of the largest and best in town, with a slowly sloping, shallow entrance that mimics the beach, a rope swing for a touch of playfulness, and a large children's section. This hotel is great for families and honeymooners alike. Rooms don't have TVs, if that matters, but all have air-conditioning. The restaurant is excellent, the gardens are large and lush, and the strip of beach in front is beautiful.

On the road between Tamarindo and Playa Langosta. www.hotelcapitansuizo.com. ✆ **2653-0075** or 2653-0075. 28 units and 6 bungalows. $199–$280 double; $360–$440 bungalow; $440–$680 suite. Rates include breakfast buffet. **Amenities:** Restaurant; bar; outdoor pool and children's pool; spa; free Wi-Fi.

MODERATE

Hotel Arco Iris ★★ The charm quotient is high at this little complex of rooms and bungalows located about a 5-minute walk from the beach. Much of that has to do with the attentiveness of Richard Resnick, the U.S. owner and his staff, who make all the guests feel like VIPs. The rooms are immaculate, with white travertine tile floors and minibars. Beds have pure white linens and bedcovers, with hardwood and woven bamboo headboards. There's a small pool and the restaurant here, **Seasons by Shlomy** (see below), is excellent.

Tamarindo, 50m east and 100m south of the Banco Nacional. www.hotelarcoiris.com. ✆ **2653-0330.** 13 units. $110–$160 double, $25 each per extra person, including breakfast. **Amenities:** Restaurant; bar; small outdoor pool; free Wi-Fi.

Sueño del Mar ★★ This intimate bed-and-breakfast, in a quiet setting on Playa Langosta, has built a loyal following of guests who come back year after year for the personalized service, gorgeous sunsets, and spectacular breakfasts. It's also a great spot for a once-in-a-lifetime romantic occasion like a wedding or honeymoon. The Luna Suite is the prime room in the house (the only one with an ocean view) and is worth the splurge if it's available—it's a second-floor unit with wraparound windows facing the sea and an open-air shower that also shares the view. The standard rooms have hand-painted linens and also have cute open-air showers with small gardens and plantings providing privacy (although they all open onto the hotel's main walkway, so that privacy is somewhat limited). Hammocks are strung under shade trees, and wooden chairs in the sand facing the waves are where guests gather to toast the sunset.

Playa Langosta. www.sueno-del-mar.com. ✆ **2653-0284.** 4 units, 2 casitas. $155–$204 double; $185–$310 suite or casita, including breakfast. No children 12 and under. **Amenities:** Small outdoor pool; free snorkel equipment and boogie boards; free Wi-Fi.

INEXPENSIVE

In addition to the hotels listed below, the beachfront **Witch's Rock Surf Camp ★** (www.witchsrocksurfcamp.com; ✆ **888/318-7873** in the U.S. and Canada, or 2653-1262 in Costa Rica) caters to young, budget-minded surfers.

Hostel La Botella de Leche ★★ New management is putting this cool hostel back on the map, with a renewed emphasis on customer service and big plans to build six new upstairs units and install a hot tub. Manuel Fontana of Argentina, who bought the quaint blue hostel in 2015, says there are three pillars essential to running a hotel: hardware (air-conditioning and bathrooms in all the rooms, though no hot water); soul (decoration, lighting, music); and service (24/7 reception, very attentive management). And in case you're wondering, the hostel, established in 2000, was named after the Milk Bottle Motel in the 1996 John Travolta movie *Michael.*

50m east of the Banco Nacional. www.labotelladeleche.com. ✆ **2653-0189**. 12 units, 6 more planned. $35–$60 for private rooms for 2; dorms $11–$20, depending on season. **Amenities:** Swimming pool; concierge service; free Wi-Fi.

Mar Rey Hotel ★ For more than 40 years, the Martinez and Reyes families have run this budget favorite under the name Zullymar, but they decided on a rebranding that combines the two family names. Though the name has changed, the ambience hasn't. The two-story building is still painted a blinding white and features heavy concrete arches, balcony railings, and bannisters. The rooms continue with the all-white theme, getting their only splash of color from vibrant print bedspreads. The individually carved hardwood doors, featuring animal and native life motifs, are perhaps the most striking design element here. It's worth the small splurge for a room with air-conditioning and television. You can enjoy a small, free-form pool for cooling off, but the beach is just across the street. ***Be forewarned:*** This hotel is located on the busiest corner in Tamarindo, so this is not a good choice for those seeking a quiet getaway or a peaceful retreat.

Central Tamarindo, just south of Subway. www.hotelmarrey.com. ✆ **2653-0028.** 22 units. $61–$69 double. **Amenities:** Swimming pool; small spa; free Wi-Fi.

Where to Eat

Tamarindo has a glut of good restaurants. **El Coconut ★** (www.elcoconut-tamarindo.com; ✆ **2653-0086**), right on the main road, is an institution, specializing in fresh seafood, with a European flair. **Nogui's Café ★** (www.noguistamarindo.com; ✆ **2653-0029**) is one of the more popular places in town, and rightly so. This simple open-air cafe just off the beach on the small traffic circle serves hearty breakfasts and well-prepared salads, sandwiches, burgers, and casual meals. It also has a few tables and chairs on the beach.

Wok N Roll ★ (www.facebook.com/WokNRollCostarica; ✆ **2653-0156**), a half-block inland from the Mar Rey along the road that leads to Playa Langosta, is a lively, open-air affair, with a big menu of Asian cuisine. For pizzas, I recommend **La Baula ★** (✆ **2653-1450**), another open-air place, on the road to Dragonfly (see below), and for Mexican fare and good breakfast burritos, try **Green Papaya Taco Bar** (✆ **2653-0863**), just across the street. If you want sushi, head to the **Bamboo Sushi Club ★** (✆ **2653-4519**), on the main road, near the turnoff for Langosta. And, for hearty steaks and Argentine fare, try **Patagonia** (✆ **2653-0612**), located across from the Tamarindo Diria Hotel.

Dragonfly Bar & Grill ★★ INTERNATIONAL/FUSION The menu here features spices and flavors from around the world, with prominent influences from the Pacific Rim and southwestern United States. So you might find yourself dining on thick-cut pork loin crusted in panko and served with a brandy-Dijon cream sauce or a similarly creative fish dish. Portions are large, so don't be afraid to share. The look of the place is as fun as the food: A zinc roof is held high by columns made from locally farmed tree trunks, and finished underneath with woven mats and thin bamboo. The bar serves up fab cocktails, sometimes to live music.

Down a dirt road behind the Hotel Pasatiempo. www.dragonflybarandgrill.com. ✆ **2653-1506.** Reservations recommended. Main courses C5,500–C9,500. Mon–Sat 6–9:30pm.

Pangas Beach Club ★★★ SEAFOOD/INTERNATIONAL Chef Jean-Luc Taulere had a very successful run at Mar y Sol restaurant in Playa

Flamingo, but real estate issues forced him to close up shop there—much to the betterment of the dining scene in Tamarindo. Located on the main road near the northern end of town, his current restaurant lets out onto the beach, right about where the ocean meets the estuary, a scenic spot. Heavy wooden tables are spread on hard-packed sand under tall coconut trees, which are strung with rope lighting and bare bulbs, giving this place a rustic, romantic feel by night. While fresh seafood is the specialty here, the steak tenderloin cooked at the table on a hot volcanic stone is the sleeper hit here. Breakfast and lunch are also served.

On the waterfront, north end of Tamarindo. www.lasmareas.com/pangas-beach-club. ✆ **2653-0024.** Reservations recommended. Main courses C7,500–C18,000. Mon–Thurs noon–10pm and Sun 9am–10pm.

Seasons by Shlomy ★★ INTERNATIONAL Cordon Bleu–trained chef and owner Shlomy Koren began his time in Tamarindo at Pachangas. But since 2008 he's been serving up his tasty Mediterranean-inspired cuisine with an Asian twist out of a small kitchen at the Hotel Arco Iris (p. 113). Good menu choices include seared tuna in a honey chili marinade, red snapper with spinach, artichoke and cherry tomatoes, jumbo shrimp with coconut milk and sweet chilis, and beef tenderloin in a rosemary sauce. Don't get too attached to any item as the menu changes regularly, with daily specials and seasonal variations.

Inside the Hotel Arco Iris. www.seasonstamarindo.com. ✆ **8368-6983.** Reservations recommended in high season. Main courses $15–$22. No credit cards. Mon–Sat 6–10pm.

Exploring Tamarindo

You have to be careful when and where you swim off Tamarindo's long white-sand beach. The calmest water and best swimming are at the southern end of the beach, toward the Hotel Capitán Suizo (p. 112). Much of the sea just off the busiest part of the town is best for surfing. When the swell is up, you'll find scores of surfers in the water here. ***Be careful:*** In several places there are rocks just offshore, some exposed only at low tide. An encounter with one of these could be nasty, especially if you're bodysurfing. Also, avoid swimming near the estuary mouth, where there are two dangers: strong currents and crocodiles.

Organized Tours & Activities

Tamarindo has a host of good tour operators. The best are **Xplore CR ★** (www.xplorecostarica.com; ✆ **844/278-6877** in the U.S. and Canada, or 2653-4130 in Costa Rica), **Tamarindo Transfers & Tours ★** (www.tamarindoshuttle.com; ✆ **2653-4444**), and **Iguana Surf** (✆ www.iguanasurf.net; ✆ **2653-0613**). All offer a range of half- and full-day trips, including outboard or kayak tours through the nearby estuary and mangroves, excursions to Santa Cruz and Guaitíl, raft floats on the Corobicí River, and tours of Palo Verde and Rincón de la Vieja national parks. Rates run between $50 and $185, varying by the length of the tour and group size. All the hotel desks and tour operators here offer **turtle nesting tours** to Playa Grande, in season, or you can contact **ACOTAM** (✆ **2653-1687**), a specialized local operator.

No canopy tour is available right in Tamarindo, but the **Monkey Jungle Canopy Tour** (www.canopymonkeyjungle.com; ✆ **2653-1172**) and **Cartagena Canopy Tour** ★ (✆ **2675-0801**) are nearby. Both charge $50 per person and include transportation from Tamarindo. Of these two, the Monkey Jungle operation is much closer, but the Cartagena tour has a much more lush forest setting. But your best bet in this region is to take a day trip to Hacienda Guachipelín (p. 104) and do the zipline and canyoning tours there.

Horseback riding enthusiasts should contact **Casagua Horses** ★ (www.paintedponyguestranch.com; ✆ **2653-8041** or 8871-9266 in Costa Rica). Rates for horse rental, with a guide, are around $25 and $40 per hour.

For sailboat charters, several cruises are offered from Tamarindo, many of them with an open bar. Catch a ride on the 80-foot schooner ***Antares***, built in 1947 (www.tamarindosailing.net; ✆ **8587-3095**), or try the 40-foot catamaran ***Blue Dolphin*** ★ (www.bluedolphinsailing.com; ✆ **855/842-3204** in the U.S., or 8842-3204 in Costa Rica) or 66-foot catamaran ***Marlin del Rey*** (www.marlindelrey.com; ✆ **877/827-8275** in the U.S., or 2653-1212 in Costa Rica). A half-day snorkel or shorter sunset cruise should cost $70 to $85 per person, and a full day should run between $100 and $150. This usually includes an open bar and snacks on the half-day trip and sunset cruises, and all of that plus lunch on the full-day trip.

For sportfishing, a host of captains offer anglers a chance to go after the "big ones" that abound in the offshore waters. From the Tamarindo estuary, it takes only 20 minutes to reach the edge of the continental shelf, where the waters are filled with mostly marlin and sailfish. Although fishing is good all year, the peak season for billfish is between mid-April and August. Contact **Tamarindo Sportfishing** (www.tamarindosportfishing.com; ✆ **2653-0090**), **Capullo Sportfishing** ★ (www.capullo.com; ✆ **2653-0048**), or **Osprey Sportfishing** (www.osprey-sportfishing.com; ✆ **8754-9292**).

If you want to try snorkeling, surfing, or sea kayaking in Tamarindo, **Agua Rica Diving Center, Iguana Surf,** and **Arenas Adventure Tours** rent all the necessary equipment. They have half-day and hourly rates.

Tamarindo has a host of surf shops and surf schools, if you want to learn to catch a wave while in town. Tamarindo's got a great wave to learn on, although it can get very crowded at the popular beginners' breaks. For gear and lessons, try **Tamarindo Surf School** (www.tamarindosurfschool.com; ✆ **2653-0923**), **Kelly's Surf Shop** ★ (www.kellyssurfshop.com; ✆ **888/710-4746** in the U.S. and Canada, or 2653-1355 in Costa Rica), or **Witch's Rock Surf Camp** ★ (www.witchsrocksurfcamp.com; ✆ **888/318-7873** in the U.S. and Canada, or 2653-1262 in Costa Rica).

Especially for Kids

Bolas Locas Mini Golf (www.bolaslocas.com; ✆ **2653-1178;** daily 9am–11pm), located next to Dragonfly Bar & Grill (p. 114), is a nice change from the beach and pool. This 18-hole course features a wave wall, a waterfall, and a traditional Costa Rican oxcart as obstacles. A round of golf costs $7 for adults, $5 for children under 10.

Pretty Pots

The lack of any longstanding local Arts and Crafts tradition across Costa Rica is often lamented. One of the outstanding exceptions to this rule is the small village of Guaitíl, located on the outskirts of the regional capital of Santa Cruz. Its small central plaza—actually a soccer field— is ringed with craft shops and artisan stands selling a wide range of ceramic wares. Most are low-fired, relatively soft clay pieces, with traditional Chorotega indigenous design motifs. The local tour agencies offer day trips to Guaitíl, or you can drive, by heading first to Santa Cruz, then taking the well-marked turnoff for Guaitíl, just south of the city, on the road to Nicoya.

Shopping

Tamarindo's main boulevard is awash in souvenir stands, art galleries, jewelry stores, and clothing boutiques. For original beachwear and jewelry, try **Azul Profundo** ★ (www.azulprofundoboutique.com; ✆ **2653-0395**), in the Plaza Tamarindo shopping center. The modern **Garden Plaza** shopping center, near the entrance to town, has several high-end shops, as well as a massive **Automercado** (supermarket).

Nightlife

As a popular surfer destination, Tamarindo has a raging nightlife scene. The most happening bars in town are **El Garito** ★★ (✆ **2653-2017**), located about a block inland, on the road leading toward Playa Langosta, and **Aqua** ★ (✆ **8934-2896**), on the main road through town. Other popular spots throughout the week include the **Crazy Monkey Bar** at the Best Western Tamarindo Vista Villas (✆ **2653-0114**), and the **Dragonfly Bar & Grill** (p. 114). For a chill-out dance party, try the **Voodoo Lounge** (✆ **2653-0100**); those looking for a rocking sports bar can head to **Sharky's** ★★ (✆ **8918-4968**). These latter two places are just across from each other, a little up the road that heads to Playa Langosta. The best casino in town is at the **Barceló Playa Langosta** (✆ **2653-0363**) resort in Playa Langosta.

En Route South: Playa Avellanas & Playa Negra

Heading south from Tamarindo are several as-yet-undeveloped beaches, most of which are quite popular with surfers. Beyond Tamarindo and Playa Langosta are **Playa Avellanas** and **Playa Negra,** both with a few basic surfer *cabinas,* and little else.

PLAYAS HOTELS

JW Marriott Guanacaste Resort & Spa ★★★ This handsome resort is built around a massive pool (said to be the largest in Central America) and fronts a gorgeous but small patch of soft, white-sand beach. The rooms are ample and well-equipped, with fine dark wood furnishings and red tile floors in a herringbone pattern. The bathrobes are some of the plushest you'll ever fondle. Every room has a large balcony or patio, though some of the patios open onto heavily trafficked walkways (potted plants, palms, and bamboo have been placed to try to provide some privacy). The best rooms have ocean and sunset views. The various dining options include a semi-formal steakhouse and contemporary Asian Fusion restaurant. The hotel runs a regular shuttle to nearby Playa Langosta, where guests have access to a small beach club, with a pool, showers, restaurant, and bar, as well as boogie- and surfboard rentals.

Hacienda Pinilla. www.marriott.com. ✆ **888/236-2427** in the U.S. and Canada, or 2681-2000. 310 units. $289–$635 double; $483 and up suite. **Amenities:** 4 restaurants; 1 bar; babysitting; children's programs; championship 18-hole golf course nearby; large health club and spa; massive outdoor pool; room service; tennis courts nearby; watersports equipment; Wi-Fi for a fee.

WHERE TO EAT

In addition to the place listed below, the restaurants inside the **JW Marriott** resort (see above) are open to the general public.

Lola's ★★★ INTERNATIONAL/SEAFOOD Named for the owner's pet pig (who sometimes frolics in the waves as diners watch), this quintessential beach bar and restaurant sits on a patch of land and sand fronting the quiet and underdeveloped Playa Avellanas beach. The Belgian and U.S. owners serve up hearty, fresh food (like seared tuna atop salad with an Asian dressing) on homemade heavy wooden tables and chairs under the shade of palm trees and large linen umbrellas. Lola's is extremely popular, especially on weekends, so be prepared to wait occasionally for food or a table (sorry, no reservations). When you're finished, you might snag a siesta in one of the hammocks strung between the many coconut palms.

On the beach, Playa Avellanas. ✆ **2652-9097.** Main courses $12–$18. Tues–Sun 9am–sunset.

PLAYA SÁMARA ★

35km (22 miles) S of Nicoya; 245km (152 miles) W of San José

Playa Sámara is a long, broad beach on a gently curved, horseshoe-shaped bay. Unlike most of the other beaches along this stretch of the Pacific coast, the water here is usually relatively calm and safe for swimming because an offshore island and rocky headlands break up most of the surf. That said, there are often gentle rollers, and you'll find plenty of surf schools and lessons perfect for beginners. Playa Sámara is popular both with Tico families seeking a quick and inexpensive getaway and with young Ticos looking to do some serious beach partying. On weekends, in particular, Sámara can get crowded and rowdy. Still, the calm waters and steep cliffs on the far side of the bay make this a very attractive spot, and the beach is so long that the crowds are usually well dispersed. Moreover, if you drive along the rugged coastal road in either direction, you'll discover some truly spectacular and isolated beaches.

Essentials

ARRIVING **By Car:** Head west out of San José on the San José–Caldera Highway (CR27). When you reach Caldera, follow the signs to Puntarenas and the Inter-American Highway (CR1). You will actually follow signs for Liberia and San José, which are, in fact, leading you to the unmarked entrance to CR1. This road (CR23) ends when it hits the Inter-American Highway. Pass under the bridge and follow the on-ramp, which will put you on the highway heading north. Just 47km (29 miles) after you get on the Inter-American Highway heading north, you'll see signs and the turnoff for La Amistad Bridge (CR18). After crossing the bridge, continue on CR18 until it hits CR21. Take this road north to Nicoya. Turn into the town of Nicoya, and head more or less straight through town until you see signs for Playa Sámara. From here, it's a well-marked and paved road (CR150) all the way to the beach.

To drive to Sámara from Liberia, head out of town on the main road to the Guanacaste beaches, passing through Filadelfia, Santa Cruz, and Nicoya. Once you reach Nicoya, follow the directions outlined above.

By Bus: Alfaro express buses (www.empresaalfaro.com; ✆ **2222-2666**) leave San José daily at noon and 5pm from Avenida 5 between calles 14 and 16. The trip lasts 5 hours; the one-way fare is C4,620. Extra buses are sometimes added on weekends and during peak periods.

Alternatively, you can take a bus from this same station to Nicoya and then catch a second bus from Nicoya to Sámara. **Alfaro** buses leave San José nearly every hour between 5:30am and 5pm. The fare is C4,045. The trip can take between 4 and 5½ hours, depending if the bus goes via Liberia or La Amistad Bridge. The latter route is much faster and more frequent. **Empresa Rojas Castro** (✆ **2685-5032**) buses leave Nicoya for Sámara and Carrillo regularly throughout the day, between 5am and 9pm. The trip's duration is 1½ hours. The fare to Sámara is C1,135; the fare to Carrillo is C1,300.

Express buses to San José leave daily at 10am and noon. Buses for Nicoya leave throughout the day between 5am and 6pm. Buses leave Nicoya for San José nearly every hour between 3am and 5pm.

Interbus (www.interbusonline.com; ✆ **4100-0888**) has a daily bus that leaves San José for Playa Sámara at 8am. The fare is $50, and the bus will pick you up at most San José-area hotels.

VISITOR INFORMATION The website **www.samarabeach.com** is an excellent, all-around resource for information about Playa Sámara and the vicinity.

VILLAGE LAYOUT Sámara is a busy little town at the bottom of a steep hill. The main road heads straight into town, passing the soccer field before coming to an end at the beach. Just before the beach is a road to the left that leads to most of the hotels listed below. This road also leads to Playa Carrillo (p. 121) and the **Hotel Punta Islita.** If you turn right 3 blocks before hitting the beach, you'll hit the coastal road that goes to playas Buena Vista, Barrigona, and eventually Nosara.

GETTING AROUND If you need a ride around Sámara, or to one of the nearby beaches, have your hotel call you a taxi. Rides in town should cost $2 to $5; rides to nearby beaches might run $10 to $25.

FAST FACTS To reach the local police, dial ✆ **2656-0436.** Sámara has a small **medical clinic** (✆ **2656-0166**). A branch of **Banco Nacional** (✆ **2656-0089**) is on the road to Playa Buena Vista, just as you head out of town. For full-service laundry, head to **Green Life Laundry** (✆ **2656-1051**), about 3 blocks west of the Banco Nacional.

Playa Sámara Hotels

MODERATE

The Hideaway Hotel ★★ This two-story boutique hotel has the feel of a converted home, due in no small part to the warm welcome owner Martina and her staff give the guests. Rooms are oversize, with really handsome blue, green, and white comforters and curtains (the exact pattern varies from room to room). The color theme continues outside, where bright blue chairs and lounges ring a crescent-shaped pool. The hotel is about a block or so inland from the far southern end of Playa Sámara, so a rental car is helpful to get to and from the many restaurants, bars, and shops in town.

Playa Sámara, Nicoya, Guanacaste. www.thehideawayplayasamara.com. ✆ **2656-1145.** 12 units. $139 double. Rates include full breakfast. **Amenities:** Restaurant; bar; outdoor pool; free Wi-Fi.

Learn the Language

Sámara Language School (www.samaralanguageschool.com; ✆ **866/978-6668** in the U.S. and Canada, or 2656-3000 in Sámara) offers a range of programs and private lessons and can arrange for a home stay with a local family. The facility even features classes with ocean views, although that might be a detriment to your language learning.

INEXPENSIVE

In addition to the places listed below, **Tico Adventure Lodge ★** (www.ticoadventurelodge.com; ✆ **2656-0628**) is another good option, about 2 blocks from the beach, in the heart of town.

Hotel Belvedere ★ German emigrants Manfred and Michaela Landwehr opened the Belvedere more than 2 decades ago. It's grown over the years, but always kept to its mission of providing clean, cozy rooms at a reasonable price. In the newer rooms in the annex, a bit uphill from the original hotel, you'll find a larger pool and more exuberant gardens. These gardens, in fact, join wild forest and are occasionally visited by troops of howler and spider monkeys. No matter the location, rooms are well-kept and many feature a yellow hand-painted wash effect that serves as wainscoting. Large, filling breakfasts are served at the main lodge, where you'll also find a second, smaller pool. It's just a 1-block walk into the heart of town, and 2 blocks to the beach.

Playa Sámara. www.belvederesamara.net. ✆ **2656-0213.** 24 units. $55–$65 double. Rates include breakfast and taxes. **Amenities:** Lounge; Jacuzzi; 2 pools; free Wi-Fi.

Sámara Tree House Inn ★★ It's not possible to find a room closer to the waves in Playa Sámara. While not true treehouses, four raised-stilt wooden cabins are supported by columns made from whole tree trunks in a tight line facing the ocean. They have prized ocean views from the elevated perch of their large sitting rooms, although the bedrooms feel a bit small and spartan, and there's no air-conditioning. However, every unit here comes with a full kitchenette, as well as a large space underneath the living area equipped with a varnished wood table and chairs, as well as a couple of woven hammocks. There's a tiny, round pool at the center of the complex, and a few chaise longues on a patch of well-tended grass facing the beach.

Playa Sámara. www.samaratreehouse.com. ✆ **2656-0733.** 6 units. $89–$145 double. Rates include breakfast. **Amenities:** Jacuzzi; small outdoor pool; free Wi-Fi.

Where to Eat

Sámara has numerous inexpensive *sodas*, and most of the hotels have their own restaurants. **El Ancla** (www.isamara.co/ancla.htm; ✆ **2656-0716**), located a bit south of downtown, serves up good, simple meals, with an excellent view of the beach and waves.

El Lagarto ★ STEAK/GRILL Here's the macho way to dine! A massive fire churns out a stream of hot wood-burning coals to feed the large, long barbecue grill stations at this restaurant and bar. Tables are made from massive heavy planks and the food is served on huge, crosscut blocks of wood, which adds to the rustic vibe. Grilled grass-fed and aged meats, seafood, and organic veggies are the heart of the long menu here.

North end of Playa Sámara. www.ellagartobbq.com. ✆ **2656-0750.** Reservations recommended. Main courses $8–$32. Daily 3–11pm.

Gusto Beach ★★ ITALIAN/BISTRO This simple, Italian-run restaurant is basically a beachfront trattoria—and then some. It's also a beach club, where people rent chaise longues to hang for the day, playing volleyball and catching rays. Food choices range from pastas, panini, and thin-crust pizzas to sushi, sashimi, and curries. Presentations can be creative, like the crisp pan-fried potatoes served in the cooking pan, or the fresh gelato made and served in a mason jar and topped with shaved chocolate. At night, this becomes nightlife central, with live music or DJs.

On the beach, north end of Playa Sámara. ✆ **2656-0252.** Reservations recommended. Main courses C4,900–C14,000. Daily 9am–11pm.

Exploring Playa Sámara

Playa Sámara is a somewhat quiet and underdeveloped beach town, and most folks are content to simply hang on the beach and swim in the gentle waves. But if you're looking for something more, there's horseback riding either on the beach or through the bordering pastureland and forests. Other options include sea kayaking in the calm waters off Playa Sámara, sportfishing, snorkeling, scuba diving, boat tours, mountain biking, and tours to Playa Ostional to see the mass nesting of olive ridley sea turtles.

You'll find that the beach is nicer and cleaner down at the south end. Better yet, head about 8km (5 miles) south to **Playa Carrillo** ★★, a long crescent of soft, white sand. With almost no development here, the beach is nearly always deserted. Loads of palm trees provide shade. If you've got a good four-wheel-drive vehicle, ask for directions at your hotel and set off in search of the hidden gems of **Playa Buena Vista** and **Playa Barrigona ★★**, which are north of Sámara, less than a half-hour drive.

Organized Tours

All the hotels here can help you arrange any number of tour options, including horseback rides, boat trips, sea kayaking, scuba diving, and snorkeling outings. You might also contact **Carrillo Adventures** (www.carrilloadventures.com; ✆ **2656-0606**), an excellent all-around local tour company.

Wingnuts Canopy Tours (www.wingnutscanopy.com; ✆ **2656-0153**) offers zipline canopy tours. The 2-hour outing costs $60 per person or $45 for those under 12. If you want to repeat the adventure, Wingnuts offers a 50 percent discount on your second tour. You'll find the office by the giant strangler fig tree, or *matapalo*, toward the southern end of the beach.

Almost every hotel in the area can arrange sportfishing trips, or you can contact **Kingfisher ★** (www.costaricabillfishing.com; ✆ **800/783-3817** in the U.S., or 8358-9561 in Costa Rica). Rates run from $850 for a half-day to $1,250 for a full day.

The waves hitting Playa Sámara are somewhat muffled by an offshore reef and headlands on each side. For some this makes it a great wave to learn on. For lessons or to rent a board, check in with **C&C Surf Shop and School** (www.cncsurfschool.com; ✆ **5006-0369**) or **Choco's Surf School** (www.chocossurfschool.com; ✆ **8937-5246**). Surfboard rentals run around $10 per day. Private lessons cost $30 to $50 per hour.

For a bird's-eye view of the area, go to the **Flying Crocodile ★★** (www.flying-crocodile.com; ✆ **2656-8048** or 8330-3923) in Playa Buena Vista. It offers flights in a two-seat (one for you, one for the pilot) Gyrocopter, the ultralight equivalent of a helicopter. Although it might feel like little more than a modified tricycle with a nylon wing and lawnmower motor, these winged wonders are very safe. A 20-minute flight runs $110, while an hour-long tour costs $230.

Located near Barra Honda National Park (see below), **Rancho Humo ★★** (www.ranchohumo.com; ✆ **2233-2233**) is a private wildlife reserve that offers fabulous **bird-watching and wildlife viewing** opportunities along the Tempisque River basin and surrounding wetlands. The area is rich in waterbird species, shore lizards, and crocodiles. A full-day tour ($95) includes a river boat trip, a tour of the reeds and lowland forest in a motorized safari-style vehicle, and a tour of the neighboring cattle ranching operations, as well as lunch. Transportation can be provided, and you can choose a half-day tour that takes in only one or two of the elements of the full-day tour.

Outlying Attractions

Spelunkers should head 62km (38 miles) northeast of Playa Sámara on the road to La Amistad Bridge. Those without a car can get to Nicoya, a half-hour away by bus, then take a taxi to the park, which costs about $25. **Barra**

Honda National Park ★ (✆ **2659-1551;** daily 8am–4pm; $12 admission) is an extensive system of caves with a long history. Here human remains have been found that are thought to be 2,000 years old, believed to be Chorotega nobles. In 1967, spelunkers discovered 42 caves here, though only 19 were ever explored and only one, **Caverna Terciopelo,** is open to the public. To go inside, you'll need to hire a guide, which should cost around $30 per person, depending on the size of your group and your bargaining abilities. You begin the tour by getting harnessed and roped and then descending a scary, vertical aluminum ladder that is 17m (56 feet) long, about the height of a 5-story building. Inside you'll see an impressive array of stalactites and stalagmites, many of them named after something they resemble (like a hen and her chicks, and papaya, and fried eggs). **Cave tours** are conducted from 8am to 1pm daily, and the park is open for hiking until 4pm, though the park is closed during the rainy season (May to Mid-Nov). Headlamps and helmets are provided. Do not wear flip-flops, or you will be turned away. Even if you don't enter the cave, the trails around Barra Honda and its prominent limestone plateau are great for hiking and bird-watching. Be sure to stop at **La Cascada,** a gentle waterfall that passes through a series of calcium and limestone pools, some large enough to bathe in.

Nightlife

After dark, the most happening place in town is **Bar Arriba** ★, a second-floor affair with a contemporary vibe, located a couple of blocks inland from the beach on the main road into town. You might also check out what's going on at **Gusto Beach** ★ (see above), **La Vela Latina** (✆ **2656-2286**), or **Tabanuco** (✆ **2656-1056**), all on the beach or fronting the water, right near the center of the action, on the main road running parallel to the beach off the center of town.

PLAYA NOSARA ★★

55km (34 miles) SW of Nicoya; 266km (165 miles) W of San José

Playa Nosara is an umbrella term used to refer to several neighboring beaches, spread along an isolated stretch of coast. **Playa Guiones, Playa Pelada, Playa Garza,** and (sometimes) **Playa Ostional** are also lumped into this area. In fact, the village of Nosara itself is several kilometers inland from the beach.

Playa Guiones is one of Costa Rica's most dependable beach breaks, and surfers come here in good numbers throughout the year. Happily, the waves are much less crowded than in Tamarindo.

The best way to get to Nosara is to fly, but with everything so spread out, that makes getting around difficult after you've arrived. The roads to, in, and around Nosara are usually in very rough shape, with little sign that will improve anytime soon.

Essentials

ARRIVING **By Plane: Nature Air** (www.natureair.com; ✆ **800/235-9272** in the U.S. and Canada, or 2299-6000 in Costa Rica) has several flights daily to **Nosara airport** (airport code: NOB). Fares run between $110 and $160 each way.

It's usually about a 5- to 10-minute drive from the airport to most hotels. Taxis wait for every arrival, and fares range between C3,000 and C6,000 to most hotels in Nosara.

By Car: Follow the directions for getting to Playa Sámara (p. 118), but watch for a well-marked fork in the road a few kilometers before you reach that beach. The right-hand fork leads to Nosara over 22km (14 miles) of rough dirt road.

By Bus: An **Alfaro** express bus (www.empresaalfaro.com; ✆ **2222-2666** in San José, or 2682-0064 in Nosara) leaves San José daily at 5:30am from Avenida 5 between calles 14 and 16. The trip's duration is 5½ hours; the one-way fare is C4,805.

You can also take an Alfaro bus from San José to Nicoya and then catch a second bus from Nicoya to Nosara. **Alfaro** buses leave San José nearly every hour between 7:30am and 5pm. The fare is C3,950. The trip can take between 4 and 5½ hours, depending on whether the bus goes via Liberia or La Amistad Bridge. The latter route is much faster and much more frequent. **Empresa Rojas** buses (✆ **2685-5352**) leave Nicoya for Nosara daily at 4:45 and 10am, 12:30pm, and 3:30 and 5:30pm. The trip is about 2 hours, and the one-way fare is C1,870. Return buses leave Nosara for Nicoya at 5, 6, and 7am, noon, and 3:30pm. A direct Alfaro bus from Nosara to San José leaves daily at 12:30pm. Buses to Nicoya leave Nosara daily at 4:45 and 10am, noon, and 3 and 5:30pm. Buses leave Nicoya for San José nearly every hour from 3am to 5pm.

VILLAGE LAYOUT The village of Nosara is about 5km (3 miles) inland from the beach. The small airstrip runs pretty much through the center of town; however, most hotels listed here are on or near the beach itself. This area was originally conceived and zoned as a primarily residential community. The maze of dirt roads and lack of any single defining thoroughfare can be confusing for first-time visitors. Luckily, a host of hotel and restaurant signs in the area help point lost travelers in the direction of their final destination.

GETTING AROUND If you want to rent a car, both **Economy** (www.economyrentacar.com; ✆ **877/326-7368** in the U.S. and Canada, or 2582-1246 in Costa Rica) and **National** (www.natcar.com; ✆ **2242-7878**) have offices here. Because demand often outstrips supply, I recommend you reserve a car in advance. You could also rent an ATV from several operators around town, including **Iguana Expeditions** and **Boca Nosara Tours** (p. 127). If you need a taxi, call **Taxi Freddy** (✆ **8662-6080**) or **Gypsy Cab Company** (www.gypsycabnosara.com; ✆ **8302-1903**).

FAST FACTS You'll find the post office and police station (✆ **2682-1130**) right at the end of the airstrip. An EBAIS medical clinic (✆ **2682-0266**) and a couple of pharmacies are in the village as well. Both Banco Popular and Banco de Costa Rica have offices in Nosara with ATMs. There's even a tiny strip mall at the crossroads to Playa Guiones.

Playa Nosara Hotels

The **Nosara Beach House** ★ (www.thenosarabeachhouse.com; ✆ **2682-0019**), on Playa Guiones, has clean, comfortable rooms and a swimming pool—and it's right on the beach. For an intimate option that's also a good deal, check out the **Nosara B&B Retreat** ★ (www.nosararetreat.com; ✆ **2682-0209**).

EXPENSIVE

Harmony Hotel & Spa ★★★ With an enviable setting right on Playa Guiones, this is by far the best hotel option in Nosara. Well-heeled surfers and yogis flock here, and it's often hard to get a room. Even the entry-level "Coco" rooms are quite spacious, with high peaked wood-paneled ceilings, queen-size beds, and a private, enclosed garden deck area featuring an outdoor shower with a massive, rainwater-style shower head. The bungalows are even larger, with king beds, and there are two-bedroom suites for families or small groups of friends. A short path through thick foliage leads to the waves, and the hotel has a shower and fresh towels waiting for guests where the property lets out onto the beach. There's an excellent on-site spa and yoga facility, and the restaurant serves top-notch, locally sourced spa cuisine. This hotel was awarded the maximum "5 Leaves" by the CST Certification for Sustainable Tourism program, thanks to a comprehensive commitment to environmental protection.

Playa Guiones. www.harmonynosara.com. ✆ **2682-4114.** 25 units. $210–$330 double; $280–$380 bungalow; $560–$690 2-bedroom suite. Rates include breakfast and 1 yoga class. **Amenities:** Restaurant; bar; complimentary use of bikes; midsize outdoor pool; spa; surfboard rental; free Wi-Fi.

MODERATE

Harbor Reef Surf Resort ★ This sprawling miniresort features a mix of rooms and suites at excellent prices, and is quite popular with the surf crowd. All of the rooms are spacious and clean, although a bit bare, with very few decorative touches. Some of the suites come with full kitchens; the staff also rents out several fully equipped houses. The grounds feature tall trees, pretty gardens, and two swimming pools—one with a swim-up bar and the other with a stone waterfall that forms a small, private, grotto-like area underneath. The beach and popular surf break at Playa Guiones is about a 3-minute walk away. Attached to the resort is a well-stocked convenience store that rents bicycles, ATVs, and golf carts.

Playa Guiones. www.harborreef.com. ✆ **2682-5049.** 23 units. $120–$165 double; $175–$280 suite. Rates include continental breakfast. **Amenities:** Restaurant; bar; 2 small outdoor pools; free Wi-Fi.

INEXPENSIVE

In addition to the places mentioned below, **Kaya Sol** ★ (www.nosarahotelkayasol.com; ✆ **2682-1459**) is a popular budget option and surfer hangout.

The Gilded Iguana ★ Located in the heart of Playa Guiones, about 200m (656 ft.) inland from the beach, the Iguana features a mix of rooms, a midsize kidney-shaped pool, and one of the best restaurant and bar scenes in the area. The downside to the restaurant and bar's popularity is that it can be noisy here, especially when there's a live band or major sporting event going on. The most economical rooms are simple and worn, with low wooden beds and colorful Guatemalan textile bedspreads. It's worth a splurge for the newer rooms, which not only feature air-conditioning, but are located behind the pool and away from the restaurant and its hubbub.

Playa Guiones. www.thegildediguana.com. ✆ **2682-0450.** 12 units. $60–$65 double; $85–$110 suite. **Amenities:** Restaurant; bar; midsize outdoor pool; free Wi-Fi.

Where to Eat

In addition to the places mentioned below, **Marlin Bill's** (✆ **2682-0458**) is a popular and massive open-air haunt on the hillside of the main road, just across from **Café de Paris** (see below). You can expect to get good, fresh seafood and American classics here. **La Dolce Vita** ★★ (✆ **2682-0107**), on the outskirts of town on the road to Playa Sámara, serves up Italian fare nightly. **Robin's Ice Cream** ★ (www.robinsicecream.com; ✆ **2682-0617**) makes homemade ice cream and also serves breakfast, lunch, and dinner. Finally, **Go Juice** ★ (✆ **8682-4692**) is a semi-permanent "food truck" dishing out fresh juices, iced coffee drinks, and tuna *poki* bowls. Its signature frozen banana coffee drink has won over more than a few skeptics. For local flavor, **Doña Olga's** is a simple Costa Rican *soda* right on the beach in Playa Pelada.

Café de Paris ★ BAKERY/BISTRO You can stop here for a freshly baked croissant and cup of coffee or a full breakfast. It's also worthwhile for lunch (think burgers, nachos, or wraps) or dinner—both the steak au poivre and fish curry are excellent. A pool, minigolf course and children's play set just off the main dining area make this a good choice for families with young kids. Café de Paris is located right at the main crossroads for access to Playa Guiones.

On the main road into Nosara. www.cafedeparis.net. ✆ **2682-1036.** Main courses C6,500–C9,900. Daily 7am–5pm.

The Gilded Iguana ★★ SEAFOOD/GRILL The fare here is bar food-plus, with all the staples you'd expect—burgers, nachos, quesadillas, fajitas, and wings—as well as more substantial (chicken Parmesan) or eclectic (Thai shrimp) fare. The menu also features vegetarian, gluten-free, and low-calorie options. Try the fresh fish dishes, which are provided daily by Chiqui, the owner's husband, a Nosara-born fisherman and tour guide. There's live music here Tuesdays and Fridays, and sporting events are shown on TV daily.

About 90m (295 ft.) inland from the beach at Playa Guiones. www.thegildediguana.com. ✆ **2682-0259.** Main courses C4,000–C9,000. Daily 7am–10pm.

La Luna ★★ INTERNATIONAL This funky, oceanfront bistro enjoys the best setting of any restaurant in Nosara. From its sand and grass perch right above Playa Pelada, you can watch surfers just below from one of the outdoor tables or long couches with overstuffed pillows. This is also a great place to catch the sunset. As darkness sets in, candlelight and strings of bare bulbs running between the trees and main building are lit to create a romantic atmosphere. Wood oven–fired pizzas and Mediterranean fare are the specialties here, but nightly chalkboard specials might feature anything from pad Thai to chicken curry. For lunch, try the fish tacos. Service can be slow and a bit gruff. Playa Pelada. ✆ **2682-0122.** Main courses C6,700–C11,200. Daily noon–9pm.

Exploring Playa Nosara

Among the several beaches at Nosara are the long, curving **Playa Guiones ★★**, **Playa Nosara ★**, and the diminutive **Playa Pelada ★**. Because the village of Nosara is several miles inland, these beaches tend to be clean, secluded, and quiet. Surfing and bodysurfing are good here, particularly at Playa Guiones, which is garnering quite a reputation as a consistent beach break with a good ride. Pelada is a short white-sand beach with three deep scallops, backed by sea grasses and mangroves. There isn't too much sand at high tide, so you'll want to hit the beach when the tide's out. At either end of the beach, rocky outcroppings reveal tide pools at low tide.

When the seas are calm, you can do some decent snorkeling around the rocks and reefs just offshore. Masks, snorkels, and fins can be rented at **Café de Paris** (see above) or **Coconut Harry's** (see below). Bird-watchers should explore the mangrove swamps around the estuary mouth of the Río Nosara. Just walk north from Playa Pelada and follow the riverbank, then take the paths into the mangroves. In addition to numerous water, shore, and seabird species, you may spot hawks and other raptors, as well as toucans and parrots.

Organized Tours & Activities

All the hotels in the area can arrange **fishing charters** for $200 to $500 for a half-day, or $400 to $1,200 for a full day. These rates are for one to four people and vary according to boat size and accouterments.

The folks at **Boca Nosara Tours** (www.bocanosaratours.com; ✆ **2682-0280**) have a large stable of well-cared-for horses and a range of beach, jungle, and waterfall rides to choose from. They also run similar tours on motorized off-road quads. Rates run between $40 and $70 per person, depending on the size of your group and the length of the tour. Another good option for ATV tours and rentals is **iQuad** (www.iquadnosara.com; ✆ **8629-8349**).

If you time your trip right, you can do a night tour to nearby **Playa Ostional** to watch nesting olive ridley sea turtles. These turtles come ashore by the thousands in a mass egg-laying phenomenon known as an *arribada.* The *arribadas* are so difficult to predict that no one runs regularly scheduled turtle-viewing trips, but when the *arribada* is in full swing, several local guides and agencies offer tours. These *arribadas* take place 4 to 10 times between July and December; each occurrence lasts between 3 and 10 days. Consider yourself very lucky if you happen to be around during one of these fascinating natural phenomena. Your best bet is to ask the staff at your hotel or check in with the **Associación de Guias de Ostional** (Ostional Local Guide Association) ★ (✆ **2682-0428;** asoc.guiasostional@hotmail.com).

Tours are generally run at night, but because the turtles come ashore in such numbers, you can sometimes catch them in the early morning light as well.

Yo Quiero Hablar Español

You can brush up on or start up your Spanish at the **Rey de Nosara Language School** (www.reydenosara.itgo.com; ✆ **2682-0215**). It offers group and private lessons according to demand, and can coordinate week or multiweek packages.

Even if it's not turtle-nesting season, you might want to look into visiting Playa Ostional just to have a long, wide expanse of beach to yourself. However, be careful swimming here because the surf and riptides can be formidable. During the dry season (mid-Nov to Apr), you can usually get here in a regular car, but during the rainy season you'll need four-wheel-drive. This beach is part of **Ostional National Wildlife Refuge** (✆ **2682-0428**). At the northwest end of the refuge is **India Point,** which is known for its tide pools and rocky outcrops.

With miles of excellent beach breaks and relatively few crowds, this is a great place to surf or learn how to surf. If you want to try to stand up for your first time, check in with **Coconut Harry's Surf Shop** (www.coconutharrys.com; ✆ **2682-0574**); **Del Mar Surf Camp** (www.delmarsurfcamp.com; ✆ **855/833-5627** in the U.S. and Canada, or 2682-1433 in Costa Rica); or **Safari Surf School** (www.safarisurfschool.com; ✆ **866/433-3355** in the U.S. and Canada, or 2682-0113 in Costa Rica). All offer hourly solo or group lessons, multiday packages with accommodations and meals included, and board rentals.

HIKING & WILDLIFE VIEWING Located on land surrounding the Nosara river mouth, the **Nosara Biological Reserve** (www.lagarta.com/reserva.htm; ✆ **2682-0035**) features a network of trails and raised walkways through tropical transitional forests and mangrove swamps. More than 270 species of birds have been spotted here. This private reserve is owned and managed by Lagarta Lodge, and the trails start right at the hotel. Admission is $6. Guided tours and guided boat tours are also available.

Nosara Yoga Institute ★★ (www.nosarayoga.com; ✆ **866/439-4704** in the U.S. and Canada, or 2682-0071 in Costa Rica) offers daily yoga classes, and a host of custom-designed "retreat" options. This is an internationally recognized institute. Its daily 90-minute classes are open to the public and cost just $15, with a mat provided. You might also check to see if anything is being offered at the Harmony Hotel & Spa (see p. 125).

Nightlife

When evening rolls around, don't expect a major party scene. **Kaya Sol** (✆ **2682-1459**) has a lounge that's popular with surfers, and the **Gilded Iguana** (p. 125) often has live music. In "downtown" Nosara, you'll probably want to check out either the **Tropicana** (✆ **2682-0140**), the town's longstanding local disco, or **Legends Bar** (✆ **2682-0184**), an American-style bar with big-screen TVs and pool and foosball tables.

Outlying Attractions

Just north of Nosara lies Playa Ostional, famous for its massive nestings of olive ridley sea turtles (see above). This is an underdeveloped beach village with only a few hotels, the best of which is **Hotel Luna Azul ★** (www.hotellunaazul.com;

(© **2682-1400**), which features nice individual bungalows and a great view of the ocean—although the beach is a good distance away. If you come to Ostional to surf, try the **Ostional Turtle Lodge** (www.surfingostional.com; © **2682-0131**), a basic hostel right on the beach near the center of the village.

PLAYA MONTEZUMA ★★

166–184km (103–114 miles) W of San José (not including the ferry ride); 36km (22 miles) SE of Paquera; 54km (33 miles) S of Naranjo

For decades, this remote village and its surrounding beaches, forests, and waterfalls have enjoyed near-legendary status among backpackers, UFO seekers, hippie expatriates, natural healers, and European budget travelers. Although it maintains its alternative vibe, Montezuma is a great destination for all manner of travelers looking for a beach retreat surrounded by some stunning scenery and lush forests. Active pursuits abound, from hiking in the Cabo Blanco Absolute Nature Reserve to horseback riding to visiting a beachside waterfall. The natural beauty, miles of almost abandoned beaches, rich wildlife, and jungle waterfalls here are what first made Montezuma famous, and they continue to make this one of my favorite beach towns in Costa Rica.

Essentials

ARRIVING **By Plane:** The nearest airport is in Tambor, 17km (11 miles) away. Some of the hotels listed below might pick you up in Tambor for a reasonable fee. If not, you'll have to hire a taxi, which could cost $40 to $50. Taxis are generally waiting to meet regularly scheduled planes, but if they aren't, call **Gilberto Rodríguez** (© **8826-9055**).

By Car: The traditional route here is to first drive to Puntarenas and catch the ferry to either Naranjo or Paquera. Montezuma is about 30 minutes south of Tambor, 1 hour south of Paquera, and 2 hours south of Naranjo. The road from Paquera to Tambor is paved, and taking the Paquera ferry will save you time and some rough, dusty driving. The road from Naranjo to Paquera is all dirt and gravel and often in bad shape. For information on car ferries, see below. For driving directions to Puntarenas, see p. 111.

To drive to Montezuma from Liberia, head out of town on the main road to the Guanacaste beaches, passing through Filadelfia, Santa Cruz, and Nicoya on your way toward the turnoff for La Amistad Bridge. Continue straight at this turnoff, and follow the directions for this route as listed above.

A Time-Saving Route

The fastest route is the daily speedboat shuttle between Montezuma and Jacó (actually Playa Herradura). This 1-hour shuttle departs Montezuma for Playa Herradura at 9:30am and makes the return trip from Playa Herradura to Montezuma at 11am. **CocoZuma Traveller** (www.cocozuma.com; © **2642-0911**) or **Zuma Tours** (www.zumatours.net; © **2642-0024**) can book this, including connecting shuttle service to or from San José, Manuel Antonio, Malpaís, and other destinations. The boat shuttle itself is $40 to $45 per person, one-way.

By Bus & Ferry: Transportes Cobano (✆ **2642-1112**) runs two daily direct buses between San José and Montezuma. The buses leave from the Coca-Cola bus terminal at Calle 12 and Avenida 5 at 6am and 2pm. Fare is C7,500, including the ferry. The trip takes a bit over 5 hours.

Alternatively, it takes two buses and a ferry ride to get to Montezuma. **Empresarios Unidos de Puntarenas** express buses (✆ **2222-0064**) to Puntarenas leave San José daily every hour between 6am and 7pm from Calle 16 and Avenida 12. The trip takes 2 hours; the fare is C2,640. From Puntarenas, you can take the ferry to Paquera. A bus south to Montezuma will be waiting to meet the ferry when it arrives in Paquera. The bus ride takes about 1½ hours; the fare is C1,800. Be careful not to take the Naranjo ferry because it does not meet with regular onward bus transportation to Montezuma.

Buses are met by hordes of locals trying to corral you to one of the many budget hotels. Remember, they are getting a commission, so their information is biased. Not only that, they are often flat-out lying when they tell you the hotel you want to stay in is full.

When you're ready to head back, direct buses leave Montezuma daily at 6:30am and 2:30pm. Regular local buses to Paquera leave Cóbano roughly every 2 hours throughout the day starting around 4am. Buses to San José leave Puntarenas daily every hour between 6am and 7pm.

Buses from Montezuma to Paquera leave roughly every 2 hours between 5:30am and 5pm.

VILLAGE LAYOUT As the winding mountain road that descends into Montezuma bottoms out, you turn left onto a small dirt road that defines the village proper. On this 1-block road, you will find El Sano Banano Village Cafe and, across from it, a small shaded park with plenty of tall trees, as well as a basketball court and children's playground. The bus stops at the end of this road. From here, hotels are scattered up and down the beach and around the village's few sand streets. Around the center of town are several tour agencies among the restaurants and souvenir stores.

Playa Montezuma Hotels

EXPENSIVE

Ylang Ylang Beach Resort ★★ This pioneering rainforest resort does an excellent job of blending tropical fantasy with hints of luxury. The complex is just off the beach in a dense patch of forest and flowering gardens. Lodging options range from glamping-style tent cabins (slat wood floors, private porches, indoor plumbing, batik window coverings) to individual bungalows and geodesic domes. All are comfortable and quite pretty. The on-site restaurant serves some of the tastiest fare on this stretch of coastline. There is no regular vehicular access to the resort, so check-in is at El Sano Banano Village Cafe (p. 132) in town; you and your bags are shuttled in via Jeep or dune buggy. The owners, Lenny and Patricia, have been here for decades and have done much to promote and protect the area.

Montezuma. www.ylangylangbeachresort.com. ✆ **888/795-8494** in the U.S. and Canada, or 2642-0636 in Costa Rica. 22 units. $220–$355 double. Rates include breakfast and dinner. **Amenities:** Restaurant; bar; midsize outdoor pool; spa; free Wi-Fi.

MODERATE

Amor de Mar ★★ A little slice of paradise, Amor de Mar is a large house perched on a high spot of land that runs down to a rocky outcropping hiding a small natural swimming pool carved into the coral stones. Between this pool and the rooms is a broad lawn and a small grove of mango trees and coconut palms strung with hammocks. The rooms themselves are comfortable and pretty, awash in varnished hardwoods, with large windows (though they vary greatly in size and location; the prized choices are those on the second floor, especially those with oceanview balconies). Beside and behind the main hotel building lie Casa Luna and Casa Sol, two separate two-story, fully equipped villas perfect for families and small groups. The entrance to the trail to Montezuma's famous waterfall is directly across the dirt street from Amor de Mar, and it's a short walk into town. The in-house restaurant is open only for breakfast and lunch.

Montezuma. www.amordemar.com. ✆ **2642-0262.** 11 units. $120–$150 double; $250–$270 villa. **Amenities:** Restaurant; free Wi-Fi.

INEXPENSIVE

The folks at Ylang Ylang (see above) also run the in-town **El Sano Banano B&B** (www.elbanano.com; ✆ **866/332-3590** in the U.S. and Canada, or 2642-0636 in Costa Rica), just off their popular restaurant (see below). The rooms here feature air-conditioning (which, because of the design, you are basically forced to use) and satellite televisions. Double rooms are $75 to $95.

Hotel La Aurora ★ You'll see the stone columns and yellow archway entrance to this intimate budget lodging on your left as soon as you hit the town's main crossroad. Spread over three floors, the rooms are not as comfortable as they could be, with low wooden beds and rather thin mattresses. Still the German owner Angela Kock runs a tight ship, so rooms and common areas (including a much-used communal kitchen for the guests) are immaculate. On the top floor, you'll find a two-bedroom apartment that enjoys just a hint of a sea view through the thick trees. Guests tend to gather in the several common areas, including the well-stocked lending library. Or you can grab a siesta in one of the shady hammocks hung around the hotel.

Montezuma, Cóbano de Puntarenas. www.hotelaurora-montezuma.com. ✆ **2642-0051.** 20 units. $40 double; $50–$60 suites. **Amenities:** Lounge; free Wi-Fi.

Hotel Lucy ★ For a budget hotel, this place has some serious location cachet, as it's right on the beach a short walk south of the village, close to the Montezuma Waterfall trail entrance. However, the rooms here are very basic and only sporadically maintained, and the service and personal attention provided are minimal. Guests choose between rooms with private bathrooms or shared dorms.

Montezuma. ✆ **2642-0273.** 17 units, 6 with bathroom. $24 double with shared bathroom; $28 double with private bathroom. Rates include taxes. **Amenities:** Free Wi-Fi.

Where to Eat

You'll find several basic *sodas* and casual restaurants right in the village. The **Chelo Pizzeria** (✆ **2642-1430**), at the crossroads into town, serves thin-crust pizzas, calzones, and pastas. You might also want to check out the Spanish cuisine and fabulous setting at the downtown **Hotel Moctezuma** (✆ **2642-0058**), or the varied international fare at **Cocolores** (✆ **2642-0348**). Just outside of downtown proper, the Israeli-owned **Puggo's** ★ (✆ **2642-0325**) serves up an eclectic menu that ranges from falafel to *ceviche* to focaccia and beyond.

For breakfast, coffee, and light meals, **Orgánico** ★ (✆ **2642-1322**) is the pick, with a range of healthy sandwiches, daily specials, and freshly baked goods. The **Bakery Café** (✆ **2642-0458**) is another option, serving everything from gourmet coffee drinks to full meals. Finally, the restaurant at **Ylang Ylang Beach Resort** ★★ (see above) is excellent.

El Sano Banano Village Cafe ★★ INTERNATIONAL/VEGETARIAN El Sano Banano has always been the heart and soul and social center of Montezuma. It doesn't hurt that it's also located at the rough geographic center of town as well, just across from the small central park. The menu is focused on vegetarian and market-fresh cooking, with a long list of vegan, gluten-free, and raw food choices. The salads are huge and plentiful and the sandwiches are served on home-baked whole wheat bread and buns. No red meat is offered, but seafood and poultry make their way into a range of dishes, from Thai-style spring rolls to burritos to pasta dishes. Every evening at 7:30pm, recent releases and classic movies are shown on a large screen. ***Tip:*** There are lots of seating choices, but the prized tables are located in the back patio garden, under the tall shade trees.

Montezuma. ✆ **2642-0944.** Main courses C4,000–C8,500. Daily 7am–10pm.

Playa de los Artistas ★★★ ITALIAN/MEDITERRANEAN This is the place to go for a special occasion or a date night. Dim lighting, soft electronic music, and large wooden tables spread around the covered patio and open garden area (just a few steps from the ocean) make this a wonderfully romantic place to dine. And the food is superb. It arrives from two distinct places: a small kitchen in the owners' home behind the dining area, and a large outdoor grill and wood-burning oven. The menu is handwritten every day and varies according to what's fresh and available. You might find some fresh-caught octopus grilled and served over crostini, or slow-cooked pork ribs in a rum and honey glaze. Seafood is the main draw here, and the whole grilled fresh catch of the day is hard to top.

Across from Hotel Los Mangos, Montezuma. ✆ **2642-0920.** Reservations recommended. No credit cards. Main courses C6,000–C10,000. Mon–Fri 5pm–9:30pm, Sat noon–9:30pm. ***Note:*** Lunch is sometimes served during the high season.

Exploring Montezuma

The ocean here is a gorgeous royal blue, and idyllic beaches stretch out along the coast on either side of town. Be careful, though: The waves can occasionally be too rough for casual swimming. Be sure you know where the rocks are and what the tides are before going bodysurfing. Given the prevailing currents and winds here, Montezuma also has experienced several severe and long-lasting red tide episodes at different times over the years. During these periods of massive algae bloom, the ocean is reddish-brown in color and not recommended for swimming. The best places to swim are a couple of hundred meters north of town in front of **El Rincón de los Monos,** or several kilometers farther north at Playa Grande.

Don't miss the **Montezuma waterfall** ★★ just outside town—it's one of those tropical fantasies where water comes pouring down into a deep pool. It's a popular spot, and it's a fairly easy hike from town up the stream. Along this stream are a couple of waterfalls, but the upper falls are by far the most spectacular. You'll find the trail to the falls just over the bridge south of the village (on your right just past Las Cascadas restaurant). At the first major outcropping of rocks, the trail disappears and you have to scramble a bit up the rocks and river. A trail occasionally reappears for short stretches. Just stick close to the stream and you'll eventually hit the falls. ***Note:*** Be very careful when climbing close to the rushing water, and also if you plan on taking any dives into the pools below. The rocks are quite slippery, and several people each year get very scraped up, break bones, and otherwise hurt themselves here.

Another popular local waterfall is **El Chorro** ★, located 8km (5 miles) north of Montezuma. It cascades down into a tide pool at the edge of the ocean, making it a delightful mix of fresh water and seawater. You can bathe while gazing out over the sea and rocky coastline. When the water is clear and calm, this is one of my favorite swimming holes in all of Costa Rica. However, a massive landslide in 2004 filled in much of this pool and also somewhat lessened the drama and beauty of the falls. Moreover, the pool here is dependent upon the tides—it disappears entirely at very high tide. It's about a 2-hour hike along the beach to reach El Chorro. You can take a horseback tour here offered by any of the tour operators in town.

Organized Tours & Activities

A range of guided tours and adventure trips is available in Montezuma. **Coco-Zuma Traveller** (www.cocozuma.com; ✆ **2642-0911**) and **Sun Trails** (www.montezumatraveladventures.com; ✆ **2642-0808**) can both arrange horseback riding, boat excursions, scuba-dive and snorkel tours, ATV outings, and rafting trips.

The **Waterfall Canopy Tour** ★ (www.montezumatraveladventures.com; ✆ **2642-0808;** daily at 9am, 1pm, and 3pm; $45) is built right alongside Montezuma's famous falls. The tour, which features nine cables connecting 13 platforms, includes a swim at the foot of the falls.

HORSEBACK RIDING Several people around the village rent horses for around $10 to $20 an hour, although most people choose to do a guided 4-hour horseback tour for $30 to $50. Any of the hotels or tour agencies in town can arrange this.

Some shops in the center of the village rent bicycles by the hour or day, as well as boogie boards and snorkeling equipment (although the water must be very calm for snorkeling).

Outlying Attractions

As beautiful as the beaches around Montezuma are, the beaches at **Cabo Blanco Absolute Nature Reserve ★★** (✆ **2642-0093**), 11km (6¾ miles) south of the village, are even more stunning. At the southernmost tip of the Nicoya Peninsula, Cabo Blanco is a national park that preserves a nesting site for brown pelicans, magnificent frigate birds, and brown boobies. The beaches are backed by a lush tropical forest that is home to howler monkeys. The main trail here, Sendero Sueco (Swedish Trail), is a rugged and sometimes steep hike through thick rainforest. The trail leads to the beautiful Playa Balsita and Playa Cabo Blanco, two white-sand stretches that straddle either side of the Cabo Blanco point. The beaches are connected by a short trail. It's 4km (2.5 miles) to Playa Balsita. Alternately, you can take a shorter 2km (1.25-mile) loop trail through the primary forest here. This is Costa Rica's oldest official bioreserve and was set up thanks to the pioneering efforts of conservationists Karen Mogensen and Nicholas Wessberg. Admission is $10; the reserve is open Wednesday through Sunday from 8am to 4pm.

On your way out to Cabo Blanco, you'll pass through the tiny village of **Cabuya.** There are a couple of private patches of beach to discover in this area, off deserted dirt roads. A small offshore island serves as the town's picturesque cemetery; snorkel and kayak trips to this island are offered out of Montezuma.

Shuttle buses head from Montezuma to Cabo Blanco roughly every 2 hours beginning at 8am, and then turn around and bring folks from Cabo Blanco to Montezuma; the last one leaves Cabo Blanco around 5pm. The fare is $3 each way. These shuttles often don't run during the off-season. You can also share a taxi: The fare is around $15 to $20 per taxi, which can hold four or five passengers. Taxis tend to hang around Montezuma center. One dependable *taxista* is **Gilberto Rodríguez** (✆ **8826-9055**).

Nightlife

Montezuma has had a tough time coming to terms with its nightlife. For years, local businesses banded together to force most of the loud, late-night activity out of town. This has eased somewhat, allowing for quite an active nightlife in Montezuma proper. The local action seems to base itself either at **Chico's Bar ★** or at the bar at the **Hotel Moctezuma** (✆ **2642-0058**). Both are located on the main strip in town facing the water. If your evening tastes are mellower, **El Sano Banano Village Cafe** (p. 132) doubles as the local movie house, with nightly late-run features projected on a large screen.

MALPAÍS & SANTA TERESA ★★

150km (93 miles) W of San José; 12km (7½ miles) S of Cóbano

Malpaís (or Mal País) means "badlands," but that's hardly descriptive of this booming beach area today. Malpaís is a term sometimes used to refer to a string of neighboring beaches, including Malpaís, Playa Carmen, Santa Teresa, Playa Hermosa, and Playa Manzanillo—though the region is increasingly referred to as Santa Teresa. These beaches are long, wide expanses of light sand dotted with rocky outcroppings. This is one of Costa Rica's hottest spots, and development rages on at a dizzying pace, especially in Santa Teresa. Still, it will take some time before this place is anything like more developed destinations Tamarindo or Manuel Antonio. In Malpaís and Santa Teresa today, you'll find a mix of beach hotels and resorts, restaurants, shops, and private houses, as well as miles of often deserted beach, and easy access to virgin jungle.

Essentials

ARRIVING **By Plane:** The nearest airport is in Tambor (p. 129), about 22km (14 miles) from Malpaís; the ride takes around 20 to 25 minutes. Some of the hotels listed below might be willing to pick you up in Tambor for a reasonable fee. If not, you'll have to hire a taxi, which could cost $60 to $70. **Taxis** are generally waiting to meet most regularly scheduled planes, but if they aren't, you can call **Richard** (© **8360-8166** or 2640-0099) for a cab.

By Car: Follow the directions to Montezuma (see "Playa Montezuma," above). At Cóbano, follow the signs to Malpaís and Playa Santa Teresa. It's another 12km (7½ miles) down a rough dirt road that requires four-wheel-drive much of the year, especially during the rainy season.

To drive to Malpaís from Liberia, head out of town on the main road to the Guanacaste beaches, passing through Filadelfia, Santa Cruz, and Nicoya on your way toward the turnoff for La Amistad Bridge. Continue straight at this turnoff, and follow the directions for this route as listed above.

By Bus & Ferry: Transportes Cobano (© **2642-1112**) has two daily buses to Malpaís and Santa Teresa departing from Avenida 7 and 9, Calle 12. The buses leave at 6am and 2pm, and the fare is C7,535, including the ferry passage. The ride takes around 6 hours. The return buses leave Santa Teresa at 5:15am and 2pm.

Alternatively, you can follow the directions above for getting to Montezuma, but get off in Cóbano. From Cóbano, there are several daily buses for Malpaís and Santa Teresa running throughout the day. The fare is C950. ***Be forewarned:*** These bus schedules are subject to change according to demand, road conditions, and the whim of the bus company.

If you miss the bus connection in Cóbano, you can hire a cab to Malpaís for around $25 to $30.

VILLAGE LAYOUT Malpaís and Santa Teresa are two small beach villages laid out along a road that parallels the beach. As you reach the ocean, the road forks; Playa Carmen is straight ahead, Malpaís is to your left, and Santa Teresa is to your right. If you continue beyond Santa Teresa, you'll come to the even-more-deserted beaches of playas Hermosa and Manzanillo (not to be confused with beaches of the same names to be found elsewhere in the country). To get to playas Hermosa and Manzanillo, you have to ford a couple of rivers, which can be tricky during parts of the rainy season. ***Warning:*** Bandits have been known to lie in wait at river crossings to ambush people who get out of their cars to check the depth of the river.

GETTING AROUND If you need a taxi, call **Richard** (✆ **8360-8166** or 2640-0099). If you want to do the driving yourself, you can contact the local offices of **Alamo** (www.alamocostarica.com; ✆ **2640-0526**) or **Budget Rent A Car** (www.budget.co.cr; ✆ **2640-0500**). Or head to **Quads Rental Center** (✆ **2640-0178**), which stocks ATVs.

Malpaís & Santa Teresa Hotels

EXPENSIVE

In addition to the places listed below, **Latitude 10** ★★ (www.latitude10resort.com; ✆ **8309-2943**) is a lovely boutique beachfront resort, while **Casa Chameleon** ★★ (www.hotelcasachameleon.com; ✆ **888/705-0274** in the U.S. and Canada, or 2288-2879 in Costa Rica) is a collection of plush, individual villas, each with a private pool, set on a steep hillside overlooking Malpaís.

If you're looking to combine beachfront luxury with some serious yoga and healthful eating, **Pranamar Villas & Yoga Retreat** ★★ (www.pranamarvillas.com; ✆ **2640-0852**) on the northern end of Santa Teresa is a great option, built and run by the original owners and builders of Florblanca Resort (see below).

Florblanca Resort ★★★ This is the premier boutique luxury beach resort in this area, which is saying a lot. The resort consists of a collection of massive, elegant private villas spread around exuberant gardens. The foliage is so thick and abundant that you may get lost on the stone walkways that weave through the resort. About half the villas are designed for couples, and the rest feature a separate upstairs bedroom with two twin beds perfect for families—although no children under 6 are allowed. All feature a humongous living room that opens on an equally spacious private patio area, as well as large, open-air bathrooms with outdoor rain showers and separate free-standing tubs in a small private garden. Enjoy a morning Pilates or Ashtanga yoga class in the oceanview open-air Dojo, and follow it up with a cool dip in the large two-tiered pool. The spa is superb and the on-site Nectar restaurant is one of the best in the area.

Playa Santa Teresa. www.florblanca.com. ✆ **800/683-1031** in the U.S. and Canada, or 2640-0232 in Costa Rica. 11 units. $387–$531 double. Rates include breakfast and taxes. No children under 6. **Amenities:** Restaurant; bar; small gym; outdoor pool; room service; spa; watersports equipment rental; free Wi-Fi.

Pranamar Villas & Yoga Retreat ★★ Pranamar feels like a small village, with tight paths overflowing with tropical foliage weaving between thatched-roof buildings, with wood and bamboo walls. As is common on this coast, there's a heavy dose of Balinese, Thai, and Indonesian artwork, crafts, and furnishings, but it's mixed in with elements from Mexico, Guatemala, and Ecuador. As the name suggests, yoga is an integral part of the program here, with regular daily classes, a steady stream of visiting workshops, and a large and pretty yoga studio. The hotel's Buddha Eyes restaurant specializes in healthy and vegetarian cuisine, without skimping on flavor. This hotel is located on the far northern edge of Santa Teresa, right where it becomes Playa Hermosa.

Santa Teresa. www.pranamarvillas.com. ✆ **2640-0852.** 10 units. $235–$362 double. Rates include breakfast, daily yoga class, and taxes. **Amenities:** Restaurant; bar; saltwater pool; spa treatments; free Wi-Fi.

MODERATE

Trópico Latino Lodge ★★ This small beachfront resort is set on a large, mostly forested piece of land fronting a prime patch of sand in the center of Santa Teresa. You can opt for the older, spacious and economical garden units, or splurge for a newer beachfront room or bungalow. These latter bungalows feature roughhewn wood planks for walls and peaked wood ceilings; it's a handsome look. The expansive grounds here are covered with tall pochote trees that are often frequented by roaming bands of howler monkeys. The hotel has a small pool and yoga studio and spa, all with ocean views, and the Shambala restaurant is excellent. Some of the most coveted surf spots in Santa Teresa are directly in front of this resort.

Santa Teresa. www.hoteltropicolatino.com. ✆ **800/724-1235** in the U.S. and Canada, or 2640-0062 in Costa Rica. 21 units. $115–$145 double. Rates include breakfast and taxes. **Amenities:** Restaurant; bar; Jacuzzi; pool; small spa; free Wi-Fi.

INEXPENSIVE

Hardcore budget travelers should check out **Tranquilo Backpackers ★** (www.tranquilobackpackers.com; ✆ **2640-0589**), a bit inland off the road to Santa Teresa. It has a mix of dorm-style and private rooms.

Hotel Oasis ★ This hotel is aptly named. Individual bungalows and studio apartments are spread around shady grounds, just a short walk from the beach and some of Malpaís's most popular surf breaks. The rooms themselves are simple in decor but are well-maintained and very fairly priced. Most feature exposed beam ceilings and varnished wood lattice work over the windows. All have a usable kitchenette (three-burner stove, toaster, minifridge, rice cooker, and coffeemaker), and those in the studios are outdoors. The bungalows are fab for families, with separate master and kids' rooms. However, only the two studios have air-conditioning. There's a small pool, and the owners are very hands-on and attentive.

Malpaís. www.oasis.cr. ✆ **2640-0259.** 8 units. $75–$105 double. **Amenities:** Small outdoor pool; free Wi-Fi.

Malpaís Surf Camp & Resort ★ This multifaceted, budget-conscious resort offers a wide range of rooms and prices. You can opt for everything from bunk-bed rooms with shared bathrooms to private poolside villas. You can even pitch a tent here. Budget-conscious surfers tend to fill the garden ranchos, which have crushed-stone floors and tree-trunk columns supporting corrugated plastic roofs. This same green roofing material is used as half-walls to divide up the ranchos into separate sleeping areas. On the other end of the spectrum, there are fully equipped villas with air-conditioning and contemporary appointments. A good-size, free-form pool sits at the center of the complex, which itself is about a 5-minute walk from the waves.

Malpaís. www.malpaissurfcamp.com. ✆ **2640-0031.** 16 units, 8 with shared bathroom. $10 per person, camping; $25 double with shared bathroom; $35 double with private bathroom and $65 villa. **Amenities:** Restaurant; bar; small exercise room; midsize outdoor pool; surfboard rental; free Wi-Fi.

Where to Eat

Mary's (www.maryscostarica.com; ✆ **2640-0153**) is a very popular open-air joint that features wood-oven baked pizzas and fresh seafood. It's toward the northern end of Malpaís. The fresh creative cooking at the **Beija Flor Resort** (www.facebook.com/beijaflorresort.malpais; ✆ **2640-1007**) is another good option in Malpaís.

At the Playa Carmen Commercial Center, at the crossroads at the entrance to town, you'll find a small food court with a wide range of options, including the bistro-style **Chop It—Holy Cow Burger ★★** (✆ **2640-0000**). Open just for lunch, it serves a range of salads, wraps, and justifiably popular burgers. Gluten-free buns are even offered. Another good option here is **Product C ★★** (www.product-c.com; ✆ **2640-1026**), a seafood retail outlet that also cooks up the daily catch, makes fresh *ceviche,* and serves fresh, farm-grown, local oysters. Just across the street, you'll find **The Bakery ★★** (✆ **2640-0560**), which serves an amazing array of fresh pastries and baked goods, along with sandwiches and pizzas.

On the far northern end of Playa Santa Teresa, **El Rey Patricio ★★** (www.elreypatricio.com; ✆ **2640-0248**) has tasty tapas, drinks, and a sunset view, and **Al Chile Viola ★** (✆ **2640-0433**) is a good Italian restaurant in town. Even farther, near the start of Playa Hermosa, **Koji ★★** (✆ **2640-0815**) is the area's most popular sushi joint.

INEXPENSIVE

Caracolas ★★ SEAFOOD/COSTA RICAN/MEXICAN This place would win major points for the view and ambience alone, but the food is super fresh and tasty, and it's a great value. The ceviche here is made daily with locally caught fish and seafood, and you can't go wrong with a grilled filet of dorado in garlic sauce. And while the fish tacos are really good, they might not be exactly what you'd expect, as they're served in a crispy fried flour tortilla, more like a *flauta.* As for the ambience, patrons dine at large communal tables under trees close to the water, or in a series of more intimate pop-up shade structures and rustic thatched-roof *palapas* spread around the sloping grounds. When you're finished with your meal, feel free to stretch out in one of the hammocks hung between the coconut palms. Caracolas is also a perfect choice for sunset cocktails and appetizers.

On the beach, about 1km south of the main crossroads in Malpaís. ✆ **2291-1470.** Main courses C4,950–C9,500. Daily 7am–10pm.

Organized Tours & Activities

If you decide to do anything here besides sunbathe on the beach and play in the waves, your options include nature hikes, horseback riding, ATV tours, scuba diving, and snorkeling, which most hotels can help arrange. Surfing is a major draw, with miles of beach breaks to choose from and a few points to boot. If you want to rent a board or take a lesson, try **Costa Rica Surf & SUP** (www.costaricasurfandsup.com; ✆ **2640-0328**), **Surfing Costa Rica Pura**

Vida (www.surfingcostaricapuravida.com; ✆ **8333-7825**), or **Del Soul Surf School** (www.surfvacationcostarica.com; ✆ **8878-0880**).

If you've gotten beat up by the waves, or are sore from paddling out, you'll find several excellent spas in town. The best and most extensive (and expensive) is at the **Florblanca Resort** (see above). But you might also check in with the **Pranamar Villas & Yoga Retreat** (see above), located on the beach, at the northern end of Santa Teresa.

For zipline adventures, head to **Canopy del Pacífico** (http://canopymalpais.com; ✆ **2640-0360;** $45), which is toward the southern end of Malpaís and just slightly inland. A 2-hour tour over the nearly 2km (1.2 miles) of cables touches down on 11 platforms, features two rappels, and offers good views of both the forest and the ocean below. Round-trip transportation from an area hotel is $5 per person.

For fishing, wildlife viewing and bird-watching, I highly recommend **Sapoa Adventures ★★** (www.sapoaadventures.com; ✆ **8996-9000**).

Nightlife

The most popular bar in the area is **Coco Loco ★** (no phone), right on the beach in Malpaís. It features a mix of live bands and DJs, with weekly reggae and Latin nights, as well as a monthly full moon party. Thursday nights in Santa Teresa belong to the punk-ska-reggae band that holds forth at **Kika** (✆ **2640-0408**). Also in Santa Teresa, **La Lora Amarilla** (✆ **2640-0134**) is a classic local nightspot that heats up on Saturday night, when the locals come to dance salsa and merengue.

THE NORTHERN ZONE

7

Costa Rica's northern zone is a fabulous destination for all manner of adventurers, naturalists, and down-to-earth travelers. The region is home to several prime ecotourist destinations, including the majestic **Arenal Volcano ★★** and the misty **Monteverde Cloud Forest Biological Reserve ★★★**. Changes in elevation create unique microclimates and ecosystems throughout the region. You'll find rainforests and cloud forests, jungle rivers and waterfalls, mountain lakes, lowland marshes, and an unbelievable wealth of birds and other wildlife. In addition to these natural wonders, this region provides an intimate glimpse into the rural heart and soul of Costa Rica. Small, isolated lodges flourish, and the region's many towns and villages remain predominantly small agricultural communities.

This area is also a must for adventure travelers. The northern zone has one of the best windsurfing spots in the world, on **Lake Arenal ★**, as well as excellent opportunities for mountain biking, hiking, canyoning, and river rafting. Zipline canopy tours and suspended forest bridges abound. And after you partake these adventure activities, you'll find soothing natural hot springs in the area where you can soak your tired muscles. Most travelers would do well to include some time spent in the northern zone on any trip to Costa Rica.

ARENAL VOLCANO ★★ & LA FORTUNA ★★

140km (87 miles) NW of San José; 61km (38 miles) E of Tilarán

In July 1968, Arenal Volcano, which had lain dormant for hundreds of years, surprised everybody by erupting with sudden violence. The nearby village of Tabacón was destroyed, and nearly 80 of its inhabitants were killed. At 1,607m (5,271 ft.) high, Arenal was for many decades afterward one of the world's most regularly active volcanoes. Sometime around December 2010, it entered into a relatively quiet phase. No one knows how long this will last. Still, rising to a near-perfect cone, the volcano itself remains majestic to gaze upon. And the area offers up a rich variety of primary

The Northern Zone

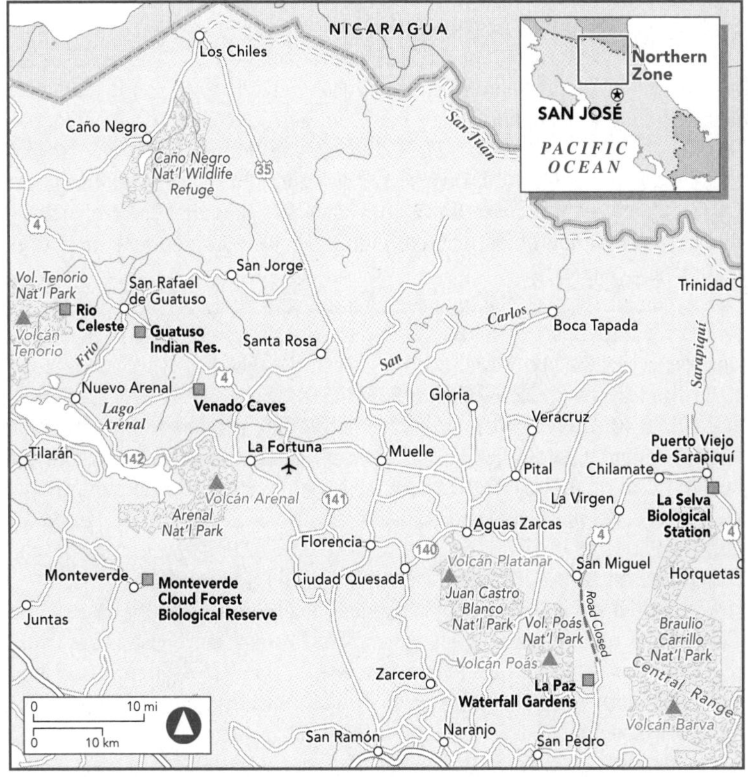

rainforests, rushing jungle rivers and waterfalls, lush natural hot springs, and a wide range of adventure activities.

Lying at the eastern foot of this natural spectacle is the town of **La Fortuna.** Once a humble little farming village, La Fortuna has become a magnet for travelers from around the world.

Essentials

ARRIVING **By Plane: Nature Air** (www.natureair.com; ✆ **800/235-9272** in the U.S. and Canada, or 2299-6000 in Costa Rica) and **Sansa** (www.flysansa.com; ✆ **877/767-2672** in the U.S. and Canada, or 2290-4100 in Costa Rica) each have one daily flight to Arenal/La Fortuna (airport code: FOR) from Juan Santamaría International Airport in San José (airport code: SJO). Fares range from $80 to $110 one-way. Nature Air also sometimes has direct flights between La Fortuna and Tortuguero, which eliminate a lot of driving and potentially long layovers.

The La Fortuna airstrip is actually in the small village of El Tanque, about a 15-minute drive from La Fortuna, and anywhere from 20 to 40 minutes from most of the popular area hotels. **Taxis** are sometimes waiting for arriving flights. If not, you can call one at © **2479-9605.** The fare to La Fortuna runs around C8,000–C15,000. Also, Nature Air can arrange to have a van waiting for you, for $62–$130 for up to six people depending upon the location of your hotel.

By Car: Several routes connect La Fortuna and San José. The most popular is to head west on the Inter-American Highway (CR1) from San José and then turn north at Naranjo, continuing north through Zarcero to Ciudad Quesada on CR141. From Ciudad Quesada, CR141 passes through Florencia, Jabillos, and Tanque on its way to La Fortuna. This route offers fab views of the San Carlos valley as you come down from Ciudad Quesada; Zarcero, with its topiary gardens and quaint church, is a good place to stop and snap a few photos (see chapter 5).

You can also stay on the Inter-American Highway (CR1) until San Ramón (west of Naranjo) and then head north through La Tigra on CR142. The travel time on any of the above routes is roughly 3 to 3½ hours.

By Bus: Buses (© **2255-0567** or 2255-4318) leave San José for La Fortuna at 6:30, 8:40, and 12:30am from the **Atlántico del Norte** bus station at Avenida 7 and 9 and Calle 12. The trip lasts 4 hours; the fare is C2,575. The bus you take might be labeled TILARÁN. Make sure it passes through Ciudad Quesada (also known as San Carlos). If so, it passes through La Fortuna; if not, you'll end up in Tilarán via the Inter-American Highway, passing through the Guanacaste town of Cañas, a long way from La Fortuna.

You can also take a bus from the same station to Ciudad Quesada (San Carlos) and transfer there to another bus to La Fortuna. These buses depart roughly every 40 minutes between 5am and 7:30pm. The fare for the 3-hour trip is C1,860. Local buses between Ciudad Quesada and La Fortuna run regularly through the day, although the schedule changes frequently, depending on demand. The trip lasts an hour; the fare is C1,300.

Buses depart La Fortuna for San José roughly every 2 hours between 5am and 6pm; in most instances, you will have to transfer in Ciudad Quesada to one of the frequent buses to San José.

boats, HORSES & TAXIS

You can travel between La Fortuna and Monteverde by boat and taxi, or on a combination of boat, horseback, and taxi. A 10- to 20-minute boat ride across Lake Arenal cuts out hours of driving around its shores. From La Fortuna to the put-in point is about a 25-minute taxi ride. It's about a 1½-hour four-wheel-drive taxi ride between the Río Chiquito dock on the other side of Lake Arenal and Santa Elena. These trips can be arranged in either direction for between $30 and $50 per person.

You can also add on a horseback ride on the Santa Elena/Monteverde side of the lake. Several routes and rides are offered. The steepest heads up the mountains and through the forest to the town of San Gerardo, only a 30-minute car ride from Santa Elena. Other routes throw in shorter sections of horseback riding along the lakeside lowlands. With the horseback ride, this trip runs around $85 per person.

Gray Line (www.graylinecostarica.com; ✆ **800/719-3105** in the U.S. and Canada, or 2220-2126 in Costa Rica) and **Interbus** (www.interbusonline.com; ✆ **4031-0888**) both have two daily buses leaving San José for La Fortuna. The fare is around $50. Both companies will pick you up at most San José-area hotels. And both companies also run routes from La Fortuna with connections to most other major destinations in Costa Rica.

CITY LAYOUT As you enter La Fortuna from the east, you'll see the massive volcano directly in front of you. The main road into town, CR142, passes through the center of La Fortuna and then out toward Tabacón and the volcano. La Fortuna is only a few streets wide, with almost all the hotels, restaurants, and shops clustered along the main street and around the small central park.

GETTING AROUND If you don't have a car, you'll need to either take a cab or go on an organized tour if you want to visit the hot springs or view the volcano. La Fortuna has tons of **taxis** (you can flag one down practically anywhere, or dial ✆ **2479-9605**), and a line of them is always ready and waiting along the main road beside the central park. Another alternative is to rent a car when you get here. **Alamo** (www.alamocostarica.com; ✆ **2479-9090**) has an office in downtown La Fortuna.

FAST FACTS You'll find several information and tour-booking offices, as well as a couple of pharmacies, general stores, banks, and laundry facilities within a few blocks of the town's central park and church. If you need assistance, call the Tourist Police at ✆ **2479-7257.**

ORGANIZED TOURS **Desafío Expeditions ★★** (www.desafiocostarica.com; ✆ **855/818-0020** in the U.S. and Canada, or 2479-0020 in Costa Rica), **Jacamar Tours** (www.arenaltours.com; ✆ **2479-9767**), and **Pure Trek Canyoning ★★** (www.puretrek.com; ✆ **866/569-5723** in the U.S. and Canada, or 2479-1313 in Costa Rica) are the main tour operators in the area. All offer most of the tours listed in this section, as well as fishing and sightseeing excursions on the lake, and transfers to and from other destinations around Costa Rica.

La Fortuna Hotels

INEXPENSIVE

Right in La Fortuna, you'll find plenty of budget options. One of the better choices is **Arenal Backpackers Resort ★** (www.arenalbackpackersresort.com; ✆ **2479-7000**), which bills itself as a "five-star hostel" for its large pool, free Wi-Fi, and volcano views. It has both shared-bathroom dorm rooms and more upscale private rooms.

Hotel La Fortuna ★ This used to be a simple, two-story, wood-and-zinc hostel, but a fire changed all that, and now it's a modern, five-story hotel. The best rooms face west and have volcano-view balconies. Of these, those on the top two floors are the best, as their views aren't blocked by Las Colinas and other nearby buildings. Inside, the rooms are fairly plain, with white tile floors and locally made furnishings that show a hint of Japanese aesthetics, with their smooth, square lines. The restaurant here is open only for breakfast, but

Arenal National Park & La Fortuna

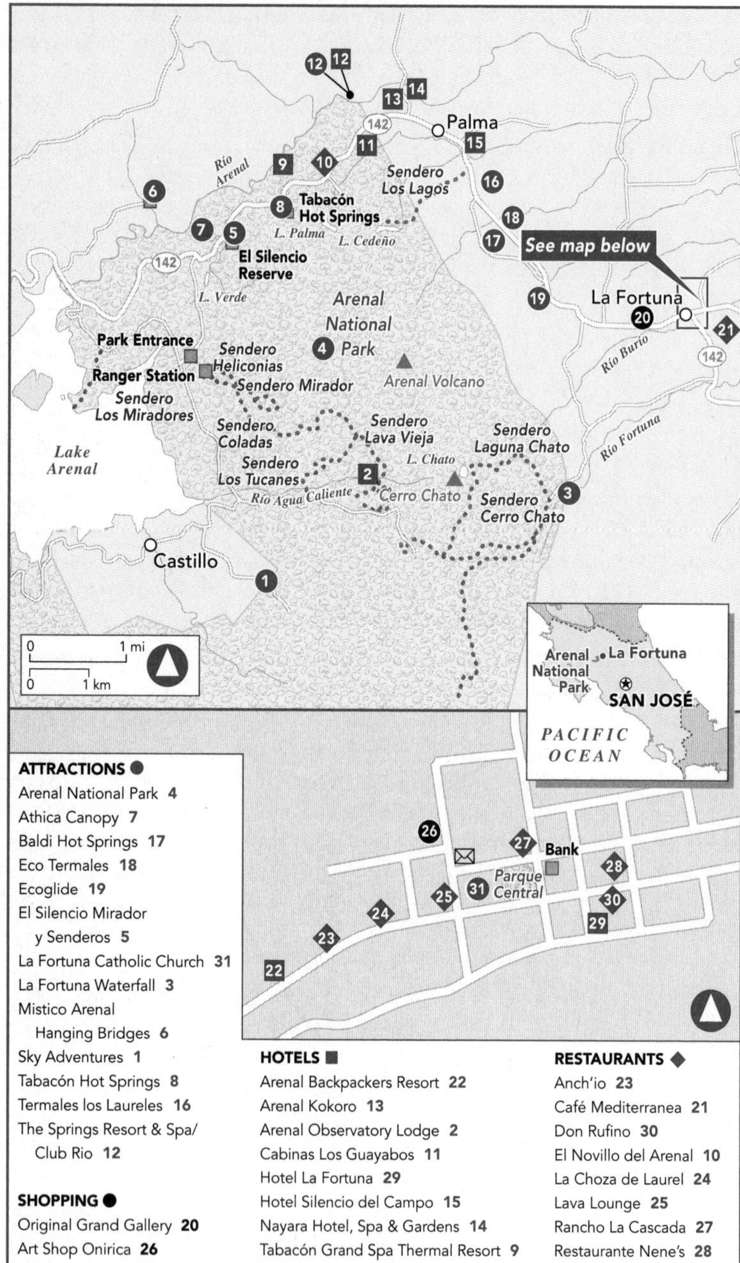

you're right in the heart of downtown and close to all of the restaurants and shops of La Fortuna.

1 block south of the gas station, downtown La Fortuna. www.lafortunahotel.com. ✆ **415/315-9595** in the U.S. and Canada, or 2479-9197 in Costa Rica. 40 units. $55–$90 double. Rates include breakfast and taxes. **Amenities:** Restaurant; free Wi-Fi.

Hotels Near the Volcano

While La Fortuna is the major gateway town to Arenal Volcano, many of the best places to stay are on the road between La Fortuna and the national park.

EXPENSIVE

Nayara Hotel, Spa & Gardens ★★★ Intimate, romantic, and pampering: Those are the words that come to mind when describing Nayara. It's a special place, with lodgings in large and luxurious private bungalows, with wide volcano-facing balconies, each with a large, two-person Jacuzzi, and both an indoor and garden shower. Units 1 through 5 are closest to the restaurants and pool and thus the least isolated and private. Around the bungalows are well-tended tropical gardens (wonderful for bird-watching); trails lead through the property and down to a river. The dining options are varied and all are well executed, from the classy wine and tapas bar to the Peruvian-influenced sushi bar. However, unlike most of the other offerings in this price category, the hotel does not have a natural hot springs on-site. In its adjoining property, **Nayara Springs Resort** (www.nayarasprings.com), there is a natural spring-fed hot pool. It's reached via a long and high suspension bridge, and populated with even larger villas, decorated with lovely Balinese-style pieces. Each comes with a hot, natural, spring-fed private pool.

On the main road btw. La Fortuna and Lake Arenal. www.arenalnayara.com. ✆ **888/332-2961** in the U.S. and Canada, or 2479-1600 in Costa Rica. 66 units. $320–$406 double. Rates includes buffet breakfast. **Amenities:** 4 restaurants; 2 bars; small spa; exercise room; 2 large outdoor pools; 3 Jacuzzis; room service; free Wi-Fi.

Tabacón Grand Spa Thermal Resort ★★★ You might want to stay here for the fab hot springs, even if the rooms were dark, dank and dingy—but they're not. Far from it. Guestrooms are large and well-maintained, with heavy, dark-stained wood furnishings and at least one wall of windows or sliding glass doors. Not all the rooms have volcano views, and the hotel maddeningly refuses to guarantee a volcano-view room. On the plus side, management has a deep commitment to locally sustainable development and environmental conservation. Plus, staying at the resort gets you unlimited access to the impressive Tabacón hot springs complex, as well as slightly extended hours and access to a private, hotel-guests-only section of the hot springs dubbed Shangri-La. If you take into account the hefty entrance fee to the springs, this place is practically a bargain.

On the main road btw. La Fortuna and Lake Arenal. www.tabacon.com. ✆ **855/822-2266** in the U.S. and Canada, 2479-2099 for reservations in San José, or 2479-2000 at the resort. 102 units. $214–$467 double. Rates include breakfast and taxes. **Amenities:** 2 restaurants; 3 bars; exercise room; Jacuzzi; pool w/swim-up bar; room service; hot springs and spa facilities across the street; free Wi-Fi.

MODERATE

Arenal Kokoro ★ This place arguably gets you the best bang for your buck in the area. The spacious individual "eco-cabinas" all have volcano views and small private balconies. The more economical "casona" rooms are a tad more rustic and housed in two-story blocks of four rooms. Inside you'll find a mix of locally milled wood-plank paneling and painted concrete walls—some with handpainted murals of birds, butterflies, and fanciful trees. The hotel has a pool, a small, natural hot springs complex and spa, and extensive and lush gardens and grounds. The staff is very friendly and helpful.

On the main road btw. La Fortuna and Lake Arenal. www.arenalkokoro.com. ✆ **800/649-5913** in the U.S. and Canada, or 2479-1222 in Costa Rica. 30 units. $115–$140 double. Rates include breakfast. **Amenities:** Restaurant; bar; outdoor pool; small hot springs complex and spa; free Wi-Fi.

Arenal Observatory Lodge ★★ Originally a scientific observatory associated with the Smithsonian to monitor volcanic activity, this is one of the closest hotels to the Arenal Volcano. The views from the rooms, restaurant, and common areas are simply spectacular. The main dining room features a massive wall of glass, with a "V"-shaped peak that perfectly frames the volcano. The lodge is a bit isolated from the hustle and bustle of this busy region, and is graced with a large, private reserve and an excellent network of trails bordering the national park. The best rooms and views are found in the suites and private villas below the main lodge building. Given the remote location, you'll want a rental car if staying here.

On the flanks of Arenal Volcano. To get here, head to the national park entrance, stay on the dirt road past the entrance, and follow the signs to the Observatory Lodge. A 4WD vehicle is recommended but not essential. www.arenalobservatorylodge.com. ✆ **877/804-7732** in the U.S. and Canada, 2290-7011 for reservations in San José, or 2479-1070 at the lodge. 48 units. $104–$128 double. Rates include breakfast and taxes. **Amenities:** Restaurant; bar; Jacuzzi; midsize outdoor pool; small spa; free Wi-Fi.

Hotel Silencio del Campo ★★ This friendly, family-run resort features a small collection of individual cabins oriented to take in the volcano view. All are quite spacious, with red tile floors, wooden walls, A/C, TVs, and mini-fridges. They are a little bit too close together, but large tropical flowers and palms planted all around give them some sense of privacy. Try for one farthest from the main road and parking area. The best feature here is the lovely pool and hot springs complex. This is by far the best hotel hot springs complex in this price range. Service is extremely personalized and attentive.

On the main road btw. La Fortuna and Lake Arenal. www.hotelsilenciodelcampo.com. ✆ **2479-7055.** 23 units. $167–$184 double. Rates include breakfast and taxes. **Amenities:** Restaurant; bar; pool and hot springs complex; free Wi-Fi.

INEXPENSIVE

If you have a car, **Cabinas Los Guayabos ★** (www.cabinaslosguayabos.com; ✆ **2479-1444**) is a good value, with views and a location that rival the pricier lodgings listed above.

Where to Eat

Dining in La Fortuna is nowhere near as inspiring as the area's natural attractions, but given the town's booming tourist business, options abound. Popular places in downtown La Fortuna include **Rancho La Cascada** (✆ **2479-9145**), **La Choza de Laurel** (✆ **2479-7063**), and **Restaurante Nene's** (✆ **2479-9192**) for Tico fare. For good pizza and Italian cuisine, try either **Café Mediterranea** (✆ **2479-7497**), just outside town on the road to the La Fortuna waterfall, or **Anch'io** (✆ **2479-7560**), just beyond Las Brasitas, on the road toward Tabacón and the national park entrance.

Don Rufino ★★ COSTA RICAN Don Rufino is the semiofficial social center of town, with a popular open-air bar overlooking the main street. The decor has rustic touches, but the menu takes Costa Rican fare and adds a lot of fusion flourishes. In addition to juicy steaks and local staples, dishes range from Szechuan chicken to Cajun shrimp pasta. Prices are on the high end but worth it.

Main road through downtown La Fortuna, 2 blocks east of the church. www.donrufino.com. ✆ **2479-9997.** Main courses $10–$50. Daily 11am–10:30pm. Reservations recommended during high season.

El Novillo del Arenal ★ COSTA RICAN/STEAKHOUSE If you want local steaks or grilled chicken, but don't need the fancier ambience or accouterments of the other places listed here, this is your spot. Portions are hearty and the price is right. The restaurant is a simple affair built on a plain concrete slab under a very high, open-air, corrugated-zinc-roof structure. When it's clear, you get an excellent view of the volcano.

On the road to Tabacón, 10km (6¼ miles) outside La Fortuna. ✆ **2479-1910.** Main courses C4,000–C12,000. Daily 11am–10pm.

Lava Lounge ★ INTERNATIONAL California meets Costa Rica at this popular downtown restaurant. Lava Lounge's menu ranges from glorified bar food—nachos, quesadillas, wings, and wraps—to a hearty Costa Rican *casado,* with dishes such as a thick-cut grilled pork chop or coconut shrimp with spicy mango salsa quite well done. Wooden picnic tables with bench seating fill the main dining room, so you might have to share your table.

Downtown La Fortuna, on the main road. www.lavaloungecostarica.com. ✆ **2479-7365.** Main courses $11–$25. Daily 11am–11pm.

Where to Stay & Eat Farther Afield

All the hotels listed are at least a half-hour drive from La Fortuna and the volcano. Most, if not all, offer both night and day tours to Arenal and Tabacón, but they also attract guests with their own natural charms.

MODERATE

South of La Fortuna

Finca Luna Nueva Lodge ★★ (www.fincalunanuevalodge.com; ✆ **800/903-3470** in the U.S. and Canada, or 2468-4006 in Costa Rica) is a fascinating sustainable farm and tourism project, and proud advocate for the international "slow food" movement.

Chachagua Rainforest Hotel & Hacienda ★★ This boutique rainforest lodge is located on 100 hectares (247 acres) of land, much of which is primary rainforest. While the rooms are certainly comfortable and cozy, consider splurging on one of the individual wooden bungalows, which are much roomier, have TVs and Jacuzzi tubs, and come with their own large, covered-deck area. Throughout you'll find lots of varnished hardwood, and handsome headboards on the beds studded with sections of hardwood tree trunks. The large central pool here is fed by a natural spring and kept chemical-free. The lodge has opened miles of excellent trails, leading through thick wildlife-rich rainforest, with waterfalls, rivers, and jungle lagoons to explore. It also offers a host of adventure tours and guided activities. The small village of Chachagua sits 10km (6 miles) south of La Fortuna, on the road to San Ramón. The lodge itself is another 2km (1¼ miles) along a dirt road from the village. The entrance is well-marked and easy to spot.

Chachagua, Alajuela. www.chachaguarainforesthotel.com. ✆ **2468-1011.** 28 units. $130–$160 double. Rates include breakfast and taxes. **Amenities:** Restaurant; bar; concierge, lounge area, large outdoor pool; mountain bike rental; free Wi-Fi.

Villa Blanca Cloud Forest & Spa ★★ Once the country retreat and family-run hotel of former Costa Rican President Rodrigo Carazo Odio, this beautiful mountain lodge features a series of individual little houses, or *casitas,* with clay-tile roofs, whitewashed stucco walls, rustic tile floors, and open-beam and cane ceilings. Each *casita* has a working wood-burning fireplace, which comes in handy in the cool, moist climate. The deluxe *casitas* and suites come with their own Jacuzzi tubs. The hotel's private reserve borders the Los Angeles Cloud Forest Reserve, a fascinating area and ecosystem, very similar to that found in Monteverde. In fact, some visitors have spotted the elusive resplendent quetzal here. This lodge has earned the maximum "5 Leaves" in the CST Certification for Sustainable Tourism program. To reach the hotel, you must first drive to the mountain city of San Ramón on the Inter-American Highway (CR1), northwest of San José. From here, drive north on CR142 toward Los Angeles, following signs to Villa Blanca.

San Ramón, Alajuela. www.villablanca-costarica.com. ✆ **877/256-8399** in the U.S. and Canada, or 2461-0300 in Costa Rica. 35 units. $184–$203 double. Rates include taxes. **Amenities:** Restaurant; bar; small spa; free Wi-Fi.

North of La Fortuna

Caño Negro Natural Lodge ★ Serious bird-watchers, nature lovers, and fishermen should consider this very remote lodging, in the tiny lagoon-side village of Caño Negro. Bordering the area's namesake Caño Negro Wildlife Refuge, this simple place offers easy access to the lakes, lagoons, and waterways of this beautiful, low-lying wetlands area (one of the best places in the region to spot a jabiru stork). The rooms themselves are roomy, clean, and cool, with large sliding glass doors opening onto a small patio overlooking the well-tended gardens. To get there, drive toward Los Chiles, and just before reaching the town of Los Chiles, follow the well-marked signs for Caño Negro Natural Lodge and the wildlife refuge. The final 18km (11 miles) is on a rugged dirt road.

Caño Negro. www.canonegrolodge.com. ✆ **2471-1426** in Costa Rica. 42 units. $111–$124 double. Rates include breakfast and taxes. **Amenities:** Restaurant; bar; midsize outdoor pool; free Wi-Fi.

Exploring Arenal Volcano & La Fortuna

It's worth a quick visit to tour the town's **Catholic Church,** a contemporary church designed by famous Costa Rican artist Teodorico Quirós. It features a soaring concrete front steeple and clock tower.

EXPERIENCING THE VOLCANO ★★★

As mentioned, the Arenal Volcano has been quiet since December 2010, with no loud eruptions or pyroclastic blasts. Still, the actual volcano remains a stunning sight, and the natural park and surrounding trails and activities make this a fabulous destination. That said, Arenal is surrounded by cloud forests and rainforests, and the volcano's cone is often socked in by clouds and fog. Many people come to Arenal and never see the exposed cone. ***Note:*** Although it's counterintuitive, the rainy season is often a better time to see the exposed cone of Arenal Volcano. For some reason, during the dry season the volcano can often be shrouded for days at a time. The bottom line is that catching a glimpse of the volcano's cone is never a sure thing.

Despite its current state of dormancy, climbing Arenal Volcano remains illegal. Over the years, many daredevil climbers have lost their lives, and others have been severely injured. This is still a very "alive" volcano, with steam vents and a molten core.

ARENAL NATIONAL PARK ★★

Arenal National Park (✆ **2461-8499;** daily 8am–3pm; $15/person) constitutes an area of more than 2,880 hectares (7,114 acres), which includes the viewing and parking areas closest to the volcano. The trails through forest and over old lava flows inside the park are gorgeous and fun. (Be careful climbing on those volcanic boulders, though.) The principal trail inside the park, **Sendero Coladas (Lava Flow Trail) ★★**, is just under 2km (1.25 miles) long and passes through secondary forest and open savanna. At the end of the trail, a short natural stairway takes you to a broad, open lava field left in the wake of a massive 1992 eruption. Scrambling over the cooled lava is a real treat, but be careful, as the rocks can be sharp in places. Many spots throughout the park offer great views of the volcano, but the closest view can be found at **El Mirador (The Lookout) ★**, where you not only can see the volcano better, but also can hear it rumble and roar on occasion. From the parking lot near the trailhead for the Lava Flow Trail, you have the option of hiking or driving the 1km (.6 mile) to El Mirador.

Organized Tours

Aside from the impressive volcanic activity, the area around Arenal Volcano is packed with other natural wonders.

The best of the area's tour operators is **Original Arenal ATV** (www.original arenalatv.com; ✆ **2479-7522**), which offers a 2½-hour ATV tour along the area around the lake and national park. The cost is $99 per person, or $130 for two people riding tandem.

You have numerous ways to get up into the forest canopy here. Perhaps the simplest is to hike the trails and bridges of **Mistico Arenal Hanging Bridges ★** (www.misticopark.com; ✆ **2479-1170;** daily 7:30am–4pm; $36 admission). Located just over the Lake Arenal dam, this attraction is a complex of gentle trails and suspension bridges through a beautiful tract of primary forest. Night tours depart at 5:30pm every evening.

Another option is the **Sky Tram ★★** (www.skyadventures.travel; ✆ **844/468-6759** in the U.S., or 2479-4100 in Costa Rica), an open gondola-style ride that begins near the shores of Lake Arenal and rises up, providing excellent views of the lake and volcano. From here, you hike a series of trails and suspended bridges. In the end, you can hike down, take the gondola, or strap on a harness and ride the zipline down to the bottom. The **zipline tour** features several very long and very fast sections, with impressive views of the lake and volcano. The cost is $93 for the combined tram ride up, a guided hike to the trails and hanging bridges, and the zipline tour back down. It's $44 to ride the tram round-trip. The tram runs daily from 7:30am to 3pm. Sky Tram also has a butterfly and orchid garden.

Ecoglide ★ (www.arenalecoglide.com; ✆ **2479-7120**) and **Athica Canopy** (✆ **2479-1405**) are two other good zipline operations close to La Fortuna.

Canyoning is an adventure sport that consists of hiking through and alongside a jungle river, punctuated with periodic rappels through and alongside the faces of rushing waterfalls. **Pure Trek Canyoning ★★★** (www.puretrek.com; ✆ **866/569-5723** in the U.S. and Canada, or 2479-1313 in Costa Rica; $101/person) and **Desafío Adventure Company ★★★** (www.desafiocostarica.com; ✆ **855/818-0020** in the U.S. and Canada, or 2479-0020 in Costa Rica; $99/person) are the primary operators in this area. Pure Trek's trip is probably better for first-timers and families with kids, while Desafío's tour is just a bit more rugged and adventurous. Both companies offer various combination full-day excursions, mixing canyoning with other adventures, and tend to have two to three daily departures.

In 2015, Desafío added a new, more extreme canyoning option called **Gravity Falls ★★★**. Although it features only one major rappel, this tour consists of a series of leaps off of high rocks into river pools below. The cost is $125.

With Lake Arenal just around the corner, fishing is a popular activity here. The big fish to catch is *guapote,* a Central American species of rainbow bass. However, you can also book **fishing trips** to Caño Negro, where snook, tarpon, and other game fish can be stalked. Most hotels and adventure-tour companies can arrange fishing excursions. Or try GetMyBoat.com. Costs run around $150 to $250 per boat, and a full day goes for around $250 to $500.

El Silencio Mirador y Senderos ★ (www.miradorelsilencio.com; ✆ **2479-9900;** daily 7am–7pm; $8) is a great place for **hiking** outside the national park. This private reserve has four well-marked and well-groomed trails, one of which takes you to a patch of the 1968 lava flow. There's a pretty pond and excellent views of the volcano.

For a more strenuous hike, climb **Cerro Chato ★★**, a dormant volcanic cone on the flank of Arenal with a beautiful little crater lake. **Desafío Adventures Company ★★** (www.desafiocostarica.com; ✆ **855/818-0020** in the U.S. and Canada, or 2479-0020 in Costa Rica) leads a 5- to 6-hour hike for $85, including lunch, though you can also do it on your own from either La Fortuna Waterfall or from Arenal Observatory Lodge.

Horseback riding is a popular activity in this area, with scores of good rides on dirt backroads and through open fields and dense rainforest. Volcano and lake views come with the terrain on most rides. Horseback trips to the La Fortuna waterfall are perhaps the most popular, but the horse will get you only to the entrance; from there, you'll have to hike a bit. A horseback ride to the falls should cost between $30 and $45, including the entrance fee. You can also book with **Cabalgata Don Tobías** (www.cabalgatadontobias.com; ✆ **2479-1780**), which runs a 2½-hour tour on its private land—a mix of farmland and forest, with terrific views of the volcano. Two tours leave daily at 8:30am and 1:30pm; cost is $65 per person.

Leading the list of side attractions in the area is the impressive **La Fortuna Waterfall ★★** (www.arenaladifort.com; ✆ **2479-8338;** daily 8am–5pm; $11 entrance), about 5.5km (3½ miles) outside of town in a dense jungle setting. A sign in town points the way to the road out to the falls. You can drive or hike to just within viewing distance. It's another 15- to 20-minute hike down a steep and often muddy path to the pool formed by the waterfall. The hike back up will take slightly longer. You can swim, but stay away from the turbulent water at the base of the falls—several people have drowned here. Instead, check out and enjoy the calm pool just around the bend, or join the locals at the popular swimming hole under the bridge on the paved road, just after the turnoff for the road up to the falls. It's also possible to reach the falls by horseback. Most tour operators in town, as well as the waterfall folks themselves, offer this option for around $45. The tour generally lasts around 3 to 4 hours.

This region is very well suited for **mountain biking.** Rides range in difficulty from moderate to extremely challenging. You can combine a day on a mountain bike with a visit to one or more of the popular attractions here. **Bike Arenal ★** (www.bikearenal.com; ✆ **866/465-4114** in the U.S. and Canada, or 2479-9020 in Costa Rica) offers top-notch bikes and equipment and a wide range of tour possibilities. Hardcore bikers come in March for the **Vuelta al Lago ★** (www.vueltaallagoarenal.com; ✆ **2695-5297**), a 2-day race around the lake.

For adventurous **whitewater rafting and kayaking tours** of the area, check out **Desafío Expeditions ★★** (www.desafiocostarica.com; ✆ **855/818-0020** in the U.S. and Canada, or 2479-0020 in Costa Rica) or **Wave Expeditions ★★** (www.waveexpeditions.com; ✆ **888/224-6105** in the U.S. and Canada, or 2479-7262 in Costa Rica). Both companies offer daily raft rides of Class I to II, III, and IV to V on different sections of the Toro, Peñas Blancas,

What's SUP?

Stand-Up Paddling (SUP) is a booming sport and fitness craze, and you can practice it on lovely Lake Arenal, in the shadow of the lake's namesake volcano, with Desafío Expeditions (see above).

and Sarapiquí rivers. If you want a wet and personal ride, try Desafío's tour in inflatable kayaks, or "duckies." For families, a gentle safari float on the Peñas Blancas may be the best bet. A half-day float trip on a nearby river costs around $70 per person; a full day of rafting on some rougher water costs around $89 per person, depending on what section of river you ride. Both companies also offer mountain biking and local guided trips.

La Fortuna is a great base for a day trip to the **Caño Negro National Wildlife Refuge ★**. This vast network of marshes and rivers (particularly the Río Frío) is 100km (62 miles) north of La Fortuna near the town of Los Chiles. The refuge is best known for its abundance of bird life, including roseate spoonbills, jabiru storks, herons, and egrets, but you can also see caimans and crocodiles. Bird-watchers should not miss this refuge, although keep in mind that the main lake dries up in the dry season (mid-Apr to Nov), which reduces the number of wading birds. Full-day tours to Caño Negro average between $70 and $80 per person. However, most of the tours run out of La Fortuna that are billed as Caño Negro never really enter the refuge but instead ply sections of the nearby Río Frío, which features similar wildlife and ecosystems. If you're interested in staying in this area and really visiting the refuge, head to Caño Negro Natural Lodge (p. 148).

You can also visit the **Venado Caverns ★★**, a 45-minute drive away. In addition to plenty of stalactites, stalagmites, and other limestone formations, you'll see bats and unique cave fish and crabs. This tour is not for the claustrophobic, and includes wading through a river, scrambling over rocks and sliding through some tight squeezes. This cave system is quite extensive, although tourists have access to only around 10 chambers. Still, these are quite striking, with impressive stone formations and ceilings over 100 feet high in places. Tours here cost between $65 and $80, including the guide and headlamps. Be prepared to get wet and muddy.

All tour agencies and hotel tour desks can arrange trips to Caño Negro and Venado Caverns.

Especially for Kids

Located a couple of miles outside La Fortuna, the **Ecocentro Danaus ★** (www.ecocentrodanaus.com; ✆ **2479-7019;** daily 8am–4pm; admission $17 with tour, $12 for self-guided visit) is a private biological reserve and sustainable tourism project, which offers educational and engaging tours. Among the attractions here are a butterfly garden and reproduction center, botanical and medicinal plant gardens, and a small museum honoring the local Maleku indigenous culture. Night tours ($37) are offered by reservation. Children 5 to 10 get a 50 percent discount, and children 4 and under are free.

A SOOTHING SOAK IN hot springs

Tabacón Grand Spa Thermal Resort ★★★ (www.tabacon.com; ✆ **2519-1900;** daily 10am–10pm) is the most luxurious, extensive, and expensive spot in the area to soak in hot springs. A series of variously sized pools, fed by natural springs, are spread out among sumptuous gardens. One of the stronger streams flows over a sculpted waterfall, with a rock ledge underneath that provides a perfect place to sit and receive a water massage. The extensive grounds are worth exploring, but the pools and springs closest to the volcano are the hottest. The resort also has an excellent spa, offering professional massages, mud masks, and other treatments, as well as yoga classes (appointments required). Most of the treatments are conducted in pretty open-air gazebos. The spa here also has several sweat lodges, based on a Native American traditional design. A full-service restaurant, garden grill, and several bars round out the offerings here.

Admission is $60 for adults and $10 for children 11 and under. A range of packages, including meals, are available. The pools are busiest between 2 and 6pm. After 6pm, you can enter for $45, not including meals. Management enforces a policy of limiting visitors, so reservations are recommended.

Baldi Hot Springs Hotel Resort & Spa (www.baldihotsprings.cr; ✆ **2479-2190;** $34 admission) are the first hot springs you'll come to as you drive from La Fortuna toward Tabacón. This place has grown substantially over the years, with many different pools, slides, and bars and restaurants spread around the expansive grounds. Baldi has more of a party vibe than other spots, with loud music blaring at some of the swim-up bars.

Just across the street from Baldi Hot Springs is the entrance of **Eco Termales ★★★** (www.ecotermalesfortuna.cr; ✆ **2479-8787;** $34 admission). Smaller and more intimate than Tabacón, this series of pools amid dense forest and gardens is almost as picturesque and luxurious, though it has far fewer pools, lacks a view of the volcano, and offers much less extensive spa services. Eco Termales runs three time periods daily—10am to 1pm, 1pm to 5pm, and 5pm to 9pm—and reservations are highly recommended, as admissions are limited to make sure the pools don't get crowded.

Termales Los Laureles (www.termaleslosl aureles.com; ✆ **2479-1395**) is located between Baldi and Eco Termales and Tabacón. This spot has the area's most local feel and is by far the most economical, charging just C6,000 for adults.

You can also enjoy the hot springs, pools, and facilities at the **Springs Resort & Spa ★★.** In addition to the main pools by the hotel, it has a few more at a beautiful riverfront area about 1km away. The Springs is open to day visitors from 8:30am to 10pm, and admission is $60 per person.

Finally, if you like your water hot, fast, and free, head to Río Chollín, a rushing river of hot water open to the public right next to Tabacón. Across from the main entrance to Tabacón, where you can park your car in its roadside spaces, walk downhill through some yellow barriers meant to keep out vehicles and you'll find the river.

Along the banks of the Arenal River, **Club Río ★★** (www.thespringscostarica.com; ✆ **954/727-8333** in the U.S., or 2401-3313 in Costa Rica; 2-day pass $99 adults, $75 for kids 12 and under) is a wonderful playground for parents and kids alike. You can go tubing on the river, ride a horse through the forest trails, visit the midsize zoo, and take a shot at the three-story climbing wall. There's also a series of naturally fed hot springs sculpted alongside the river, as well as a restaurant. It's part of the **Springs Resort & Spa,** but you don't have to stay at the resort to enjoy the activities and facilities here. The pass gets you access to the facilities and two of the above-mentioned adventure activities, as well as a full lunch and free run of all the pools and waterslides at the resort itself.

Finally, the newest attraction on the block is the **Kalambu Hot Springs & Water Park ★** (www.kalambu.com; ✆ **2479-0170;** daily 9am–10pm; $32 adults, $16 children). While most of the other hot springs in the area might have a waterslide or two, this place is a true water park, with several large waterslides and a massive and very entertaining children's play area and pools. The latter includes a giant bucket that is constantly filled and then dumped on everyone below. There are also a few quieter pool and hot springs areas. If you enter after 5pm, the entrance is $20 adult and $10 children.

Shopping

La Fortuna is chock-full of souvenir shops selling standard tourist fare. However, the town also has an authentic crafts shop, **Original Grand Gallery** (✆ **8946-0928**). This local artisan and his family produce sculptures in a variety of styles, specializing in faces, many of them larger than a typical home's front door. You can also find a host of animal figures, ranging in style from purely representational to rather abstract. To get there: As you leave the town of La Fortuna toward Tabacón, keep your eye on the right-hand side of the road. When you see a massive collection of wood sculptures, slow down. **Art Shop Onirica** (✆ **2479-7589**), located next to La Fortuna's post office, is another good shop, featuring original oil paintings and acrylics, as well as one-off jewelry and jade pieces.

ALONG THE SHORES OF LAKE ARENAL ★

200km (124 miles) NW of San José; 20km (12 miles) NW of Monteverde; 70km (43 miles) SE of Liberia

Despite its many charms, this remains one of the least developed tourism regions in Costa Rica. Lake Arenal, the largest lake in Costa Rica, is the centerpiece here. The long, beautiful lake is surrounded by rolling hills that are partly pastured and partly forested. Loads of adventures are available both on the lake and in the surrounding hills and forests. While the towns of Tilarán and Nuevo Arenal remain quiet rural communities, several excellent hotels spread out along the shores of the lake.

Locals here used to curse the winds, which often come blasting across this end of the lake at 60 knots or greater. However, since the first sailboarders caught wind of Lake Arenal's combination of warm, fresh water, steady gusts, and spectacular scenery, that's changed. Even if you aren't a fanatical sailboarder, you might enjoy hanging out by the lake, hiking in the nearby forests, riding a mountain bike on dirt farm roads and one-track trails, and catching glimpses of Arenal Volcano.

The lake's other claim to fame is its rainbow-bass fishing. These fighting fish are known in Central America as *guapote* and are large members of the cichlid family. Their sharp teeth and bellicose nature make them a real challenge.

Essentials

ARRIVING **By Car:** From San José, you can either take the Inter-American Highway (CR1) north all the way from San José to Cañas, or first head west out of San José on the San José–Caldera Highway (CR27). When you reach Caldera, follow the signs to Puntarenas and the Inter-American Highway (CR1). You will actually follow signs for Liberia and San José, which are, in fact, leading you to the unmarked entrance to CR1. This road (CR23) ends when it hits the Inter-American Highway. You'll want to pass under the bridge and follow the on-ramp, which will put you on the highway heading north. This latter route is a faster and flatter drive, with no windy mountain switchbacks to contend with. In Cañas, turn east on CR142 toward Tilarán. The drive takes 3 to 4 hours. If you're continuing on to Nuevo Arenal, follow the signs in town, which will put you on the road that skirts the shore of the lake. Nuevo Arenal is about a half-hour drive from Tilarán. You can also drive here from La Fortuna, along a scenic road that winds around the lake. From La Fortuna, it's approximately 1 hour to Nuevo Arenal and 1½ hours to Tilarán.

By Bus: Transportes Tilarán buses (✆ **2222-3854**) leave San José for Tilarán roughly five times throughout the day between 7:30am and 6:30pm from Calle 20 and Avenida 3. The trip lasts from 4 to 5½ hours, depending on road conditions; the fare is C4,400.

Morning and afternoon buses connect **Puntarenas** to Tilarán. The ride takes about 3 hours; the fare is C1,300.

The daily bus from **Monteverde** (Santa Elena) leaves at 7am. The fare for the 2½-hour trip is C1,150.

Buses from **La Fortuna** leave for Tilarán daily at 8am and 12:15 and 5:30pm, returning at 7am and 12:20 and 4:30pm. The trip takes around 2 to 3 hours; the fare is C2,300.

Direct buses to San José leave from Tilarán beginning at 5am. Buses to Puntarenas leave at 6am and 1pm daily. The bus to Santa Elena (Monteverde) leaves daily at 12:30pm. Buses also leave regularly for Cañas, and can be caught heading north or south along the Inter-American Highway.

GETTING AROUND Both Tilarán and Nuevo Arenal are very small towns, and you can easily walk most places in the compact city centers. If you need a taxi to get to a lodge on Lake Arenal, call **Taxis Unidos Tilarán** (✆ **2695-5324**) in Tilarán, or either **Taxis Nuevo Arenal** (✆ **8388-3015**) or **Pencho** (✆ **8817-6375**) in Nuevo Arenal.

Arenal Hotels

La Mansion Inn Arenal (www.lamansionarenal.com; ✆ **877/660-3830** in U.S. and Canada, or 2692-8018 in Costa Rica) is one upscale option with an excellent setting and cozy cabins.

MODERATE

Mystica ★★ This Italian-owned hilltop retreat is a primo place to unwind. Rooms are simple but immaculate, with wood or tile floors, large windows, and a shared common lake-view veranda, with brightly varnished decking and columns made from whole tree trunks. Settle into one of the cushioned Adirondack chairs here to soak in the view or read a book. The best rooms are the private villa and the individual cabin, which offer more space and a greater sense of privacy. Families or small groups can book the two-bedroom Ra Ma Da Sa house, with a full kitchen. It's on the highest spot on the property and features an outdoor bathroom with a mosaic-tiled hot tub and waterfall shower. The expansive grounds and gardens include a nice river-stone pool and open-air yoga platform, as well as a massage room in a treehouse.

On the road btw. Tilarán and Nuevo Arenal. www.mysticacostarica.com. ✆ **2692-1001.** 9 units. $110–120 double. Rates include breakfast and taxes. **Amenities:** Restaurant; outdoor pool; yoga center and small spa; free Wi-Fi.

Villa Decary ★★ The original owners of Villa Decary were hardcore palm enthusiasts, so the grounds and gardens are planted with scores of unique species, including the Madagascar three-sided palm, or *Dypsis decaryi*, named for the French botanist Raymond Decary, who is also the namesake of this B&B. The grounds are beautiful, but you'll also like the cozy rooms, which are decorated with panache (bright Guatemalan bedspreads, and walls adorned with wildlife photos and primitive-style nature paintings). Rooms in the main building feature picture windows and private balconies with wonderful views of Lake Arenal; there are also three private *casitas* with full kitchens and more space.

Nuevo Arenal. www.villadecary.com. ✆ **800/556-0505** in the U.S. and Canada, or 2694-4330 in Costa Rica. 5 units, 3 casitas. $109 double; $142–$164 casita for 2. Rates include full breakfast. **Amenities:** Free Wi-Fi.

INEXPENSIVE

Lucky Bug Bed & Breakfast ★★ Set back from the road, on a small hill above a small lake, this intimate bed-and-breakfast is a swell pick. Though rooms don't have any views to speak of, they are spacious, cheery, and creative, featuring handmade furniture, hand-painted tiles, and unique artwork. All of this handiwork was done by the owner and her triplet daughters. The handcrafted iron and steel headboards are particularly captivating, and the one in the Flower room is filled in with colored stained glass. Even better are the Butterfly and Frog rooms, which have small private balconies. There's a nice restaurant attached.

Nuevo Arenal. www.luckybugcr.net. ✆ **2694-4515.** 5 units. $89–$109 double. Rates include breakfast and taxes. **Amenities:** Restaurant; free Wi-Fi.

Where to Eat

Tilarán has numerous inexpensive places to eat, including the restaurant at **Hotel La Carreta** (✆ **2695-6593**) and **Cabinas Mary** (✆ **2695-5479**).

Another couple of good options are the brewpub and **La Huerta** restaurant at the **Lake Arenal Hotel**. In Nuevo Arenal, **Tom's Pan German Bakery** (✆ **6694-4547**) is a popular spot for breakfast, snacks, and lunch.

Gingerbread ★★★ MEDITERRANEAN/INTERNATIONAL Israeli-born chef Eyal Ben-Menachem is a gregarious, gracious host who keeps the needs of his guests foremost. Therefore the menu changes regularly, based on which local ingredients are at their peak, though the duck quesadillas, seared tuna salad, and shrimp risotto are a few regularly occurring specials. Portions are large, often big enough to share. In fact, depending on your group size, you may just be served a family-style meal, with no menu or selections offered—although the food will be abundant, with plenty of variety and pizzazz. If you want a touch of romance and privacy, choose patio seating. Most guests, however, prefer to be close to Eyal's amusing banter, and grab seats at one of the heavy wooden tables inside. The large U-shape bar stays open long after the kitchen has closed.

On the road btw. Tilarán and Nuevo Arenal. www.gingerbreadarenal.com. ✆ **2694-0039.** Main courses $27–$32. No credit cards. Reservations recommended. Tues–Sat 5–8pm.

Moya's Place ★★ INTERNATIONAL/VEGETARIAN/PIZZA This cozy spot is the top pick right in the town of Nuevo Arenal for its delicious wood-oven pizzas, hearty wraps, and meal-size fresh salads. And who wouldn't like a place that's covered with kooky hand-painted murals of Mayan temples and a giant Aztec calendar? There's an on-site lending/exchange library, and if there's any live music happening in Nuevo Arenal, it's most likely to be happening here.

Downtown Nuevo Arenal. ✆ **2694-4001.** Main courses $5–$12. Daily 6:30am–9pm.

Organized Tours & Activities

If you want to try your hand at fishing for *guapote,* call **Captain Ron** at **Arenal Fishing Tours** (www.arenalfishing.com; ✆ **2694-4678**), or just ask at your hotel. A half-day fishing trip should cost around $150 to $300 per boat, and a full day goes for around $300 to $500. The boats will usually accommodate up to three people.

Any of the hotels in the area can hook you up with a **horseback-riding** tour for around $10 to $20 per hour.

Lake Arenal is a big lake with plenty of calm quiet corners to practice **wakeboarding**. If you're interested in lessons, or just a reliable pull on a wakeboard or water skis, contact **Fly Zone** (www.flyzone-cr.com; ✆ **8339-5876**). Simple pulls behind its specialized boat run around $125 per hour, including boards, skis, and any other necessary gear.

If you want to try **windsurfing or kiteboarding**, check in with **Tico Wind** ★ (www.ticowind.com; ✆ **2692-2002**), which sets up shop on the shores of the lake each year from December 1 to the end of April. Rates run $88 per day, including lunch; multiday and lesson packages are also available. This is also the place to rent **stand-up paddle boards** and equipment.

Shopping

About halfway between Nuevo Arenal and Tilarán is **Casa Delagua ★** (**© 2692-1324**), the studio, gallery, and coffee shop of Costa Rican artist Juan Carlos Ruiz. The **Lucky Bug Gallery ★★** is an excellent roadside Arts and Crafts and souvenir shop, attached to the **Lucky Bug Bed & Breakfast** (see above). This place sells a host of functional and decorative pieces produced locally.

MONTEVERDE ★★

167km (104 miles) NW of San José; 82km (51 miles) NW of Puntarenas

Monteverde, which translates to "Green Mountain," is one of the world's first and finest ecotourism destinations. The mist-shrouded and marvelous Monteverde Cloud Forest Biological Reserve and the extensive network of neighboring private reserves are rich and rewarding. Bird-watchers flock here for a chance to spot the myth-inspiring resplendent quetzal and scientists come to study the bountiful biodiversity. On top of all that, Monteverde is arguably the best place in Costa Rica for extreme adventure (rivaled perhaps by Arenal). It boasts a zipline where you can fly facedown like Superman for almost a mile, and the only bungee-jumping left in Costa Rica.

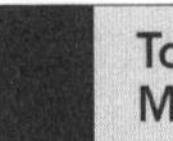

Today's Forecast . . . Misty & Cool

The climatic conditions that make Monteverde such a biological hot spot can leave many tourists feeling chilled to the bone. More than a few visitors are unprepared for a cool, windy, and wet stay in the middle of their tropical vacation, and can find Monteverde a bit inhospitable, especially from August through November.

Cloud forests are a mountaintop phenomenon. Moist, warm air sweeping in from the ocean is forced upward by mountain slopes, and as this moist air rises, it cools, forming clouds. The mountaintops around Monteverde are blanketed almost daily in dense clouds, and as the clouds cling to the slopes, moisture condenses on forest trees. This constant level of moisture has given rise to an incredible diversity of innovative life forms and a forest in which nearly every square inch of space has some sort of plant growing. Within the cloud forest, the branches of huge trees are draped with epiphytic plants: orchids, ferns, and bromeliads. This intense botanical competition has created an almost equally diverse population of insects, birds, and other wildlife. Beyond the **resplendent quetzal,** the Monteverde area boasts more than 2,500 species of plants, 450 types of orchids, 400 species of birds, and 100 species of mammals.

Essentials

ARRIVING **By Car:** The principal access road to Monteverde is located along the Inter-American Highway (CR1); about 20km (12 miles) north of the exit for Puntarenas is a marked turnoff for Sardinal, Santa Elena, and Monteverde. From this turnoff, the road is paved for 15km (9½ miles), to just beyond

Monteverde

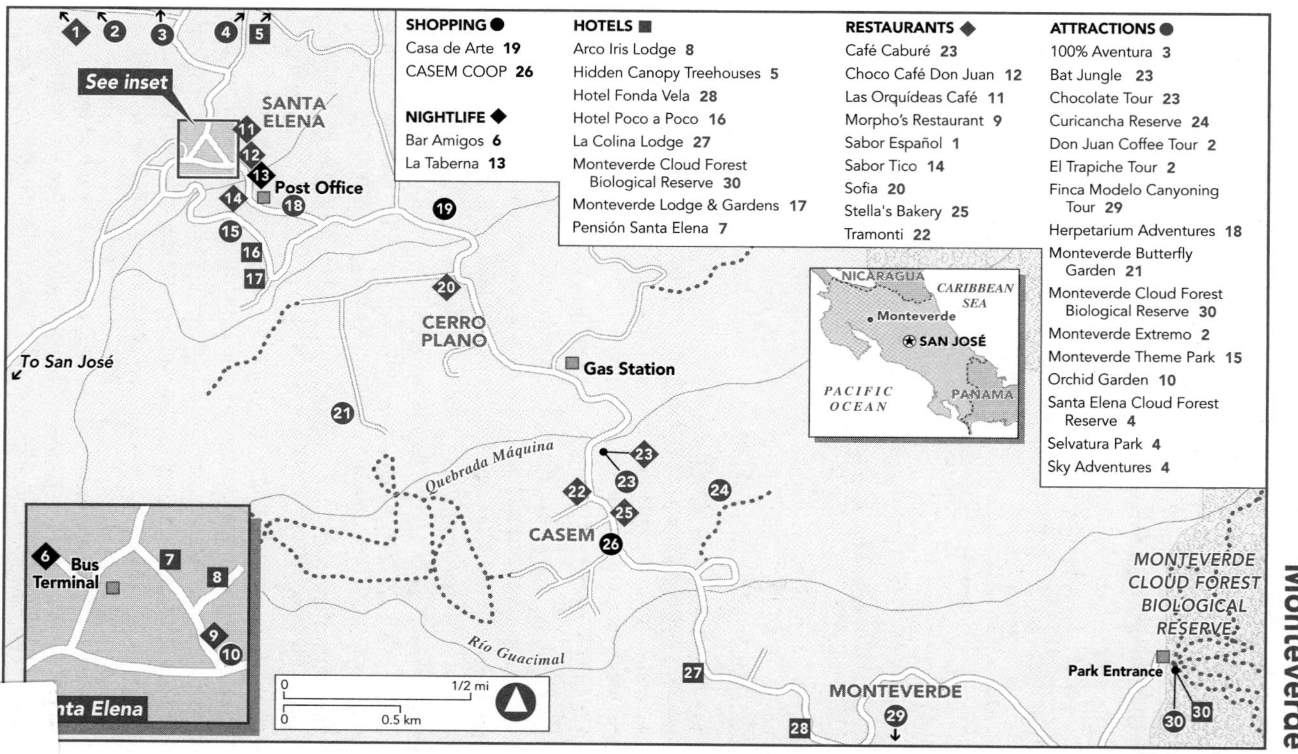
SHOPPING
Casa de Arte 19
CASEM COOP 26
NIGHTLIFE
Bar Amigos 6
La Taberna 13
HOTELS
Arco Iris Lodge 8
Hidden Canopy Treehouses 5
Hotel Fonda Vela 28
Hotel Poco a Poco 16
La Colina Lodge 27
Monteverde Cloud Forest Biological Reserve 30
Monteverde Lodge & Gardens 17
Pensión Santa Elena 7
RESTAURANTS
Café Caburé 23
Choco Café Don Juan 12
Las Orquídeas Café 11
Morpho's Restaurant 9
Sabor Español 1
Sabor Tico 14
Sofia 20
Stella's Bakery 25
Tramonti 22
ATTRACTIONS
100% Aventura 3
Bat Jungle 23
Chocolate Tour 23
Curicancha Reserve 24
Don Juan Coffee Tour 2
El Trapiche Tour 2
Finca Modelo Canyoning Tour 29
Herpetarium Adventures 18
Monteverde Butterfly Garden 21
Monteverde Cloud Forest Biological Reserve 30
Monteverde Extremo 2
Monteverde Theme Park 15
Orchid Garden 10
Santa Elena Cloud Forest Reserve 4
Selvatura Park 4
Sky Adventures 4
See inset
SANTA ELENA
Post Office
To San José
CERRO PLANO
Gas Station
Quebrada Máquina
Río Guacimal
CASEM
MONTEVERDE
MONTEVERDE CLOUD FOREST BIOLOGICAL RESERVE
Park Entrance
NICARAGUA
CARIBBEAN SEA
Monteverde
SAN JOSÉ
PACIFIC OCEAN
PANAMA
Bus Terminal
nta Elena
0 1/2 mi
0 0.5 km

the tiny town of Guacimal. From here, it's another 20km (12 miles) to Santa Elena, the gateway town to Monteverde.

Another access road to Santa Elena is found just south of the Río Lagarto Bridge. This turnoff is the first you will come to if driving from Liberia. From the Río Lagarto turnoff, it's 38km (24 miles) to Santa Elena, and the road is unpaved the entire way.

Once you arrive, the roads in and around Santa Elena are paved, including all the way to Cerro Plano, and about halfway to the reserve.

By Car: Transmonteverde express buses (✆ **2256-7710** in San José, or **2645-7447** in Santa Elena) leave San José daily at 6:30am and 2:30pm from Calle 12 between avenidas 7 and 9. The trip takes around 4 hours; the fare is C2,905. Buses arrive at and depart from Santa Elena. If you're staying at one of the hotels or lodges near the reserve, arrange pickup if possible, or take a taxi or local bus. Return buses for San José also depart daily at 6:30am and 2:30pm.

A daily bus from **Tilarán (Lake Arenal)** leaves at 12:30pm. Trip duration, believe it or not, is 2 hours (for a 40km/25-mile trip); the fare is C1,150. The Santa Elena/Tilarán bus leaves daily at 7am.

Gray Line (www.graylinecostarica.com; ✆ **800/719-3105** in the U.S. and Canada, or 2220-2126 in Costa Rica) and **Interbus** (www.interbusonline.com; ✆ **4031-0888**) both offer two daily buses that leave San José for Monteverde, one in the morning and one in the afternoon. The fare is around $50. Both of the above companies will pick you up and drop you off at most San José and Monteverde area hotels. Both Gray Line and Interbus offer routes with connections to most major destinations in Costa Rica.

VILLAGE LAYOUT The tiny town of **Santa Elena** is the gateway to the Monteverde Cloud Forest Biological Reserve, 6km (3¾ miles) outside of town along a windy road that dead-ends at the reserve entrance. As you approach Santa Elena, take the right fork in the road if you're heading directly to Monteverde. If you continue straight, you'll come into the little town center of tiny **Santa Elena,** which has a bus stop, a health clinic, a bank, a supermarket, and a few general stores, plus a collection of simple restaurants, budget hotels, souvenir shops, and tour offices. Heading just out of town, toward Monteverde, is a small strip mall with a large and prominent Megasuper supermarket. **Monteverde,** on the other hand, is not a village in the traditional

Alternative Transport

You can travel between Monteverde and La Fortuna by boat and taxi, or on a combination boat, horseback, and taxi trip. See "Boats, Horses & Taxis," on p. 142, for details. Any of the trips described there can be done in the reverse direction departing from Monteverde. Most hotels and **Desafío Expeditions ★★** (www.desafiocostarica.com; ✆ **855/818-0020** in the U.S. and Canada, or 2479-0020 in Costa Rica) can arrange this trip for you. Desafío offers multiday hikes from Monteverde to Arenal; you spend the night in rustic research facilities inside the Bosque Eterno de los Niños.

> **Peace, Love & Ecotourism**
>
> Monteverde was settled in 1951 by Quakers from the United States who wanted to leave behind the fear of war, as well as their obligation to support continued militarism through taxes and the draft. They chose Costa Rica, a country that had abolished its army in 1948. Although Monteverde's founders came here to farm, they wisely recognized the need to preserve the rare cloud forest that covered the mountain slopes above their fields, and to that end, they dedicated the largest adjacent tract of cloud forest as the Monteverde Cloud Forest Biological Reserve.

sense of the word. There's no center of town—only dirt lanes leading off from the main road to various farms. This main road has signs for all the hotels and restaurants mentioned here.

GETTING AROUND Five or so daily buses connect the town of Santa Elena and the Monteverde Cloud Forest Biological Reserve. The first bus leaves Santa Elena for the reserve at 6:15am and the last bus from the reserve leaves at 4pm. The fare is C500. Periodic van transportation also runs between the town of Santa Elena and the Santa Elena Cloud Forest Reserve. Ask around town and you should be able to find the current schedule and book a ride for around C1,000 per person. A **taxi** (✆ **2645-6969** or 2645-6666) between Santa Elena and either the Monteverde Reserve or the Santa Elena Cloud Forest Reserve costs around C5,500 for up to four people. You may have to pay about the same for a ride from Santa Elena to your lodge in Monteverde. Finally, several places around town rent **ATVs,** or all-terrain vehicles, for around $60 to $90 per day.

Monteverde Hotels

When choosing a place to stay in Monteverde, be sure to check whether the rates include a meal plan. In the past, almost all the lodges included three meals a day in their prices, but this practice is waning.

EXPENSIVE

Hidden Canopy Treehouses ★★★ For an intimate, unique, in-touch-with-nature experience in the Monteverde area, you can't beat this place. While a couple of perfectly lovely rooms are off the main lodge building, you'll definitely want one of the individual "tree houses." Set in the forest canopy, these are all ample, individual bungalows built on raised stilts, featuring polished hardwoods, slate bathrooms with waterfall showers, canopy beds, large picture windows, and a balcony or outdoor deck. You can take in superb sunset views from the main lodge, where afternoon tea is served daily. This lodge has excellent in-house guides and provides very personalized service.

On the road to the Santa Elena Cloud Forest Reserve. www.hiddencanopy.com. ✆ **2645-5447.** 7 units. $225 double; $285–$445 double tree house. Rates include breakfast and afternoon happy hour. No children 14 or under. 2-night minimum. **Amenities:** Afternoon tea; free Wi-Fi.

MODERATE

Hotel Fonda Vela ★★ This longstanding hotel is one of the closest you'll find to the Monteverde reserve, just a 15-minute or so walk away, and it's recommendable also for its unique and pretty look. Owner Paul Smith's paintings, stained-glass works, and large sculptures are scattered throughout the hotel and grounds. Rooms, in several separate blocks of buildings, have views over the forests to the Gulf of Nicoya. Locally milled tongue-and-groove wood planking is used for walls, floors, ceilings, and wainscoting. A short walk from the rooms is a pool, a couple of Jacuzzis, pool and Ping-Pong tables, board games, and a casual bar, all housed under a high, curving atrium roof.

On the road to the Monteverde Biological Cloud Forest Reserve. www.fondavela.com. ✆ **2645-5125.** 40 units. $124–$156 double. Rates include breakfast and taxes. **Amenities:** 2 restaurants; 2 bars; Jacuzzi; pool; free Wi-Fi.

Hotel Poco a Poco ★★ A good choice for families with kids, the "Little by Little Hotel" is a hive of activity, with a pool, small playhouse, restaurant, heated Jacuzzi, and small spa. Located on the outskirts of Santa Elena, Poco a Poco has clean, comfortable rooms (cream tiled floors, quality beds) with all the modern amenities, including TV/DVD systems and access to a massive DVD library. Some are a bit tight in terms of size, so ask to move if you're not happy. The restaurant is excellent and features live music nightly.

Santa Elena. www.hotelpocoapoco.com. ✆ **855/557-7262** in U.S. and Canada, or 2645-6000 in Costa Rica. 32 units. $120–$145 double. Rates include breakfast and taxes. **Amenities:** Restaurant; bar; Jacuzzi; small indoor pool; spa; sauna; Jacuzzi; free Wi-Fi.

Monteverde Lodge & Gardens ★★★ Some things do get better with age, and that's true of this pioneering ecolodge, which is run by Michael Kaye and Costa Rica Expeditions. Rooms are large and cozy, with hardwood floors, orthopedic beds, and a wall of windows or French doors with views of the gardens and forest. Meals are served in a large central dining room with walls of windows all around and a large, open fire burning under a suspended conical steel chimney. There are well-marked trails through the lush and beautiful gardens, and there's a midsize heated outdoor pool with slate decking all around, as well as butterfly, orchid. and hummingbird attractions. These folks also operate one of the best guide and tour operations in the area.

Santa Elena. www.monteverdelodge.com. ✆ **2257-0766** San José office, or 2645-5057 at the lodge. 27 units. $201–$240 double. Rates include breakfast and taxes. **Amenities:** Restaurant; bar; swimming pool; free Wi-Fi.

INEXPENSIVE

For real budgeteers, there are quite a few backpacker havens in Santa Elena and spread along the road to the reserve. The best of these is the **Pensión Santa Elena** (www.pensionsantaelena.com; ✆ **2645-5051**), which also offers swankier rooms with private bathrooms in its new annex. Owned and operated by Texan Ran Smith, and right next to the popular **Taco Taco** takeout counter run by his sister, this affordable hotel is centrally located in Santa Elena's triangular, three-street downtown.

It's also possible to stay in a room right at the **Monteverde Cloud Forest Biological Reserve** (www.cct.or.cr; ✆ **2645-5122**). A bunk bed, shared bathroom, and three meals per day here run $70 per person. For an extra $11, you can get a room with a private bathroom. Admission to the reserve is included in the price.

Arco Iris Lodge ★★ This small hotel is actually right in the town of Santa Elena, but you'd never know it. The expansive grounds and gardens give it a great sense of isolation and privacy (though you can still walk to shops and restaurants). The rooms come in a variety of shapes and sizes from simple standards, some with bunk beds, to individual cabins and superior rooms with a kitchenette and sleeping loft.

Santa Elena. www.arcoirislodge.com. ✆ **2645-5067.** 24 units. $99–$130 double. Rates include breakfast and taxes. **Amenities:** Lounge; free Wi-Fi.

La Colina Lodge ★ This rustic old lodge (originally the Pensión Flor Mar) is fairly close to the Monteverde reserve, and it radiates a friendly, homey vibe. Guests from all over the world gather in the common lounge area or cook together in the communal kitchen. The walls, tables, and chairs here are painted bright colors, with fanciful hand-painted patterns and designs. Rooms are basic but well-kept and cozy. You have a choice of shared bathroom dorm accommodations or rooms with their own private bath. You can even pitch a tent on the grounds, while enjoying kitchen and bathroom privileges.

Monteverde. ✆ **2645-5009.** 11 units, 6 with private bathroom. $25 double with shared bathroom; $35 double with private bathroom; $8 per person camping. Rates include taxes. **Amenities:** Restaurant; free Wi-Fi.

Where to Eat

Because most visitors want to get an early start, they usually grab a quick breakfast at their hotel. It's also common for people to have their lodge pack them a bag lunch to take to the reserve, though there's a decent little *soda* at the reserve entrance.

You can get good pizzas and pastas at **Tramonti ★** (www.tramonticr.com; ✆ **2645-6120**), along the road to the reserve, and great paella and other Spanish specialties at **Sabor Español ★** (✆ **2645-5387**), a few miles outside of Santa Elena on the road to Tilarán. Also, the restaurant at the **Hotel Poco a Poco** (✆ **2645-6000**) gets high marks for its wide range of international dishes.

A popular choice for lunch is **Stella's Bakery** (✆ **2645-5560**), across from the CASEM gift shop. Bright and inviting, its selection changes regularly but might include vegetarian quiche, eggplant *parmigiana,* and different salads. Stella's also features a number of decadent baked goods.

EXPENSIVE

Sofia ★★★ COSTA RICAN/FUSION Here's your splurge choice, a happy change from typical Costa Rican cooking. The Nuevo Latino cuisine here is based on classic Tico dishes and local ingredients, but with intriguing twists, like tenderloin in chipotle butter salsa or guava-glazed chicken. Owner and restaurateur Karen Nielsen has created a sophisticated and romantic ambience here, with solid wooden tables and chairs, soft lighting, and cool jazz in the background.

Cerro Plano, just past the turnoff to the Butterfly Farm, on your left. ✆ **2645-7017.** Reservations recommended during high season. Main courses $14–$20. Daily 11:30am–9:30pm.

Moderate

Café Caburé ★★★ INTERNATIONAL/CHOCOLATES Set on the second floor of a small complex also housing the Bat Jungle (p. 169), with open-air seating on a broad wooden veranda, this is a good place for a decadent dessert break (though lunches and dinners here are also solid). The homemade chocolates and fancy, flavored truffles here are truly scrumptious. On the savory side, the main menu features a wide range of international dishes, with everything from chicken mole to shrimp curry to more straightforward but very tasty sandwiches, wraps, and fresh empanadas.

On the road btw. Santa Elena and the reserve, at the Bat Jungle. www.cabure.net. ✆ **2645-5020.** Reservations recommended during high season. Main courses C2,900–C9,500. Mon–Sat 9am–9pm.

Inexpensive

Morpho's Restaurant ★ COSTA RICAN/VEGETARIAN Although it's moved around over the years, Morpho's is a local institution, serving up hearty meals at reasonable prices. The large and varied *casado* (a local blue-plate special) is quite popular, as are the fresh fruit smoothies and home-baked desserts. For something a bit fancier, try the thick pork chop in a plum/cherry sauce. There are also a host of excellent vegetarian selections. You can't miss this place, with its painted exterior covered with oversize, fluttering blue morpho butterflies.

In downtown Santa Elena, next to the Orchid Garden. www.morphosrestaurant.com. ✆ **2645-5607.** Main courses C2,500–C9,200. Daily 11am–9pm.

Take a Break

If all the activities in Monteverde have worn you out, stop in at **Las Orquídeas Café** (✆ **2645-6850**) or the **Choco Café Don Juan ★** (✆ **2645-7444**), two excellent local coffee shops just off the main drag in Santa Elena. The latter is connected to the Don Juan Coffee Farm (p. 168) and has a small gift shop attached.

Sabor Tico ★★ COSTA RICAN The name means "Tico Flavor," and that's what you get at this family-run, traditional joint. The portions are huge, and everything is extremely tasty and well prepared, although service can be slow (but friendly) when the place is busy. The *casados, arroz con pollo,* and fresh fruit juices are all excellent.

In downtown Santa Elena, across from the soccer field. ✆ **2645-5827.** Main courses C2,700–C4,900. Daily 7am–9pm.

Seeing the Forest for the Trees, Bromeliads, Monkeys, Hummingbirds . . .

Because the entrance fee to Monteverde is valid for a full day, consider taking an early-morning walk with a guide and then heading off on your own either directly after that hike or after lunch. A guide will certainly point out and explain a lot, but there's also much to be said for walking quietly through the forest on your own or in a small group. This will also allow you to stray from the well-traveled paths in the park.

Exploring Monteverde Cloud Forest Biological Reserve ★★★

The **Monteverde Cloud Forest Biological Reserve** (www.reservamonteverde.com; ✆ **2645-5122**) is one of the most developed and well-maintained natural attractions in Costa Rica. The trails are clearly marked, regularly traveled, and generally gentle in terms of ascents and descents. The cloud forest here is lush and largely untouched. Still, keep in mind that most of the birds and mammals are rare, elusive, and nocturnal. Moreover, to all but the most trained eyes, those thousands of exotic ferns, orchids, and bromeliads tend to blend into one large mass of indistinguishable green. However, with a guide hired through your hotel, or on one of the reserve's official guided 2- to 3-hour hikes, you can see and learn far more than you could on your own. At $18 per person, the reserve's tours might seem like a splurge, especially after you pay the entrance fee, but I strongly recommend that you go with a guide.

Perhaps the most famous resident of the cloud forests of Costa Rica is the quetzal, a bird with iridescent green wings and a ruby-red breast, which has become extremely rare due to habitat destruction. The male quetzal has two long tail feathers that can reach nearly .6m (2 ft.) in length, making it one of the most spectacular birds on earth. The best time to see quetzals is early morning to midmorning, and the best months are February through April (mating season).

Other animals that have been seen in Monteverde, although sightings are extremely rare, include jaguars, ocelots, and tapirs. After the quetzal, Monteverde's most famous resident used to be the golden toad (*sapo dorado*), a rare native species. However, the golden toad has disappeared from the forest and is feared extinct. Competing theories of the toad's demise include adverse effects of a natural drought cycle, the disappearing ozone layer, pesticides, and acid rain.

The reserve is open daily from 7am to 4pm; the entrance fee is $20 for adults, $10 for students and children. Only 220 people are allowed into the reserve at any one time, so you might be forced to wait. Most hotels can reserve a guided walk and entrance to the reserve for you on the following

A self-guided HIKE THROUGH THE RESERVE

If you're intent on exploring the reserve on your own, I suggest starting off on the **Sendero El Río (River Trail) ★★**. This trail, which heads north from the reserve office, puts you immediately in the midst of dense primary cloud forest, where heavy layers of mosses, bromeliads, and epiphytes cover every branch and trunk. This very first section of trail is a prime location for spotting a resplendent quetzal.

After 15 or 20 minutes, you'll come to a little marked spur leading down to a ***catarata,*** or waterfall. This diminutive fall fills a small, pristine pond and is quite picturesque, but if you fail in your attempts to capture its beauty, look for its image emblazoned on postcards at souvenir stores all around the area. The entire trek to the waterfall should take you an hour or so.

From the waterfall, turn around and retrace your steps along the River Trail until you come to a fork and the **Sendero Tosi (Tosi Trail).** Follow this shortcut, which leads through varied terrain, back to the reserve entrance.

Once the River Trail and waterfall are behind you, consider a slightly more strenuous hike to a lookout atop the Continental Divide. The **Sendero Bosque Nuboso (Cloud Forest Trail) ★** heads east from the reserve entrance. As its name implies, the trail leads through thick, virgin cloud forest. Keep your eyes open for any number of bird and mammal species, including toucans, trogons, honeycreepers, and howler monkeys. The trail has some great specimens of massive strangler fig trees, which start as parasitic vines and eventually engulf their host tree. After 1.9km (1.2 miles), you will reach the Continental Divide. This might sound daunting, but there's a modest elevation gain of only some 65m (213 ft.).

A couple of lookout points on the divide are through clearings in the forest, but the best is **La Ventana (The Window) ★**, just beyond the end of this trail and reached via a short spur trail. Here you'll find a broad, elevated wooden deck with panoramic views. Be forewarned: It's often misty and quite windy up here.

On the way back, take the 2km (1.2-mile) **Sendero Camino (Road Trail),** much of which was once used as a rough all-terrain road. Since it is wide and open in many places, this trail is particularly good for bird-watching. About halfway along, you'll want to take a brief detour to a **suspended bridge ★**. Some 100m (330 ft.) long, this midforest bridge gives you a bird's-eye view of the forest canopy. The entire loop should take around 3 hours.

day, or you can get tickets in advance directly at the reserve entrance. Night tours of the reserve leave every evening at 6:15pm. The cost is $17, and includes admission to the reserve, a 2-hour hike, and, most importantly, a guide with a high-powered searchlight.

Some of the trails can be very muddy, depending on the season, so ask about current conditions.

Exploring Outside the Reserve

You'll find ample **bird-watching** and **hiking** opportunities outside the reserve boundaries. Avoid the crowds at Monteverde by heading 5km (3 miles) north from the village of Santa Elena to the **Santa Elena Cloud Forest Reserve ★★**

(www.reservasantaelena.org; ✆ **2645-5390;** daily 7am–4pm). This 310-hectare (765-acre) reserve has a maximum elevation of 1,680m (5,510 ft.), making it the highest cloud forest in the Monteverde area. The reserve has 13km (8 miles) of hiking trails, as well as an information center. Because it borders the Monteverde reserve, a similar richness of flora and fauna is found here, although quetzals are not nearly as common. The $14 entry fee at this reserve goes directly to support a variety of good causes, including conservation and improving the local schools. The 3-hour guided tours are $15 per person, not including the entrance fee.

Located just before the Monteverde Cloud Forest Biological Reserve, and sharing many of the same ecosystems and habitats, the **Curicancha Reserve ★★★** (www.reservacuricancha.com; ✆ **2645-6915;** daily 7am–3pm and 5:30–7:30pm) is an excellent alternative, especially if you're looking to avoid the crowds that can sometimes be found at the area's namesake attraction. The reserve covers some 86 hectares (240 acres), of which almost half is primary cloud forest. The trails here are rich in flora and fauna, and quetzals are frequently spotted here. Entrance is $14, and a 3- to 4-hour guided hike can be arranged for an additional $15 per person.

Organized Tours & Activities

100% Aventura ★★★ (www.aventuracanopytour.com); ✆ **2645-6388;** daily 8am–3pm), claims to have Latin America's longest zipline, at 1,590m (64 ft. short of a mile)—a "Superman flight" where you fly facedown between two mountains with a spectacular valley far below. If that didn't scare you enough, try the terrifying (and optional) Tarzan swing at the end of the **canopy tour** ($45).

Monteverde Extremo ★★★ (www.monteverdeextremo.com); ✆ **2645-6058** or 2645-6981, offers Costa Rica's only **bungee-jumping** ($60)—the most extreme adventure possible in this adventure-rich place—as well as Tarzan swings, Superman flights, and ordinary ziplines. If you thrive on adrenaline, just jump off the aerial tram suspended 143m (469 ft.) above the ground, attached to either a bungee cord or a Tarzan swing.

Selvatura Park ★★ (www.selvatura.com; ✆ **2645-5929;** daily 7am–4:30pm), located close to the Santa Elena Cloud Forest Reserve, is a good one-stop shop for various adventures and attractions in the area. In addition to an **extensive canopy tour,** with 13 cables connecting 15 platforms, it has a network of trails and suspended bridges, a huge butterfly garden, a hummingbird garden, a snake exhibit, and a wonderful insect display and museum. Prices vary depending upon how much you want to see and do. Individually, the canopy tour costs $45; the walkways and bridges $30; the snake and reptile exhibit, the butterfly garden, and the insect museum, $15 each. Packages to combine the various exhibits are available.

Another popular option is offered by **Sky Adventures ★★** (www.sky adventures.travel; ✆ **2479-4100**), which is part of a large complex of **aerial adventures** and hiking trails. This is one of the most extensive canopy tours in the country, and begins with a cable car ride (or **Sky Tram**) up into the cloud forest, where the zipline tour features 10 cables. There are no rappel descents, and you brake using the pulley system for friction. Nearby, the **Sky Walk ★★** is a network of forest paths and suspension bridges that can easily be combined with this adventure tour. Also here: a serpentarium and hummingbird garden. The Sky Walk is open daily from 7am to 1pm; admission is $35, which includes a knowledgeable guide. For $89 per person, you can do the Sky Trek canopy tour and Sky Tram, and then walk the trails and bridges of the Sky Walk.

Finally, if you want to add a bit more excitement to your adventure, and definitely more water, try the **Finca Modelo Canyoning Tour ★★** (www.familiabrenestours.com; ✆ **2645-5581**). This tour involves a mix of hiking and then rappelling down the face of a series of forest waterfalls. The tallest of these waterfalls is around 40m (132 ft.). You will get wet on this tour. The cost is $70.

Monteverde has excellent terrain for horseback riding. **Horse Trek Monteverde ★** (www.costaricahorsebackridingvacations.com; ✆ **866/811-0522** in U.S and Canada, or 2645-5874 in Costa Rica) and **Sabine's Smiling Horses ★** (www.smilinghorses.com; ✆ **2645-6894**) are the most established operators, offering guided rides for around $20 to $23 per hour. Horseback/boat trips link Monteverde/Santa Elena with La Fortuna.

If you're looking for a glimpse into the practices and processes of daily life in this region, the **Don Juan Coffee Tour ★★** (www.donjuancoffeetour.com; ✆ **2645-7100**) is a local, family-farm operation that offers a 2-hour tour of its sprawling farm. Coffee is the primary crop and the focus of the tour, although there are a range of crops, including macadamia; a trapiche, or sugar cane mill; and a small boutique-chocolate production area. As a bonus, you get a snack and coffee tasting, and you may even get to meet the farm's namesake septuagenarian, Don Juan. The tour costs $35/adults and $15/children.

El Trapiche Tour ★★ (www.eltrapichetour.com; ✆ **2645-7780** or 2645-7650) is another **family-run tour,** which gives you insight into the traditional means of harvesting and processing sugar cane, as well as the general life on a farm that includes bananas, macadamia, and citrus groves. Back at the farmhouse, you get to see how the raw materials are turned into cane liquor, raw sugar, and local sweets. The 2-hour tour includes a ride in an ox-drawn cart, and a visit to the family's coffee farm and roasting facility. Depending on the season, you may even get to pick a bushel of raw coffee beans. Tours run daily at 10am and 3pm, and cost $32 for adults, and $12 for children 10 through 12, and include transportation.

Finally, if you want a detailed explanation of the processes involved in growing, harvesting, processing, and producing chocolate, be sure to stop by Café Caburé (p. 164) for its **Chocolate Tour.** You'll take some chocolate beans right through the roasting, grinding, and tempering processes during the 45-minute tour. The tour is offered most days at 1:30pm, and by appointment. The cost is $10.

Other Attractions in Monteverde

Butterflies abound here, and the long-established **Monteverde Butterfly Garden** ★ (www.monteverdebutterflygarden.com; ✆ **2645-5512;** daily 8:30am–4pm), located near the Pensión Monteverde Inn, displays many of Costa Rica's most beautiful species. Aside from seeing the hundreds of preserved and mounted butterflies, you can watch live butterflies in the garden and greenhouse. Admission, including a guided tour, is $15/adults, $10/students, and $5 for kids ages 4 to 6. If you can, visit between 9 and 11am, when the butterflies tend to be most active.

If your taste runs toward the slithery, check out the informative displays at the **Herpetarium Adventures** ★ (www.skyadventures.travel/herpetarium.com; ✆ **2645-6002;** daily 9am–8pm), in Santa Elena on the road to the reserve. It charges $13 for adults, $11 for students and $8 for children.

Monteverde Theme Park ★ (www.ranariomonteverde.com; ✆ **2645-6320;** daily 9:30am–8pm), a couple of hundred meters north of the Monteverde Lodge, has several attractions. A variety of amphibians populates a series of glass terrariums; nearby is a butterfly garden and canopy tour. The entrance fee ($14 for adults and $12 for students) gets you a 45-minute guided tour, and your ticket is good for 1 week, allowing for multiple visits. Stop by at least once after dark, when the tree frogs are active.

The **Bat Jungle** ★★★ (www.batjungle.com; ✆ **2645-7701;** daily 9am–7:30pm) provides an in-depth look into the life and habits of these odd flying mammals. A visit here includes several different types of exhibits, from skeletal remains to a large enclosure where you get to see various live species in action—the enclosure and room are kept dark, and the bats have had their biological clocks tricked into thinking that it's night. The last tour starts at 6:45pm. Admission is $13/adults and $11/students. Children under 6 are free.

If you've had your fill of critters, you might want to stop at the **Orchid Garden** ★★ (www.monteverdeorchidgarden.net; ✆ **2645-5308;** daily 8am–5pm), in Santa Elena across from the Pensión El Tucano. This botanical garden has more than 425 species of orchids. Admission is $10 for adults, $7 for students and free for children under 12.

Shopping

The **Monteverde Cloud Forest Biological Reserve** has a well-stocked gift shop, just off the entrance. You'll find plenty of T-shirts, postcards, and assorted crafts here, as well as science and natural history books. Another top shop is **CASEM COOP** ★ (http://casemcoop.blogspot.com; ✆ **2645-5190;** daily 7am–5pm), on the right side of the main road, just across from Stella's Bakery. This crafts cooperative sells embroidered clothing, T-shirts, posters, and postcards, Boruca weavings, locally grown and roasted coffee, and many other items to remind you of your visit to Monteverde. CASEM COOP is open daily 7am to 5pm.

Over the years, Monteverde has developed a nice little community of artists. Around town, you'll see paintings by local artists Paul Smith and Meg Wallace, whose works are displayed at Hotel Fonda Vela and Stella's Bakery. You should also check out **Casa de Arte** ★★ (www.monteverdearthouse.com; ✆ **2645-5275**), which has a mix of Arts and Crafts.

Nightlife

Perhaps the most popular after-dark activities in Monteverde are night hikes in one of the reserves. However, if you want a taste of the local party scene, head to **Bar Amigos** (www.baramigos.com; ✆ **2645-5071**), a large and often loud bar in the heart of Santa Elena. You'll find a bunch of flat-screen TVs showing sporting events, a couple of pool tables, and occasional live bands. There's also **La Taberna** ★ (✆ **8839-5569**), on the edge of Santa Elena town, below the Serpentarium. With a more contemporary club vibe, this place attracts a mix of locals and tourists, cranks its music loud, and often gets people dancing.

THE CENTRAL PACIFIC COAST

8

After Guanacaste, the beaches of Costa Rica's central Pacific coast are the country's most popular. Options here range from the surfer and snowbird hangout of Jacó, to the ecotourist mecca of Manuel Antonio, to remote and largely undeveloped Dominical and Uvita, with their jungle-clad hillsides and rainforest waterfalls. With a dependable highway connecting San José to the coast, and improvements along the Costanera Sur highway heading south, this region is now even easier to visit.

Jacó and Playa Herradura are the closest major beach destinations to San José. They have historically been the first choice for young surfers and city-dwelling Costa Ricans. Just north of Playa Herradura sits **Carara National Park ★★**, one of the few places in Costa Rica where you can see the disappearing dry forest join the damp, humid forests that extend south down the coast. It's also a place to see scarlet macaws in the wild.

Just a little farther south, Manuel Antonio is one of the country's foremost ecotourist destinations, with a host of hotel and lodging options and an easily accessible national park that combines the exuberant lushness of a lowland tropical rainforest with several gorgeous beaches. **Manuel Antonio National Park ★★** is home to all four of Costa Rica's monkey species, as well as a wealth of other easily viewed flora and fauna. This is one of the country's most visited destinations, and for good reason. The wildlife is fabulous, and a wide range of tours and activities is open to travelers of all styles and ages.

If you're looking to get away from it all, **Dominical** and the **beaches south of Dominical ★** should be your top destination on this coast. Still a small village, the beach town of Dominical is flanked by even more remote and undeveloped beaches, including those found inside **Ballena Marine National Park ★★**.

Central Pacific Coast

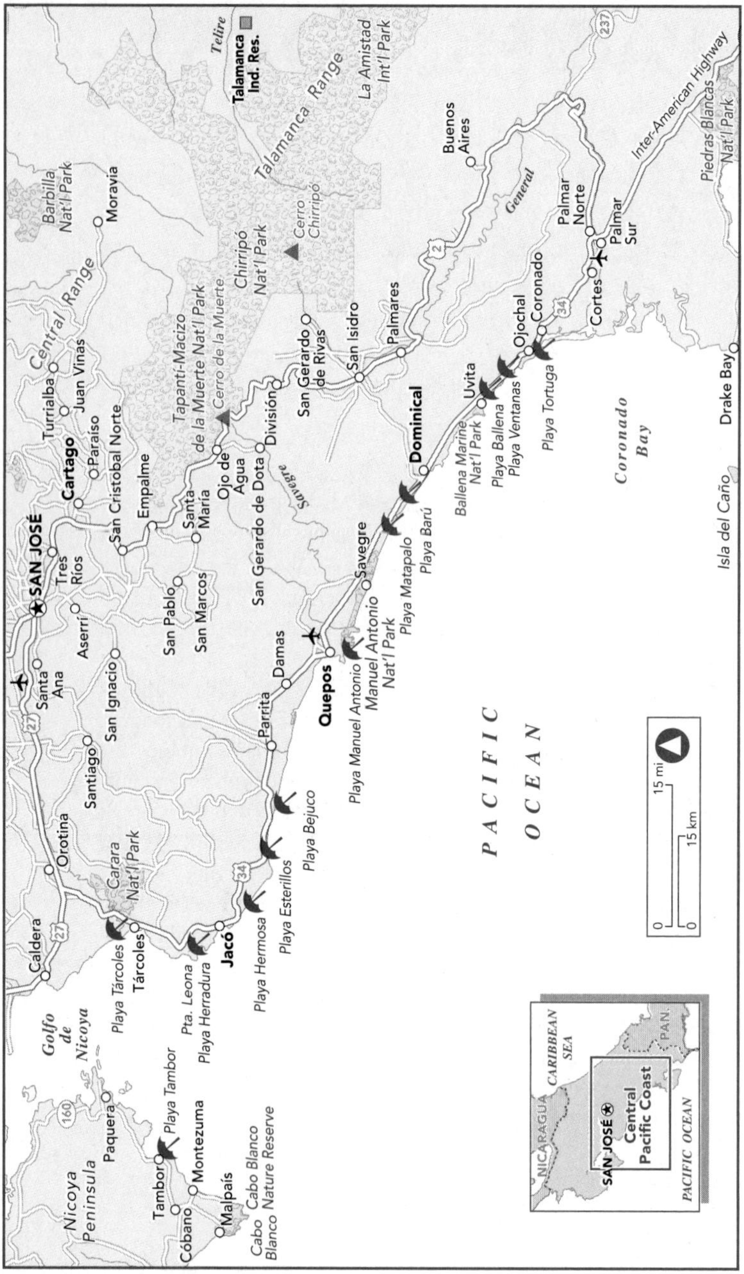

PLAYA HERRADURA & JACÓ

Jacó: 117km (73 miles) W of San José; 75km (47 miles) S of Puntarenas; Playa Herradura: 108km (67 miles) W of San José; 9km (6 miles) NW of Playa de Jacó

If you're coming from San José, **Playa Herradura** is the first major beach you'll hit as you head south along the coastal highway. Playa Herradura is a long stretch of brown sand that is home to the massive **Los Sueños Resort,** which is anchored by the **Los Sueños Marriott Ocean & Golf Resort ★★** as well as a sprawling complex of condos and private homes and its attached marina. North of Herradura you'll find a few other small beaches and resorts, including the elegant **Villa Caletas ★★★** (p. 175).

Jacó is a long stretch of beach strung with a dense hodgepodge of hotels in all price categories, souvenir shops, seafood restaurants, pizza joints, and rowdy bars. The top attraction here is the surf, and this is definitely a surfer-dominated beach town. However, the beach itself is not particularly appealing, consisting of dark-gray sand with lots of little rocks (it's often pretty rough for swimming). Still, given its proximity to San José, Jacó is almost always packed with a mix of foreign and Tico vacationers. Known for its nightlife, Jacó has raging bars that include everything from live music venues to chill lounge environments to beachfront sports bars with pool and foosball tables.

Essentials

ARRIVING **By Car:** Head west out of San José on the San José–Caldera Highway (CR27). Just past the fourth toll booth at Pavón, follow the signs to Jacó and you'll turn onto the Costanera Sur (CR34), the Southern Coastal Highway. From here it's a straight shot down the coast to Jacó. The trip should take a little over an hour.

By Bus: Transportes Jacó express buses (www.transportesjacoruta655.com; ✆ **2290-2922**) leave San José daily every 2 hours between 7am and 7pm

croc SPOTTING

The Costanera Highway passes over the Tárcoles River just outside the entrance to **Carara National Park,** about 23km (14 miles) south of Orotina. This is a popular place to pull over and spot gargantuan crocodiles. Some can reach 3.7 to 4.6m (12–15 ft.) in length. Usually anywhere from 10 to 20 are easily visible, either swimming in the water or sunning on the banks. But be careful. First, you'll have to brave walking on a narrow sidewalk along the side of the bridge with cars and trucks speeding by. And second, car break-ins are common here, including in the seemingly safe restaurant parking lots at the north end of the bridge. Although a police post has somewhat reduced the risk, it's not a good idea to leave your car or valuables unguarded. Consider leaving someone at the car and taking turns watching the crocs.

from the Coca-Cola bus terminal at Calle 16 between avenidas 1 and 3. The trip takes between 2½ and 3 hours; the fare is C2,445. On weekends and holidays, extra buses are sometimes added, so it's worth calling to check. No direct buses run all the way into Playa Herradura. All buses to Jacó will drop off passengers at the entrance to Playa Herradura, which is about 1km (½ mile) or so from the beach.

The Jacó bus station is at the north end of town, at a small mall across from the Jacó Fiesta Hotel. Buses for San José leave daily roughly every 2 hours between 5am and 5pm. Buses returning to San José from Quepos pass periodically and pick up passengers on the highway. Because schedules can change, it's best to ask at your hotel about current departure times.

Gray Line (www.graylinecostarica.com; ✆ **800/719-3105** in the U.S. and Canada, or 2220-2126 in Costa Rica) and **Interbus** (www.interbusonline.com; ✆ **4100-0888**) both offer two buses daily (one in the morning, one in the afternoon) leaving San José for Jacó and Playa Herradura. Call or check the websites for times. The fare is around $40. Both companies will pick you up at most San José–area hotels. Both also have connections to most major tourist destinations in the country.

Buses from San José to **Quepos** and Manuel Antonio also pass by Jacó. (They let passengers off on the highway about 1km/½ mile from town.) However, during the busy months, some of these buses will refuse passengers getting off in Jacó or will accept them only if they pay the full fare to Quepos or Manuel Antonio.

VILLAGE LAYOUT Playa Herradura is a short distance off the Southern Coastal Highway. Just before you hit the beach, you'll see the entrance to the Los Sueños resort complex and marina on your right. One dirt road runs parallel to the beach, with a few restaurants and a makeshift line of parking spaces all along its length.

Jacó is also located a short distance off the Southern Coastal Highway. One main road runs parallel to the beach, with a host of arteries heading toward the water; you'll find most of the town's hotels and restaurants off these roads.

GETTING AROUND Almost everything is within walking distance in Jacó, but you can call **Asotaxi** (✆ **2643-2020** or 2643-1919) for a cab.

Bikes and scooters are for rent from a variety of shops and streetside stands along the main street. Bicycle rental should run around $10 to $15 per day, and a scooter should cost between $40 and $70 per day.

For longer excursions, you can rent a car from **Budget** (www.budget.co.cr; ✆ **2643-2665**), **Economy** (www.economycarrentals.com; ✆ **2643-1719**), **National** (www.natcar.com/main.cfm; ✆ **2643-3224**), or **Zuma** (www.zumarentacar.com; ✆ **2643-1528**).

FAST FACTS Playa Herradura has no real town. At the main intersection with the Southern Coastal Highway, you'll find a modern strip mall, with a large Automercado supermarket, some restaurants, shops, and a couple of ATMs. A handful of banks have branches along the main road in Jacó. The

health center (✆ **2643-3667**) and **post office** (✆ **2643-2175**) are at the Municipal Center at the south end of town. You'll find a half-dozen or so pharmacies along the town's main drag.

A gas station is on the main highway, between Playa Herradura and Jacó, and another station, **El Arroyo,** on the highway on the southern edge of Jacó. Both are open 24 hours.

Playa Herradura & Jacó Hotels

EXPENSIVE

Besides the Marriott resort, the Los Sueños complex has scores of condominium units for rent. All come with kitchens, access to swimming pools, and rights to golf here. These are excellent options for families who want to do some cooking, and for longer stays. If you want to rent a condo here, contact **Stay In Costa Rica** (www.stayincostarica.com; ✆ **866/439-5922** in the U.S. and Canada, or 2637-2661 in Costa Rica).

Croc's Casino Resort ★★ This 17-story, 152-room behemoth, which opened in February 2015, has been a game-changer in Jacó, and not just for the skyline. The luxurious rooms are decorated in a modern, not-too-splashy style, and the ocean views are awesome. Here you can choose from three restaurants: Adacus, serving Peruvian-Mediterranean fusion cuisine, with a nice wine list; Parsley & Pepper, with Italian, Mexican, Japanese, and other international foods; and El Zarpe Pool Bar and Grill, for poolside snacking on buffalo wings, quesadillas, and seafood. The Liquidity Casino Bar is happy to serve up tropical cocktails to gamblers, while the Holy Moly! Disco Club has become the hottest spot in town for late-night revelers. The Las Vegas–style casino has new slots and gaming tables. The big, oceanfront swimming pool features a waterslide and three cold-water Jacuzzis. The hotel even has a couple of rescued crocodiles named Paco and Lola.

800m west of the Banco de Costa Rica, Jacó. www.crocscasinoresort.com. ✆ **800/809-5503** in the U.S. and Canada, or 2105-3200 in Costa Rica. 152 units. $179–$398 double, including $12 voucher for breakfast. **Amenities:** 3 restaurants and 1 coffee shop; 3 bars; casino; spa; concierge; laundry service; free Wi-Fi.

Villa Caletas ★★★ Whimsy and luxury go hand in hand at this cliff-top hideaway, which includes the Villa Caletas Hotel and the Zephyr Palace. Villa Caletas is a tropical Victorian mansion in the rainforest overlooking the Pacific Ocean. Here you'll find an exclusive pebble beach (15-min. shuttle provided), inviting pools, a bar, and two restaurants. Guests can sip cocktails while enjoying the sunset from a recreated Greek amphitheater, and the suites and junior suites come with plunge pools or private outdoor Jacuzzis; most have great views of the Pacific Ocean.

Btw. Tárcoles and Playa Herradura. www.hotelvillacaletas.com. ✆ **2630-3000.** 52 units. $200–$235 double; $280 villa; $352–$680 suite; $365–$1,600 Zephyr Palace suites; taxes not included. Extra person $42 at Villa Caletas; $85 at Zephyr Palace. **Amenities:** 2 restaurants; 1 bar; concierge; 3 midsize outdoor pools; Jacuzzi; spa; gym; free Wi-Fi.

MODERATE

The oceanfront **Apartotel Girasol ★★** (www.girasol.com; ✆ **800/923-2779** in the U.S. and Canada, or 2643-1591 in Costa Rica), with 16 fully equipped one-bedroom apartments, is a good option, especially for longer stays, while **Canciones del Mar ★** (www.cancionesdelmar.com; ✆ **888/260-1523** in the U.S. and Canada, or 2643-3273 in Costa Rica) and **Hotel Catalina ★** (www.hotelcatalinacr.com; ✆ **2643-1237**) are two other good beachfront choices.

Club del Mar ★★★ A great option on the outskirts of Jacó, Club del Mar is located at the far southern end of the beach, so it feels far removed from the crowds and craziness in the thick of town. This is also one of the safest parts of the beach for swimming, as it's somewhat protected by the rocky headlands. It's not a party hotel, but families flock here, drawn both by the calmer waters and the fact that all the comfortable, well-maintained one- and two-bedroom condos here come with fully equipped kitchens, large living rooms, and washers and dryers. Standard rooms are all air-conditioned and have mini-fridges. All are housed in a series of two- and three-story buildings spread around gardens that are chock-full of flowering heliconia and ginger. There's also a midsize pool with a volleyball net that often attracts a pickup game, and a very good on-site restaurant, Las Sandalias.

Jacó. www.clubdelmarcostarica.com. ✆ **866/978-5669** in the U.S. and Canada, or 2643-3194 in Costa Rica. 34 units. $117–$188 double; $160–$354 for 1- or 2-bedroom condos, taxes included. **Amenities:** Restaurant; bar; babysitting; outdoor pool; room service; small spa; bike, paddleboard and surfboard rental; free Wi-Fi.

Hotel Nine ★ Though it's called the Hotel Nine, I'd rank this place a 10. The staff is incredibly efficient and friendly, the hotel is on the serene and (usually) swimmable southern end of the beach and the place has a happy dose of "South Beach Miami" style in the architectural details and decor. That means rooms with handsome rattan and wood furnishings and colorful throws on the beds. A small multitiered pool with a swim-up bar, waterfall, and Jacuzzi is at the center of the complex, and ocean views can be had from the narrow shared veranda that fronts most rooms. The on-site restaurant is terrific.

Jacó. www.hotelnine.com. ✆ **800/477-2486** in the U.S. and Canada, or 2643-5335 in Costa Rica. 14 units. $118–$143 double; $273–$398 suite. Rates include breakfast. No children under 6. **Amenities:** Restaurant; bar; Jacuzzi; midsize outdoor pool; room service; surfboards; free Wi-Fi.

INEXPENSIVE

There are quite a few budget hotels around town, so if you're looking to stay on the cheap, simply walk the strip and see who's got the best room at the best price.

Room2Board ★★ This hip hostel at the southern end of the Jacó beach can make an old guy feel young again, with happy, drinking 20-somethings filling the pool and bar as if it's perpetually spring break. Despite the gaudy outcroppings on the exterior of the four-story building, meant to resemble waves, the hotel has a futuristic feel thanks to its motion-sensing lights and sleek, glass-and-steel design. Established in 2014, Room2Board has a big poolside screen that displays games, events, and surfing, and there's a room upstairs that doubles as movie theater and yoga space, plus a communal kitchen. Call ahead if you're eager to save money, as the $16 shared dorms can fill up and leave you looking at a private room closer to $80. Room2Board has a surf school and board rentals and is a block from the ocean. Just a few rules: No pets, no prostitutes, and no children under 14.

Jacó. www.room2board.com. ✆ **2643-4949.** 21 units, with capacity for 87 people. Dorm rooms $16–$28; private room with shared bathroom $62–$84; with private bathroom $59–$86. **Amenities:** Restaurant; bar; outdoor pool; surf school; laundry service; bike rental; free Wi-Fi.

Where to Eat

Jacó has a wide range of restaurants, many catering to surfers and budget travelers. In addition to the places listed below, if you're looking for simply prepared fresh seafood, **El Barco de Mariscos** (✆ **2643-2831**) and **El Recreo** (✆ **2643-1172**) are both good bets. For traditional Costa Rican food, **Jacó Rustico** (✆ **2643-2727**) is super-popular and cheap, and for Italian food at a nice price, try **Chinita Pacific** (✆ **8501-6651**) or **Peccati Di Gola** (✆ **2643-5867**). Sushi lovers should head to **Tsunami Sushi** (✆ **2643-3678**), in the Jacó Walk Shopping Center. For a coffee break and freshly baked pastries, head to **Café del M@r** (✆ **2643-1250**) or the **Pachi's Pan** (✆ **2643-6068**).

At the Los Sueños marina, you'll find **El Galeón,** an upscale fusion restaurant; **Bambu,** a sushi bar and Pan-Asian restaurant; **La Linterna,** a fancy Italian restaurant; and **Hook Up,** an excellent American-style grill and restaurant. You can make reservations at any of the marina restaurants by calling ✆ **2630-4050.**

EXPENSIVE

Lemon Zest ★★ SEAFOOD/FUSION Chef/owner Richard Lemon left a teaching gig at the famed Le Cordon Bleu culinary school to open this superb eatery. His food, not surprisingly, is complex and sophisticated, ranging over a number of world influences. Among the many excellent appetizers are the buffalo lobster bites with blue cheese dipping sauce and the Korean-style beef skewers with a homemade banana ketchup. Main courses are impressive, especially the green curry shrimp and the jerk pork chop with pineapple-chipotle sauce. The terrible dining room acoustics leave something to be desired, so try to grab one of the few wooden tables on the outdoor balcony.

Downtown Jacó. www.lemonzestjaco.com. ✆ **2643-2591.** Reservations recommended during high season. Main courses $11–$29. Daily 5–10pm; closed Mon in low season. Closed mid-Sept through Oct 31.

MODERATE

El Pelícano ★★ SEAFOOD/COSTA RICAN Just across the single-lane dirt road that runs along the beach, this simple, open-air spot serves up fresh ceviche, fish, seafood, and other Tico standards. You can also get steak and chicken, but I recommend the seafood, as it's caught and brought in daily. Most lunch meals (11am–4pm) come with a visit to the small salad bar. There is sometimes live music at night.

On the beach in Playa Herradura. www.elpelicanorestaurante.com. ✆ **2637-8910.** Reservations recommended during high season. Main courses C6,500–C38,000. Daily 11am–10pm.

Graffiti Resto Café & Wine Bar ★★★ FUSION It's a little hard to find Graffiti Resto, as it's wedged in the far back corner of a strip mall near the center of Jacó. But it's worth the search for food that's at the apex of what you'll find in Costa Rica. Each night a short selection of specials is written on a chalkboard, based on the chef's whims and what's fresh. On top of the specials, the regular menu is also excellent, featuring Graffiti's signature cacao- and coffee-crusted tenderloin and Asian-spiced seared tuna. Occasionally there's live music here, and it's worth visiting the attached gift shop, which features hand-carved wooden surfboards and unique body surfing paddles. As you might expect, it's a hip-looking place with graffiti art covering the walls. Along with the interior dining rooms, there's limited outdoor seating in the front of the restaurant, abutting the parking lot.

Centro Comercial Pacific Center, downtown Jacó. www.graffiticr.com. ✆ **2643-1708.** Reservations recommended during high season. Main courses C5,000–C18,500. Mon–Sat 5–10pm.

MODERATE

Caliche's Wishbone ★ SEAFOOD/MEXICAN This landmark was the brainchild of a local surfing legend, Caliche. It serves up hearty fare, everything from pizzas, burritos, and stuffed potatoes to fresh, seared tuna in a soy-wasabi sauce. Surf videos play on TVs in the main dining room, but you may prefer the tables closest to the busy sidewalk, on the covered veranda.

On the main road in Jacó. ✆ **2643-3406.** Main courses C3,500–C13,000. Thurs–Tues noon–10pm.

INEXPENSIVE

Taco Bar ★ MEXICAN/INTERNATIONAL Taco Bar is so popular that it's opened several branches in San José, and is looking to expand elsewhere around the country. This is the original, an open-air joint featuring two long, wooden bars with seating on "swings" supported by heavy ropes (you can also choose from more traditional tables and picnic tables). It serves up a wide range of tacos, burritos, and pizzas; seafood varieties are prepared using freshly caught fish. After choosing the main plate, you also have ample choices at the well-stocked and inventive salad bar. Also open for breakfast. ***Note:*** Don't confuse this place with Jacó Taco, which is located on the main strip and is not as good.

½ block inland from the POPS ice cream shop, central Jacó. www.tacobar.info. ✆ **2643-0222.** Main courses C3,675–C7,000. Mon 11–10pm; Tues–Sun 7:00am–10pm.

Exploring Jacó & Playa Herradura

Playa Herradura is a calm and protected beach, although the dark sand is rocky in places and not very attractive. The calmest section of beach is toward the north end, where you'll find the Los Sueños Marriott Ocean & Golf Resort. When the swell is big, the center section of beach here can be a good place to body-surf, boogie-board, or try some beginning surf moves.

Punta Leona, just a few kilometers north of Playa Herradura, is a cross between a hotel, a resort, and a private country club, and it has some of the nicer beaches in the area. Although Punta Leona has effectively restricted access to its beaches for years, this is technically illegal in Costa Rica, and you have the right to enjoy both playas **Manta** ★ and **Blanca** ★, two very nice white-sand beaches inside the Punta Leona complex. The public access beach road is south of the main Punta Leona entrance and is not very well marked.

The beach in **Jacó** has a reputation for dangerous riptides (as does most of Costa Rica's Pacific coast). Even strong swimmers have been known to drown in the powerful rips. In general, the far southern end of the beach is the calmest and safest place to swim.

As an alternative to Jacó, you may want to visit other nearby beaches, like **Playa Manta, Playa Blanca, Playa Hermosa, Esterillos,** and **Playa Bejuco.** These beaches are just south of Jacó and easily reached by car or even bicycle—if you've got a lot of energy.

In addition to the tours and activities mentioned below, Manuel Antonio is only about an hour south of Jacó, making it an easy day trip. Most local operators offer a variety of tours in **Manuel Antonio,** including trips to the national park and the Damas Island estuary.

Organized Tours & Activities

Several operations run **ATV tours** through the surrounding countryside. Tours range in length from 2 to 4 hours up to a full day, and cost between $70 and $175 per person. Contact **Adventure Tours Costa Rica** (www.adventuretours costarica.com; ✆ **2643-5720**).

The easiest way to get up into the **canopy** here is on the **Rain Forest Aerial Tram Pacific** ★ (www.rfat.com; ✆ **866/759-8726** in the U.S. and Canada, or 2257-5961 in Costa Rica; see map "Central Pacific Coast" on p. 172). A sister project to the original Rain Forest Aerial Tram, this attraction features modified ski-lift type gondolas that take you through and above the transitional forests bordering Carara National Park. The $60 entrance fee includes the guided 50-minute tram ride and a guided 45-minute hike on a network of trails, which feature an orchid garden and serpentarium. You can also hike the company's trails for as long as you like. There's a zipline canopy tour on the same grounds. The Aerial Tram is a few kilometers inland from an exit just north of the first entrance into Jacó.

Quite a few **zipline** and **harness-style canopy tours** are in this area. **Vista Los Sueños Canopy Tour** ★ (www.canopyvistalossuenos.com; ✆ **321/220-9631** in the U.S. and Canada, or 2637-6020 in Costa Rica) is located in the hills above Playa Herradura. The tour features 12 ziplines, some excellent views, and the longest cable in the area (almost ½-mile in length). The cost is $60 per person, and round-trip transportation can be added. Horseback-riding tours to a nearby waterfall are also available.

For those eager to see **crocodiles,** several companies offer **boat tours** of the river and mangroves, and every hotel and tour agency in the area can make arrangements for you. Many operators bring along freshly killed chickens to attract the crocs, though it's irresponsible to feed any wild animals in Costa Rica. That's why I suggest going with **Eco Jungle Cruises ★** (www.ecojungle cruises.com/eng/index; ✆ **2582-0181;** 2-hr. tour $75 adults, $37.50 kids 4–10). Its staff doesn't believe in feeding the crocs or altering their behaviors, a policy recognized with "2 Leaves" in Costa Rica's Certification for Sustainable Tourism evaluation. There are plenty (hundreds, in fact) of crocodiles to be seen along this stretch of river and mangrove, and plenty of photo opportunities. Transportation is available from Jacó, Playa Herradura, Manuel Antonio, or San José.

Horseback riding tours take travelers away from all the development in Jacó to see some nature. The best operator in the area is **Discovery Horseback** (www.horseridecostarica.com; ✆ **8838-7550**) in Playa Hermosa. It's $75 per person for a 2½-hour tour. Options range from beach riding to trails through the rainforest with stops at a jungle waterfall.

Kayak Jacó (www.kayakjaco.com; ✆ **2643-1233**) operates several outings in either single or tandem sea kayaks, as well as eight-person outrigger canoes. Customers can admire the beautiful coastline and, when conditions permit, take a snorkel break. Kayak fishing tours and sailing trips aboard 25-foot trimarans are also available. Most tours run around 4 hours and include transportation to and from the put-in, as well as fruit and soft drinks during the trip. The tours cost $55 to $140 per person, depending on the tour and group size.

A number of dependable fishing and scuba-diving operators base themselves at Los Sueños Marriott Ocean & Golf Resort and its adjacent 250-slip marina. Dependable operators include **Maverick Sportfishing Tours** (www. mavericksportfish.com; ✆ **800/405-8206** in the U.S., or 8712-9683 in Costa Rica) and **Costa Rica Dreams** (www.costaricadreams.com; ✆ **337/205-0665** in the U.S., or 2637-8942 in Costa Rica). A full day of fishing runs from around $1,250 for four people up to $2,800 for six people.

The same waves that often make Playa Jacó a bit rough for swimmers make it one of the most popular beaches in the country with surfers. Nearby Playa Hermosa, Playa Tulin, and Playa Escondida are also excellent surfing beaches. Those who want to challenge the waves can **rent surfboards and boogie boards** for around $3 an hour or $10 to $20 per day, from any of the numerous surf shops along the main road. If you want to learn how to surf, try the **Del Mar Surf Camp ★★** (www.delmarsurfcamp.com; ✆ **855/833-5627** in the U.S or 2643-3197 in Costa Rica) or **Jacó Surf School** (www.jacosurf school.com; ✆ **8829-4697**).

The excellent **La Iguana,** an 18-hole golf course at Los Sueños Marriott Ocean & Golf Resort (www.golflaiguana.com; ✆ **2630-9028**), is open to non-guests. Greens fees are $150. Club and shoe rentals are available.

Carara National Park ★★

A little more than 17.5km (11 miles) north of Playa Herradura is **Carara National Park** (✆ **2637-1054;** daily 7am–4:30pm; $10/person), a nesting ground for **scarlet macaws.** It has a few kilometers of trails open to visitors. The **Sendero Acceso Universal (Universal Access Trail),** which heads out from the national park office, is broad, flat, and wheelchair-accessible. The first half of this 1km (.6-mile) stretch leads into the forest and features various informative plaques, in both English and Spanish, pointing out prominent flora. About 10 or 15 minutes into your hike, you'll see that the trail splits, forming a loop (you can go in either direction). The entire loop trail should take you about an hour. The macaws migrate daily, spending their days in the park and their nights among the coastal mangroves. It's best to view them in the early morning when they arrive, or around sunset when they head back to the coast for the evening, but a good guide can usually find them for you during the day. Whether or not you see them, you should hear their loud squawks. Among the other wildlife that you might see are caimans, coatis, armadillos, pacas, peccaries, and, of course, hundreds of species of birds.

Bring along insect repellent or, better yet, wear light cotton long sleeves and pants.

Although you can certainly hike the gentle and well-marked trails of Carara independently, my advice is to take a **guided tour;** you'll learn a lot more about your surroundings. Most hotel desks can arrange for a guided hike to Carara National Park, or you can contact **Vic Tours** (www.victourscostarica.com; ✆ **8723-3008**) for one. Also, there are almost always bilingual naturalist guides available to hire at the park entrance.

Nightlife

Jacó is the central Pacific's party town, with tons of bars and several discos. One standout is the new **Holy Moly! Disco Club** at Croc's Casino Resort, which features DJs from around the world, and where you may feel like you've stepped into another country. This place gets to hopping around 11:30pm.

Other options are the **Loro Loco,** which has live music and DJs, the **Surf Dogs** sports bar, and the **Orange Pub,** which has live music, as well as pool and foosball tables.

Jacó Blu, located right on the beach near the center of town, is a mellow beach club, with a pool, cabanas, and restaurant service by day, but at night it becomes a fairly raucous bar and dance spot, especially on Wednesdays (ladies' night). **Le Loft,** on the main street near the center of town, attracts a more sophisticated and chic clubbing crowd.

Sports freaks can catch the latest games at **Clarita's Beach Bar & Grill,** on the beach toward the north end of town.

If you're into casino games, head to **Croc's Casino Resort,** which has a Las Vegas–style casino and the **Liquidity Casino Bar.**

Note: Jacó has a lot of legal prostitution and it's not uncommon to find working women at any of the bars around town.

Side Trips from Jacó: Playas Hermosa, Esterillos & Bejuco

South of Jacó, Costa Rica's coastline is a long, almost entirely straight stretch of largely undeveloped beach backed by thick forests and low-lying rice and African palm plantations.

Playa Hermosa ★, 10km (6¼ miles) southeast of Jacó, is the first beach you'll hit as you head down the Southern Coastal Highway. This is primarily a surfers' choice, but it is still a lovely spot to spend some beach time. Aside from a small grouping of hotels and restaurants, most of Playa Hermosa is protected, as **olive ridley sea turtles** lay eggs here from July to December. During turtle nesting season, all the hotel tour desks and local tour agencies can help arrange a nighttime turtle nesting tour for around $40 to $50 per person.

Playa Hermosa is the only beach in this section located right along the Southern Coastal Highway; all of the rest are a kilometer or so in from the road and reached by a series of dirt access roads. If you exit the highway in Playa Hermosa, you can follow a dirt-and-sand access road that runs parallel to the shore along several miles of deserted, protected beach, as Playa Hermosa eventually becomes **Playa Tulin,** near the Tulin River mouth. This is another popular surf spot, but watch out for crocodiles.

As you continue down the coastal highway from Playa Hermosa, you will hit Esterillos. **Playa Esterillos,** 22km (14 miles) south of Jacó, is long and wide and has three separate sections, Esterillos Oeste, Centro, and Este—west, center, and east, in order as you head away from Jacó.

If you keep heading south (really southeast), you next come to **Playa Bejuco,** another long, wide, nearly deserted stretch of sand with mangroves and swampland behind it.

Safety note: While beautiful, isolated, and expansive, the beaches of Hermosa, Esterillos, and Bejuco can be quite rough at times and dangerous for swimming. Caution is highly advised here.

MANUEL ANTONIO NATIONAL PARK ★★

140km (87 miles) SW of San José; 69km (43 miles) S of Playa de Jacó

Manuel Antonio was Costa Rica's first major ecotourism destination and remains one of its most popular. The views from the hills overlooking the park are spectacular, the beaches are idyllic, and the rainforest is crawling with howler, white-faced, spider, and squirrel monkeys, among other exotic wildlife. The downside is the abundance of the species *Homo sapiens* you'll find

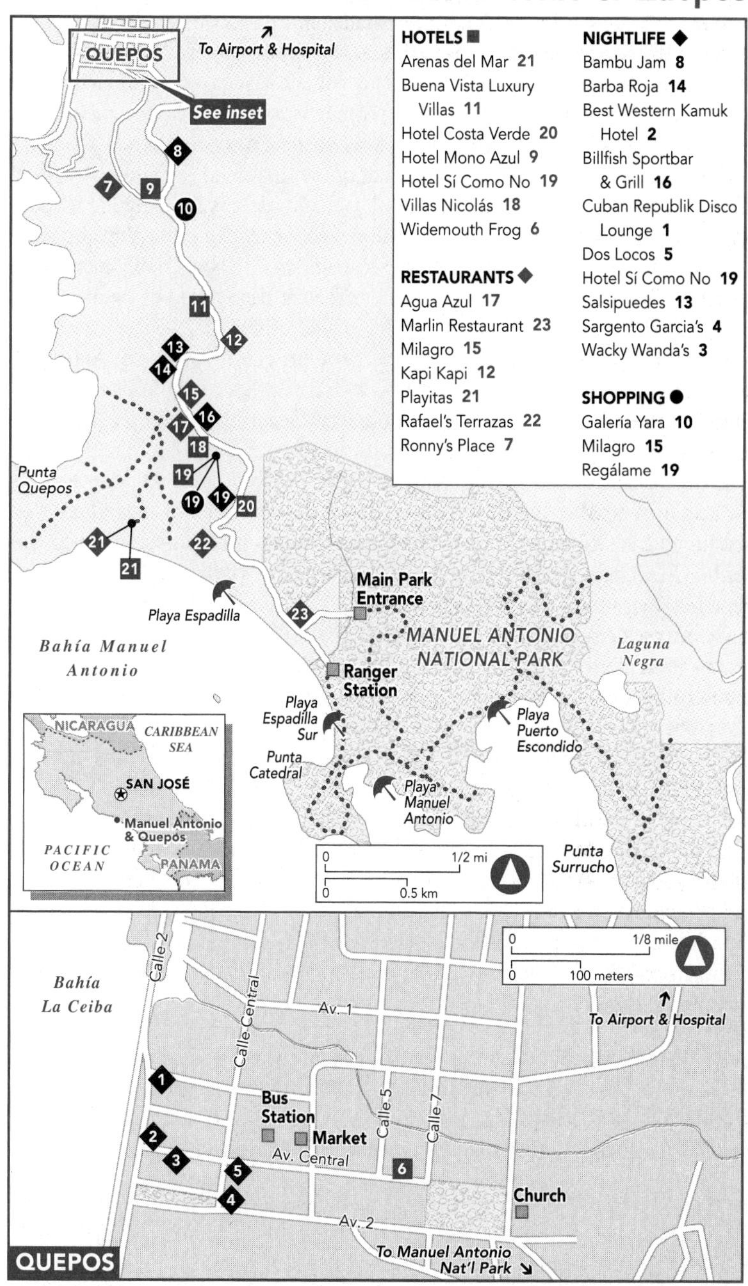

HOTELS ■
Arenas del Mar 21
Buena Vista Luxury Villas 11
Hotel Costa Verde 20
Hotel Mono Azul 9
Hotel Sí Como No 19
Villas Nicolás 18
Widemouth Frog 6
RESTAURANTS ◆
Agua Azul 17
Marlin Restaurant 23
Milagro 15
Kapi Kapi 12
Playitas 21
Rafael's Terrazas 22
Ronny's Place 7
NIGHTLIFE ◆
Bambu Jam 8
Barba Roja 14
Best Western Kamuk Hotel 2
Billfish Sportbar & Grill 16
Cuban Republik Disco Lounge 1
Dos Locos 5
Hotel Sí Como No 19
Salsipuedes 13
Sargento Garcia's 4
Wacky Wanda's 3
SHOPPING ●
Galería Yara 10
Milagro 15
Regálame 19
QUEPOS
To Airport & Hospital
See inset
Punta Quepos
Playa Espadilla
Bahía Manuel Antonio
Main Park Entrance
MANUEL ANTONIO NATIONAL PARK
Laguna Negra
Ranger Station
Playa Espadilla Sur
Punta Catedral
Playa Puerto Escondido
Playa Manuel Antonio
Punta Surrucho
NICARAGUA
CARIBBEAN SEA
SAN JOSÉ
Manuel Antonio & Quepos
PACIFIC OCEAN
PANAMA
0
1/2 mi
0.5 km
Bahía La Ceiba
Calle 2
Calle Central
Av. 1
1/8 mile
100 meters
To Airport & Hospital
Bus Station
Market
Calle 5
Calle 7
Av. Central
Church
Av. 2
To Manuel Antonio Nat'l Park
QUEPOS

here. Booming tourism and development have adversely affected the natural appeal of this place, which is often criticized because it's so touristy. What was once a smattering of small hotels tucked into the forested hillside has become a string of lodges along the 7km (4⅓ miles) of road between Quepos and the national park entrance. A jumble of snack shacks, souvenir stands, and makeshift parking lots choke the beach road just outside the park, making the entrance road look more like a shantytown than a national park.

Still, this remains a beautiful destination, with a wide range of attractions and activities that make it perfect for all sorts of travelers. Gazing down on the blue Pacific from high on the hillsides of Manuel Antonio, you'll realize there's a good reason so many people come here. Offshore, rocky islands dot the vast expanse, and in the foreground, the rich, deep green of the rainforest sweeps down to the water.

One of the most popular national parks in the country, Manuel Antonio is also one of the smallest, covering fewer than 680 hectares (1,680 acres). Its several nearly perfect small beaches are connected by trails that meander through the rainforest. The mountains surrounding the beaches quickly rise as you head inland from the water; however, the park was created to preserve not its beautiful beaches but its forests, home to rare squirrel monkeys, three-toed sloths, purple-and-orange crabs, and hundreds of other species. Once this entire stretch of coast was a rainforest teeming with wildlife, but now only this small rocky outcrop of forest remains.

Those views that are so bewitching also have their own set of drawbacks. If you want a great view, you aren't going to be staying on the beach—in fact, you probably won't be able to walk to the beach. This means that you'll be driving back and forth, taking taxis, or riding the public bus. Also bear in mind that it's hot and humid here, and that all that lush rainforest means there's a lot of rain.

If you're traveling on a rock-bottom budget or are mainly interested in sportfishing, you might end up staying in the nearby town of **Quepos,** which was once a quiet banana port and now features a wide variety of restaurants, shops, and lively bars. Disease wiped out most of the banana plantations, and now the land is planted primarily with African palm trees (see "Profitable Palms," below).

Essentials

ARRIVING **By Plane:** Both **Nature Air** (www.natureair.com; ✆ **800/235-9272** in the U.S. and Canada, or 2299-6000) and **Sansa** (www.flysansa.com; ✆ **877/767-2672** in the U.S. and Canada, or 2290-4100 in Costa Rica) offer several daily direct flights to the **Quepos airport** (airport code: XQP). The flight is 30 minutes long; the fare is $60 to $90 each way.

Both **Sansa** (✆ **2777-1912** in Quepos) and **Nature Air** (✆ **2777-2548** in Quepos) provide minivan airport-transfer service coordinated with their arriving and departing flights. The service costs around $8 per person each way. Taxis meet incoming flights and may be more economical. Expect to be

Travel Tips

If you plan carefully, you can avoid many of the problems that detract from Manuel Antonio's appeal. Steer clear of the peak months (Dec–Mar), and you can miss most of the crowds. If you must come during the peak period, try to avoid weekends, when the beach is packed with families and young Ticos from San José. Plan to arrive early in the morning, and then leave when the crowds begin to show up at midday.

charged between $10 and $20 per car for up to four people, depending on the distance to your hotel.

By Car: Head west out of San José on the San José–Caldera Highway (CR27). Just past the fourth toll booth at Pavón, follow the signs to Jacó and you'll turn onto the Costanera Sur (CR34), the Southern Coastal Highway. From here it's a straight shot down the coast to Quepos and Manuel Antonio. The trip should take a little over an hour.

If you're coming from Guanacaste or any point north, take the Inter-American Highway to the Puntarenas turnoff and follow signs to the San José–Caldera Highway (CR27). Take this east toward Orotina, where it connects with the Costanera Sur (CR34). It's about a 4½-hour drive from Liberia to Quepos and Manuel Antonio.

By Bus: Tracopa buses (www.tracopacr.com; ✆ **2221-4214** or 2290-1308) to Manuel Antonio leave San José regularly throughout the day between 6am and 7:30pm from Calle 5 between avenidas 18 and 20. Trip duration is around 3 hours; the fare is C4,675. These buses go to the park entrance and will drop you off at any of the hotels along the way.

For your return trip, the **Quepos bus station** (✆ **2777-0263**) is next to the market, 3 blocks east of the water and 2 blocks north of the road to Manuel Antonio. Buses depart for San José daily between 4am and 5pm.

Gray Line (www.graylinecostarica.com; ✆ **800/719-3105** in the U.S. and Canada, or 2220-2222 in Costa Rica) and **Interbus** (www.interbusonline.com; ✆ **4031-0888**) both have two buses daily leaving San José for Quepos and Manuel Antonio, one in the morning and one in the afternoon. The fare is around $50. Both companies will pick up at most San José-area hotels. Both also offer connections to most major tourist destinations in the country.

Many of the buses for Quepos stop to unload and pick up passengers in **Jacó.** If you're in Jacó heading toward Manuel Antonio, you can try your luck at one of the covered bus stops on the Inter-American Highway.

In the busy winter months, tickets sell out well in advance, especially on weekends; if you can, purchase your ticket several days in advance. However, you must buy your Quepos-bound tickets in San José and your San José return tickets in Quepos. If you're staying in Manuel Antonio, you can buy your return ticket for a direct bus in advance in Quepos, and then wait along the road to be picked up. There is no particular bus stop; just make sure you are

Profitable Palms

On any drive to or from Quepos and Manuel Antonio, you'll pass through miles and miles of African palm plantations. Native to West Africa, *Elaeis guineensis* was planted along this stretch in the 1940s by the United Fruit Co., in response to a blight that was attacking its banana crops. The palms took hold and soon proved quite profitable, being blessed with copious bunches of plum-size nuts that are rich in oil. This oil is extracted and processed in plantations that dot the road between Jacó and Quepos. The smoke and distinct smell of this processing is easily noticed. The processed oil is eventually shipped overseas and used in a wide range of products, including soaps, cosmetics, lubricants, and food products.

These plantations are a major source of employment in the area—note the small, orderly "company towns" built for workers—but their presence is controversial. The palm trees aren't native, and the farming practices are thought by some to threaten Costa Rica's biodiversity.

out to flag down the bus and give it time to stop—you don't want to be standing in a blind spot when the bus comes flying around a tight corner.

CITY LAYOUT Quepos is a small port city at the mouth of the Boca Vieja Estuary. If you're heading to Manuel Antonio National Park, or any hotel on the way to the park, after crossing the bridge into town, take the lower road (to the left of the high road). In 4 blocks, turn left, and you'll be on the road to Manuel Antonio. This road winds through town a bit before starting over the hill to all the hotels and the national park.

FAST FACTS The telephone number of the **Quepos Hospital** is ✆ **2777-0922.** In case of emergency, you can also call the **Cruz Roja** (Red Cross; ✆ **2777-0116**). For the **local police,** call ✆ **2777-3608.** The **post office** (✆ **2777-1471**) is in downtown Quepos. Several pharmacies are in Quepos, as well as a pharmacy at the hospital, and another close to the park entrance. A half-dozen or so laundromats and laundry services are in town. Several major Costa Rican banks have branches and ATMs in downtown Quepos, and a couple of ATMs have sprung up along the road to the national park.

Getting Around

By Taxi: A taxi between Quepos and Manuel Antonio (or any hotel along the road toward the park) costs between C4,000 and C5,000, depending upon the distance. At night or if the taxi must leave the main road (for hotels such as La Mariposa, Parador, Makanda, and Arenas del Mar), the charge is a little higher. If you need to call a taxi, dial ✆ **2777-0425** or 2777-1207. Taxis are supposed to use meters, although they don't always. If your taxi doesn't have a meter, or the driver won't use it, try to negotiate in advance. Ask your hotel what a taxi ride should cost.

By Bus: The bus between Quepos and Manuel Antonio (✆ **2777-0318**) takes 15 minutes each way and runs roughly every half-hour from 5:30am to

9:30pm daily. The buses, which leave from the main bus terminal in Quepos, near the market, go all the way to the national park entrance before turning around and returning. You can flag down these buses from any point on the side of the road. The fare is C250.

By Car: You can also rent a car from **Adobe** (✆ **2777-4242**), **National/Alamo** (✆ **2777-3344**), **Economy** (✆ **2777-5260**), or **Hertz** (✆ **2777-3365**) for between $53 and $150 a day. All have offices in downtown Quepos or Manuel Antonio, but with advance notice, someone will meet you at the airport with your car for no extra charge.

If you rent a car, never leave anything of value in it. Car break-ins are common here. A couple of parking lots just outside the park entrance cost around $3 for the entire day. You should definitely keep your car in one of these while exploring the park or soaking up sun on the beach. And although these lots do offer a modicum of protection, you still should not leave anything of value exposed in the car. The trunk is probably safe.

Where to Stay

EXPENSIVE

Buena Vista Luxury Villas ★★ (www.buenavistaluxuryvillas.net; ✆ **866/569-6241** in the U.S. and Canada, or 2777-0580 in Costa Rica) is the current incarnation of the former Tulemar Resort. It features a wide range of private villas and bungalows in a gated community; each unit has access to Buena Vista's own secluded and protected bit of beach.

If you're coming for an extended stay with the family or a large group, consider **Escape Villas ★★★** (www.escapevillas.com; ✆ **888/771-2976** in the U.S., or 2203-4401 in Costa Rica) or **Manuel Antonio Rentals ★★** (www.manuelantoniovacationrentals.com; ✆ **985/247-4558** in the U.S., or 8913-9415 in Costa Rica). Both outfits rent a broad selection of large and luxurious private villas and homes, with all the amenities and some of the best views in Manuel Antonio.

Arenas del Mar ★★★ This beachfront resort is in a league of its own, with handsome rooms, fabulous views, great dining, and direct access to two beaches. All rooms are wonderfully spacious, featuring pale yellow antique-style tile floors, cushy beds complete with leaf-print headboards and sleek, minimalist decor. Many rooms come with a private outdoor Jacuzzi tub on a private balcony. There are two main centers of operation—one near the highest point of the property, the other down by one of the beaches—and each has its own pool, restaurant, and bar. This property is a leader in sustainable tourism and conservation, and all stays include a guided tour on sustainable living.

Manuel Antonio. www.arenasdelmar.com. ✆ **2777-2777.** 38 units. $350–$470 double; $590–$780 suite. Additional person $70. Rates include full breakfast and free local and international calls. **Amenities:** 2 restaurants; 2 bars; babysitting; concierge; 2 small outdoor pools; room service; spa; free Wi-Fi.

Hotel Sí Como No ★★ This boutique resort occupies a privileged position on a high ridge about midway between Quepos and the Manuel Antonio

National Park. Upon arrival you'll be drawn to the jutting triangular lookout point just off the lobby. It's all dense rainforest below, with spectacular views of the Pacific Ocean. You'll enjoy the same view from most of the rooms, almost all of which feature private balconies. Monkey sightings are quite common here. There are two restaurants, two pools (one is adults only, the other has a fun little waterslide for the kids), and an air-conditioned theater with nightly movie showings. Sí Como No's friendly owner, Jim Damalas, was an early leader in sustainable tourism in Costa Rica and the hotel was awarded "5 Leaves" in the CST Certification for Sustainable Tourism program.

Manuel Antonio. www.sicomono.com. ✆ **888/742-6667** in the U.S., or 2777-0777 in Costa Rica. 57 units. $242–$350 double; $400–$450 suite. Rates include full breakfast. Extra person $30. Children 5 and under stay free in parent's room. **Amenities:** 2 restaurants; 2 bars; babysitting; concierge; 1 Jacuzzi; 2 midsize outdoor pools, including 1 w/ small waterslide; modest spa; free Wi-Fi.

MODERATE

Hotel Costa Verde ★ Make sure your tray table is in the upright and locked position if you stay in the converted Boeing 727 that serves as a two-bedroom suite here, with the nose appearing to be flying straight out of the rainforest. Most of the rooms in this sprawling complex are found in two tall buildings (one for families, one adults only), featuring large balconies with wonderful rainforest and ocean views. The studio and studio-plus rooms all have kitchenettes and flat-screen TVs. Not all rooms have air-conditioning or televisions and some can be quite a hike to the main restaurant, so be sure to check before making your choice. The hotel has a series of trails, one of which leads to the beach. It's about a 10-minute walk, but since the complex is located on a steep hillside, the return trip from the beach and to some of the rooms can be strenuous. Breakfast is served at the main hotel complex, and there are three restaurants across the street.

Manuel Antonio. www.costaverde.com. ✆ **866/854-7958** in the U.S. and Canada, or 2777-0584 in Costa Rica. 70 units. $79–$200 double; $180–$350 bungalows. **Amenities:** 4 restaurants; 4 bars; 3 small outdoor pools; free Wi-Fi.

Villas Nicolás ★★ This collection of spacious condo units offers up the very same classic Manuel Antonio views at near bargain prices. Virtually all of the rooms here come with large balconies, reached via arched wooden French doors. Every balcony comes equipped with a sleep-inducing rope hammock, and monkey sightings are common. Some units have full kitchens, and many can be combined to accommodate families or groups. All have different owners, so interior decor can vary from tropical casual to contemporary chic. The pretty pool is surrounded by blooming gardens. The service is friendly and personal.

Manuel Antonio. www.villasnicolas.com. ✆ **2777-0481.** 19 units. $152–$192 double; $170–$210 suite; $300–$400 upstairs-downstairs villa. Rates include taxes and breakfast. No children under 6. **Amenities:** Restaurant; bar; pool; free Wi-Fi.

INEXPENSIVE

True budget hotels are hard to come by in and around Quepos and Manuel Antonio. Those on a tight budget should look at **Widemouth Frog ★** (www.widemouthfrog.org; ✆ **2777-2798**), a hostel in downtown Quepos, which offers everything from bunk-bed dorm rooms with shared bathrooms to cozy double rooms with private facilities, plus a swimming pool.

Hotel Mono Azul ★ Under new ownership as of December 2014, the "Blue Monkey" has a hostel-like feel and very social vibe, with slightly more upscale accommodations than you'd find in a typical hostel. Husband-and-wife owners Paige Cain and John Westgard have made several renovations, included making two rooms, a public restroom, and one swimming pool accessible to the disabled, and they are in the process of replacing televisions, air conditioners, linens, and mattresses. Rooms, which can be somewhat dated, vary quite a bit in size and amenities; larger and higher-priced rooms have air-conditioning and television. The two pool areas are quite nice, with pretty gardens and plenty of shade, and you can often spot toucans and sloths here. The little restaurant is a hub of activity and a great place to meet fellow travelers.

Manuel Antonio. www.monoazul.com. ✆ **2777-1548.** 20 units. $65–$95 double. **Amenities:** Restaurant; bar; lounge; 2 outdoor pools; free Wi-Fi.

Where to Eat

Scores of dining options are available around Manuel Antonio and Quepos, and almost every hotel has some sort of restaurant. For the cheapest meals around, try a simple *soda* in Quepos, or head to one of the open-air joints on the beach road before the national park entrance. Here the standard Tico menu prevails, with prices in the C3,500-to-C6,500 range. Of these, **Marlin Restaurant ★** (✆ **2777-1134**), right in front of Playa Espadilla, is your best bet. **Mi Lugar,** or **"Ronny's Place" ★** (www.ronnysplace.com; ✆ **2777-5120**), on the outskirts of Quepos, is another fine spot.

For lunch, try the beachfront **Playitas ★★** at Arenas del Mar (p. 187); in addition to its great location and secure parking, you get pool privileges for the price of an excellent meal.

EXPENSIVE

Kapi Kapi ★★★ FUSION/NUEVO LATINO Ready to propose? Kapi Kapi is the place to pick. Dim lighting, an elegant, almost Asian decor, and generous space between tables make Kapi Kapi romantic and private. And the food won't break the spell. It's very fresh, making use of local produce and seafood whenever possible, and highly inventive. Favorites on the menu include local shrimp skewered on spikes of sugar cane, grilled, and then bathed in a glaze of rum, tamarind, and coconut; and the mahimahi crusted in macadamia nuts, and served with a sweet plum-chili sauce and jasmine rice. The wide-ranging wine list includes selections from Italy, France, Argentina, and Chile.

On the road from Quepos to Manuel Antonio. www.restaurantekapikapi.com. ✆ **2777-5049.** Main courses C8,500–C14,500. Daily 4–10pm.

MODERATE

Agua Azul ★★ INTERNATIONAL Sitting high above the rainforest with sweeping views over the trees to the Pacific Ocean below, this corrugated zinc-roofed, open-air restaurant has one of the best settings in town. There's little in the way of decor, but there really doesn't need to be when the sunsets are so pretty (grab a table at the railing if you can for an unobstructed view). Agua Azul's menu seems, at first glance, to be heavy in bar food standards, but dishes often have a creative twist (like the signature tuna margarita, seared tuna over a cucumber salad with a lime vinaigrette, all served in a salt-rimmed margarita glass). You can also get burgers and a few more substantial plates, like whole snapper in a tamarind sauce, and the chef's nightly pasta special.

Manuel Antonio, near Villas del Parque. www.cafeaguaazul.com. ✆ **2777-5280.** Main courses C4,500–C10,500. Tues–Mon 11am–9:30pm.

Milagro ★★★ NUEVO LATINO/FUSION A local institution, this offshoot of the coffee-roasting operation offers a full range of barista-brewed concoctions. But the appeal here goes well beyond java—breakfast, lunch, and dinner are served in the crayon-colored dining room and patios here, and they're all top-notch. For lunch, I like Milagro's take on a traditional Cuban sandwich, replacing the pork with fresh, local mahimahi. The dinner menu features fusion-inspired Latin fare with everything from jerk chicken to shrimp in a coconut-rum sauce served over mango-infused rice. Creative, contemporary cocktails, as well as excellent South American wines, can be ordered at the bar or at the tables. There's often live music in the evening.

On the road from Quepos to Manuel Antonio. www.cafemilagro.com. ✆ **2777-2272.** Reservations recommended. Main courses C6,300–C13,000. Daily 7am–10pm.

Rafael's Terrazas ★ SEAFOOD/COSTA RICAN This simple open-air restaurant has a stunning location, clinging to a steep hillside with a perfect view of the Pacific over a small patch of thick rainforest. The hillside is so steep that the dining rooms are terraced (hence the name) and spread over three floors connected by steep steps. The menu features a host of Tico classics and is heavy on fresh seafood. Try the excellent ceviche as a starter, then a *casado* of fish, chicken, or beef. More worldly options include seared tuna

Yo Quiero Hablar Español

Academia de Español D'Amore (www.academiadamore.com; ✆ **877/434-7290** in the U.S. and Canada, or 2777-0233 in Costa Rica) offers language-immersion programs out of a former hotel with a fabulous view on the road to Manuel Antonio. A 2-week conversational Spanish course, including a home stay and two meals daily, costs $1,100. Or you can try the **Costa Rica Spanish Institute** (**COSI;** www.cosi.co.cr; ✆ **2234-1001** or 2777-0021), which charges $1,180 for a similar 2-week program with a home stay.

with a ginger, soy, and wasabi sauce, or the bacon-wrapped tenderloin in a fresh mushroom sauce.

On the road from Quepos to Manuel Antonio. ✆ **2777-6310.** Reservations recommended. Main courses C5,300–C15,000. Tues–Sun 11am–11pm.

Exploring the National Park

Manuel Antonio is a small park with three major trails. Most visitors come primarily to lie on a beach and check out the white-faced monkeys. A guide is not essential here, but unless you're experienced in rainforest hiking, you'll see and learn a lot more with one. You can always stay on inside the park after your guided tour is over. A 2- or 3-hour guided hike should cost between $40 and $75 per person. Almost any hotel in town can help you set up a tour of the park. Avoid hawkers dressed as guides stopping you on the street for a hard sell.

ENTRY POINT, FEES & REGULATIONS In 2015, the park (✆ **2777-5185**) announced that it would be closed Mondays, but it remains open Tuesday through Sunday from 7am to 4pm. The entrance fee is $16 per person. The **main park entrance** is located almost about 1.5km (almost a mile) inland, at the end of the road that leads off perpendicular to Playa Espadilla at the corner featuring the popular Marlin Restaurant.

Another ranger station and exit point is at the end of the road from Quepos. This ranger station is located across a small stream that's little more than ankle-deep at low tide but that can be knee- or even waist-deep at high tide. It's even reputed to be home to a crocodile or two. For years there has been talk of building a bridge over this stream; in the meantime, access to or from the park via this point is prohibited.

MINAE, the national ministry that oversees the park, has been frustratingly inconsistent about which entrance visitors may use. However, for the past several years, tickets have been sold and entry allowed only at the inland entrance. This requires about 20 to 30 minutes of hiking along an often muddy access road before you get to the beach and principal park trails. ***Note:*** The Parks Service allows only 800 visitors to enter each day, which could mean that you won't get in if you arrive in midafternoon during the high season. Camping is not allowed.

People feeding monkeys, and monkeys and raccoons stealing food, have become a serious problem, and the park service no longer allows visitors to bring in many types of foods.

BEACHES **Playa Espadilla Sur** (as opposed to Playa Espadilla, which is just outside the park; see below) is the first beach within the actual park boundaries. It's usually the least crowded and one of the best places to find a quiet shade tree to plant yourself under. However, if there's any surf, this is also the roughest beach in the park. If you want to explore further, you can walk along this soft-sand beach or follow a trail through the rainforest parallel to the beach. **Playa Manuel Antonio,** which is the most popular beach inside the park, is a short, deep crescent of white sand backed by lush rainforest. The water here is sometimes clear enough to offer good snorkeling along the rocks at either end, and it's usually fairly calm. At low tide, Playa Manuel Antonio shows a very interesting relic: a circular stone turtle trap left by its pre-Columbian residents. From Playa Manuel Antonio, a slightly longer trail leads to **Puerto Escondido,** where a blowhole sends up plumes of spray at high tide.

HIKING TRAILS From either Playa Espadilla Sur or Playa Manuel Antonio, you can take a circular loop trail (1.4km/.9 mile) around a high promontory bluff. The highest point on this hike, which takes about 25 to 30 minutes round-trip, is **Punta Catedral ★★**, where the view is spectacular. The trail is a little steep in places, but anybody in average shape can do it. This is a good place to spot monkeys, as is the **trail inland** from Playa Manuel Antonio. A linear trail, it's mostly uphill, but it's not too taxing. It's great to spend hours exploring the steamy jungle and then take a refreshing dip in the ocean.

Finally, a trail connects Puerto Escondido (see above) and **Punta Surrucho,** which has some sea caves. Be careful when hiking beyond Puerto Escondido: What seems like easy beach hiking at low tide becomes treacherous to impassable at high tide. Don't get trapped.

BEACHES OUTSIDE THE PARK **Playa Espadilla,** the gray-sand beach just outside the park boundary, is often perfect for board surfing and bodysurfing. At times it's a bit rough for swimming, but with no entrance fee, it's the most popular beach with locals and visiting Ticos. Some shops by the water rent boogie boards, beach chairs, and umbrellas. A full-day rental of a beach umbrella and two chaise longues costs around $10. (These are not available inside the park.) This beach is actually a great spot to learn how to surf, because several open-air shops renting surfboards and boogie boards are along the beachfront road. Rates run $5 to $10 per hour, and around $20 to $30 per day. For a lesson, check with **Blue Horizon Surf School** (www.bluehorizonsurfschool.com; ✆ **8994-1424**), which provides excellent attention for individuals, small groups, and families.

Helping Out

If you want to help protect the local environment and the vulnerable squirrel monkey, make a donation to the **Titi Conservation Alliance** (www.monotiti.org; ✆ **2777-2306**), an organization supported by local businesses, or to **Kids Saving the Rainforest** (www.kidssavingtherainforest.org; ✆ **2777-2592**), which was started in 1999 by local children.

Organized Tours

Iguana Tours (www.iguanatours.com; ✆ **2777-2052**) is the most established tour operator in the area, offering **river rafting, sea kayaking, mangrove tours,** and guided hikes. Iguana as well as **Amigos del Río** (www.amigosdelrio.net; ✆ **877/393-8332** in the U.S., or 2777-0082 in Costa Rica) offer full-day rafting trips for around $90 to $95. Large multiperson rafts are used during the rainy season, and single-person "duckies" are broken out when the water levels drop. Both companies also offer half-day rafting adventures and sea-kayaking trips for around $65 to $90. Depending on rainfall and demand, they will run either the Naranjo or Savegre rivers. The **Savegre River ★★** is highly recommended for its stunning scenery.

Another good option in this area is the **mangrove tour** of the **Damas Island estuary.** These trips generally include lunch, a stop on Damas Island, and roughly 3 to 4 hours of cruising the waterways. You'll see lots of wildlife. The cost is usually $65 to $70. **Manuel Antonio Expeditions** (www.manuelantonioexpeditions.blogspot.com; ✆ **8365-1057**) is a good choice for this tour.

Among the other **boating options** around Quepos/Manuel Antonio are excursions in search of dolphins and sunset cruises. **Iguana Tours** (see above) and **Planet Dolphin ★** (www.planetdolphin.com; ✆ **800/943-9161** in the U.S., or 2777-1647 in Costa Rica) offer these tours for around $80 per person, depending on the size of the group and the length of the cruise. Most tours include a snorkel break, and you may see dolphins. For more of a booze cruise experience, you could try the 100-foot **Ocean King** (www.catamaranadventurescr.com; ✆ **4000-5740**).

Quepos is one of Costa Rica's **sportfishing** centers, and sailfish, marlin, and tuna are all common in these waters. In recent years, freshwater and brackish water fishing in the mangroves and estuaries has also become popular. If you're into sportfishing, hook up with **Blue Fin Sportfishing** (www.bluefinsportfishing.com; ✆ **2777-0000**) or **Luna Tours Sportfishing** (✆ **272/242-5982** in the U.S., or 2777-0725 in Costa Rica). A full day of fishing should cost between $600 and $1,900, depending on the size of the boat, distance traveled, tackle provided, and amenities. With so much competition here, it pays to stop by the marina and shop around.

For ATV enthusiasts, **Midworld ★★** (www.midworldcostarica.com; ✆ **2777-7181**) offers a range of **ATV tours** through forests and farmlands at its center on the outskirts of Quepos and Manuel Antonio. ATV tours are $105 for one person, $135 for two.

Manuel Antonio Nature Park ★★ (www.manuelantonionaturepark.com; ✆ **888/742-6667** in the U.S. and Canada, or 2777-0850 in Costa Rica) is just across from (and run by) Hotel Sí Como No (p. 187). A nice bi-level **butterfly garden ★** is the centerpiece attraction here, but there is also a private reserve and a small network of well-groomed trails through the forest. A 1-hour guided **tour of the butterfly garden** costs $15 per person. This is also a good place for a night tour ($39).

The most exciting local **canopy tour** is **Midworld ★★** (www.midworldcostarica.com; ✆ **2777-7181**). Its main zipline tour features 10 cables, including the longest cables in the area. It also has a face-down "Superman" cable, which is long and fast, as well as a ropes course. ATV tours through the surrounding rainforest stop at a waterfall pool for a dip. **Canopy Safari ★** (www.canopysafari.com; ✆ **888/765-8475** in the U.S. and Canada, or 2777-0100 in Costa Rica) is another good option, featuring 18 treetop platforms connected by a series of cables and suspension bridges, with a "Tarzan swing" and two rappels. The on-site butterfly garden and serpentarium are an added bonus. A canopy tour should cost around $85 per person, and up to $125 for a combo package that includes lunch.

While you can sometimes find locals renting horses on the beaches outside the national park, the crowded beach is too short to enjoy a nice ride, and the horse droppings are problematic. Better yet, head back into the hills and forests. Both **Finca Valmy** (✆ **2779-1118**) and **Brisas del Nara** (www.horsebacktour.com; ✆ **2779-1235**) offer **horseback excursions** that pass through both primary and secondary forest and feature a swimming stop or two at a jungle waterfall. Full-day tours, including breakfast and lunch, cost between $70 and $75 per person. Finca Valmy also offers an overnight tour for serious riders, with accommodations in rustic cabins in the Santa María de Dota Mountains.

The **ADR Adventure Park ★★** (www.adradventurepark.com; ✆ **877/393-8332** in the U.S. and Canada, or 2777-0082 in Costa Rica) is an excellent one-stop spot for thrill seekers. Billing itself as a 10-in-1 adventure tour, ADR offers a **7-hour full-day tour** that includes a zipline, waterfall rappels, a high plunge into a jungle river pool, horseback riding, and more. The cost is $130, and includes transportation and lunch.

Located 16km (10 miles) outside of Quepos, **Villa Vanilla ★★** (www.rainforestspices.com; ✆ **2779-1155** or 8839-2721) offers an informative and tasty **tour of its open-air botanical gardens and spice farm.** The commercial vanilla operation is the centerpiece, but you'll also learn about a host of other tropical spices and assorted flora, and you'll sample some sweet and savory treats and drinks. The half-day guided tour runs daily at 9am and 1pm and costs $50, including round-trip transportation from any area hotel. A small shop sells pure vanilla, cinnamon, and locally grown pepper.

Especially for Kids

For a taste of local Tico rural culture, mixed in with fabulous scenery and adventure, sign up for the **Santa Juana Mountain Tour & Canopy Safari ★★** (www.sicomono.com; ✆ **888/742-6667** in the U.S. and Canada, or 2777-0777 in Costa Rica). This full-day tour starts off with a visit to the Canopy Safari (p. 193) and then takes you to a local farming village in the mountains outside of Quepos. Here you can tour coffee and citrus farms, go for a horseback ride, hike trails, swim in rainforest pools, fish for tilapia, or see how sugar cane is processed. A traditional Tico lunch is included. Rates are $129 to $155 per person, depending on your group size, and $89 for kids under 12.

Shopping

If you're looking for souvenirs, you'll find plenty of beach towels, beachwear, and handmade jewelry in a variety of small shops in Quepos and at the rows of open-air shops and impromptu stalls near the national park. The gift shop inside **Milagro** ★★ (p. 190) features a host of excellent, locally sourced craft items, as well as freshly roasted coffee. For higher-end gifts, check out Hotel Sí Como No's **Regálame** (www.regalameart.com; ✆ **2777-0777**) gift shop, which has a wide variety of craft works, clothing, and original paintings and prints, or **Galería Yara** (✆ **2777-4846**), a contemporary art gallery in the Plaza Yara shopping center.

Nightlife

For evening entertainment, the bars at the **Barba Roja** restaurant, about midway along the road between Quepos and Manuel Antonio, and the **Hotel Sí Como No** (p. 187) are good places to hang out and meet people. To shoot some pool, head to the **Billfish Sportbar & Grill** ★ at the Byblos Resort (on the main road from Quepos to the park entrance). For tapas and local *bocas,* try **Salsipuedes** (roughly midway along the same road), which translates as "get out if you can." If you want live music, **Bambu Jam** ★ (along the same road) and **Dos Locos** (in the heart of downtown) are your best bets. You might also try **Hawg & Bill,** which fronts the beach in Playa Espadilla. In downtown Quepos, **Sargento Garcia's, Wacky Wanda's,** and the **Fish Head Bar** at El Gran Escape are all popular hangouts.

Night owls and people looking to dance can find live salsa and merengue music at **Bambu Jam,** and for real late-night action, the hottest club in town is the **Cuban Republik Disco Lounge,** in the heart of Quepos. The **Best Western Kamuk Hotel** in Quepos and the **Byblos Resort** both have small casinos and will even foot your cab bill if you try your luck gaming. If you want to see a movie, check what's playing at **Hotel Sí Como No**'s (p. 187) little theater, although you have to eat at the restaurant or spend a minimum amount at the bar for admission.

A Day Trip South of Manuel Antonio ★★

With a stunning setting and miles of nearly deserted beaches backed by rainforest-covered mountains, the coastline south of Manuel Antonio is an excellent place to find uncrowded stretches of sand, spectacular views, and remote jungle.

Leaving Manuel Antonio, the well-paved Costanera Sur highway (CR34) runs by mile after mile of palm-oil plantations, until just before the village of Dominical, where the mountains again meet the sea. From Dominical south, the coastline is dotted with tide pools, tiny coves, and cliffside vistas. Dominical is the largest town in the area, with an enviable location on the banks of Río Barú, right where it widens considerably before emptying into the ocean. The banks of the river and throughout the surrounding forests provide good birding. Along the coast and rivers, you're likely to see numerous shore and seabirds, including herons, egrets, and kingfishers, while the forests are home to colorful and lively tanagers, toucans, and trogons. Dominical is also one of the prime surf destinations in Costa Rica, with both right and left beach breaks. When the swell is big, the wave here is a powerful and hollow tube.

EXPLORING DOMINICAL & BALLENA MARINE NATIONAL PARK

This area is best explored with a rental car, although it can be done by local bus. A short distance south of Dominical lies **Dominicalito,** a small beach and cove that can be a decent place to swim. Farther south is **Playa Hermosa,** a long stretch of isolated beach with fine sand. The beach is unprotected and can be rough, but it's a nicer place to sunbathe and swim than Dominical.

At the village of Uvita, 16km (10 miles) south of Dominical, you'll reach the northern end of the **Ballena Marine National Park ★★**, which protects a coral reef that stretches from Uvita south to Playa Piñuela and includes the little Isla Ballena, just offshore. To get to **Playa Uvita,** which is inside the park, turn in at the village of Bahía and continue until you hit the ocean. The beach here is actually well protected and good for swimming. At low tide, an exposed sandbar allows you to walk about and explore another tiny island. This park is named for the whales that are sometimes sighted close to shore in the winter months. If you ever fly over this area, you'll notice that this little island and the spit of land that's formed at low tide compose the perfect outline of a whale's tail. An office at the entrance here regulates the park's use and even runs a small turtle-hatching shelter and program. Entrance to the national park is $10 per person. Camping is allowed here for $2 per person per day, including access to a public restroom and shower.

ORGANIZED TOURS

Adventures in Dominical include **kayak tours** of the mangroves, river floats in inner tubes, and day tours to Caño Island and Corcovado National Park. To arrange any of these activities, contact **Dominical Adventures** (www.dominicalsurfadventures.com; ✆ **2787-0431**) or the staff at the **Hotel Roca Verde** (www.rocaverde.net; ✆ **2787-0036**).

For **diving** the rocky sites off Ballena National Park or all the way out to Isla del Caño, call **Mystic Dive Center** (www.mysticdive.com; ✆ **2786-5217;** Dec 1–Apr 15 only), which has its main office in a small roadside strip mall down toward Playa Tortuga and Ojochal. Prices for Ballena National Park are $80 for snorkeling and $100 for a two-tank dive; rates for Isla del Caño are $130 for snorkeling and $170 for a two-tank dive.

Several local farms offer **horseback tours** through forests and orchards, and some of these farms provide overnight accommodations. **Hacienda Barú ★** (www.haciendabaru.com; ✆ **2787-0003**) offers several hikes and tours, including: a walk through mangroves and along the riverbank (for some good birdwatching); a rainforest hike through 80 hectares (198 acres) of virgin jungle; an all-day trek from beach to mangrove to jungle that includes a visit to some Indian petroglyphs, an overnight camping trip, and a combination horseback-and-hiking tour. The operation, which is dedicated to conservation and reforestation, even has **tree-climbing tours** and a small canopy platform 30m (98 ft.) above the ground, as well as one of the more common **zipline canopy tours.** Tour prices range from $25 for the mangrove hike to $125 for an

slithery FUN

Parque Reptilandia ★★ (www.crreptiles.com; ✆ **2787-0343;** daily 9am–4:30pm; $12 adult, $6 children 14 and under) is among the best snake and reptile attractions in Costa Rica. With more than 70 well-designed and spacious terrariums and other enclosures, the collection includes a wide range of snakes, frogs, turtles, and lizards, as well as a crocodile. Both native and imported species are on display, including the only Komodo dragon in Central America and a huge anaconda. For those looking to spice up their visit, Fridays are feeding days. The park is a few miles outside Dominical on the road to San Isidro.

overnight stay in the jungle. If you're traveling with a group, you'll be charged a lower per-person rate, depending on the number of people.

In addition to its eco- and adventure tourism activities, Hacienda Barú has 12 comfortable rooms at prices ranging from $75 to $107 double, including taxes and breakfast. Hacienda Barú is 3km (2 miles) north of Dominical on the road to Manuel Antonio.

The jungles just outside of Dominical are home to two spectacular waterfalls. The most popular and impressive is the **Santo Cristo** or **Nauyaca Waterfalls ★**, a two-tiered beauty with an excellent swimming hole and some good cliff-jumping. Most of the hotels in town can arrange for the horseback ride up here, or you can contact operator **Don Lulo** (www.cataratasnauyaca.com; ✆ **2787-0541**). A full-day tour, with both breakfast and lunch, should cost around $70–$90 per person, including transportation to and from Dominical. The tour is a mix of hiking, horseback riding, and hanging out at the falls. It is also possible to reach these falls by horseback from an entrance near the small village of Tinamaste. (You will see signs on the road.) Similar tours at similar prices are offered to the **Diamante Waterfalls,** which are a three-tiered set of falls with a 360m (1,180-ft.) drop, but a pool that's not quite as spacious and inviting as the one at Nauyaca.

THE SOUTHERN ZONE

9

Costa Rica's southern zone is an area of jaw-dropping beauty, with vast expanses of virgin lowland rainforest, loads of wildlife, tons of adventure opportunities, and few cities or towns. Lush, forested mountains tumble into the sea, streams run clear and clean, scarlet macaws squawk in the treetops, and dolphins and whales frolic in the Golfo Dulce. The Osa Peninsula is the most popular attraction in this region and one of the premier ecotourism destinations in the world. It's home to **Corcovado National Park ★★★**, the largest single expanse of lowland tropical rainforest in Central America, and to its neighbor, **Piedras Blancas National Park ★★**, both connected by the Golfo Dulce Forestry Reserve. Scattered around the edges of these national treasures and along the shores of the Golfo Dulce are some of the country's finest nature lodges.

The southern zone's remoteness is often emphasized, and perhaps exaggerated. You can fly into any of four airstrips here from San José in less than an hour, or you can drive here in about 6 hours on good, paved roads. Beyond the population centers, though, the roads get rough and four-wheel drive is often a must. Some places can be reached only by boat, and the prime attraction, Corcovado National Park, has no roads. However, you can fly into the heart of the park, take a boat, or undertake some of the most scenic (if grueling) hiking in the country to get there. You may find that even the most luxurious lodges here are rustic and lacking in amenities like air-conditioning, TVs, and telephones, but their stunning settings more than make up for it.

DRAKE BAY ★★

145km (90 miles) S of San José; 32km (20 miles) SW of Palmar

While Drake Bay (Bahía Drake in Spanish, pronounced *Ba-ee-ah Drah-keh*) remains one of the more isolated spots in Costa Rica, the small town located at the mouth of the **Río Agujitas** has boomed

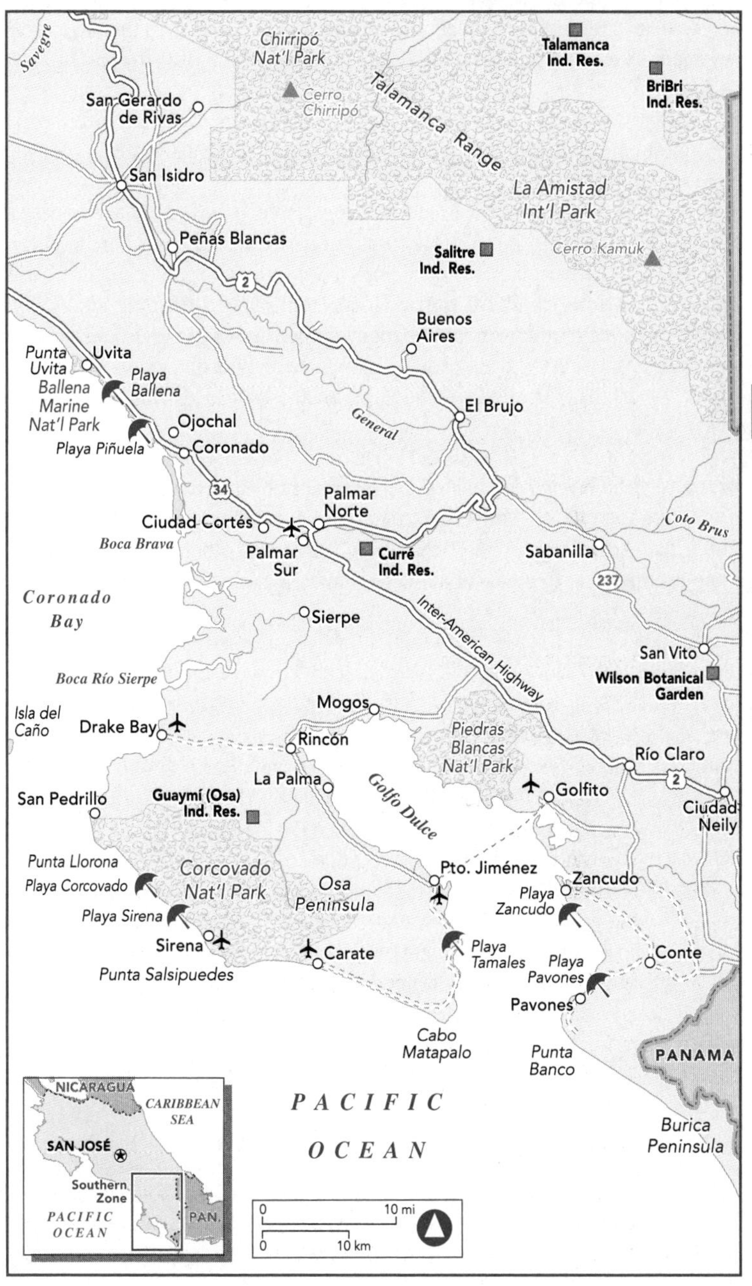
Savegre
Chirripó Nat'l Park
Cerro Chirripó
Talamanca Ind. Res.
BriBri Ind. Res.
Talamanca Range
San Gerardo de Rivas
San Isidro
La Amistad Int'l Park
Peñas Blancas
Salitre Ind. Res.
Cerro Kamuk
2
Buenos Aires
Punta Uvita
Uvita
Ballena Marine Nat'l Park
Playa Ballena
El Brujo
General
Ojochal
Playa Piñuela
Coronado
34
Palmar Norte
Ciudad Cortés
Boca Brava
Palmar Sur
Curré Ind. Res.
Sabanilla
Coto Brus
237
Coronado Bay
Sierpe
Inter-American Highway
San Vito
Wilson Botanical Garden
Boca Río Sierpe
Mogos
Isla del Caño
Drake Bay
Rincón
Piedras Blancas Nat'l Park
Río Claro
La Palma
Golfo Dulce
Golfito
Ciudad Neily
San Pedrillo
Guaymí (Osa) Ind. Res.
Punta Llorona
Playa Corcovado
Corcovado Nat'l Park
Osa Peninsula
Pto. Jiménez
Zancudo
Playa Zancudo
Playa Sirena
Sirena
Carate
Playa Tamales
Playa Pavones
Conte
Punta Salsipuedes
Pavones
Cabo Matapalo
Punta Banco
PANAMA
NICARAGUA
CARIBBEAN SEA
SAN JOSÉ
Southern Zone
PACIFIC OCEAN
PAN.
PACIFIC OCEAN
0
10 mi
0
10 km
Burica Peninsula

over the years. Some 25 years ago, there was no road, and the nearest regularly functioning airstrip was in Palmar Sur. Today a small airstrip operates here year-round, and the gravel road connecting Drake Bay to the paved road at Rincón is usually passable. Still, the village of Drake Bay, formally known as Agujitas, remains small, and most of the lodges here are quiet and remote getaways catering to wildlife lovers and scuba divers. Tucked away on the northwest corner of the Osa Peninsula, Drake Bay is a great place to get away from it all.

The bay is named after Sir Francis Drake, who is believed to have anchored here in 1579. The tiny Río Agujitas flows into a protected bay where boats are moored. It's a great place for canoeing or swimming, and a number of **dolphin- and whale-watching tours** depart from here. Stretching south from Drake are miles of remote beaches, rocky points, and stretches of primary and secondary rainforest. Adventurous explorers will find tide pools, spring-fed rivers, waterfalls, forest trails, and some of the best bird-watching in all of Costa Rica.

If you want to go to Drake Bay, be advised that almost all the visitors here have advance bookings at an all-inclusive resort. This is not the place to come if you like to "wing it," traveling first and seeking lodging later, nor will you find a lively community here where you'll run into other backpackers bumming around. The tourism model here is almost exclusively pre-booked with all-inclusive packages.

South of Drake Bay are the wilds of the **Osa Peninsula,** including **Corcovado National Park,** which is often described as the crown jewel of Costa Rican parks. It covers about a third of the Osa Peninsula and contains the largest single expanse of virgin lowland rainforest in Central America. For this reason, Corcovado is well known among naturalists and researchers studying rainforest ecology. If you come here, you'll learn firsthand why they're called rainforests: Some parts of the peninsula receive up to 700cm (23 ft.) of rain per year.

Puerto Jiménez (p. 206) is the best jumping-off place if you want to spend time hiking and camping in Corcovado National Park. Drake Bay is primarily a collection of high-end hotels, very isolated and mostly accessible by boat. These hotels offer great day hikes and guided tours into the park, but Puerto

Helping Out

If you want to help local efforts to protect the fragile rainforests and wild areas of the Osa, contact the **Corcovado Foundation** (www.corcovadofoundation.org; ✆ **2297-3013**) or **Osa Conservation** (www.osaconservation.org; ✆ **2735-5756**). If you're looking to really lend a hand, both of these groups have volunteer programs, ranging from trail maintenance to environmental and English-language education to sea-turtle protection programs.

Jiménez is the place to go if you want to spend more time in the park. (It has hotels for all budgets, the parks office, and land transportation to Carate and Los Patos, from which visitors can hike into the various stations.) From the Drake Bay side, you're more dependent on a boat ride/organized tour from one of the lodges to explore the park, but these lodges offer many other guided outings in addition to visits to the park.

Essentials

Because Drake Bay is so remote, I recommend that you have a room reservation and transportation (often arranged with your hotel) before you arrive. Most of the lodges listed here are scattered along several kilometers of coastline, and it is impossible to wander from one to another looking for a room.

Tip: A flashlight and rain gear are always useful to have on hand in Costa Rica, and during the rainy season in Drake Bay they're absolutely essential.

ARRIVING **By Plane:** Most visitors fly directly into the little airstrip at Drake Bay (airport code: DRK), although the more adventurous can fly to Palmar Sur and then boat down the Sierpe River through the Térraba-Sierpe wetlands, the largest mangrove swamp in the Northern Hemisphere. All lodges will either arrange transportation for you or include it in their packages. Both **Nature Air** (www.natureair.com; ✆ **800/235-9272** in the U.S. and Canada, or 2299-6000 in Costa Rica) and **Sansa** (www.flysansa.com; ✆ **877/767-2672** in the U.S. and Canada, or 2290-4100 in Costa Rica) fly directly to Drake Bay from San José's Juan Santamaría International Airport. Flights also depart San José daily from the same airport for Palmar Sur. Fares range from $120 to $210 each way by air; a taxi to Sierpe runs about $30 and a boat ride to Drake $20.

If your travels take you to Drake Bay via Palmar Sur, you must then take a 15-minute bus or taxi ride over dirt roads to the small town of **Sierpe.** This bumpy route runs through several **banana plantations** and past an important archaeological site featuring the stone spheres of the Diquís indigenous group. In Sierpe, you board a small boat for a 40km (25-mile) ride to Drake Bay; see "By Taxi & Boat from Sierpe," below. The first half of this trip snakes through a maze of mangrove canals and the main river channel before negotiating the mouth of the Sierpe River and heading out to sea for the final leg to the bay. ***Warning:*** Entering and exiting the Sierpe River mouth is often treacherous.

By Bus: Tracopa buses (www.tracopacr.com; ✆ **2221-4214** or 2290-1308) leave San José daily for the southern zone throughout the day, between 5am and 6:30pm from Calle 9 and Avenida 18. Almost all stop in Palmar Norte, but make sure to ask. The ride takes around 6 hours; fares are around C8,000. Once in Palmar Norte, ask when the next bus leaves for Sierpe. If it doesn't leave for a while (buses aren't frequent), consider taking a taxi.

By Taxi & Boat from Sierpe: When you arrive at either the Palmar Norte bus station or the Palmar Sur airstrip (airport code: PMZ), you'll most likely first need to take a taxi to the village of Sierpe. The fare should be around $35. If you're booked with one of the main lodges, chances are your transportation is included. Even if you're not booked with one of the lodges, a host of taxi and minibus drivers offer the trip. When you get to Sierpe, head to the river dock at either the Las Vegas Restaurant or the Hotel Oleaje Sereno to book passage on the collective water taxis. This will cost you an additional $20, or you can charter a private boat for your party for $200 or so. Collective water taxis are timed to coincide with the twice-daily Sansa flights from San José.

By Car: Driving to Drake Bay is not for the faint of car. Four-wheel drive is essential on the sometimes steep gravel road, and you have to cross three streams and one fair-size river, plus there's a scary little bridge with two planks for your tires and no rails. If you do drive here from the capital, take the San José–Caldera Highway (CR27) to the first exit after the fourth toll booth and follow the signs to Jacó, where you will pick up the Southern Highway, or Costanera Sur (CR34). Take this south past Jacó, Quepos, Dominical, and Uvita, and turn right onto the Inter-American Highway (CR2) at Palmar Norte. Take this road south to the junction at Chacarita, where you can gas up before turning right toward the Osa Peninsula, following the signs for Puerto Jiménez and Corcovado. Just before the Rincón River bridge, turn right to follow the signs to Drake.

About 5km from Drake, there's one fairly wide river that can become impassable in the rainy season, but you can leave your car at the Drake Bay Backpackers Hostel and catch a ride the rest of the way for $20 or so. The road ends in the town of Drake Bay, formally known as Agujitas, so from there you must take a boat to reach destinations to the south. The only hotels that you can actually drive up to are very basic cabins in town.

DEPARTING If you're not flying directly out of Drake Bay, have your lodge arrange a boat trip back to Sierpe for you. Be sure that the lodge also arranges for a taxi to meet you in Sierpe for the trip to Palmar Sur or Palmar Norte. (If you're on a tight budget, you can ask around to see whether a late-morning public bus is still running from Sierpe to Palmar Norte.) In Palmar Sur you can catch your round-trip return flight, and from Palmar Norte you can catch north- and southbound buses along the Inter-American and Costanera highways.

Drake Bay Hotels

Given the remote location and logistics of reaching Drake Bay, as well as the individual isolation of each hotel, nearly all the hotels listed below deal almost exclusively in package trips that include transportation, meals, tours, and taxes. I list the most common packages, although all the lodges will work with you to accommodate longer or shorter stays. Nightly room rates are listed only where they're available and practical, generally at the more moderately priced hotels.

EXPENSIVE

La Paloma Lodge ★★★ This is one of the top nature lodges in Costa Rica—the views are superb, the setting sublime, and the wildlife viewing and adventure opportunities are as good as it gets. Rooms are beautiful, with gleaming hardwood decks and interiors, and most are two-story, with a bedroom and bathroom upstairs and down connected by a spiral staircase. The food and service are top-notch, with guests seated together at long tables, swapping tales over four-course dinners. A small pool sits on the edge of a jungle-clad hillside, and Cocalito Beach is a short hike down a winding trail through the rainforest.

Drake Bay. www.lapalomalodge.com. ✆ **2293-7502.** 11 units. $990–$1,245 per person for 4 days/3 nights with 2 tours; $1,235–$1,575 per person for 5 days/4 nights with 2 tours. Rates are based on double occupancy and include all meals, park fees, and indicated tours. Rates slightly lower in off-season. Closed around Sept 15–Nov 1. **Amenities:** Restaurant; bar; small pool; free use of kayaks; free Wi-Fi.

MODERATE

In addition to the spot listed below, you might check out **Finca Maresia ★** (www.fincamaresia.com; ✆ **2775-0279**), a pretty boutique property located between Drake Bay and the national park.

Drake Bay Wilderness Resort ★★ This has one of the best locations of all the lodges in Drake Bay, on a large chunk of land with the Agujitas River and Drake Bay on one side and the open Pacific Ocean on the other. Rooms feature hand-painted murals on concrete walls, and comfortable beds. A couple of budget rooms share bathrooms and shower facilities. The shoreline right at the lodge is a bit too rocky for swimming, but there's a nice pool naturally fed and filled with seawater. Owner Marleny's chocolate-chip cookies are regionally renowned.

Drake Bay. www.drakebay.com. ✆ **2775-1716** or 2775-1715. 20 units. $865 per person for 4 days/3 nights with 2 tours, including all meals and taxes. **Amenities:** Restaurant; bar; small saltwater pool; free use of canoes and kayaks; free Wi-Fi.

INEXPENSIVE

Hotel Jinetes de Osa ★★ Just off the water at the far southern end of the Drake Bay shore, this is an excellent budget to mid-priced option. Many of the rooms have splendid ocean views, all have hot water, and some are air-conditioned. In the rooms up the hill, be prepared for a bit of a climb. The hotel specializes in dive trips and is recognized as a full-service PADI (Professional Association of Diving Instructors) resort.

Drake Bay. www.jinetesdeosa.com. ✆ **866/553-7073** in the U.S. and Canada, or 2231-5806 in Costa Rica. 13 units. $65–$160 double plus tax, breakfast included. **Amenities:** Restaurant; bar; free Wi-Fi.

Exploring Drake Bay

Beaches, forests, wildlife, and solitude are the main reasons to visit Drake Bay. Although Corcovado National Park (see "Puerto Jiménez: Gateway to

THOSE MYSTERIOUS stone spheres

Although Costa Rica lacks the great cities, giant temples, and bas-relief carvings of the Maya, Aztec, and Olmec civilizations of northern Mesoamerica, its pre-Columbian inhabitants left a unique legacy that has archaeologists and anthropologists still scratching their heads. Over a period of several centuries, hundreds of painstakingly carved and carefully positioned stone spheres were left by the peoples who lived throughout the Diquís Delta, which flanks the Térraba River in southern Costa Rica. The orbs, which range from grapefruit size to more than 2m (6½ ft.) in diameter, can weigh up to 15 tons, and all are nearly perfect spheres.

Archaeologists believe that the spheres were created during two defined cultural periods. The first, called the Aguas Buenas period, dates from around A.D. 100 to 500. Few spheres survive from this time. The second phase, during which spheres were created in apparently greater numbers, is called the Chiriquí period and lasted from approximately A.D. 800 to 1500. The "balls" believed to have been carved during this time frame are widely dispersed along the entire length of the lower section of the Térraba River. To date, only one known quarry for the spheres has been discovered, in the mountains above the Diquís Delta, which points to a difficult and lengthy transportation process.

Some archaeologists believe the spheres were hand-carved in a very time-consuming process, using stone tools. Another theory holds that granite blocks were placed at the base of powerful waterfalls, and the hydraulic beating of the water eventually turned and carved the rock into these near-perfect spheres. And more than a few theories have credited extraterrestrial intervention for the creation of the spheres.

Most of the stone balls have been found at the archaeological remains of defined settlements and are associated with either central plazas or known burial sites. Their size and placement have been interpreted to have both social and celestial importance, although their exact significance remains a mystery. Unfortunately, many of the stone balls have been plundered and are currently used as lawn ornaments in the fancier neighborhoods of San José. Some have even been shipped out of the country. The **Museo Nacional de Costa Rica** has a nice collection, including one massive sphere in its center courtyard. It's a never-fail photo op. You can also see the stone balls near the small **airports in Palmar Sur** and **Drake Bay,** and on **Isla del Caño** (which is 19km/12 miles off the Pacific Coast near Drake Bay).

The best place to see the spheres is the **Finca 6 Archaeological Museum ★★** (**✆ 2100-6000;** daily 8am–4pm; $6), located between Palmar Sur and Sierpe. (The blue sign saying FINCA 6, right next to a one-lane bridge, is easy to miss.) It's estimated that nearly 10 percent of all stone spheres produced in Costa Rica can be found on the 10 or so acres that comprise Finca 6. A small museum building provides background and displays of some smaller spheres and other artifacts. From here, trails lead out to several excavations of archeological finds where a range of large stone spheres and other relics are displayed in their original positioning. Finca 6 is located 6km (about 3.8 miles) south of Palmar Sur. This unique archeological site is easily visited by anyone arriving or departing Drake Bay via Sierpe.

Corcovado National Park," p. 206) is the area's star attraction, there are plenty of other nearby options. The Osa Peninsula is home to an unbelievable variety of plants and animals: more than 140 species of mammals, some 400 species of birds, and 130 species of amphibians and reptiles. You can expect to see as many as four species of monkeys, coatis, scarlet macaws, parrots, and hummingbirds. Other park inhabitants include jaguars, tapirs, peccaries, sloths, anteaters, and crocodiles.

Organized Tours & Activities

All lodges in the area have their own **in-house tour operations** and offer a host of half- and full-day tours and activities, including hikes in Corcovado, snorkeling trips to Caño Island, horseback rides, and wildlife-viewing treks. In some cases, tours are included in your room rate or package; in others, they must be bought a la carte. Other options include mountain biking and sea kayaking. Most of these tours run between $60 and $120; scuba diving costs about $150 for a two-tank dive with equipment, and sportfishing runs $900 to $1,800, depending on the size of the boat and other amenities.

If you want to try a zipline canopy adventure, the **Drake Bay Canopy Tour** (www.canopytour.com/drakebay.html; ✆ **8314-5454** or 2231-5806) has six cable runs, several "Tarzan swings," and a hanging bridge, all set in lush forests just outside Drake Bay. The 2-hour tour costs $55.

One of the most popular excursions from Drake Bay is a trip to **Isla del Caño** and the **Caño Island Biological Reserve ★★** for snorkeling or scuba diving or hiking on the island. Caño Island, about 19km (12 miles) off the Drake shore, was once home to a pre-Columbian culture about which little is known. Few animals or birds live on the island, but the coral reefs that ring the island teem with life, making this one of Costa Rica's prime **scuba diving sites ★★**. Visibility is often very good, especially during the dry season, and the beach has easily accessible snorkeling. All the lodges listed above offer trips to Isla del Caño. Since 2014, the Costa Rican National Park service has been severely restricting access to the island, and visiting groups are no longer allowed to picnic there. Typically, tours arrive in the morning, conduct their snorkel and scuba excursions, and then head back to the mainland for a picnic lunch and some beach time.

One of the most compelling tour options in Drake Bay is a 2-hour **night tour ★★★** (www.thenighttour.com; ✆ **8701-7356** or 8701-7462; $40 per person) offered by Tracie Stice, the "Bug Lady," and her partner Gianfranco Gómez. Equipped with headlamps, participants get a bug's-eye view of the forest at night. You might see some larger forest dwellers, but most of the tour is a fascinating exploration of the nocturnal world of insects, arachnids, frogs, toads, and snakes. Among the highlights is watching Tracie pry open the portal of a trapdoor spider, and you might see an orange-kneed tarantula.

Drake Bay is one of the best places in Costa Rica for **whale-watching;** Northern Pacific humpback whales are commonly spotted in the area from March to April and Southern Pacific populations during September and October. All the hotels listed above can arrange whale-watching and dolphin-spotting trips. Two resident marine biologists, Shawn Larkin and Roy Sancho, are often hired by the better hotels, but depending on demand and availability, the hotels may send you out with one of their own captains. If you want more information on the local whale-watching scene, or to contact Shawn Larkin directly, go to **www.costacetacea.com.** This crew also offers deep-water free diving and snorkel tours aimed at providing the chance to swim in close proximity to large pelagic fish, mammals, and reptiles.

PUERTO JIMÉNEZ: GATEWAY TO CORCOVADO NATIONAL PARK

35km (22 miles) W of Golfito by water (90km/56 miles by road); 85km (53 miles) S of Palmar Norte

Don't let its small size and languid pace fool you. **Puerto Jiménez ★** is a bustling little burg, where rough jungle gold-panners mix with wealthy eco-tourists, budget backpackers, serious surfers, and occasionally a celebrity seeking anonymity and escape. Located on the Golfo Dulce shoreline in the eastern **Osa Peninsula,** the town itself is just a few streets wide in any direction, with a soccer field, a handful of general stores, budget hotels, tourism offices, an airstrip, some inexpensive *sodas,* and several bars. Scarlet macaws fly overhead, and mealy parrots provide wake-up calls.

Corcovado National Park has its park service headquarters here, and the town makes an excellent base for exploring this vast wilderness area. Signs in English on walls around town advertise a variety of tours, including a host of activities outside the park. If the in-town accommodations are too basic, you'll find several far more luxurious places farther south on the Osa Peninsula. **Cabo Matapalo** (the southern tip of the peninsula) is a prime surf spot, home to several dependable right point breaks. Sometimes the waves at Pan Dulce and Backwash actually connect, and can provide rides almost as long as those to be had in the more famous Pavones.

Essentials

ARRIVING **By Plane:** Both **Nature Air** (www.natureair.com; ✆ **800/235-9272** in the U.S. and Canada, or 2299-6000 in Costa Rica) and **Sansa** (www.flysansa.com; ✆ **877/767-2672** in the U.S. and Canada, or 2290-4100 in Costa Rica) have daily direct flights to Puerto Jiménez from San José. The flight duration is around 55 minutes, although this flight often includes brief stops in Golfito or Drake Bay. Fares range from $80 to $140, one-way. Because of the remoteness of this area and the unpredictable flux of traffic, both Sansa and Nature Air sometimes improvise on scheduling, so it's always best to confirm.

Taxis are generally waiting to meet all incoming flights. A ride into downtown Puerto Jiménez should cost around C2,000. If you're staying at a hotel outside of town, it's best to have the hotel arrange for a taxi to meet you. Otherwise you can hire one at the airstrip. Depending on how far away you are staying, it could cost up to $90 for a four-wheel-drive vehicle to Carate or Los Patos, or $125 to Drake.

By Car: Take the San José–Caldera Highway (CR27) to the first exit past the fourth toll booth and follow the signs to Jacó, where you will pick up the Southern Highway, or Costanera Sur (CR34). Take this south through Jacó, Quepos, Dominical and Uvita, and turn right onto the Inter-American Highway (CR2) at Palmar Norte. Take this road south to the junction at Chacarita, turn right and follow the signs to Puerto Jiménez and Corcovado.

By Bus: Transportes Blanco-Lobo express buses (✆ **2257-4121** in San José, or 2771-4744 in Puerto Jiménez) leave San José daily at 8am and noon from Calle 12, between avenidas 7 and 9. The trip takes 7 to 8 hours; the fare is C7,500. Buses depart Puerto Jiménez for San José daily at 5am and 9am.

By Boat: A passenger ferry that seats about 20 makes several runs a day between Golfito and Puerto Jiménez. The fare is C3,000, and the ride takes a half-hour. The ferry operates between the *muellecito* (little dock) in Golfito and the *muelle* (public dock) in Puerto Jiménez. You can also charter a boat taxi between the two places.

VILLAGE LAYOUT The public pier is over a bridge past the north end of the soccer field, and the bus stop is a block west of the center of town. You'll find a couple of Internet cafes in town; the best is **CafeNet El Sol** (www.soldeosa.com; ✆ **8632-8150**), which is a great place to book tours and get information, and is also a Wi-Fi hot spot.

GETTING AROUND Four-wheel-drive taxis are plentiful in Puerto Jiménez. You'll find them cruising or parked along the main street of town, or have your hotel call one. You can rent a car here from **Solid Car Rental** (www.solidcarrental.com; ✆ **800/390-7065** in U.S. and Canada, or 2442-6000 in Costa Rica), or from **Alamo** (www.alamocostarica.com; ✆ **2735-5175** in Costa Rica).

Puerto Jiménez Hotels

EXPENSIVE

Iguana Lodge ★★ Located on the outskirts of Puerto Jiménez, this beachfront mini-resort is backed by tall rainforest trees and fronts a calm section of beach where the Golfo Dulce and Pacific Ocean meet. You'll find rooms in a wide range of prices here. I prefer the second-floor units of the two-story casitas, although the club rooms are a good value. There's a large, open-air, wood-floor studio, and yoga is a big attraction. Often there are yoga classes or a visiting group conducting a retreat. The gardens are lush, and gentle Platanares Beach is just steps away.

Playa Platanares. www.iguanalodge.com. ✆ **800/259-9123** in the U.S. and Canada, or 8848-0752 in Costa Rica. 19 units. $180 double club room; $440 casita double; $650 3-bedroom beach house. Rates for club room include breakfast. Rates for casita include breakfast and dinner; villa rates do not include meals. All rates include taxes. **Amenities:** 2 restaurants; bar; outdoor pool; spa; Jacuzzi; watersports equipment rental; free Wi-Fi.

INEXPENSIVE

In addition to the hotel listed below, **Cabinas Marcelina** (✆ **2735-5007**) is a clean, dependable budget lodging right in the heart of town.

Cabinas Jiménez ★★ On the waterfront 2 blocks from town, this hotel offers 15 air-conditioned rooms with fridges and a deck with hammocks. Some cabinas have kitchens and private decks overlooking the water, and there's a private waterfront 2-bedroom, 2-bath house with kitchen and deck. Rooms and common areas are enlivened by local arts and crafts, including hand-painted murals, carved animal sculptures, and complex iron works on the windows. The hotel offers guests complimentary use of kayaks and bicycles. The owner has a few boats and offers excellent tours of the Golfo Dulce and the nearby mangroves.

Puerto Jiménez, 50m (165 ft.) north of the soccer field. www.cabinasjimenez.com. ✆ **2735-5090.** 15 units. $57 double. **Amenities:** Small pool; free Wi-Fi.

Where to Eat in Puerto Jiménez

In addition to the places listed below, you might head to the waterfront **Marisquería Corcovado** (✆ **2735-5659**), a lively local joint serving up excellent seafood and local specialties. They'll even cook up your fresh catch if you've been fishing.

Il Giardino ★★ ITALIAN/INTERNATIONAL/SEAFOOD For years, this has been the best restaurant in Puerto Jiménez, and now it's got a waterfront location that matches the fine cooking. The pastas and ravioli are all homemade and delicious, and the seafood is freshly caught and perfectly prepared. Although it's an odd combination, these folks also frequently do sushi nights, and are even open for breakfast. Everything is made fresh to order, so the kitchen can be a bit slow at times.

On the beachfront, just down from the public pier, Puerto Jiménez. www.ilgiardinoitalianrestaurant.com. ✆ **2735-5129.** Main courses C5,000–C14,000. No credit cards. Daily 7am–10pm.

Pizza Mail.it ★ ITALIAN Nadia Zollia of Trieste, Italy, opened this great restaurant with the strange name in 2008, and it soon became the most popular pizza in town. It serves roughly 20 types of pizza, the most popular being the

Pizza Tica, with ground beef among several other ingredients. Pasta bolognesa is a great choice among the heaping plates of pasta. As for the name Pizza Mail.it, there's a myth that it comes from the fact that the post office is next door. It actually comes from Zollia's original intention of opening a small takeout place, with ".it" being the Italian suffix for e-mail addresses.

Across from the soccer field in Puerto Jiménez. ✆ **2735-5483.** Main courses C4,000–C9,000. Daily 3:30–10:30pm in high season.

Exploring Puerto Jiménez

While Puerto Jiménez has typically been a staging ground for adventures farther out toward Carate and Corcovado, quite a few activities and tours can be undertaken closer to town.

If you're looking to spend some time on the beach, head south of town on the airstrip road for a long, pretty stretch of sand called **Playa Platanares.** Here there are a couple of nice hotels, the **Iguana Lodge** and the **Agua Dulce Lodge.** Swimmers beware: The surf can be very powerful. If you head farther south on the peninsula, you'll come to the beaches of **Pan Dulce, Backwash,** and **Matapalo,** all major surf spots with consistently well-formed right point breaks and wave size depending on the swells coming in from the South Pacific. Backwash has a spectacular, long wave for intermediate and advanced surfers and an internal wave that is optimal for learners. **Pollo Surf School** offers year-round surf lessons ($55).

Osa Peninsula Lodges

As with most of the lodges in Drake Bay, the accommodations listed in this section include three meals a day in their rates and do a large share of their bookings in package trips. Per-night rates are listed, but the price categories have been adjusted to take into account the fact that all meals are included. Ask about package rates if you plan to take several tours and stay awhile: They could save you money.

In addition to the lodges listed below, other options range from small B&Bs to fully equipped home rentals. Surfers, in particular, might want to inquire into one of several rental houses located close to the beach at Matapalo. Your best bet for alternative accommodations is to contact **Jiménez Hotels** (www.jimenezhotels.com; ✆ **8632-8150**), which also handles a host of house rentals around the area.

Finally, Carate has several lodges. In addition to the lodges listed below, you can look into **Finca Exótica Eco-Lodge** ★ (www.fincaexotica.com; ✆ **4070-0054**), a delightful oceanview lodge, and **La Leona Eco-Lodge** ★ (www.laleonaecolodge.com; ✆ **2735-5705**), a tent-camp option on the outskirts of the national park.

This is a very isolated area, with just one gravel road connecting all the lodges, nature reserves, and parks. Almost all visitors here take all their meals at their lodge. If you want to venture away for some good simple home cooking, head to Martina Hoffman's **Buena Esperanza,** on the main road at Carbonera, near Matapalo.

EXPENSIVE

The following lodges are some of the best ecolodges Costa Rica has to offer, and most are pretty pricey. Bear in mind that the rooms have no TVs, telephones or air-conditioning, the roads are not paved, and there are no towns to speak of. Consequently, there are also no crowds and few modern distractions. The lodges listed below are 40 minutes to 2 hours outside Puerto Jimenez, along a rough dirt road, with several river crossings.

Bosque del Cabo Rainforest Lodge ★★★ Among the most spectacular of the Matapalo ecolodges, Bosque del Cabo is perched some 500 feet above the water on more than 750 acres, with neatly manicured grounds, multiple nature trails, a cool hanging bridge, and access to both the Pacific Ocean and the Golfo Dulce. The 13 elegant bungalows and three fully equipped houses have great ocean views, and others are surrounded by tropical gardens. All are done up in hardwoods, cane, and tile, and some of the bungalows have thatched roofs. There are two nice pools (one is an adult quiet pool) and many miles of wildlife trails, but also a thrillingly high zipline and tree platform set in a Manu tree. Guests may take a tree-climbing tour inside a hollowed-out tree, waterfall-rappelling courses, massage and reflexology treatments, and more.

Matapalo, Osa Peninsula. www.bosquedelcabo.com. ✆ **2735-5206** or 8389-2846. 18 units. $170–$350 per person. Rates include 3 meals daily and taxes. Round-trip transportation from Puerto Jiménez airport, $30 per person. **Amenities:** Restaurant; bar; 2 midsize pools; surfboard rental; on-site guide; free Wi-Fi.

El Remanso ★★ This magnificent collection of rooms, private cabins, and duplexes is just past Cabo Matapalo, 22km (14 miles) from Puerto Jiménez. It features a large main lodge and bamboo restaurant structure with a Pacific Ocean view, surrounded by towering rainforest trees. Rooms are spread around the sprawling gardens and grounds, and a few have ocean views. The lodge offers a variety of internal tours, including guided walks, waterfall rappelling, and a canopy tour with five cables and four platforms, plus a new 300-foot suspension bridge.

Matapalo, Osa Peninsula. www.elremanso.com. ✆ **2735-5569** or 8814-5775. 14 units. $170–$380 per person. Rates include 3 meals daily and all taxes. **Amenities:** Restaurant; bar; small outdoor pool; free Wi-Fi.

Lapa Ríos ★★ Luxury in the jungle doesn't get much better than this. Built by owners John and Karen Lewis and now managed by the Cayuga chain of ecolodges, this trailblazing hotel was one of the first to put ecotourism in the Osa Peninsula on the map. Rooms are spacious, private, and oriented toward the ocean, with high-peaked thatched roofs and open screen walls (no glass). A small tropical garden and large deck, complete with outdoor shower and hammock, more than double the living space. Rooms are housed in a series of units stretching in a line down the spine of a mountain ridge. As is common in the area, the main lodge and restaurant feature a high thatched roof overhead. There's a large spiral staircase leading up to a great lookout, and even if you can't afford to stay here, it's a great place to stop for a cocktail with a view. Lapa Ríos sits on a 400-hectare (988-acre) private rainforest reserve, with a well-maintained trail system and an abundance of flora and fauna. Activities included with lodging range from birding tours, jungle and waterfall hikes to night walks and tours of a local school. Note that there's no Wi-Fi here.

Matapalo, Osa Peninsula. www.laparios.com. ✆ **2735-5130.** 17 bungalows. $340–$470 per person based on double occupancy. Rates include 3 meals daily and round-trip transportation from Puerto Jiménez. Discounts for children between 6 and 11; no children under 6. **Amenities:** Restaurant; bar; outdoor pool; spa; on-site tours.

Organized Tours & Activities

Osa Aventura (www.osaaventura.com; ✆ **2735-5758** or 8372-6135) is a local tour company that offers a host of guided tours and **wildlife-watching expeditions** around the Osa Peninsula and into Corcovado National Park. Rates run between $80 and $300 per person, depending on group size and the tour.

Osa Corcovado Tour and Travel (www.soldeosa.com); ✆ **8632-8150**) also arranges Corcovado tours, guides, transportation, lodging and, if you're looking for your own slice of paradise, real estate, through its affiliate Osa Pen Realty.

Finca Kobo ★ (www.fincakobo.com; ✆ **8398-7604**), near La Palma, 17km (11 miles) northwest of Puerto Jiménez, offers an informative tour of this **organic cacao plantation.** You'll learn about and see all the stages involved in growing cacao and transforming these precious beans (used as currency by pre-Columbian cultures) into chocolate. At the end of the tour, you'll get to sample some of the handiwork, dipping local fruit into fresh chocolate fondue. The tour costs $32; children 8 and under are half-price. Finca Kobo also has a few rooms and bungalows for rent.

If you'd like to do some inshore (inside the gulf) or offshore (deep-sea) **sportfishing,** look up **Crocodile Bay Resort** (www.crocodilebay.com; ✆ **800/733-1115** in the U.S. and Canada, or 2735-5631 in Costa Rica). This upscale fishing lodge, one of the **largest fishing outfitters** in Central America, is close to the Puerto Jiménez airstrip. The owners have plans to build a condominium project starting in 2016 and a state-of-the-art marina and hotel starting in 2018. Three-day fishing packages start at $1,985 per person based on double occupancy. Another top outfitter is **Las Islas Lodge** (www.lasislas lodge.com; ✆ **2735-5510**), 1km west of downtown Puerto Jiménez, which offers half- and full-day inshore and offshore fishing trips for $1,200 to $1,800 for up to six anglers, or surf fishing (from the shore) for $135 to $185 per person with two to four people.

Pollo's Surf School ★ (www.pollosurfschool.com; ✆ **8366-6559**) is located near some excellent learning waves on Pan Dulce Beach. Pollo's is also the place to try **stand-up paddling (SUP).** A 2-hour surfing lesson runs $55.

If you want to get your adrenaline flowing, check in with **Everyday Adventures,** also known as **Psycho Tours ★★★** (www.psychotours.com; ✆ **8353-8619**). Andy Pruter and his guides specialize in two **adventure tours** in Matapalo, **waterfall rappelling and tree climbing.** The latter features a free climb (with safety rope) up a 60m (200-ft.) strangler fig, where you reach a natural platform at around 18m (60 ft.), ring a cowbell, and then take a deep breath for the Tarzan swing, belayed down by your guide. This is accompanied by an informative hike through primary rainforest and can be paired with a couple of rappels down jungle waterfalls, the highest of which is around 30m (100 ft.), and is scary good fun. You can do either one of the above adventures separately, but I recommend the 5- to 6-hour combo tour, which costs $120.

Reachable only by boat, the **Osa Wildlife Sanctuary ★★★** (www.osawildlife.org; ✆ **8348-0499**) is a delightful animal rescue center on the shore of the northern Golfo Dulce, completely surrounded by Piedras Blancas National Park. Here you can see an ocelot, kinkajous, sloths, tayras, peccaries, scarlet macaws, a porcupine, and capuchin and spider monkeys, most of them rescued from the pet trade or from crippling accidents. **Daily tours** are offered by volunteers or founder Carol Patrick, who is as charming as her wards. A donation of $25 per person is requested for the tour.

Shopping

Jagua Arts & Craft Store ★★ (✆ **2735-5267**) stocks excellent local and regional art and craft works, including some fine jewelry and blown glass. ***Tip:*** Many folks head to this store while waiting for their departing flight out of Puerto Jiménez, as the store is near the airstrip. Be sure to give yourself enough time to explore the extensive collection here. Jagua also has an inviting open-air lounge area with locally made ice cream for sale and free coffee. It's a great place to wait for a flight or a transfer to your lodge.

Corcovado National Park ★★★

Exploring Corcovado National Park is not something to be undertaken lightly, but neither is it the expedition that some people make it out to be. The weather is the biggest obstacle to overnight backpacking trips through the park. The heat and humidity are often extreme, and frequent rainstorms can make trails fairly muddy. Within a couple of hours of Puerto Jiménez (by 4WD vehicle) are two entrances to the park, at La Leona and Los Patos; however, the park has no roads, so before you reach the entrances, you'll have to start hiking. Note that all Corcovado visitors must be accompanied by licensed, professional guides.

Corcovado National Park

Corcovado National Park is amazingly rich in biodiversity. It is one of the only places in Costa Rica that is home to all four of the country's monkey species—howler, white-faced, squirrel, and spider. Its large size makes it an ideal habitat for wildcat species, including the endangered jaguar, as well as other large mammals, like the Baird's tapir. Apart from the jaguar, other cat species found here include the ocelot, margay, jaguarundi, and puma. More than 390 species of birds have been recorded inside the park. Scarlet macaws are commonly sighted here. Other common bird species include antbirds, manakins, toucans, tanagers, hummingbirds, and puffbirds. Once thought extinct in Costa Rica, the harpy eagle has been spotted here as well in recent years. Most rivers in Corcovado are home to crocodiles and at high tide are frequented by bull sharks. For this reason, river crossings must be coordinated with low tide. Your guide will know the ropes.

Because of its size and remoteness, Corcovado National Park is best explored over 2 to 3 days; no more than 5 days are permitted at one time. Still, it is possible to enter and hike the park on a day trip. The best way to do this is to book a tour with your lodge on the Osa Peninsula, from a tour company in Puerto Jiménez, or through a lodge in Drake Bay (see "Osa Peninsula Lodges," above).

ARRIVING The park has four primary ranger stations, two of which serve as entry and exit points for multi-day expeditions. You can drive all the way to Los Patos Ranger Station, but La Leona is a 3km hike past the end of the road. Perhaps the easiest to reach from Puerto Jiménez is **La Leona Ranger Station,** a 20-minute hike past Carate, which is accessible by car, taxi or the twice-daily *colectivo* truck.

If you choose to drive, take the dirt road from Puerto Jiménez to Carate, where the road ends. From Carate, it's a 3km (1.75-mile) hike to La Leona. To travel there by "public transportation," pick up one of the collective buses (actually, a 4WD pickup truck with a tarpaulin cover and slat seats in the back) that leave Puerto Jiménez for Carate daily at 6am and 1:30pm, returning at 8am and 4pm. The one-way fare is $9. A small fleet of these trucks leaves 1 block south of the bus terminal, and will stop to pick up anyone who flags them down along the way. Your other option is to hire a taxi to suit your schedule, which will charge about $90 to or from Carate.

You can also travel to **El Tigre,** about 14km (8¾ miles) by dirt road from Puerto Jiménez, site of a newly opened ranger station. But note that trails from El Tigre go only a short distance into the park and do not connect to the heart of Corcovado, where most of the wildlife is.

Another entrance is in **Los Patos,** which is reached from the town of La Palma, northwest of Puerto Jiménez. From here, a 19km (12-mile) trail runs through the center of the park to **Sirena,** a ranger station and research facility (see "Beach Treks & Rainforest Hikes," below). Sirena has a landing strip used by charter flights.

The northern entrance to the park is **San Pedrillo,** which you can reach by taking a boat from Drake Bay or Sierpe (p. 201). It's 14km (8¾ miles) from Drake Bay.

If you're not into hiking in the heat, you can charter a plane in Puerto Jiménez to take you to Carate ($180) or Sirena ($360). Contact **Alfa Romeo Air Charters** (www.alfaromeoair.com; ✆ **8632-8150**).

FEES & REGULATIONS Park admission is $15 per person per day. Only the Sirena station is equipped with dormitory-style lodgings and camping platforms with bathrooms and showers and cafeteria-style meal service. Meals are costly ($20–$25), so you might consider packing your own breakfast and lunch and perhaps splurging on dinner. Sirena is the only place in Corcovado where camping and overnight dorm lodging are allowed. All must be reserved in advance by contacting the **ACOSA** (Area de Conservacion de Osa) in Puerto Jiménez (✆ **2735-5036;** pncorcovado@gmail.com). However, its offices, adjacent to the airstrip, are notoriously poor at answering e-mails and attending to reservations. Only a limited number of people are allowed to camp or to enter on day trips and all must be accompanied by a certified guide, so make your reservations well in advance. Your best bet is probably to contact full-service outfitters **Osa Corcovado Tour & Travel** (www.corcovado guide.com; ✆ **8632-8150**) or **Osa Aventura** (www.osaaventura.com; ✆ **2735-5758** or 8372-6135).

BEACH TREKS & RAINFOREST HIKES Corcovado has some of the best hiking trails in the world, with animals so acclimated to humans that they barely glance at you, much less run away (most aren't a threat to humans, but keep your distance from the peccaries). The most popular trail starts at La Leona, near Carate, and leads to Sirena. Between any two ranger stations, the hiking is arduous and takes all or most of a day. In 2006, the environment minister of Costa Rica was lost in Corcovado for 3 days after a mother tapir attacked him. Today, nobody is allowed into the park without a licensed guide, and for good reason. This is a wild place where you shouldn't expect neat trails or clear signage. At times you have to cross rivers inhabited by crocodiles, with bull sharks drifting in at high tide looking for dinner.

The **Sirena** ranger station is a fascinating destination. As a research facility, it attracts scientists studying the rainforest, but most of the visitors here are hardcore ecotourists and backpackers, who can be a surprisingly cheerless lot. If you were looking for a big party, you've come to the wrong place. But for a wild, buggy, snaky, hot, wet adventure, Corcovado is unsurpassable.

WHERE TO STAY & EAT IN THE PARK Reservations are essential at the various ranger stations if you plan to eat or sleep inside the park (p. 214). **Sirena** has dormitory-style accommodations for 28 people, as well as a campground, cafeteria, and landing strip for charter flights. Camping inside Corcovado is currently available only at Sirena. Every ranger station has potable water, but it's advisable to pack in your own. You should never drink from a river. Campsites in the park are $4/person per night. A dorm bed at the Sirena station runs $11, but you must bring your own sheets, and a mosquito net is also a good idea. Meals here are $20 for breakfast and $25 for lunch and dinner. Everything must be reserved in advance.

Golfo Dulce Lodge

EXPENSIVE

Playa Nicuesa Rainforest Lodge ★★★ This exquisite lodge is one of the most remote ecolodges in the southern zone, accessible only by boat, about a 30-minute ride from Golfito deep inside the Golfo Dulce. The wildlife and nature viewing here is fabulous (it's a good place to find the endemic Golfo Dulce frog), as are the hikes through primary forest on the lodge's own 66-hectare (163-acre) private reserve adjoining the much larger Piedras Blancas National Park. From here you can go kayaking or snorkeling in the Golfo Dulce, where dolphins are common and whale sharks are occasionally spotted. Rooms are rich in local varnished hardwoods, and each has an element that makes guests feel like they're one with nature. Tasty family-style meals are served in the large main lodge building, which soars over two floors with sitting areas, a library, and a reception desk that are all entirely open to the surrounding forest. Please note that this lodge does not have Wi-Fi.

Golfo Dulce. www.nicuesalodge.com. ✆ **866/504-8116** in the U.S., or 2258-8250 in Costa Rica. 9 units. $235–$280 per person per night, double occupancy; $120–$150 children 6–12; no children under 6. Rates include all meals, taxes, and transfers btw. Golfito or Puerto Jiménez. 2-night minimum stay required year-round, except 4-night minimum stay required Dec 22–Jan 1. Closed Oct 1–Nov 15. **Amenities:** Restaurant; bar; free kayaks, snorkeling gear, and fishing equipment.

THE CARIBBEAN COAST

10

Costa Rica's Caribbean coast is a world apart from the rest of the country. The pace is slower, the food is spicier, the tropical heat is more palpable, and the rhythmic lilt of patois and reggae music fills the air. This remains one of Costa Rica's least explored regions, with more than half the coastline still inaccessible except by boat or small plane. This isolation has helped preserve large tracts of virgin lowland rainforest, which are now set aside as **Tortuguero National Park ★★** and **Barra del Colorado National Wildlife Refuge ★**. These two parks, on the coast's northern reaches, are among Costa Rica's most popular destinations for adventurers and ecotourists. Of particular interest are the sea turtles that nest here. Farther south, **Cahuita National Park ★★** is another popular park, located just off its namesake beach village. It was set up to preserve 200 hectares (494 acres) of coral reef, but its palm tree–lined white-sand beaches and gentle trails are stunning. And when you're ready for nice lodging, fine dining, and a hearty party, the hopping village of **Puerto Viejo ★★** is hard to top anywhere in Costa Rica.

So remote was the Caribbean coast from Costa Rica's population centers in the Central Valley that it developed a culture all its own. The original inhabitants of the area included people of the Bribri and Cabécar tribes, which proudly maintain their cultures on indigenous reserves in the Talamanca Mountains. In fact, until the 1870s, this area had few non-Indians. However, when Minor Keith built a railroad from San José to Limón and began planting bananas, he brought in black laborers from Jamaica and other Caribbean islands to lay the track and work the plantations. These workers and their descendants established fishing and farming communities up and down the coast. Today dreadlocked Rastafarians, reggae music, Creole cooking, and the English-based patois of this Afro-Caribbean culture give the region a quasi-Jamaican flavor, a striking contrast with Latino Costa Rican culture.

The Caribbean Coast

0 15 mi
0 15 km

NICARAGUA
SAN JOSÉ
Caribbean Coast
PACIFIC OCEAN

NICARAGUA
Boca del Río Colorado
Barra del Colorado
Barra del Colorado Wildlife Refuge
Boca del Río Tortuguero
Tortuguero
Tortuguero
Tortuguero Nat'l Park
CARIBBEAN SEA
Tortuguero Canal
Cariari
Parismina
Reventazón
Guacimo
Carmen
Guápiles
Pacuare
Vol. Turrialba Nat'l Park
Siquirres
32
Matina
Volcán Turrialba
Playa Bonita
Moín
Limón
Guayabo Nat'l Monument
Westfalia
Vol. Irazú Nat'l Park
Central Range
Barbilla Nat'l Park
Atlantico
Juan Viñas
Turrialba
Moravia
36
Chirripó
Playa Cahuita
Cahuita
Cahuita Nat'l Park
Tapantí (Orosí) Nat'l Park
Playa Cocles
Punta Uva
Puerto Viejo
Uatsi
Cerro de la Muerte
Telire
Hitoy-Cerere Biological Res.
Manzanillo
Talamanca Ind. Res.
Chirripó Nat'l Park
Talamanca Range
Bratsi
Gandoca-Manzanillo NWR
2
Sixaola
Cerro Chirripó
BriBri Ind. Res.
San Gerardo de Rivas
La Amistad Int'l Park
PANAMA
Buenos Aires

Caribbean Weather

The Caribbean coast has a unique weather pattern. It's said that there are two seasons: the rainy season and the very rainy season. Whereas you'll almost never get even a drop of rain in Guanacaste during Costa Rica's typical dry season (mid-Nov to Apr), on the Caribbean coast it can rain almost any day of the year. However, the months of September and October, when torrential rains pound most of the rest of the country, are two of the drier and more dependably sunny months along the Caribbean coast. Visit during these months and you'll find lower prices and fewer tourists.

The Caribbean coast has only one big city, **Limón,** a major commercial port and popular cruise ship port of call. However, the city itself is of little interest to most visitors, who often head south to the coast's spectacular beaches, or north to the jungle canals of Tortuguero.

Over the years, the Caribbean coast has garnered a reputation as being a dangerous, drug-infested zone, rife with crime. And though there have been several high-profile crimes in the area and petty theft is a common problem, this reputation is exaggerated. The same crime and drug problems found here exist in San José and most of the popular beach destinations on the Pacific coast. Use common sense and take normal precautions, and you should have no problems on the Caribbean coast.

TORTUGUERO ★★

250km (155 miles) NE of San José; 79km (49 miles) N of Limón

Tortuguero is a tiny fishing village connected to the rest of mainland Costa Rica by a series of rivers and canals. This aquatic highway is lined with a mix of farmland and dense tropical rainforest that is home to howler and spider monkeys, three-toed sloths, toucans, and green macaws. A trip through the canals surrounding Tortuguero is a lot like cruising the Amazon basin, though on a much smaller scale.

"Tortuguero" comes from the Spanish name for the giant sea turtles (*tortugas*) that nest on the beaches of this region every year from early March to mid-October (prime season is July–Oct, and peak months are Aug–Sept). The chance to see this nesting attracts many people to this remote region, but just as many come to explore the intricate network of jungle canals that serve as the region's main transportation arteries.

Independent travel is not the norm here, although it's possible. Most travelers rely on their lodge for boat transportation through the canals and into town. At most of the lodges around Tortuguero, almost everything is done in groups, including the bus rides to and fro, boat trips through the canals, and family-style meals.

Tortuguero

HOTELS ■
- Cabinas Miss Junie 5
- Cabinas Miss Miriam 5
- Casa Marbella 5
- Hotel El Icaco 5
- Hotel Tortuguero Natural 5
- Laguna Lodge 3
- Tortuga Lodge 2

RESTAURANTS ◆
- Budda Café 5
- Miss Junie's 5
- Wild Ginger 5

ATTRACTIONS ●
- Sea Turtle Conservancy Visitors' Center and Museum 4
- Cerro de Tortuguero 1
- Tortuguero National Park 6

Important: More than 508cm (200 in.) of rain falls here annually, so you can expect a downpour at any time of the year. Most of the lodges will provide you with rain gear (including ponchos and rubber boots), but it can't hurt to carry your own.

Essentials

ARRIVING **By Plane: Nature Air** (www.natureair.com; ✆ **800/235-9272** in the U.S. and Canada, or 2299-6000 in Costa Rica) has one daily flight at 6am for **Tortuguero** airstrip from Juan Santamaría International Airport in San José. The flight takes about 30 minutes; the fare is $107 each way. The return flight leaves Tortuguero daily at 7:05am for San José. Additional flights are often added during the high season, and departure times can vary according to weather conditions. In addition, many local lodges operate charter flights as part of their package trips. Be sure to arrange with your hotel to pick you up at the airstrip. Otherwise you'll have to ask one of the other hotels' boat captains to give you a lift, which they'll usually do for a few dollars.

By Car: It's not possible to drive to Tortuguero.

By Boat: Flying to Tortuguero is convenient if you don't have much time, but a boat trip through the canals and rivers of this region is often the highlight of any visit. You'll first have to ride by bus or minivan from San José to Moín, Caño Blanco, or one of the other embarkation points; then it's 2 to 3 hours on a boat, usually with hard wooden benches or plastic seats. All of the more expensive lodges listed offer their own bus and boat transportation packages, which include the boat ride through the canals. However, if you're coming here on the cheap and plan to stay at one of the less expensive lodges or at a budget *cabina* in Tortuguero, you will have to arrange your own transportation. In this case, you have a few options.

One option is to get yourself to Limón and then to the public docks in **Moín,** just to the north, and try to find a boat on your own. At the docks, you should be able to negotiate a fare of between $60 and $90 per person roundtrip with one of the boats docked here. These boats tend to depart between 8 and 10am every morning. You can stay as many days as you like in Tortuguero, but be sure to arrange with the captain to be there to pick you up when you're ready to leave. The trip from Moín to Tortuguero takes between 3 and 4 hours.

It is possible to get to Tortuguero by bus and boat from Cariari. For backpackers and budget travelers, this is the cheapest and most reliable means of reaching Tortuguero from San José. To take this route, begin by catching the 9 or 10:30am direct bus to Cariari from the **Gran Terminal del Caribe,** on Calle Central, Avenida 13 (✆ **2222-0610**). The fare is C1,715. This bus will actually drop you off at the main bus terminal in Cariari, from which you'll have to walk 4 blocks east to a separate bus station, known locally as *"la estación vieja,"* or the old station. Here, you can buy your bus ticket for La Pavona, also known as Rancho El Suerte. The bus fare is around C1,300. Buses to La Pavona leave at 6 and 11am, and 3pm.

A boat or two will be waiting to meet the bus at the dock at the edge of the river. These boats leave after a bus arrives, or when they fill up. The boat fare to Tortuguero is C1,600 each way. You can buy your ticket for the boat at the cashier of the very prominent (and only) restaurant at La Pavona. Return boats leave Tortuguero for La Pavona every morning at 6 and 11:30am, and 3pm, making return bus connections to Cariari.

Warning: Beware of unscrupulous operators providing misinformation by offering to sell you "packaged transportation" to Tortuguero, when all they are doing is charging you extra to buy the tickets described above. Be especially careful if people selling you boat transportation aggressively steer you to a specific hotel option, claim that your first choice is full, or insist that you must buy a package with them that includes the transportation, lodging, and guide services. If you have doubts or want to check on the current state of this route, check out **www.tortuguerovillage.com,** which has detailed directions to Tortuguero by a variety of routes.

VILLAGE LAYOUT Tortuguero is one of the most remote locations in Costa Rica. With no roads into this area and no cars in the village, all transportation is by boat, foot, or bicycle. Most of the lodges are spread out over several kilometers to the north of Tortuguero Village on either side of the main canal; the small airstrip is at the north end of the beachside spit of land. At the far northern end of the main canal, you'll see the **Cerro de Tortuguero (Tortuguero Hill),** which, at some 119m (390 ft.), towers over the area. The hike to the top of this hill is a popular half-day tour and offers some good views of the Tortuguero canal and village, as well as the Caribbean Sea.

The village of Tortuguero is a small collection of houses and shops connected by footpaths. The village is spread out on a thin spit of land, bordered on one side by the Caribbean Sea and on the other by the main canal. At most points, it's less than 300m (984 ft.) wide. In the center of the village, you'll find a small children's playground, the town's health clinic, and a soccer field.

If you stay at a hotel on the ocean side of the canal, you'll be able to walk into and explore the village at your leisure; if you're across the canal, you'll be dependent on the lodge's boat transportation. However, some of the lodges across the canal have their own network of jungle trails that might appeal to naturalists.

FAST FACTS Tortuguero has no banks, ATMs, or currency-exchange houses, so be sure to bring enough cash in colones to cover any expenses and incidental charges. The local hotels and shops generally charge a commission to exchange dollars.

Tortuguero Hotels

Although the room rates below may appear high, keep in mind that they usually include round-trip transportation from San José (which amounts to about $100 per person), plus all meals, taxes, and usually some tours. When broken down into nightly room rates, most of the lodges are really charging only $60 to $150 for a double room. ***Note:*** Package rates below are for the least expensive travel option, which is a bus and boat combination in and out. All lodges also offer packages with a plane flight, either one or both ways.

EXPENSIVE

Tortuga Lodge ★★★ This was one of the first upscale resorts to set up shop here, and it remains one of the best. Like the other better lodges, it has amenities like ceiling fans and landscaped gardens—plus a snazzy stone-lined pool, a waterfront dining room with some of the better local cuisine, and 20 hectares (50 acres) of grounds and jungle. The paths snaking through the property are superb for hiking. The bamboo-furnished rooms are class acts, the best ones being on the upper floor, with sleek varnished wood, verandas, and hammocks. The large, canal-front deck is built on several levels stepping up from the water and joining with the large dining room and bar, and it serves as the social hub for the lodge. Service is impeccable.

Tortuguero. www.tortugalodge.com. ✆ **2257-0766** for reservations in San José, or 2709-8136 at the lodge. 27 units. $190 double, tax included; more for packages including meals, tours, and transportation. **Amenities:** Restaurant; bar; pool; free Wi-Fi.

MODERATE

Laguna Lodge ★★ Think of this as "summer camp for adults." Rooms are adequate but basic, with screened rather than glass windows (which means that they can get noisy, as all the guest rooms are in a series of one-story buildings with shared verandas). It's also double the size of the other lodges in the area, so it can feel a bit too bustling. But does that really matter when you're surrounded by all this glorious nature? Laguna Lodge sits on the ocean side of the main canal, about a 20- to 30-minute walk north of Tortuguero Village. It boasts splendid gardens, including a butterfly and a frog garden, and two pools; the beach is just a couple hundred yards away. Meals are served buffet-style in a large, covered, open-air dining room overlooking Tortuguero's main canal.

Tortuguero. www.lagunatortuguero.com. ✆ **888/259-5615** in the U.S. and Canada, or 2272-4943 in Costa Rica. 100 units. $235 per person for 2 days/1 night; $298 per person for 3 days/2 nights. Rates are double occupancy and include round-trip transportation from San José, tours, taxes, and 3 meals daily. Children 5–11 half-price; children under 5 free. **Amenities:** Restaurant; 2 bars; 2 outdoor pools; free Wi-Fi.

INEXPENSIVE

Several basic cabinas in the village of Tortuguero offer budget lodgings for $25 to $55 per person. **Cabinas Miss Junie** (✆ **2709-8102**) and **Cabinas Miss Miriam** (✆ **2709-8002**) are the traditional favorites, although you may prefer Casa Marbella (below), with the second and third choices being **Hotel El Icaco** (www.hotelelicaco.com; ✆ **2709-8044**) and **Hotel Tortuguero Natural** (www.hoteltortugueronatural.com; ✆ **2767-0466**).

Casa Marbella ★ Co-owned by Daryl Loth, one of the most respected local guides around, this B&B occupies a converted clapboard home right on the canal in the heart of the village. All rooms come with one or two low-lying wooden beds, large windows, hardwood floors, and little else. The best rooms have views of the water. There's a small covered canal-front patio where breakfast is served, and which also serves as a nice spot to relax, read, or watch birds. Beyond leading tours, Daryl can also help arrange a wide variety of activities in the area.

Tortuguero. http://casamarbella.tripod.com. ✆ **2709-8011** or 8833-0827. 11 units. $40–$45 double; $55–$65 superior. Rates include breakfast. No credit cards. **Amenities:** Small communal kitchen; free Wi-Fi.

Where to Eat

The town has a couple of simple *sodas* and restaurants. The best of these is **Miss Junie's** (✆ **2709-8102**).

Budda Café ★ INTERNATIONAL With an appropriately Zen atmosphere of canal-front outdoor seating—try and grab one of the tables on the over-the-water deck—this happy cafe has been in business for years, despite the fact that most visitors to the area take all three meals at their lodges. I'd say that speaks to the solid quality of the food here, which consists of fresh ceviche, pizzas, pastas, stuffed crepes, and a range of main dishes (plus excellent desserts).

On the main canal, next to the ICE building, Tortuguero. www.buddacafe.com. ✆ **2709-8084.** Main courses C4,500–C13,000. Daily noon–9pm.

Wild Ginger ★ INTERNATIONAL Welcome to Tortuguero's one real fine dining option. Here that means "California meets Costa Rica" fare on a menu that features everything from seasonal lobster and mango ceviche to a beef tenderloin in a coffee rub. The ginger-marinated chicken with passion fruit sauce is a highlight. Wild Ginger also creates a number of options for vegetarians and vegans. The setting is nice, too: polished concrete floors, hand-painted murals, and lots of open air. Service is stellar, and you may feel like the owners are old friends by the time you pay the check.

On the ocean-side path, north end of Tortuguero. www.wildgingercr.com. ✆ **2709-8240.** Main courses C6,000–C13,000. Daily 12:30-3pm and 6–9pm.

Exploring Tortuguero Village

The most popular attraction in town is the small **Sea Turtle Conservancy Visitors' Center and Museum** ★ (www.conserveturtles.org; ✆ **2767-1576**). The museum has information and exhibits on a whole range of native flora and fauna, but its primary focus is on the life and natural history of the sea turtles. Most visits to the museum include a short, informative video on the turtles. All the proceeds from the small gift shop go toward conservation and turtle protection. The museum is open daily from 10am to noon and 2 to 5pm. Admission is $2, but more generous donations are encouraged.

In the village, you can also rent dugout canoes, known in Costa Rica as *cayucos* or *pangas*. Be careful before renting and taking off in one of these; they tend to be heavy, slow, and hard to maneuver.

You'll find a handful of souvenir shops spread around the center of the village. The **Paraíso Tropical Gift Shop** has the largest selection of gifts and souvenirs, while the **Jungle Shop** has a higher-end selection of wares and donates 10 percent of its profits to local schools.

Exploring Tortuguero National Park ★★

Today, four species of sea turtles nest here: the green turtle, the hawksbill, the loggerhead, and the giant leatherback. The park's beaches are excellent places to watch sea turtles nest, especially at night. As appealingly long and deserted as they are, however, the beaches are not appropriate for swimming. The surf is usually very rough, and the river mouths attract sharks that feed on the turtle hatchlings and the many fish that live here.

Green turtles are the most common turtle found in Tortuguero, so you're more likely to see one of them than any other species if you visit during the prime nesting season from **July to mid-October** (Aug–Sept are peak months). **Loggerheads** are very rare, so don't be disappointed if you don't see one. The **giant leatherback** is perhaps the most spectacular sea turtle to watch laying eggs. The largest of all turtle species, the leatherback can grow to 2m (6½ ft.) long and weigh well over 1,000 pounds. They nest from late February to June, predominantly in the southern part of the park.

You can explore the park's rainforest, either by foot or by boat, and look for some of the incredible varieties of wildlife that live here: jaguars, anteaters, howler monkeys, collared and white-lipped peccaries, some 350 species of birds, and countless butterflies, among others. Some of the more colorful and common bird species you might see in this area include the rufescent and tiger herons, keel-billed toucan, northern jacana, red-lored parrot, and ringed kingfisher. Boat tours are far and away the most popular way to visit this park, although one frequently very muddy trail starts at the park entrance and runs for about 2km (1.25 miles) through the coastal rainforest and along the beach.

ENTRY POINT, FEES & REGULATIONS The Tortuguero National Park entrance and ranger station are at the south end of Tortuguero Village. The ranger station is inside a landlocked old patrol boat, and a small, informative open-air kiosk explains a bit about the park and its environs. Admission to the

Tiptoeing Around Turtles & Other Recommendations

- Visitors to the beach at night must be accompanied by a licensed guide. Tours generally last between 2 and 4 hours.
- Sometimes you must walk quite a bit to encounter a nesting turtle. Wear sneakers or walking shoes rather than sandals. The beach is very dark at night, and it's easy to trip or step on driftwood or other detritus.
- Wear dark clothes. White T-shirts are not permitted.
- Flashlights, flash cameras, and lighted video cameras are prohibited on turtle walks, as is smoking on the beach at night.

park is $15. However, most people visit Tortuguero as part of a package tour. Be sure to confirm whether the park entrance is included in the price. Moreover, only certain canals and trails leaving from the park station are actually within the park. Many hotels and private guides take their tours to a series of canals that border the park and are very similar in terms of flora and fauna but don't require park entrance. When the turtles are nesting, arrange a night tour in advance with either your hotel or one of the private guides working in town. These guided tours generally run between $10 and $20. Flashlights and flash cameras are not permitted on the beach at night because the lights discourage the turtles from nesting.

Organized Tours

All the lodges listed above, with the exception of the most inexpensive accommodations in Tortuguero Village, offer package tours that include various hikes and river tours; this is generally the best way to visit the area.

In addition, several San José–based tour companies offer budget 2-day/1-night excursions to Tortuguero, including transportation, all meals, and limited tours around the region. Prices for these trips range between $150 and $300 per person, and—depending on the price—guests are lodged either in one of the basic hotels in Tortuguero Village or in one of the nicer lodges listed below. Reputable companies offering these excursions include **Exploradores Outdoors** ★ (www.exploradoresoutdoors.com; ✆ **646/205-0828** in the U.S. and Canada, or 2222-6262 in Costa Rica), **Jungle Tom Safaris** (www.jungletomsafaris.com; ✆ **2221-7878**), and **Iguana Verde Tours** (www.iguanaverdetours.com; ✆ **2231-6803**). Some operators offer 1-day trips in which tourists spend almost all their time coming and going, with a quick tour of the canals and lunch in Tortuguero. These trips generally run $100 to $120 per person, but if you really want to experience Tortuguero, I recommend staying for at least 2 nights.

Alternatively, you could go with **Fran and Modesto Watson** ★ (www.tortuguerocanals.com; ✆ **2226-0986**), who are pioneering guides in this region and operate their own boat. The couple offers a range of overnight and multiday packages to Tortuguero, with lodging options at most of the major lodges here.

Aside from watching turtles nest, the unique thing to do in Tortuguero is **tour the canals by boat,** keeping your eye out for tropical birds and native wildlife. Most lodges can arrange a canal tour for you, but you can also arrange a tour through one of the operators in the village of Tortuguero. I recommend **Daryl Loth** (http://casamarbella.tripod.com; ✆ **8833-0827**), who runs the Casa Marbella in the center of town. I also recommend **Ernesto Castillo** (✆ **8343-9565**). If neither of these guides is available, ask for a recommendation at the **Sea Turtle Conservancy Visitors' Center and Museum** (✆ **2767-1576**). Most guides charge $20 to $25 per person for a tour of the canals. If you travel through the park, you'll also have to pay the park entrance fee of $15 per person.

CAHUITA ★, PUERTO VIEJO ★★ & THE SOUTH CARIBBEAN COAST ★★★

Cahuita: 200km (124 miles) E of San José; 42km (26 miles) S of Limón; 13km (8 miles) N of Puerto Viejo

A single two-lane highway heads south from the port town of Limón. Along this stretch, you'll find some of Costa Rica's best beaches and a couple of unique Caribbean towns. The villages here trace their roots to Afro-Caribbean fishermen and laborers who settled in this region in the mid-1800s, and today much of the population is English-speaking, black Costa Ricans whose culture and language set them apart from most of the country.

Cahuita is a tiny town and the first beach destination south of Limón. The few dirt and gravel streets here are host to a languid parade of pedestrian traffic, parted occasionally by a bicycle, car, or bus. People come to Cahuita for the miles of pristine beaches that stretch both north and south from town. The southern beaches, the forest behind them, and the coral reef offshore (one of just a handful in Costa Rica) are all part of **Cahuita National Park ★★**. Silt and pesticides washing down from nearby banana plantations have taken a heavy toll on the coral reefs, so don't expect the snorkeling to be world-class. But on a calm day, it can be pretty good, and the beaches are idyllic every day.

Puerto Viejo is the Caribbean coast's top destination. Not to be confused with the landlocked Puerto Viejo de Sarapiquí in the north, this beach town is sometimes called Puerto Viejo de Limón or Puerto Viejo de Talamanca. Hotels, restaurants, bars, and shops abound, and the streets teem with bicycles, cars, trucks, tourists, expats, and locals. Here you can feel perfectly normal strolling the main street in a bikini, and don't be surprised if someone offers you something to smoke. The town is popular with surfers who come to ride its famous and fearsome Salsa Brava wave, and the only slightly mellower Playa Cocles beach break.

As you continue south on the coastal road from Puerto Viejo, you'll come to several of Costa Rica's best beaches. Soft white sands are fronted by the Caribbean Sea and backed by thick rainforest. **Playa Cocles** is a popular surf spot, with a powerful and dependable beach break. South of here, the isolated **Playa Chiquita** is characterized by small pocket coves and calm pools formed by dead coral reefs raised slightly above sea level by the 1991 earthquake. Beyond this lies **Punta Uva,** a long curving swath of beach punctuated by its namesake point (*punta*), a rainforest-clad mound of land that looks vaguely like a bunch of grapes from the distance. The tiny village of Manzanillo is literally the end of the road. The shoreline heading south from Manzanillo, located inside the **Gandoca–Manzanillo Wildlife Refuge,** is especially beautiful, with a series of pocket coves and small beaches, with small islands and rocky outcroppings offshore. This park stretches all the way to the Panama border.

Essentials

ARRIVING **By Car:** The Guápiles Highway (CR32) heads north out of San José on Calle 3 before turning east and passing through Braulio Carrillo National Park en route to Limón. The drive takes about 2½ hours and is beautiful in places, especially when it's not raining.

As you enter Limón, about 5 blocks from the busiest section of downtown, watch for a marked intersection with signs pointing toward Cahuita and Puerto Viejo on your right, just before the railroad tracks. Take this road (CR36) south to Cahuita, passing the airstrip and the beach on your left as you leave Limón.

To reach Puerto Viejo, continue south from Cahuita on CR36 for another 16km (10 miles). Watch for a prominent and well-marked fork in the highway. The right-hand leg continues on to Bribri, Sixaola, and Panama. The left-hand leg (it actually appears to be a straight shot) takes you into Puerto Viejo on 5km (3 miles) of sporadically paved road.

A single two-lane paved road runs south out of Puerto Viejo and ends in Manzanillo. A few dirt roads lead off this road, both toward the beach and into the mountains.

By Bus: Mepe express buses (www.mepecr.com; ✆ **2257-8129**) to Cahuita and Puerto Viejo leave San José daily at 6 and 10am, noon, and 2 and 4pm from the Caribbean bus terminal (Gran Terminal del Caribe) on Calle Central, Avenida 13. The trip's duration is 4 to 5 hours; the fare is C4,650 to Cahuita and C5,810 to Puerto Viejo. During peak periods, extra buses are sometimes added. Always ask if the bus is continuing on to **Manzanillo** (especially helpful if you're staying in a hotel south of town). If not, local buses to **Punta Uva** and **Manzanillo** leave Puerto Viejo about a half-dozen times throughout the day.

Interbus (www.interbusonline.com; ✆ **2283-5573**) has a daily shuttle from San José to the Caribbean coast beaches. The fare is $50.

VILLAGE LAYOUT Cahuita has about eight dirt streets. The highway runs parallel to the coast, with three main access roads running perpendicular. The northernmost of these access roads bypasses town and brings you to the northern end of Playa Negra. It's marked with signs for the Magellan Inn and other hotels. The second road brings you to the southern end of Playa Negra, about 1km (a half-mile) closer to town. The third road is the principal entrance into town. The village's main street in town, which runs parallel to the highway, dead-ends at the national park entrance (a footbridge over a small stream).

Buses drop passengers off at a terminal at the back of a small strip mall on the main entrance road into town. Cabs will be waiting to take you to the lodges on Playa Negra. Or you can walk north on the street that runs between

Coco's Bar and the small park. This road curves to the left and continues 1.6km (1 mile) or so out to Playa Negra.

As you reach Puerto Viejo, the road runs parallel to Playa Negra, or Black Sand Beach (not to be confused with Playa Negra in Cahuita), for about 200m (650 ft.) before entering the town of Puerto Viejo, which has all of about 10 streets, some of them paved.

As you drive south from town, the first beach you will hit is **Playa Cocles ★**, which is 2km (1¼ miles) from Puerto Viejo. A little farther, you'll find **Playa Chiquita ★**, which is 5km (3 miles) from Puerto Viejo, followed by **Punta Uva ★★** at 8.4km (5¼ miles) away, and **Manzanillo ★★**, some 13km (8 miles) away.

GETTING AROUND Both Cahuita and Puerto Viejo are tiny villages and you'll have no problem navigating each. You can rent scooters and bicycles from a handful of roadside stands in either town.

Taxis are also fairly easy to come by. In Cahuita, for a taxi, call **Alejandro** (✆ **8875-3209**) or **Dino** (✆ **2755-0012**). In Puerto Viejo, you can try calling **Taxi PV** (✆ **2750-0439**).

FAST FACTS There are a couple of banks and ATMs, as well as pharmacies, in the heart of both Puerto Viejo and Cahuita.

Cahuita Hotels

In addition to the places listed below, **El Encanto B&B** (www.elencantocahuita.com; ✆ **2755-0113**) is a lovely, well-run little B&B on the outskirts of the village. **Coral Hill Bungalows ★** (www.coralhillbungalows.com; ✆ **2755-0479**) has three individual bungalows and a separate two-story house, in a lush garden setting, about a block or so inland from the beach at Playa Negra.

INEXPENSIVE

Magellan Inn ★ Canadian Terry Newton is the second-generation owner/manager of this quaint boutique hotel, and she's kept the balance of elements that makes this place special. Service is friendly but not intrusive; rooms are spacious, clean and fairly priced (perhaps because they're not the most modern-looking); and the grounds are beautiful, with abundant flowers and a lovely pool built into the local coral. ***Note:*** Four of the six rooms have air-conditioning and it's definitely worth this small upgrade. One room has TV, with satellite reception, for an additional fee.

At the far end of Playa Negra, about 2km/1¼ miles north of Cahuita. www.magellaninn.com. ✆ **2755-0035**. 6 units. $55–$65 double plus tax; with A/C $65–$75 plus tax; deluxe $85–$95 plus tax. Rates include breakfast. **Amenities:** Bar; lounge; small outdoor pool; yoga/meditation/massage center; horseback riding; free Wi-Fi.

Playa Negra Guesthouse ★★★ The best beachfront hotel in Cahuita by a long shot, Playa Negra Guesthouse is just across a dirt-and-sand lane from a quiet and palm-lined stretch of beach. The hotel has well-tended, exuberant gardens, rooms with lots of personality, and plantation-style cottages (love the art on the walls and the unusual bedspreads). A couple of these cottages, painted in Crayola colors and adorned with intricate, bright white gingerbread trim, come with full kitchens, making them ideal for families or those planning on an extended stay.

On Playa Negra, about 1.5km/1 mile north of Cahuita. www.playanegra.cr. ✆ **2755-0127.** 7 units. $69–$79 double; cottages for 2–3, $89–$144, plus tax. **Amenities:** Small outdoor pool; laundry service; free Wi-Fi.

Puerto Viejo Hotels

In addition to the places below, **Mother Dear Cottages ★★** (www.motherdearcr.com) offers two fully equipped, raised-stilt cottages right on the beach in Playa Negra.

MODERATE

Hotel Banana Azul ★★ Colin Brownlee of Canada says he's not renting rooms, he's selling experiences, and it seems to be a winning formula at this popular beachfront hotel. It's located on the far northern end of Playa Negra, a vast stretch of beach backed by thick forest that stretches north from here all the way to Cahuita National Park. One of the top draws here is the Azul Beach Club, which serves food and drinks on the beach, with shaded lounge chairs and a great ocean view. Banana Azul calls itself "straight-friendly," with a clientele that's 20 percent gay, and caters mostly to couples.

Playa Negra. www.bananaazul.com. ✆ **2750-2035.** 15 units. $99–$135 double; $150–$170 suite, plus tax. Rates include full breakfast. No children under 16. **Amenities:** Restaurant; bar; bike rental; Jacuzzi; outdoor pool; free Wi-Fi.

INEXPENSIVE

True budgeteers will find an abundance of basic hotels in downtown Puerto Viejo in addition to what's listed below. Of these, **Hotel Pura Vida** (www.hotel-puravida.com; ✆ **2750-0002**) is a good pick in the heart of town, while **Rocking J's ★** (www.rockingjs.com; ✆ **2750-0665**) is a backpacker's fave on the southern outskirts of town.

Casa Verde Lodge ★★ Under new management as of 2016, Casa Verde is an eye-pleasing, tranquil place with spa services and a lovely, landscaped pool area. Budget travelers are catered to in the Heliconia and Bromelia rooms, which come with shared bathroom facilities and are somewhat spartan. Larger cabins and rooms with private baths are available for those who want more privacy. All have dark, well-worn wooden floors, and most have a private balcony or patio. The flowering gardens are nice, and the rooms, grounds, and even shared bathrooms and showers are immaculately maintained. Casa Verde is in the town center.

Puerto Viejo. www.cabinascasaverde.com. ✆ **2750-0015.** 17 units, 9 with private bathroom. $60–$68 double with shared bathroom; $84 double with private bathroom. Rates include taxes; discounts offered for cash. **Amenities:** Outdoor pool; massage hut; free Wi-Fi.

Hotels South of Puerto Viejo

Rent a car if you plan to stay at one of these hotels; public transportation is sporadic and taxis aren't always available. If you arrive by bus, however, a rented bicycle or scooter might be all you need to get around.

EXPENSIVE

Tree House Lodge ★★★ Everything has a funky, fun Gilligan's Island feel to it here, and artistic touches and distinct architectural feats make each unit memorable. The namesake Tree House is built on high stilts, reached via a suspension bridge, and features a toilet in the middle of a hollowed-out tree. The three-bedroom Beach Suite features a massive, domed bathroom lit by fanciful portholes and skylights of multicolored glass. Each of the units has a full kitchen, and two are air-conditioned. The whole compound is surrounded by tall rainforest trees, and anyone with a decent eye should be able to spot monkeys and perhaps even a three-toed sloth.

Punta Uva. www.costaricatreehouse.com. ✆ **2750-0706.** 5 units. $177–$345 double, taxes included. No credit cards. **Amenities:** Free Wi-Fi.

MODERATE

Lanna Ban Hotel ★★ Open since December 2014, Lanna Ban has a unique, Zen-like design meant to resemble a 12th-century Thai village, with Buddha statues, lotus flowers imported from Thailand blooming in the fish pond, and high peaked roofs topped with golden decorations that symbolize protection. Rooms come with one queen bed or two and are beautifully designed with Eastern wood carvings, while bathrooms are done in marble imported from India. Elaborate wooden window shutters can be opened wide like doors or propped open vertically for more privacy, and cable TV and ceiling fans add to the creature comforts. A swimming pool will soon be installed on the property.

Playa Cocles. www.lannaban.com. ✆ **2750-3053**. 9 units. $120 for rooms with 1 bed; $140 for rooms with 2 beds, plus tax; continental breakfast included. **Amenities:** Free Wi-Fi.

INEXPENSIVE

La Costa de Papito ★ This string of stylish bungalows is right in the Goldilocks zone—close to Puerto Viejo but not too close, inexpensive but not too cheap, surrounded by jungle but right across from the beach. Built by New York transplant Eddie Ryan in the mid-1990s, the hotel has 12 stilt-raised bungalows and one budget cabin where arches and curves are favored over 90-degree angles. Furniture is handmade from local lumber, often using whole tree limbs, roots, and trunk sections. Rooms are equipped with ceiling fans and stand-up fans and have hot water and safes, and some have delightfully whimsical Flintstones-style bathrooms. Guests can rent bikes and boogie boards, and take surf and aerial silks lessons.

Playa Cocles. www.lacostadepapito.com. ✆ **2750-0704** or 2750-0080. 13 units. $99–$107 double plus tax. $17 per additional person; $7 for children. Rates include breakfast. **Amenities:** Restaurant; bar; spa and beauty salon; free Wi-Fi.

Where to Eat

Coconut meat and milk figure into a lot of the regional cuisine here. Most nights, local women cook up pots of local specialties and sell them from the front porches of the two discos or from streetside stands; a full meal will cost you around $5.

IN CAHUITA

In addition to the places listed below, for good, fresh Italian fare, try **El Girasol** (✆ **2755-1164**), a small, elegant family-run joint on the main road into town. Another popular Italian option is **Pizzeria Cahuita** (✆ **2755-0179**), located between the police station and Restaurant Edith.

La French Riviera ★★ PIZZA/SANDWICHES/CREPES A welcome change from the standard Tico eatery, this place is run by a friendly French couple. The specialties here are very well executed, especially the serious *croque monsieur* and both the sweet and savory crepes. Knowing their audience, the owners also bring Gallic flair to fab thin-crust pizzas and juicy burgers (served on home-baked sesame seed buns with crisp, twice-cooked potatoes). The restaurant is open-air, with a thatched roof and loads of charm.

On the main road into Cahuita, across from the bus station. ✆ **2755-0050.** Main courses C3,000–C6,000; sandwiches C2,000–C3,000; pizzas C3,000–C3,800. No credit cards. Daily 10am–9pm.

Restaurant Edith ★ CREOLE/COSTA RICAN Back when tourists were just starting to make their way to Cahuita, a well-known local lady named Miss Edith Brown started serving them down-home Caribbean cooking from her front porch. Now she and her daughters (and other family members) run Restaurant Edith, which may not be long on decor but delivers the goods, made to order.

By the police station, Cahuita. ✆ **2755-0248.** Main courses C3,000–C18,000. No credit cards. Tues–Sun 7:30am–10pm.

Sobre Las Olas ★★★ SEAFOOD/ITALIAN Not only does this small, oceanfront restaurant have one of the best settings in the region (if not the country), with the sea just steps away, but the food is excellent. The Italian owners prepare the freshest local seafood in a variety of ways, touching on their home-country heritage and Caribbean cuisine in equal measure. So you might choose between a ceviche or a carpaccio of fresh snapper to start, perhaps followed by Sicilian-style pasta with locally caught shrimp, or a filet of mahimahi in a coconut cream sauce.

Just north of Cahuita on the road to Playa Negra. ✆ **2755-0109.** Main courses C5,000–C10,500. Wed–Mon noon–10pm.

IN PUERTO VIEJO & SOUTH OF PUERTO VIEJO

To really sample the local cuisine, you need to look up a few local women. Ask around for **Miss Dolly, Miss Sam, Miss Isma,** and **Miss Irma,** who all dish out sit-down meals in their modest little *sodas.* In addition to locally

THAT run-down FEELING

Rondon soup is a spicy coconut milk–based soup or stew made with anything the cook can "run down"—it usually includes a mix of local tubers (potato, sweet potato, or yucca), other vegetables (carrots or corn), and often some seafood. Be sure to try this authentic taste of the Caribbean.

seasoned fish and chicken served with rice and beans, these joints are usually a great place to find *pan bon* (a local sweet, dark bread), ginger cakes, *pati* (meat-filled turnovers), and *rondon* (see above).

In addition to the restaurants listed below, **Cabinas Selvin** (✆ **2750-0664**) at Punta Uva is an excellent option for local cuisine and fresh seafood, while **Pita Bonita** (✆ **2756-8173**) serves up wonderful Middle Eastern cuisine at an open-air spot between Playa Chiquita and Punta Uva. The intimate **El Refugio Grill ★★** (✆ **2759-9007**) is an Argentine-owned restaurant that serves grilled steaks, sausages, and seafood in a romantic rainforest setting.

Finally, near the end of the line, where the road first hits the beach at Manzanillo, **Cool & Calm Café** (✆ **2750-3151**) is winning faithful fans with its local cuisine and friendly atmosphere.

EXPENSIVE

La Pecora Nera ★★★ ITALIAN This is among the very best restaurants not only on the Caribbean coast but in all of Costa Rica. Chef/owner Ilario Gionnoni is a master and a marvel of perpetual motion. He is constantly innovating, raises his own chickens and pigs, and grows as much of his own fresh fruits, vegetables, and herbs as he can. Among the memorable dishes here are shrimp cocktail with a beet-based spicy dipping sauce; and rooster ragù over homemade gnocchi. The large, multilevel, open-air dining room is dimly lit and romantic, with heavy wooden tables spread widely for privacy.

50m (164 ft.) inland from a well-marked turnoff on the main road south just beyond the soccer field in Cocles. ✆ **2750-0490.** Reservations recommended. Main courses C6,000–C17,500. Tues–Sun 5:30–10pm.

MODERATE

Stashu's Con Fusion ★★★ INTERNATIONAL Stash Golas is a local legend, and his cooking and restaurant have been a Puerto Viejo mainstay for years, albeit with a couple of different locations and names. The current incarnation serves up his classic mix of world fusion cuisines, with fresh fish, seafood, beef, chicken, and vegetables featured in spicy curries or with Thai- or Mexican-tinged sauces. One of his more popular recurring specials is a macadamia-crusted fish filet with a white wine and white chocolate sauce. The tandoori chicken is also excellent, with a homemade spicy sauce consisting of 18 ingredients. Thanks to the painted paper lanterns, creative artwork, and sculptures, Stashu's is a good place for a romantic dinner.

On the main road just southeast of downtown Puerto Viejo. ✆ **2750-0530.** Main courses C3,500–C9,800. Thurs–Tues 5–10pm.

INEXPENSIVE

Bread & Chocolate ★★ BREAKFAST/AMERICAN Take your menu guidance from the name: The bread (biscuits, bagels, and such) is topnotch and baked here; and the chocolate can't be beat, whether you have it as a drink, in a range of truffles, or flavoring brownies. But this eatery also offers a range of tasty breakfast plates, as well as sandwiches and salads. The open-air dining room is small, with just a handful of wooden tables and chairs, and it fills up fast. It's not uncommon to have to wait a little on weekends and during high season. If you don't want to wait, you can always get an order to go.

½ block south of Café Viejo, downtown Puerto Viejo. ✆ **2750-0723.** Main courses C3,200–C4,500. No credit cards. Tues–Sat 6:30am–6:30pm; Sun 6:30am–2:30pm.

Exploring the South Caribbean Coast

CAHUITA NATIONAL PARK ★★

This little gem of a national park sits at the southern edge of the town of **Cahuita.** Although the pristine white-sand beach, with its picture-perfect line of coconut palms and lush coastal forest backing it, is the main draw here, the park was actually created to preserve the 240-hectare (787-acre) **coral reef** that lies just offshore. The reef contains 35 species of coral and provides a haven for hundreds of brightly colored tropical fish. You can walk on the beach itself or follow the trail that runs through the forest just behind the beach. The trail behind the beach stretches a little more than 9km (5.6 miles) to the southern end of the park at **Puerto Vargas** (**✆ 2755-0302**), where you'll find a lovely white-sand beach. The best section of reef is off the point at Punta Cahuita, and you can snorkel here if accompanied by a local guide. If you don't dawdle, the 3.8km (2.3-mile) hike to Punta Cahuita should take a little over an hour each way—although I'd allow plenty of extra time to enjoy the flora and fauna, and take a dip or two in the sea.

Although you can snorkel from the shore at Punta Cahuita, it's best to have a boat take you out to the nicest coral heads just offshore. A 3-hour **snorkel trip** costs between $20 and $35 per person, with equipment. You can arrange one with any of the local tour companies listed below. ***Note:*** These trips are best taken when the seas are calm—for safety's sake, visibility, and comfort.

ENTRY POINTS, FEES & REGULATIONS The **in-town park entrance** is just over a footbridge at the end of the village's main street. It has restroom facilities, changing rooms, and storage lockers. This is the best place to enter for a day hike and some beach time.

The alternate park entrance is at the southern end of the park in **Puerto Vargas.** This is where you should come if you don't feel up to hiking a couple of hours to reach the good snorkeling spots. The road to Puerto Vargas is approximately 5km (3 miles) south of Cahuita.

Officially, **admission** is $5 per person per day, but this is collected only at the Puerto Vargas entrance. You can enter the park from the town of Cahuita for free or with a voluntary contribution. The park is open from dawn to dusk for day visitors.

> **Damaged & Endangered**
>
> While patches of living, vibrant reef survive off Costa Rica's Caribbean coast, much of it has been killed off, or is severely threatened by overfishing, pollution, rain, and mud runoff during the rainy season. Much of the damage can be traced to the massive banana plantations that line this coastline, which have had a direct role in increasing the amount of muddy runoff and have dumped tons of plastic and pesticides into the fragile, inshore reef systems.

BEACHES & ACTIVITIES OUTSIDE THE PARK

Outside the park, the best place for swimming is **Playa Negra,** especially the stretch right in front of the Playa Negra Guesthouse (p. 229). The waves here are often good for bodysurfing, boogie boarding, or surfing. If you want to rent a board or try a surf lesson, check in with Rennie at **Willie's Tours** (see below).

Cahuita has plenty of options for organized adventure trips or tours. I recommend **Cahuita Tours** (www.cahuitatours.com; © **2755-0101**), **Willie's Tours** ★ (www.williestourscostarica.com; © **2755-1024** or 8917-6982), and **Roberto Tours** (© **2755-0117**). All are located along Cahuita's main road, and offer a wide range of tours, from snorkeling and rainforest hikes to visits to nearby indigenous reserves. Most also offer multiday trips to Tortuguero, as well as to Bocas del Toro, Panama.

Exploring Puerto Viejo & the Beaches South

THE BEACHES & SURF

Surfing has historically been the main draw in Puerto Viejo, but increasing numbers of visitors are coming for the miles of beautiful and uncrowded **beaches** ★★, acres of lush rainforests, and laid-back atmosphere. For swimming and sunbathing, locals like to hang out on the small patches of sand in front of Lazy Mon and Johnny's Place. Small, protected tide pools are in front of each of these bars for cooling off.

Just offshore of Puerto Viejo is a shallow reef where powerful storm-generated waves sometimes reach 6m (20 ft.). **Salsa Brava** ★★★, as it's known, is the prime surf break on the Caribbean coast. Even when the waves are small, this spot is recommended only for very experienced surfers because of the danger of the reef. Other popular beach breaks are south of town on Playa Cocles.

If you want a more open patch of sand and sea, head north to **Playa Negra,** along the road into town, or, better yet, to the beaches south of town around Punta Uva and all the way down to Manzanillo, where the coral reefs keep the surf much more manageable.

To the south, the first beach is **Playa Cocles** ★★, also known as Beach Break. This long, white-sand beach is popular with surfers. As you head south, the coastline is broken up by coral outcroppings and tide pools in an area generally called **Playa Chiquita ★★**. Beyond Playa Chiquita lies **Punta Uva ★★★**, or "Grape Point." Characterized by a large, rainforest-covered bit of land jutting out into the sea, the beach just north of Punta Uva is a gently curving stretch of white sand that is excellent for swimming. At the end of the line, you'll reach **Manzanillo ★★★**, the last beach before the Gandoca-Manzanillo Wildlife Refuge (see below). Manzanillo is a long, straight stretch of white sand backed by coconut palms and protected by a coral reef that makes this a top spot for swimming and snorkeling.

GANDOCA–MANZANILLO WILDLIFE REFUGE ★★

The Gandoca–Manzanillo Wildlife Refuge encompasses the small village and extends all the way to the Panamanian border. Manatees, crocodiles, and more than 350 species of birds live within the boundaries of the reserve. The reserve also includes the coral reef offshore—when the seas are calm, this is the best **snorkeling** and **diving** spot on this entire coast. Four species of **sea turtles** nest on one 8.9km (5½-mile) stretch of beach within the reserve between March and July. Three species of dolphins (Atlantic spotted, bottlenose, and the rare tucuxi) also frolic in the waters just off Manzanillo. This tucuxi species favors the brackish estuary waters, but has actually been observed in mixed species mating with local bottlenose dolphins. Many local tour guides and operators offer boat trips out to spot them.

If you want to explore the refuge, you can easily find the single, well-maintained trail by walking along the beach just south of town until you have to wade across a small river. On the other side, you'll pick up the trail head. Still, this is a wild and remote area, and it's best to do this hike with a guide.

PRESERVING THE ENVIRONMENT

The **Asociación Talamanqueña de Ecoturismo y Conservación ★★** (ATEC; Talamancan Association of Ecotourism and Conservation; www.ateccr.org; ✆ **2750-0398**), across the street from the Soda Tamara in Puerto Viejo, is a local organization dedicated to preserving the environment and cultural heritage of this area and promoting ecologically sound development. If you plan to stay in Puerto Viejo for an extended period of time and would like to contribute to the community, ask about volunteering. In addition to functioning as the local info center, Internet cafe, and traveler's hub, ATEC runs a little shop that sells T-shirts, maps, posters, and books.

Organized Tours & Activities

ATEC also offers quite a few tours, including **half-day walks** that focus on nature and either the local Afro-Caribbean culture or the indigenous Bribri culture. These walks pass through farms and forests; along the way, you'll learn about local history, customs, medicinal plants, and Indian mythology, and have an opportunity to see sloths, monkeys, iguanas, keel-billed toucans, and other wildlife. A range of different walks lead through the nearby **Bribri Indians' Kéköldi Reserve,** as well as more strenuous hikes through the primary rainforest. **Bird walks** and **night walks** will help you spot more of the area wildlife; there are even overnight treks. The local guides have a wealth of information and make a hike through the forest a truly educational experience. ATEC can arrange snorkeling trips to the nearby coral reefs, as well as **snorkeling and fishing trips** in dugout canoes, and everything from surf lessons to dance classes.

ATEC can also help you arrange overnight and multiday **camping trips** into the Talamanca Mountains and through neighboring indigenous reserves, as well as trips to Tortuguero and even a 7- to 10-day transcontinental trek to the Pacific coast. Half-day tours and night walks are $25 to $60, and full-day tours run between $75 and $120. Some tours require minimum groups of three or four people and several days' advance notice. The ATEC office is open Monday through Saturday from 8am to 8pm and Sunday from 11am to 7pm.

Local tour operators **Exploradores Outdoors** ★★ (www.exploradoresoutdoors.com; ✆ **2750-2020**), **Gecko Trail Adventures** ★★ (www.geckotrail.com; ✆ **2756-8412**), and **Terraventuras** ★ (www.terraventuras.com; ✆ **2750-0750**) all offer a host of half- and full-day **adventure tours** into the jungle or sea for between $40 and $280 per person. One especially popular tour is Terraventuras' **zipline canopy tour,** which features 22 treetop platforms, a large harnessed swing, and a rappel.

Caribe Horse Riding Club (located between Punta Uva and Manzanillo; www.caribehorse.com; ✆ **8705-4250;** $50–$160/person) runs one of the better and more interesting **horseback riding** operations in the country. It offers a range of rides, from short 90-minute beach jaunts to full-day excursions into the mountains and nearby reserves, and even night rides. The Hippo Camp Tour features human and equine wading in the warm waters of the Caribbean Sea.

The **Punta Mona Center For Regenerative Design & Botanical Studies** (inside the Gandoca–Manzanillo refuge; www.puntamona.org) offers **day visits** to its fascinating organic permaculture gardens.

Scuba divers can check in with **Reef Runners Dive Shop** (www.reefrunnerdivers.com; ✆ **2750-0480**) or **Punta Uva Dive Center** (www.puntauvadivecenter.com; ✆ **2759-9191**). Both of these operations frequent a variety of dive sites between Puerto Viejo and Punta Mona, and if you're lucky the seas will be calm and visibility good—although throughout most of the year, it can be a bit rough and murky here. Reef Runners has an office in downtown Puerto Viejo, while Punta Uva Dive Center has its operations center right off the beach in Punta Uva. Rates run between $80 and $110 for a two-tank boat dive.

Caribeans Chocolate Tour (www.caribeanschocolate.com; ✆ **8836-8930** or 8341-2034; Mon 10am, Tues and Thurs 10am and 2pm, Fri–Sat 2pm; $26–$30) explores a working organic cacao plantation and chocolate production facility. The tour illustrates the entire process of growing, harvesting, and processing cacao, and of course there's a tasting at the end. When you get around to the tasting, organic wine pairings are also available.

Several wildlife rescue centers and animal preservation centers operate in the area. The **Jaguar Rescue Center ★★** (www.jaguarrescue.com; ✆ **2750-0710;** guided tours Mon–Sat 9:30 and 11:30am; $18 adults, free for kids under 11) is the most extensive of the batch. Located in Playa Chiquita, it features a broad assortment of local animals, including monkeys, sloths, snakes, caimans, turtles, birds, and more. Just don't expect to see a jaguar; the center was named after an orphaned jaguar that died years ago.

Also in Playa Chiquita, at the Tree House Lodge (see p. 231), is the **Green Iguana Conservation Tour ★** (www.iguanaverde.com; ✆ **2750-0706;** Tues and Thurs at 8:30am; $15/person). This educational tour focuses on the life cycle, habits, and current situation of this reptile, which is listed as a threatened species. The tour features a walk around a massive natural enclosure, as well as a video presentation. Additional tours may be arranged by appointment.

Shopping

Cahuita and Puerto Viejo attract a lot of local and international bohemians, who seem to survive solely on the sale of handmade jewelry, painted ceramic trinkets (mainly pipes and cigarette-lighter holders), and imported Indonesian textiles. You'll sometimes find a score or so of them at makeshift stands set up by Puerto Viejo's *parquecito* (little park), which comprises a few wooden benches in front of the sea near the Lazy Mon.

In addition to the makeshift outdoor stands, a host of well-stocked gift and crafts shops are spread around town. **Luluberlu ★** (✆ **2750-0394**), located inland across from Cabinas Guaraná, features locally produced craftwork, including shell mobiles and mirrors with mosaic-inlaid frames, as well as imports from Thailand and India.

Tip: Locally produced chocolate, made by several local chocolatiers, can be found for sale at many gift shops and restaurants around town.

Nightlife

Cahuita is a rather quiet little town. **Coco's Bar ★**, a classic Caribbean watering hole at the main crossroads in town, has traditionally been the place to spend your nights (or days, for that matter) if you like cold beer and very loud reggae and soca music. Toward the park entrance, the **National Park Restaurant** has a popular bar, with loud music and dancing on most nights during the high season and on weekends during the off season. Out toward Playa Negra, the **Reggae Bar ★** has a convivial vibe, blasting thumping tropical tunes most nights.

Puerto Viejo is a much more happening place. Probably the hottest night spot is **Hot Rocks ★★** (✆ **8708-3183**), with its big stage, live music, karaoke, packed bar, and pool and foosball tables, conveniently located in the center of town, where the main road meets the harbor. Another contender is the **Lazy Mon ★** (www.thelazymon.com), a bit farther southeast, with pool and Ping-Pong tables and regular live bands or DJs. Also popular is the nearby oceanfront **Salsa Brava** ★ (✆ **2750-0241**). At all three of these, you can kick off your shoes and stand in the warm Caribbean waves while sipping a beer and chatting with other visitors.

There's also **Johnny's Place** ★ (✆ **2750-2000**) next to the police station, and **Mango Sunset Bar** ★ near the water, beside the bus station, featuring either live music or a DJ most nights. For a more sophisticated ambience, try the oceanfront **Koki Beach** ★ (www.kokibeach.com; ✆ **2250-0902**).

Finally, heading south of town, at the start of Playa Cocles, **Tasty Waves Cantina** (✆ **2750-0507**) has a very lively scene, with live bands, karaoke, trivia nights, and open jam sessions.

An Isolated Ecolodge in the Talamanca Mountains

Selva Bananito Lodge ★★ This remote ecolodge is as "eco" as they come, with its own private nature preserve and owners who are committed to conservation. The 1,750-hectare property was purchased in 1974 for farming and logging, but a decade later Jürgen Stein and his sisters persuaded their father to stop cutting down trees and start saving them. The lodge opened in 1995 as an alternate source of income, in hopes of promoting conservation through tourism. The bird-watching here is fabulous, and video cameras in the preserve routinely capture jaguars, ocelots, and pumas on the prowl. The gorgeous superior rooms on stilts offer two queen-size beds, louvered windows, and fold-away doors opening on a broad veranda with pristine rainforest views. Solar power provides electric light, hot showers, and a ceiling fan, though there are no power outlets in the rooms, and Internet and cellphone service are unreliable. Meals are served family-style in the *rancho*, which has ceiling fans but no lighting except candles. To get here, cross the wide Bananito River in your own 4WD vehicle if you dare, or arrange for the staff to pick you up on the other side of the river.

Near Bananito, southwest of Limón. www.selvabananito.com. ✆ **2253-8118.** 15 units. $100–$130 per person per day, based on double occupancy, all meals and taxes included; $160–$180 per person per day with meals, a tour, transportation from Bananito, and taxes included. **Amenities:** Wide range of tours.

11

PLANNING YOUR TRIP

Costa Rica is no longer the next new thing. Neither is it old hat. As Costa Rica has matured as a tourist destination, things have gotten easier and easier for international travelers. That said, most travelers—even experienced travelers and repeat visitors—will want to do some serious pre-trip planning. This chapter provides a variety of planning tools, including information on how to get there, tips on accommodations, and quick, on-the-ground resources.

GETTING THERE

By Plane

It takes 3 to 7 hours to fly to Costa Rica from the U.S., the origin of most of the direct and connecting flights to this country. The majority of these land at San José's **Juan Santamaría International Airport** (www.fly2sanjose.com; ✆ **2437-2626** for 24-hr. airport information; airport code SJO). However, more and more international flights are touching down at Liberia's **Daniel Oduber International Airport** (www.liberiacostaricaairport.net; ✆ **2668-1010;** airport code LIR).

Liberia is the gateway to the beaches of the Guanacaste region and the Nicoya Peninsula, and a direct flight here eliminates the need for a separate commuter flight in a small aircraft or many hours in a car or bus. If you're planning to spend most or all of your vacation in Guanacaste, you'll want to fly in and out of Liberia. However, San José is a much more convenient gateway if you're planning to head to the Pacific beaches, the Caribbean coast, or the southern zone.

By Bus

Buses make regular runs to San José and back from Panama City and Managua, Nicaragua. You'll thank yourself if you spend a little extra for a deluxe, express, or direct bus, saving you a lot of stops and improving your chances of finding a bus with a restroom. Some even show movies.

THE BEST websites ABOUT COSTA RICA

- **The *Tico Times*** (www.ticotimes.net): Established in 1956, the *Tico Times* is the oldest and most trusted English-language news source in Central America. The print edition stopped publishing in 2014 and is now only online, but it continues to be a robust source for news, sports, business, travel, and real estate coverage.
- **Latin American Network Information Center** (http://lanic.utexas.edu/la/ca/cr): This site houses a vast collection of information about Costa Rica, and is a good one-stop shop for browsing, with helpful links to a diverse range of tourism and general information sites.
- **The U.S. Embassy in Costa Rica** (http://costarica.usembassy.gov): The official site of the U.S. Embassy in Costa Rica has a good base of information and regular updates of concern to U.S. citizens abroad, as well as about Costa Rica in general.
- ***La Nación Digital*** (www.nacion.com): If you can read Spanish, this is an excellent site to visit regularly. The entire content of the country's paper of record is placed online daily, and there's an extensive searchable archive.

Several bus lines with regular daily departures connect the major capitals of Central America. Call **King Quality** (**© 2258-8834**), **Transnica** (www.transnica.com; **© 2223-4242**), or **Tica Bus Company** (www.ticabus.com; **© 2296-9788**) for further information. None of these companies reserves seats by phone, and schedules change frequently, so buy your ticket in advance. From Managua, it's 11 hours and 450km (280 miles) to San José, and the one-way fare is around $30 to $50. From Panama City, it's a 20-hour, 900km (560-mile) trip. The one-way fare is around $40 to $60.

Whenever you're traveling by bus in Central America, try to keep a watchful eye on your belongings, especially at rest and border stops.

GETTING AROUND

By Plane

Flying is one of the best ways to get around Costa Rica. Because the country is quite small, flights are short and not too expensive. Sansa and Nature Air are the country's domestic airlines. In the high season (late Nov to late Apr), be sure to book reservations well in advance.

Sansa (www.flysansa.com; **© 877/767-2672** in the U.S. and Canada, or 2290-4100 in Costa Rica) operates from a private terminal at San José's **Juan Santamaría International Airport** (see above).

Nature Air (www.natureair.com; **© 800/235-9272** in the U.S. and Canada, or 2299-6000 in Costa Rica) operates from the main terminal at the **Juan Santamaría International Airport** in San José (see above).

By Car

Renting a car in Costa Rica is no idle proposition. The roads are riddled with potholes, most rural intersections are unmarked, and, for some reason, sitting behind the wheel of a car seems to turn peaceful Ticos into homicidal maniacs. But unless you want to see the country from the window of a bus or pay exorbitant amounts for private transfers, renting a car might be your best option for independent exploring.

Be forewarned, however: Although rental cars no longer bear special license plates, they are still readily identifiable to thieves and are frequently targeted. (Nothing is ever safe in a car in Costa Rica, although parking in guarded parking lots helps.) Transit police also seem to target tourists; never pay money directly to a police officer who stops you for any traffic violation.

Before driving off with a rental car, be sure that you inspect the exterior and point out to the rental-company representative every tiny scratch, dent, tear, or any other damage. It's a common practice with many Costa Rican car-rental companies to claim that you owe payment for minor dings and dents that the company finds when you return the car. Also, if you get into an accident, be sure that the rental company doesn't try to bill you for a higher amount than the deductible on your rental contract.

These caveats aren't meant to scare you off from driving in Costa Rica. Tens of thousands of tourists rent cars here every year, and the large majority of them encounter no problems. Just keep your wits about you and guard against car theft, and you'll do fine. Also, keep in mind that four-wheel-drives are particularly useful in the rainy season (May to mid-Nov) and for navigating the poorly paved roads year-round.

Among the major international agencies operating in Costa Rica are **Alamo, Avis, Budget, Hertz, National, Payless,** and **Thrifty.**

GASOLINE (PETROL) Gasoline is sold as "regular" and "super." Both are unleaded; super is just higher octane. Diesel is available at almost every gas station, as well. Most rental cars run on super, but always ask your rental agent what type of gas your car takes. When going off to remote places, try to leave with a full tank of gas because gas stations can be hard to find. If you need to gas up in a small town, you can sometimes get gasoline from enterprising families who sell it by the liter from their houses. Look for hand-lettered signs that say GASOLINA. At press time, regular gasoline costs $3.11 (C1,662) per gallon.

ROAD CONDITIONS The awful road conditions throughout Costa Rica are legendary, and deservedly so. Despite constant promises to fix the problem and sporadic repair attempts, the hot sun, hard rain, and rampant corruption outpace any progress made toward improving the condition of roads. Even paved roads are often badly potholed, so stay alert. Conditions get especially tricky during the rainy season, when heavy rains and runoff can destroy a stretch of pavement in the blink of an eye.

Route numbers are somewhat sporadically and arbitrarily used. You'll also find frequent signs listing the number of kilometers to various towns or cities. Still, your best bets for on-road directions are billboards and advertisements for hotels. It's always a good idea to know the names of a few hotels at your destination, just in case your specific hotel hasn't put up any billboards or signs.

Most car-rental agencies now offer the opportunity to rent out GPS units along with your car rental. Rates run between $8 and $15 per day. If you have your own GPS unit, several maps to Costa Rica are available. While you still can't simply enter a street address, most commercial GPS maps of Costa Rica feature hundreds of prominent points of interest (POI), and you should be able to plug in a POI close to your destination.

RENTER'S INSURANCE Third Party Waiver, or Supplemental Liability Insurance (SLI) is mandatory in Costa Rica, regardless of your home policy or credit card coverage. Supplemental collision and damage insurance is optional. Even if you hold **your own car-insurance policy** at home, coverage doesn't always extend abroad. Be sure to find out whether you'll be covered in Costa Rica, whether your policy extends to all persons who will be driving the rental car, how much liability is covered in case an outside party is injured in an accident, and whether the type of vehicle you are renting is included under your contract.

DRIVING RULES A current foreign driver's license is valid for the first 3 months you are in Costa Rica. Seat belts are required for the driver and front-seat passengers. Motorcyclists must wear helmets. Highway police use radar, so keep to the speed limit (usually 60–90kmph/35–55 mph) if you don't want to be pulled over. Speeding tickets can be charged to your credit card for up to a year after you leave the country if they are not paid before departure.

To reduce congestion and fuel consumption, a rotating ban on rush-hour traffic takes place in the central core of San José Monday through Friday from 7 to 8:30am and from 4 to 5:30pm. The ban affects cars with licenses ending in the digits 1 or 2 on Monday; 3 or 4 on Tuesday; 5 or 6 on Wednesday; 7 or 8 on Thursday; and 9 or 0 on Friday. If you are caught driving a car with the banned license plate during these hours on a specified day, you will be ticketed.

BREAKDOWNS Be warned that emergency services, both vehicular and medical, are extremely limited outside San José, and their availability is directly related to the remoteness of your location at the time of breakdown. You'll find service stations spread over the entire length of the Inter-American Highway, and most of these have tow trucks and mechanics. The major towns of Puntarenas, Liberia, Quepos, San Isidro, Palmar, and Golfito all have hospitals, and most other moderately sized cities and tourist destinations have some sort of clinic or health-services provider.

If you're involved in an accident, contact **National Insurance Institute (INS)** at © **800/800-8000.** You should probably also call the **Transit Police**

(✆ **2222-9330**); if they have a unit close by, they'll send one. An official transit police report will greatly facilitate any insurance claim. If you can't get help from any of these, try to get written statements from any witnesses. Finally, you can also call ✆ **911,** and they should be able to redirect your call to the appropriate agency.

If the police do show up, you've got a 50-50 chance of finding them helpful or downright antagonistic. Many officers are unsympathetic to the problems of what they perceive to be rich tourists driving around in fancy cars with lots of expensive toys and trinkets. Success and happy endings run about equal with horror stories.

If you don't speak Spanish, expect added difficulty in any emergency or stressful situation. Don't expect that rural (or urban) police officers, hospital personnel, service-station personnel, or mechanics will speak English.

Finally, although not endemic, there have been reports of folks being robbed by seemingly friendly Ticos who stop to give assistance. To add insult to injury, there have even been reports of organized gangs who puncture tires of rental cars at rest stops or busy intersections, only to follow them, offer assistance, and make off with belongings and valuables. If you find yourself with a flat tire, try to ride it to the nearest gas station. If that's not possible, try to pull over into a well-lit public spot. Keep the doors of the car locked and an eye on your belongings while changing the tire.

By Bus

This is by far the most economical way to get around Costa Rica. Buses are inexpensive and relatively well maintained, and they go nearly everywhere. There are two types. **Local buses,** the cheapest and slowest, stop frequently and are generally a bit dilapidated. **Express buses** run between San José and most beach towns and major cities; these tend to be newer units and more comfortable, although very few are so new or modern as to have restroom facilities, and they sometimes operate only on weekends and holidays.

Two companies run regular, fixed-schedule departures in passenger vans and small buses to most of the major tourist destinations in the country. **Gray Line** (www.graylinecostarica.com; ✆ **800/719-3105** in the U.S. and Canada, or 2220-2126 in Costa Rica) has about 10 departures leaving San José each morning and heading or connecting to Jacó, Manuel Antonio, Liberia, Playa Hermosa, La Fortuna, Tamarindo, and playas Conchal and Flamingo. There are return trips to San José every day from these destinations and a variety of interconnecting routes. A similar service, **Interbus** (www.interbusonline.com; ✆ **4100-0888**) has a similar route map and connections. Fares run between $50 and $95, depending on the destination. Gray Line offers an unlimited weekly pass for all of its shuttle routes for $198.

Beware: Both of these companies offer pickup and drop-off at a wide range of hotels. This means that if you are the first picked up or last dropped off, you might have to sit through a long period of subsequent stops before finally hitting the road or reaching your destination. Moreover, I've heard some

New Bus Terminal

San José's newest bus terminal, the **Terminal Central 7-10** (www.terminal7-10.com; ✆ **2519-9743**), is a modern, four-story facility with scores of bus bays, a food court, and a centralized counter area for purchasing tickets. It has buses to Jacó, Arenal, Guanacaste, the Nicoya Peninsula, and Nicaragua, and the website has a complete listing of destinations and departure times. The terminal is located at Avenida 7 and Calle 10; you can tell your taxi driver it's *"diagonal al antiguo Cine Libano"* ("diagonal to the old Cine Libano").

disheartening stories about both bus lines concerning missed or severely delayed connections and rude drivers. For details on how to get to various destinations from San José, see the "Arriving" sections in the preceding chapters.

By Taxi

Taxis are readily available in San José and most popular tourist towns and destinations. In San José, your best bet is usually just to hail one on the street. However, during rush hour and rainstorms, and in more remote destinations, it is probably best to call a cab. Throughout the book, I list numbers for local taxi companies in the "Getting Around" sections. If no number is listed, ask at your hotel, or, if you're out and about, at the nearest restaurant or shop; someone will be more than happy to call you a cab.

All city taxis, and even some rural cabs, have meters (called *marías*), although drivers sometimes refuse to use them, particularly with foreigners. If this is the case, be sure to negotiate the price upfront. Always try to get drivers to use the meter first (say, *"ponga la maría, por favor"*). The official rate at press time is C640 per kilometer (½ mile). If you have a rough idea of how far it is to your destination, you can estimate how much it should cost from these figures, or you can ask at your hotel how much a specific ride should cost. After 10pm, taxis are legally allowed to add a 20 percent surcharge. Some of the meters are programmed to include the extra charge automatically, but be careful: Some drivers will use the evening setting during the daytime (or at night) to charge an extra 20 percent on top of the higher meter setting.

STAYING HEALTHY

Staying healthy on a trip to Costa Rica is mainly a matter of being a little cautious about what you eat and drink, and using common sense. Know your physical limits and don't overexert yourself in the ocean, on hikes, or during athletic activities. As you climb above 3,000m (10,000 ft.), you may feel the effects of altitude sickness. Be sure to drink plenty of water and not overexert yourself. Limit your exposure to the tropical sun, especially during the first few days of your trip and, thereafter, from 11am to 2pm. Use sunscreen with a high protection factor, and apply it liberally. Remember that kids need more protection than adults. I recommend buying and drinking bottled water or soft drinks, but the water in San José and in most of the country's heavily visited spots is safe to drink.

General Availability of Healthcare

In general, Costa Rica has a high level of medical care and services for a developing nation. The better private hospitals and doctors in San José are very good. In fact, given the relatively budget nature of care and treatment, a sizable number of Americans come to Costa Rica each year for elective surgery and other care.

Pharmacies are widely available and generally well stocked. In most cases, you will not need a doctor's script to fill or refill a prescription.

Additional **emergency numbers** are listed in the various destination chapters, as well as in "Fast Facts: Costa Rica," below.

If You Get Sick

Your hotel front desk should be your best source of information and assistance if you get sick while in Costa Rica. In addition, your local consulate in Costa Rica can provide a list of area doctors who speak English. I list the best hospitals in San José in "Fast Facts: San José" in chapter 5; these have the most modern facilities in the country. Most state-run hospitals and walk-in clinics around the country have emergency rooms that can treat most conditions, although I highly recommend the private hospitals in San José if your condition is not life-threatening and can wait for treatment until you reach one of them.

Regional Health Concerns

TROPICAL ILLNESSES Your chance of contracting any serious tropical disease here is slim, although there have been a few cases of the **Zika virus,** the mosquito-borne virus linked to birth defects. Another concern is the mosquito-borne **chikungunya virus,** which is rarely fatal but can cause joint pain for up to a year.

Malaria is found in the lowlands on both coasts and in the northern zone. Although it's rarely found in urban areas, it's still a problem in remote wooded regions and along the Caribbean coast. Malaria prophylaxes are available, but several have side effects, and others are of questionable effectiveness. Consult your doctor regarding what is currently considered the best preventive treatment for malaria. Be sure to ask whether a recommended drug will cause you to be hypersensitive to the sun. Because malaria-carrying mosquitoes usually come out at night, you should do as much as possible to avoid being bitten after dark. If you are in a malaria-prone area, wear long pants and long sleeves, use insect repellent, and either sleep under a mosquito net or burn mosquito coils.

Of greater concern is **dengue fever,** which has had periodic outbreaks in Latin America since the mid-1990s. Dengue fever is similar to malaria and is spread by an aggressive daytime mosquito. This mosquito seems to be most common in lowland urban areas, and Puntarenas, Liberia, and Limón have been the worst-hit cities in Costa Rica. Dengue is also known as "bone-break fever" because it is usually accompanied by severe body aches. The first infection with dengue fever will make you very sick but should cause no serious damage. However, a second infection with a different strain of the dengue virus can lead to internal hemorrhaging and could be life-threatening.

One tropical fever you should know about is **leptospirosis.** There are more than 200 strains of leptospires, which are animal-borne bacteria transmitted to humans via contact with drinking, swimming, or bathing water. This bacterial infection is easily treated with antibiotics; however, it can quickly cause very high fever and chills, and should be treated promptly.

If you develop a high fever accompanied by severe body aches, nausea, diarrhea, or vomiting during or shortly after a visit to Costa Rica, consult a physician as soon as possible.

DIETARY RED FLAGS Even though the water in San José and most popular destinations in Costa Rica is generally safe, water quality varies outside the city. Stick to bottled drinks as much as possible, and avoid ice. Even if you're careful to buy bottled water, order *frescos en leche* (fruit shakes made with milk rather than water), and drink your soft drink without ice cubes, you still might encounter some intestinal difficulties. Most of this is just due to tender stomachs coming into contact with slightly more aggressive Latin American intestinal flora. In extreme cases of diarrhea or intestinal discomfort, it's worth taking a stool sample to a lab for analysis. The results will usually pinpoint the amoebic or parasitic culprit, which can then be readily treated with available over-the-counter medicines.

Except in the most established and hygienic of restaurants, it's also advisable to avoid *ceviche,* a raw seafood salad, especially if it has any shellfish in it. It could be home to any number of bacterial critters.

BUGS, BITES & OTHER WILDLIFE CONCERNS Although Costa Rica has Africanized bees (the notorious "killer bees" of fact and fable) and several species of venomous snakes, your chances of being bitten are minimal, especially if you refrain from sticking your hands into hives or under rocks in the forest. If you know that you're allergic to bee stings, consult your doctor before traveling.

At the beaches, you'll probably be bitten by *purrujas* (sand fleas), especially on the lower part of your legs. These nearly invisible insects leave an itchy welt. Try not to scratch because this can lead to open sores and infections. *Purrujas* are most active at sunrise and sunset, so you might want to cover up or avoid the beaches at these times.

Snakebites are rare, and the majority of snakes in Costa Rica are nonvenomous. If you do encounter a snake, keep your distance. Avoid sticking your hands under rocks, branches, and fallen trees, and avoid brushing up against vegetation.

Scorpions, black widow spiders, tarantulas, bullet ants, and biting insects of many types can all be found in Costa Rica. In general, they are not nearly the danger or nuisance most visitors fear. Watch where you stick your hands; in addition, you might want to shake out your clothes and shoes before putting them on to avoid any painful surprises.

RIPTIDES Many of Costa Rica's beaches have riptides: strong currents that can drag swimmers out to sea. A riptide occurs when water that has been dumped on the shore by strong waves forms a channel back out to open water. These channels have strong currents. If you get caught in a riptide, you can't escape the current by swimming toward shore; it's like trying to swim upstream in a river. To break free of the current, swim parallel to shore and use the energy of the waves to help you get back to the beach.

[FastFACTS] COSTA RICA

ATMs/Banks You can change money at all banks in Costa Rica, though you must produce your passport to do so. Costa Rica has a modern and widespread network of ATMs. You should find ATMs in all but the most remote tourist destinations and isolated nature lodges. In response to several "express kidnappings" in San José, in which people were taken at gunpoint to an ATM to clean out their bank accounts, some banks shut down ATM service between 10pm and 5am. Others dispense money 24 hours a day.

It's probably a good idea to change your PIN to a four-digit PIN. While many ATMs in Costa Rica will accept five- and six-digit PINs, some will only accept four-digit PINs.

Business Hours Banks are usually open Monday through Friday from 9am to 4pm, although many have begun to offer extended hours. Post offices are generally open Monday through Friday from 8am to 5:30pm, and Saturday from 7:30am to noon. (In small towns, post offices often close on Saturday.) Stores are generally open Monday through Saturday from 9am to 6pm (many close for 1 hr. at lunch), but stores in modern malls generally stay open until 8 or 9pm and don't close for lunch. Most bars are open until 1 or 2am, although some go later.

Customs Visitors to Costa Rica are permitted to bring in all manner of items for personal use, including cameras, video cameras and accessories, tape recorders, personal computers, and music players. Customs officials in Costa Rica seldom check tourists' luggage.

Dentists Consult with your hotel or consulate in case of a dental emergency. The U.S. Embassy provides a list of medical providers, including dentists, at its website, www.costarica.usembassy.gov. Click on "U.S. Citizen Services" and scroll down to "Lawyers and Doctors."

Disabled Travelers Although Costa Rica does have a law mandating Equality of Opportunities for People with Disabilities, and some facilities have been adapted, in general, there are relatively few buildings, bathrooms, public buses, or taxis specifically designed for travelers with disabilities in the country. In San José, sidewalks are particularly crowded and uneven, and they are nonexistent in most of the rest of the country. Few hotels offer wheelchair-accessible accommodations, though this is gradually changing.

Many travel agencies offer customized tours and itineraries for travelers with disabilities. Among them are **Eco Adventure International** (www.eaiadventure.com; ✆ **888/710-9453** in the U.S. and Canada); **Flying Wheels Travel** (www.flyingwheelstravel.com; ✆ **507/451-5005**); and **Accessible Journeys** (www.disabilitytravel.com; ✆ **800/846-4537** or 610/521-0339).

Doctors Your hotel front desk will be your best source of information on what to do if you get sick and where to go for treatment. Most have the number of a trusted doctor on hand. In addition, your local consulate in Costa Rica can provide a list of area doctors who speak English. Also see "Staying Healthy," above.

Drinking Laws Alcoholic beverages are sold every day of the week throughout the year, although some local governments ban the sale of alcohol in the days before Easter. The legal drinking age is 18, though it's sporadically enforced. Liquor, beer, and wine are sold in liquor stores called *licoreras*, and in most supermarkets and convenience stores.

Electricity The standard in Costa Rica is the same as in the United States and Canada: 110 volts AC (60 cycles). However, three-pronged outlets can be scarce, so it's helpful to bring along an adapter.

Embassies & Consulates The following are located in San José: **United States Embassy,** Calle 98 and Avenida Central, Pavas (http://costarica.usembassy.gov; ✆ **2519-2000**); **Canadian Embassy,** Oficentro Ejecutivo La Sabana, Edificio 5 (www.costarica.gc.ca; ✆ **2242-4400**); and **British Embassy,** Edificio Colón, 11th Floor, Paseo Colón between calles 38 and 40 (www.gov.uk/government/world/costa-rica; ✆ **2258-2025**). San José does not have an Australian, Irish, or New Zealand embassy.

Emergencies In case of any emergency, dial ✆ **911** (which should have an English-speaking operator); for an ambulance, call ✆ **1028;** and to report a fire, call ✆ **1118.** If 911 doesn't work, you can contact the police at ✆ **2222-1365** or 2221-5337, and hopefully they can find someone who speaks English.

Family Travel Hotels in Costa Rica often give discounts for children, and allow children to stay for free in a parent's room. Still, these discounts and the cut-off ages vary according to the hotel; in general, don't assume that your kids can stay in your room for free. Some hotels, villas, and *cabinas* come equipped with kitchenettes or full kitchen facilities. These can be a real money-saver for those traveling with children. Hotels offering regular, dependable babysitting service are few and far between. If you will need babysitting, make sure that your hotel offers it, and be sure to ask whether the babysitters are bilingual. In many cases, they are not. This is usually not a problem with infants and toddlers, but it can be problematic for older children.

Health No shots or inoculations are required to enter Costa Rica. The exception to this is for those who have recently been traveling in a country or region known to have yellow fever. In this case, proof of a yellow fever vaccination is required. Also see "Staying Healthy," above.

Insurance For information on traveler's insurance, trip-cancellation insurance, and medical insurance while traveling, visit www.frommers.com/planning.

Internet & Wi-Fi Internet cafes were once ubiquitous but are increasingly rare, as most hotels and restaurants offer high-speed Wi-Fi access, usually for free.

Language Spanish is the official language of Costa Rica. However, in most tourist areas, you'll be surprised by how well Costa Ricans speak English. See chapter 13 for some key Spanish terms and phrases.

Legal Aid If you need legal help, your best bet is to first contact your local embassy or consulate. See "Embassies & Consulates," above, for contact details.

LGBT Travelers Costa Rica is a Catholic, conservative, macho country where public displays of same-sex affection are rare and considered somewhat shocking. However, gay and lesbian tourism to Costa Rica is quite robust, and gay and lesbian travelers are generally treated with respect and should not experience any harassment. If you speak Spanish, you might want to connect with the **Comunidad Arco Iris (CARI;** www.caricr.com), which serves as a meeting place and information clearinghouse for the LGBT community.

Mail & Postage It costs less than $1 to mail a letter to the United States or Europe. You can get stamps at post offices and at some gift shops in large hotels. San José's main post office is located in a historic building on Calle 2 between Av. 1 and 3. Given the Costa Rican postal service's track record, it's best to pay extra to have anything of value certified. Better yet, use an international courier service or wait until you get home to post it. Contact **DHL,** on Paseo Colón between calles 30 and 32 (www.dhl.com; ✆ **2209-6000**); **EMS Courier,** with desks at most post offices (www.correos.go.cr; ✆ **2223-9766**); **FedEx,** which is based in Heredia but will arrange pickup anywhere in the metropolitan area (www.fedex.com; ✆ **2239-0576**); or **United Parcel Service,** in Pavas (www.ups.com; ✆ **2290-2828**).

Mobile Phones Costa Rica uses **GSM** (Global System for Mobile Communications) networks. If your cellphone is on a GSM system, and you have a world-capable multiband phone, you should be able to make and receive calls in Costa Rica. Just call your wireless operator and ask for "international roaming" to be activated on your account. Per-minute charges can be high, though—up to $5 in Costa Rica, depending on your plan.

Costa Rica has three main cellphone companies and a couple of smaller outfits. The main providers are the government-run ICE/Kolbi and the international giants Claro and Movistar. All offer a range of prepaid and traditional phone plans.

You can purchase a **prepaid SIM card for an unlocked GSM phone** at the airport and at shops all around the country. A prepaid SIM card costs around $2 to $4. Cards usually come loaded with some minutes, and you can buy additional minutes separately either online or at cellphone stores and ICE offices around the country.

If you don't have your own unlocked GSM phone, you might consider buying one here. Shops around the country offer basic, functional phones with a local line, for prices beginning at around $35.

In addition, most of the major car rental agencies offer cellphone rentals. Rates run around $5 to $7 per day or $25 to $50 per week for the rental, with charges of 50¢ to $1.50 per minute for local calls and $1 to $3 per minute for international calls.

Money & Costs The unit of currency in Costa Rica is the **colón.** In this book, prices are listed in the currency you are most likely to see quoted. Hence, nearly all hotel prices and most tour and transportation prices are listed in dollars, since the hotels, airlines, tour agencies, and transport companies quote their prices in dollars. Many restaurants do as well. Still, a good many restaurants, as well as taxis and other local goods and services, are advertised and quoted in colones. In those cases, prices listed are in colones (C).

THE VALUE OF THE COLÓN VS. OTHER POPULAR CURRENCIES

Colones	Aus$	Can$	Euro (€)	NZ$	UK£	US$
526	A$1.41	C1.39	€.90	NZ$1.51	69p	$1.00

The colón is divided into 100 **céntimos,** though the smallest coins are silverish 5- and 10-colón coins, followed by gold-hued 25-, 50-, 100-, and 500-colón coins.

Paper notes come in denominations of 1,000, 2,000, 5,000, 10,000, and 20,000 colones. You might hear people refer to a *rojo* or *tucán*, which are slang terms for the red 1,000- and yellow 5,000-colón bills,

WHAT THINGS COST IN COSTA RICA	US$	COSTA RICAN COLONES
Taxi from the airport to downtown San José	25.00–40.00	C13,250–C21,200
Double room, moderate	120.00	C63,600
Double room, inexpensive	70.00	C37,100
Three-course dinner for one without wine, moderate	20.00–30.00	C10,600–C15,900
Bottle of beer	1.50–3.00	C795–C1,590
Cup of coffee	1.00–1.50	C530–C795
1 gallon/1 liter of premium gas	3.86 per gallon; 1.02 per liter	2,029 per gallon; 536 per liter
Admission to most museums	2.00–5.00	C1,060–C2,650
Admission to most national parks	15.00	C7,950

respectively. The 100-colón denominaions are called *tejas,"* so *cinco tejas* is 500 colones.

Forged bills are not entirely uncommon. When receiving change in colones, it's a good idea to check the larger-denomination bills, which should have protective bands or hidden images that appear when held up to the light.

Since banks handle money exchanges, Costa Rica has very few exchange houses. One major exception to this is the **Global Exchange** (www.globalexchange.co.cr; ✆ **2431-0686**) offices at the international airports. However, be forewarned that they change money at more than 10 percent below the official exchange rate. Airport taxis accept U.S. dollars, so there isn't necessarily any great need to exchange money the moment you arrive.

Hotels will often exchange money and cash traveler's checks, as well; there usually isn't much of a line, but they might shave a few colones off the exchange rate.

If you plan on carrying around dollars to pay for goods and services, be aware that most Costa Rican businesses, be they restaurants, convenience stores, or gas stations, will give a very unfavorable exchange rate.

Your best bet for getting colones is usually by direct withdrawal from your home account via a bank card or debit card, although check in advance if you will be assessed any fees or charges by your home bank. In general, ATMs in Costa Rica still don't add on service fees. Paying with a credit card will also get you the going bank exchange rate. But again, try to get a credit card with no foreign transaction fees.

Be very careful about exchanging money on the streets; it's extremely risky. In addition to forged bills and short counts, street money-changers frequently work in teams that can leave you holding neither colones nor dollars. Also be very careful when leaving a bank. Criminals are often looking for foreigners who have just withdrawn or exchanged cash.

The currency conversions provided in "The Value of the Colón vs. Other Popular Currencies" box above were correct at press time. However, rates fluctuate, so before departing, consult a currency exchange website such as **www.oanda.com/currency/converter** to check up-to-the-minute rates.

MasterCard and **Visa** are the most widely accepted credit cards in Costa Rica, followed by American Express. Most hotels and restaurants accept all of these, especially in tourist destination areas. Discover and Diners Club are far less commonly accepted.

Beware of hidden credit card fees while traveling. Check with your credit or debit card issuer to see what fees, if any, will be charged for overseas transactions. Recent reform legislation in the U.S., for example, has curbed some exploitative lending practices. But many banks have responded by increasing fees in other areas, including fees for customers who use credit and debit cards while out of the country—even if those charges were made in U.S. dollars. Fees can amount to 3 percent or more of the purchase price. Check with your bank before departing to avoid any surprise charges on your statement.

Newspapers & Magazines The *Tico Times* (www.ticotimes.net) is your best bet for news about Costa Rica in English. There are also a half-dozen or so Spanish-language dailies, and you can get *Time* magazine and several U.S. newspapers at some hotel gift shops and a few of the bookstores in San José. If you read Spanish, *La Nación* is the paper you'll want. Its "Viva" and "Tiempo Libre" sections list what's going on in the world of music, theater, dance, and more.

Packing Be sure to pack the essentials: sunscreen, insect repellent, camera, bathing suit, a wide-brimmed hat, all prescription medications, and so forth. You'll want good hiking shoes and/or beach footwear, depending upon your itinerary. It's also a good idea to bring a waterproof headlamp or flashlight and refillable water bottle. Lightweight, long-sleeved shirts and long pants are good protection from both the sun and insects. Surfers use "rash guards," quick-drying Lycra or polyester shirts, which provide great protection from the sun while swimming.

If you're just heading to Guanacaste between December and March, you won't need anything for rain. Otherwise, bring an umbrella and rain gear. Most high-end hotels provide umbrellas. If you plan to do any wildlife-viewing, bringing your own binoculars is a good idea, as is a field guide.

Passports Citizens of the United States, Canada, Great Britain, and most European nations may visit Costa Rica for a maximum of 90 days. No visa is necessary, but you must have a valid passport, which you should carry with you at all times while you're in Costa Rica. Citizens of Australia, Ireland, and New Zealand can enter the country without a visa and stay for 30 days, although once in the country, visitors can apply for an extension.

It is advised to always have at least one or two consecutive blank pages in your passport to allow space for visas and stamps that need to appear together. It is also important to note when your passport expires. Many countries require your passport to have at least 6 months left before its expiration in order to allow you in.

Pharmacies Pharmacies are abundant in Costa Rica, typically providing only health care supplies and not the myriad consumer goods often available at pharmacy chains elsewhere. You may find that many drugs are available without a prescription that would be required in your home country. Some of the largest pharmacy chains include Fischel, Chavarria, and Sucre. The Clinica Biblica Hospital in San José (www.clinicabiblica.com) has a 24-hr. pharmacy (✆ **2522-1100**) that offers home delivery in the Central Valley.

Police In most cases, dial ✆ **911** for the police, and you should be able to get someone who speaks English on the line. Other numbers for the **Judicial Police** are ✆ **2222-1365** and 2221-5337. The numbers for the **Traffic Police (Policía de Tránsito)** are ✆ **800/8726-7486** toll-free nationwide, or 2222-9245.

Safety Although most of Costa Rica is safe, petty crime and robberies committed against tourists are endemic. San José, in particular, is known for its pickpockets. A woman should keep a tight grip on her purse (keep it tucked under your arm). Thieves also target gold chains, cameras and video cameras, prominent jewelry, and nice sunglasses. Be sure not to leave valuables unsecured in your hotel room, or unattended—even for a moment—on the beach. Given the high rate of stolen passports in Costa Rica, mostly as collateral damage in a typical pickpocketing or room robbery, it is recommended that, whenever possible, you leave your passport in a hotel safe and travel with a photocopy of the pertinent pages. Avoid parking a car on the street in Costa Rica, especially in San José; plenty of public parking lots are around the city.

Rental cars generally stand out and are easily spotted by thieves. Don't leave anything of value in a car parked on the street, not even for a moment. Be wary of solicitous strangers who stop to help you change a tire or take you to a service station. Although most are truly good Samaritans, there are bandits who prey on roadside breakdowns. See "Getting Around: By Car," earlier in this chapter, for more info.

Inter-city buses are also frequent targets of stealthy thieves. Try not to check your bags into the hold of a bus if they will fit in the rack above your seat. If it can't be avoided, keep your eye on what leaves the hold. If you put your bags in an overhead rack, keep an eye on them.

Single women should use common sense and take precautions, especially after dark. Men and women should avoid walking alone at night, especially on deserted beaches or dark streets.

Senior Travelers Be sure to mention that you're a senior when you make your travel reservations. Although it's not common policy in Costa Rica to offer senior discounts, don't be shy about asking for one anyway. You never know. Always carry some kind of identification, such as a driver's license, that shows your date of birth, especially if you've kept your youthful glow.

Many reliable agencies and organizations target the 50-plus market. **Road Scholar,** formerly known as Elderhostel (www.roadscholar.org; ✆ **800/454-5768** in the U.S. and Canada), arranges Costa Rica study programs for those ages 55 and older, as well as intergenerational trips good for families. **ElderTreks** (www.eldertreks.com; ✆ **800/741-7956** in the U.S. and Canada; 0808-234-1714 in the U.K.) offers small-group tours to Costa Rica, restricted to travelers 50 and older.

Smoking Many Costa Ricans smoke, but in March 2012, Costa Rica's legislature passed a strict anti-smoking law. Under this law, smoking is prohibited in all public spaces, including restaurants, bars, offices, and such outdoor areas as public parks and bus stops. The law also raises taxes on cigarettes and places restrictions on advertising.

Student Travelers Although you won't find any discounts at the national parks, most museums and other attractions around Costa Rica do offer discounts for students. It can't hurt to ask.

Taxes The national 13 percent value added tax (often written IVA in Costa Rica) is added to all goods and services. This includes hotel and restaurant bills. Restaurants also add on a 10 percent service charge, for a total of 23 percent more on your bill, and some hotels add a 10 percent "resort fee." The airport departure tax is $29, and it must be paid prior to check-in. Recent changes have incorporated this tax into most airline ticket prices at time of purchase. If not, you will be able to pay it at check-in.

Telephones Costa Rica has an excellent and widespread phone system, but it doesn't have area codes. All phone numbers are eight-digit numbers. A phone call within the country costs around C10 per minute. Pay phones are relatively scarce. If you do find one, it might take a calling card or coins. Calling cards are much more practical. You can purchase calling cards in a host of gift shops and pharmacies.

However, there are several competing calling-card companies, and certain cards work only with certain phones. **CHIP** calling cards work with a computer chip and just slide into specific phones, although these phones aren't widely available. Better bets are the **197** and **199** calling cards, which are sold in varying denominations. These have a scratch-off PIN and can be used from any phone in the country. Generally, the 197 cards are sold in smaller denominations and are used for local calling, while the 199 cards are deemed international and are easier to find in larger denominations. Either card can be used to make any call, provided the card can cover the cost. Another perk of the 199 cards is the fact that you can get the instructions in English. For local calls, it is often easiest to call from your hotel, although you may be charged around C150 to C300 per call.

You might also see about getting yourself a local mobile phone; see "Mobile Phones," above.

To call Costa Rica from abroad:

1. Dial the international access code: 011 from the U.S. and Canada; 00 from the U.K., Ireland, or New Zealand; or 0011 from Australia.
2. Dial the country code 506.
3. Dial the eight-digit number.

To make international calls: First dial 00 and then the country code (U.S. or Canada 1, U.K. 44, Ireland 353, Australia 61, New Zealand 64). Next dial the area code and number. For example, if you want to call the British Embassy in Washington, D.C., you would dial 00-1-202-588-7800.

For directory assistance: Dial 1113 if you're looking for a number inside Costa Rica, and dial 1024 for numbers to all other countries.

For operator assistance: If you need operator assistance in making a call, dial 1116 if you're trying to make an international call, and 0 if you want to call a number in Costa Rica.

Toll-free numbers: Numbers beginning with 0800 or 800 within Costa Rica are toll-free, but calling a 1-800 number in the States from Costa Rica is not toll-free. In fact, it costs the same as an overseas call.

Time Costa Rica is on Central Standard Time (same as Chicago and St. Louis), 6 hours behind Greenwich Mean Time. Costa Rica does not use daylight saving time, so the time difference is an additional hour from early March through early November.

Tipping Tipping is not necessary in restaurants, where a 10 percent service charge is always added to your bill (along with 13 percent tax). If service was particularly good, you can leave a little at your own discretion, but it's not mandatory. Porters and bellhops get around C500 to C1,000 per bag. You don't need to tip a taxi driver unless the service has been superior; a tip is not usually expected.

Toilets To find a bathroom, ask for the *baño* or the *servicio*. They are marked DAMAS (women) and HOMBRES or CABALLEROS (men). Public restrooms are hard to come by. You will almost never find a public restroom in a city park or downtown area. Public restrooms are usually at most national park entrances, and much less frequently inside the national park. In towns and cities, it gets much trickier, and sometimes you have to count on a hotel or restaurant. The same goes for most beaches. Bus and gas stations often have restrooms, but many of these are pretty grim. In some restrooms around the country, especially more remote and natural areas, it's common practice not to flush any foreign matter, aside from your business, down the toilet. This includes toilet paper, sanitary napkins, cigarette butts, and so forth. You will usually find a little sign advising you of this practice in the restroom.

Visitor Information In the United States or Canada, you can get basic information on Costa Rica by contacting the **Costa Rican Tourism Board (ICT,** or Instituto Costarricense de Turismo; www.visitcostarica.com; ✆ **866/267-8274** in the U.S. and Canada, or 2299-5827 in Costa Rica). Travelers from the United Kingdom, Australia, and New Zealand will have to rely primarily on this website, or call direct to Costa Rica, because the ICT does not have toll-free access in these countries.

You can pick up a map at the ICT's information desk at the airport when you arrive, or at its downtown San José offices (although the destination maps that come with this book are sufficient for most purposes). Perhaps the best map to have is the waterproof country map of Costa Rica put out by **Toucan Maps** (www.mapcr.com), which can be ordered directly from its website or any major online bookseller, like Amazon.com.

Women Travelers For lack of better phrasing, Costa Rica is a typically "macho" Latin American nation. Single women can expect catcalls, hisses, whistles, and honking horns, especially in San José. In most cases, while annoying, this is harmless and intended by Tico men as a compliment. Nonetheless, women should be careful walking alone at night throughout the country. Also, see "Safety," earlier in this section.

12 SPECIAL-INTEREST TRIPS & TOURS

Active and adventure travelers will have their hands full and hearts pumping in Costa Rica. From scuba diving with whitetip sharks and manta rays off Isla de Caño to kiteboarding over the whitecaps of Lake Arenal, opportunities abound. And Costa Rica is not just for thrill seekers. You can search for a rare green macaw in a Caribbean rainforest, or spend some time with a local family learning the language.

This chapter lays out your options, from tour operators who run multi-activity package tours that often include stays at ecolodges, to the best places in Costa Rica to pursue active endeavors. Educational and volunteer travel options are also listed for those who desire to actively contribute to the country's social welfare, or assist Costa Rica in the preservation of its natural wonders.

ORGANIZED ADVENTURE TRIPS

Because many travelers have limited time and resources, organized ecotourism or adventure-travel packages, arranged by tour operators in Costa Rica or the United States, are a popular way of combining several activities. Bird-watching, horseback riding, rafting, and hiking can be teamed with visits to Monteverde Cloud Forest Biological Reserve and Manuel Antonio National Park.

Traveling with a group has several advantages over traveling independently: Your accommodations and transportation are arranged, and most (if not all) meals are included in the package cost. If your tour operator has a reasonable amount of experience and a decent track record, you should proceed to each of your destinations quickly without snags and long delays. You'll have the opportunity to meet like-minded souls who are interested in nature and active sports. You'll also pay more for having your arrangements handled in advance.

In the best cases, group size is kept small (10–20 people), and tours are escorted by knowledgeable guides who are either naturalists or biologists. Ask about difficulty levels when you're choosing a tour—most companies offer "soft adventure" packages for those in moderately good shape, while others focus on hard-core activities geared toward seasoned athletes.

Costa Rican Tour Agencies

Because many U.S.-based companies subcontract portions of their tours to established Costa Rican companies, smart travelers cut out the middleman and set up their tours directly with these companies. That means these packages are often less expensive than those offered by U.S. companies, but it doesn't mean they're cheap. You're still paying for the convenience of having your arrangements handled for you. Still, these local operators tend to be less expensive than their international counterparts, with 10-day tours costing from $1,900 to $4,500 per person, not including airfare to Costa Rica.

ACTUAR ★★ (www.actuarcostarica.com; ✆ **866/393-5889** in the U.S., or 2290-7514 in Costa Rica), the Costa Rican Rural Tourism Association, is a great option for budget travelers and anyone looking to get a taste of real, rural Costa Rica. It manages a network of small, often family-run rural lodges and tour operators. Bunk beds and thin foam mattresses are common.

Costa Rica Expeditions ★★ (www.costaricaexpeditions.com; ✆ **2221-6099**) offers everything from 10-day tours covering the entire country to 3-day/2-night and 2-day/1-night tours of Monteverde Cloud Forest Biological Reserve and Tortuguero National Park, where it runs its own lodges. It also offers 1- to 2-day whitewater rafting trips and other excursions. Its tours are some of the most expensive in the country, but it is the most consistently reliable outfitter (customer service is excellent). If you want to strike out on your own, Costa Rica Expeditions can supply you with transportation.

Horizontes Nature Tours ★★, Calle 32 between avenidas 3 and 5 (www.horizontes.com; ✆ **888/786-8748** in the U.S. and Canada, or 2222-2022 in Costa Rica), is not a specifically adventure-oriented operator, but it offers a wide range of individual, group, and package tours, including those geared toward active and adventure travelers, as well as families and even honeymooners. The company hires responsible and knowledgeable guides, and is a local leader in sustainable tourism practices.

International Tour Operators

These agencies and operators are known for well-organized and coordinated tours. ***Be warned:*** Most of these operators are not cheap, with 10-day tours generally costing in the neighborhood of $3,000 to $5,000 per person, not including airfare to Costa Rica.

U.S.-BASED TOUR OPERATORS

Nature Expeditions International ★ (www.naturexp.com; ✆ **800/869-0639**) specializes in educational and "low-intensity adventure" trips tailored to independent travelers and small groups.

Overseas Adventure Travel ★★ (www.oattravel.com; ✆ **800/955-1925**) provides natural-history and "soft adventure" itineraries with optional add-on excursions. Tours are limited to a maximum of 16 people and are guided by naturalists. All accommodations are in small hotels, lodges, or tent camps.

Tauck ★★ (www.tauck.com; ✆ **800/788-7885**) is a soft-adventure company catering to higher-end travelers. It offers various Costa Rica options, including a family tour, and Costa Rica–Panama Canal package.

In addition to these companies, many environmental organizations, including the **Sierra Club** (www.sierraclub.org; ✆ **415/977-5522**) and the **Smithsonian Institute** (www.smithsonianjourneys.org; ✆ **855/330-1542**), regularly offer organized trips to Costa Rica.

U.K.-BASED TOUR OPERATORS

Journey Latin America ★ (www.journeylatinamerica.co.uk; ✆ **020/3432-9325** in the U.K.) is a large British operator specializing in Latin American travel. It offers a range of escorted tours around Latin America, including a few that touch down in Costa Rica. It also designs custom itineraries, and often has excellent deals on airfare.

ACTIVITIES A TO Z

Each listing in this section describes the best places to practice a particular sport or activity and lists tour operators and outfitters.

Adventure activities, by their very nature, carry certain risks and dangers. Over the years, there have been several deaths and dozens of injuries in activities ranging from mountain biking to whitewater rafting to canopy tours, and drowning in the ocean is also sadly common.

Book with safe, reputable companies, but also know your limits and don't try to exceed them.

Biking

Costa Rica hosts significant regional and international touring races each year, but as a general rule, the major roads are dangerous and inhospitable for cyclists. Roads are narrow and without a shoulder, and most drivers show little care or consideration for those on two wheels. The options are much more

Ruta de los Conquistadores

Each year, Costa Rica hosts what many consider to be the most challenging and grueling mountain-bike race on the planet. **La Ruta de los Conquistadores** (The Route of the Conquerors; www.adventurerace.com) retraces the path of the 16th-century Spanish conquistadores from the Pacific Coast to the Caribbean Sea—all in 4 days. The race usually takes place in mid-November, and draws hundreds of competitors from around the world.

appealing for mountain bikers and off-track riders. If you plan to do a lot of biking and are very attached to your rig, bring your own. However, several companies in San José and elsewhere rent bikes, and the quality of the equipment is improving. Bike rental shops are listed in the regional chapters.

Arguably, **Arenal** has the best mountain biking in Costa Rica. The scenery's great, with primary forests, waterfalls, and plenty of trails. And the hot springs at nearby Tabacón Grand Spa Thermal Resort are a perfect place to unwind after the ride. However, the **Río Perdido** ★★ (www.rioperdido.com; ✆ **888/326-5070** in the U.S. and Canada, or 2673-3600 in Costa Rica) offers many of the same attractions, including incredible hot springs, but also features the country's best specifically designed mountain bike park, with an extensive network of trails and different level circuits. Finally, **Hacienda Guachipelin** (p. 104) also has an extensive network of bike trails and some excellent rental bikes.

TOUR OPERATORS & OUTFITTERS

Bike Arenal ★ (www.bikearenal.com; ✆ **866/465-4114** in the U.S. and Canada, or 2479-9020 in Costa Rica) is based in La Fortuna and specializes in 1-day and multiday trips around the Arenal area.

Coast to Coast Adventures ★ (www.ctocadventures.com; ✆ **2280-8054**) offers mountain-biking itineraries among its many tour options.

Bird-Watching

With more than 850 species of resident and migrant birds identified throughout the country, Costa Rica abounds with great bird-watching sites. Some of the best parks and preserves for serious birders are **Monteverde Cloud Forest Biological Reserve** (for resplendent quetzals and hummingbirds); **Corcovado National Park** (for scarlet macaws); **Caño Negro Wildlife Refuge** (for wading birds, including jabiru storks); **Wilson Botanical Gardens** and **Las Cruces Biological Station,** near San Vito (the thousands of flowering plants here are bird magnets); **Guayabo, Negritos,** and **Pájaros Islands biological reserves** in the Gulf of Nicoya (for magnificent frigate birds and brown boobies); **Palo Verde National Park** (for ibises, jacanas, storks, and roseate spoonbills); **Tortuguero National Park** (for great green macaws); and **Rincón de la Vieja National Park** (for parakeets and curassows). Rafting trips down the Corobicí and Bebedero rivers near Liberia, boat trips to or at Tortuguero National Park, and hikes in any cloud forest also provide good bird-watching opportunities.

COSTA RICAN TOUR AGENCIES

Costa Rica Expeditions ★★ (www.costaricaexpeditions.com; ✆ **2221-6099**) and **Costa Rica Sun Tours** ★ (www.crsuntours.com; ✆ **866/271-6263** in the U.S. and Canada, or 2296-7757 in Costa Rica) are well-established companies with very competent and experienced guides who offer a variety of tours to some of the better birding spots in Costa Rica.

PLANNING A COSTA RICAN wedding

Marriage may be an adventure, but getting married in Costa Rica is pretty straightforward. You'll have to provide some basic information, including a copy of each passport, your dates of birth, your occupations, your current addresses, and the names and addresses of your parents. Two witnesses are required to be present at the ceremony. If the two of you are traveling alone, your hotel or wedding consultant will provide the required witnesses.

Things are slightly more complicated if one or both partners were previously married. In such a case, the previously married partner must provide an official copy of the divorce decree.

Most travelers who get married in Costa Rica do so in a civil ceremony officiated by a local lawyer. After the ceremony, the lawyer records the marriage with Costa Rica's National Registry, which issues an official marriage certificate. This process generally takes between 4 and 6 weeks. Most lawyers or wedding coordinators then have the document translated and certified by the Costa Rican Foreign Ministry and at the embassy or consulate of your home country before mailing it to you. From here, it's a matter of bringing this document to your local civil or religious authorities, if necessary.

Because Costa Rica is more than 90 percent Roman Catholic, arranging for a church wedding is usually easy in all but the most isolated and remote locations. To a lesser extent, a variety of denominational Christian churches and priests are often available to perform or host the ceremony. If you're Jewish, Muslim, Buddhist, or a follower of some other religion, bringing your own officiant is a good idea.

Tip: Officially, the lawyer must read all or parts of the Costa Rican civil code on marriage during your ceremony. This is a rather uninspired and somewhat dated legal code that, at some weddings, can take as much as 20 minutes to slog through. Most lawyers and wedding coordinators are quite flexible and can work with you to design a ceremony and text that fits your needs and desires. Insist on this.

INTERNATIONAL TOUR OPERATORS

Costa Rican Bird Route ★★ (www.costaricanbirdroute.com; ✆ **608/698-3448** in the U.S. and Canada) is a bird-watching and conservation effort that has created several bird-watching specific itineraries, with guided tours and self-guided adventures.

Victor Emanuel Nature Tours ★★ (www.ventbird.com; ✆ **800/328-8368** in the U.S. and Canada) is a well-respected, longstanding small group tour operator specializing in bird-watching trips.

WINGS ★ (www.wingsbirds.com; ✆ **866/547-9868** in the U.S. and Canada) is a specialty bird-watching travel operator with more than 30 years of field experience. Group size is usually between 4 and 16.

Camping

Heavy rains, difficult access, and limited facilities make camping a challenge in Costa Rica. Nevertheless, a backpack and tent will get you far from the crowds and into some of the most pristine and undeveloped parts of the country.

Undoubtedly the country's best camping adventure is **Corcovado National Park,** a wild and rugged place teeming with animals, where you can camp at Sirena Ranger Station, pitching a tent on the wooden platforms or on the grass (but watch out for snakes), or you could just rent a *cabina.* Corcovado is an expensive place to visit because you have to hire a guide, but it's unforgettable.

You could also pitch a tent at **Santa Rosa National Park** and **Ballena Marine National Park.** At both spots you're likely to have miles of unspoiled beach and very few fellow campers around. But in such isolated environments, be certain you are safe.

To inquire about organized camping trips, contact **Coast to Coast Adventures** ★ (www.ctocadventures.com; ✆ **2280-8054**).

Canopy Tours

Costa Rica has a genuine claim to fame as birthplace of both the jungle canopy zipline (invented by U.S. biology student Donald Perry in 1979 at Finca La Selva) and the **jungle canopy zipline tour** (invented by Canadian entrepreneur Darren Hreniuk in 1997 in Monteverde). From these modest beginnings, ziplining exploded worldwide into one of the most popular forms of extreme adventure there is.

It's a simple concept: String a cable from a high place to a low, clip some weight to it, and watch what happens. You never know what the weather will be like, but you can always count on gravity.

For its size, Costa Rica has a staggering number of canopy tours. The designers of these courses became geniuses at stringing together multiple trees and platforms over broad valleys and rivers, giving guests the heart-fluttering sensation of flying, often at alarming speeds. Many tours include terrifying "Tarzan swings," face-down "Superman flights," controlled rappels, scary suspended bridges, and sometimes rock climbing. See the chapters on your chosen destination for recommendations on canopy tours, and expect to pay somewhere between $40 and $85.

Canyoning Tours

Canyoning means exploring a fast river by rappelling, climbing, swimming, scrambling, and rock-climbing, and it's an exhilarating adventure. The word "rappel" here typically means a fast descent controlled by a guide, while "waterfall rappelling" puts adrenaline junkies in charge of their own ropes. One of Costa Rica's best canyoning operators is **Hacienda Guachipelín** ★★ in Rincón de la Vieja, where you rappel into a big river and then grab gigantic staples in the side of a vertical cliff and climb back to safety. After that comes a Tarzan swing in which you're bashed (safely) into a waterfall, but it's all in good fun.

Waterfall rappelling is a perfected art at **Everyday Adventures,** also known as Psycho Tours ★★★ (p. 212), in Matapalo de Osa, where you can rappel down two big waterfalls and also climb a giant *matapalo* strangler fig, all in the same day. Other canyoning operators in Costa Rica are **Pure Trek**

Canyoning ★★ (p. 143) and **Desafío Expeditions** ★★ (p. 143), both in La Fortuna, and **Explornatura** ★★ in Turrialba.

Diving & Snorkeling

Costa Rica is not considered a world-class dive spot except in one extremely remote location, **Isla del Coco,** which Jacques Cousteau called "the most beautiful island in the world." It's famous for big schools of hammerhead sharks and Galapagos-like isolation. But it takes a few thousand dollars and a couple of weeks on a live-aboard boat to get there and back, and you have to be an expert diver.

For the ordinary person certified to dive, the waters off **Isla del Caño,** near Drake Bay, are the prime destination in the country. But other options abound at Pacific dive spots like **Playa del Coco, Islas Murciélagos** (Bat Islands), and the **Catalina Islands,** where you may spot manta rays, moray eels, and white-tipped sharks. On the Caribbean coast, runoff from banana plantations has destroyed much of the reefs, although **Isla Uvita,** the landing place of Columbus just off the coast of Limón, and **Manzanillo,** near the Panamanian border, still have good diving. A two-tank dive should cost around $90, and snorkelers should pay as little as $35.

For snorkelers, the same rain, runoff, and wave conditions that drive scuba divers offshore tend to make coastal and shallow-water conditions less than optimal, but sometimes the weather is calm and the water is clear. Ask around for snorkeling options; there are some good ones at **Manzanillo Beach** on the southern Caribbean coast, especially in September and October.

DIVING OUTFITTERS & OPERATORS

Diving Safaris de Costa Rica ★★ (www.costaricadiving.net; ✆ **2670-0603**) is perhaps the largest, most professional, and best-established dive operation in the country. Based out of Playa Hermosa, this outfitter is also a local pioneer in nitrox diving.

Aggressor Fleet Limited ★★ (www.aggressor.com; ✆ **800/348-2628** in the U.S. and Canada) runs the 36m (118-ft.) live-aboard *Okeanos Aggressor* on regular trips to Isla del Coco and Isla del Caño. **Undersea Hunter** ★★ (www.underseahunter.com; ✆ **800/203-2120** in the U.S., or 2228-6613 in Costa Rica) offers the *Undersea Hunter* and its sister ship, the *Sea Hunter,* two pioneers of the live-aboard diving excursions to Isla del Coco.

On the Caribbean side of the country, look up **Reef Runner Divers** (www.reefrunnerdivers.com; ✆ **2750-0480** or 8796-8898) in Puerto Viejo. On the Pacific, Playa del Coco is a top diving spot, and one of the major outfitters is **Rich Coast Diving** (www.richcoastdiving.com; ✆ **2670-0176** or 2670-0004).

Fishing

Anglers in Costa Rican waters have landed over 100 world-record catches, including blue marlin, Pacific sailfish, dolphin, wahoo, yellowfin tuna, *guapote,* and snook. Whether you want to head offshore looking for a big sailfish, wrestle a tarpon near a Caribbean river mouth, or choose a quiet spot on a lake to cast for *guapote,* you'll find it here. You can raise a marlin anywhere along the Pacific coast, while feisty snook can be found in estuaries along both coasts.

Many of the Pacific port and beach towns—Quepos, Puntarenas, Playa del Coco, Tamarindo, Flamingo, Golfito, Drake Bay, Zancudo—support large charter fleets and have hotels that cater to anglers; see chapters 6 to 9 for recommended boats, captains, and lodges. Fishing trips usually range between $400 and $2,500 per day (depending on boat size) for the boat, captain, tackle, drinks, and lunch, so the cost per person depends on the size of the group.

Costa Rican law requires that all fishermen purchase a license. The cost ranges from $15 to $50 depending upon the length of the license and whether it covers saltwater or freshwater fishing, or both. All boats, captains, and fishing lodges listed here and throughout the book will help you with the technicalities of buying your license.

Aguila de Osa Inn ★★ (www.aguiladeosa.com; ✆ **866/924-8452** in the U.S. and Canada, 2296-2190 in San José, or 8840-2929 at the lodge) is a fabulous ecolodge on the shores of Drake Bay with a top-notch fishing operation. This is a great choice for those looking to ply the Pacific Ocean in search of big-game marlin, sailfish, roosterfish, dorado, tuna, and more.

Silver King Lodge ★ (www.silverkinglodge.net; ✆ **877/335-0755** in the U.S.) is a dedicated fishing lodge in the Barra del Colorado (mouth of the Colorado River) region. Come here to land some very large tarpon, as well as snook and other game fish.

Zancudo Lodge ★★ (www.thezancudolodge.com; ✆ **800/854-8791** in the U.S. and Canada, or 2776-0008 in Costa Rica) is a beautiful boutique lodge set on the tip of remote Playa Zancudo. The food, service, and fishing here are excellent.

Golfing

Costa Rica doesn't have a lot of golf courses, but those it does have offer stunning scenery and almost no crowds. Be aware that strong seasonal winds make playing most of the Guanacaste courses challenging from December through March. The most spectacular course is at Four Seasons Resort ★★★ (p. 89), designed by Arnold Palmer. Greens fees run $250.

Another good option is the **Reserva Conchal** course ★★ at the **Westin Playa Conchal Resort & Spa** (p. 98) in Guanacaste. Greens fees here are $150, including a cart. **Hacienda Pinilla ★★** is an 18-hole links-style course located south of Tamarindo. This might just be the most challenging course in the country. Greens fees run around $200 for 18 holes, including a cart.

Another major resort course is at the **Los Sueños Marriott Ocean & Golf Resort ★★** in Playa Herradura (p. 181). Greens fees, including a cart, run around $150 for the general public; guests pay slightly less. Currently, the best option for golfers staying in and around San José is **Parque Valle del Sol ★** (www.vallesol.com; ✆ **2282-9222**), an 18-hole course in the western suburb of Santa Ana. Greens fees are $99, including a cart.

Golfers who are interested in a package deal that includes play on a variety of courses should contact **Costa Rica Golf Adventures** ★ (www.golfcr.com; ✆ **888/536-8510** in the U.S. and Canada) or **Tee Times Costa Rica** (www.teetimescostarica.com; ✆ **866/448-3182** in the U.S. and Canada).

Horseback Riding

Costa Rica's rural roots are evident in the continued use of horses for real work and transportation throughout the country. Visitors will find that horses are easily available for riding, whether for a sunset trot along the beach, a ride through the cloud forest, or a multiday trek across the northern zone.

Most travelers saddle up for a couple of hours. Rates run between $15 to $30 per hour, depending upon group size and the length of the ride, with full-day rides running around $60 to $90, usually including lunch and refreshments. In the Jacó area, look up **Discovery Horseback Tours** (www.horseridecostarica.com; ✆ **8838-7550**). In Monteverde, try **Horse Trek Monteverde** (www.horsetrekmonteverde.com; ✆ **8359-3485**). And in Guanacaste, consider **Hacienda Guachipelín** (www.guachipelin.com; ✆ **2690-2900**), a working horse and cattle ranch.

Paragliding & Ballooning

If you spend much time in Costa Rica, you'll be surprised how often you look up and see someone hanging from a parachute or standing in a balloon. Paragliding is a popular diversion in the cliff areas around Caldera, just south of Puntarenas, as well as other spots along the Central Pacific coast. Check in with **Grandpa Ninja's B&B** (www.paraglidecostarica.com; ✆ **908/545-3242** in the U.S., or 8950-8676 in Costa Rica). This place caters to paragliders and offers lessons and tandem flights. Lessons run around $60 per day, including equipment, while a 20-minute tandem flight with an experienced pilot will run you around $95.

Serendipity Adventures ★ (www.serendipityadventures.com; ✆ **888/226-5050** in the U.S. and Canada, or 2556-2222 in Costa Rica) will take you up, up, and away in a hot-air balloon near Arenal Volcano. A basic flight costs around $385 per passenger, with a two-person minimum, and a five-person or 800-pound maximum.

Spas & Yoga Retreats

Prices for spa treatments in Costa Rica are generally less expensive than those in the United States or Europe, although some of the fancier options, like the Four Seasons Resort or Tabacón Grand Spa Thermal Resort, rival the services, facilities, and prices found anywhere on the planet.

- **Florblanca Resort** ★★★ in Santa Teresa has some beautiful spa facilities, with two large treatment rooms over a flowing water feature (p. 136).
- **Four Seasons Resort** ★★★ on the Papagayo Peninsula has ample and luxurious facilities and treatment options, as well as classes in yoga, Pilates, and other disciplines (p. 89).

- **Pranamar Villas & Yoga Retreat ★★★** in Santa Teresa is a new, upscale, beachfront resort, with a beautiful, open-air yoga space. A range of daily classes is offered, and a steady stream of visiting teachers and groups use the spot for longer retreats and seminars (p. 136).
- **Tabacón Grand Spa Thermal Resort ★★★** is a top-notch spa in Arenal with spectacular hot springs, lush gardens, and a volcano view. A complete range of spa services and treatments is available at reasonable prices (p. 145).

Surfing

Significant sections of the movie *Endless Summer II* (1994), the sequel to the all-time surf classic, were filmed in Costa Rica. All along Costa Rica's immense coastline are point and beach breaks that work year-round. **Playas Hermosa, Jacó,** and **Dominical,** on the Central Pacific coast, and **Tamarindo** and **Playa Guiones,** in Guanacaste, are mini surf meccas. **Salsa Brava** in Puerto Viejo is a steep and fast wave that peels off both right and left over shallow coral. It has a habit of breaking boards, but the daredevils keep coming back. Beginners should stick to the mellower sections of **Jacó** and **Tamarindo**—surf lessons are offered at both beaches. Crowds are starting to gather at the more popular breaks, but you can still stumble onto secret spots on the **Osa** and **Nicoya peninsulas** and along the northern **Guanacaste** coast. Costa Rica's signature wave is still at **Pavones,** said to have the second-longest left in the world. Surfers also swear by **Playa Grande, Playa Negra, Matapalo, Malpaís,** and **Witch's Rock.**

If you're looking for an organized surf vacation, contact **Tico Travel** (www.ticotravel.com; ✆ **800/493-8426** in the U.S. and Canada), or check out **www.crsurf.com.** For swell reports, general surf information, live wave-cams, and great links pages, point your browser to **www.surfline.com.** Although killer sets are possible at any particular spot at any time of the year, depending upon swell direction, local winds, and distant storms, in broad terms, the northern coast of Guanacaste works best from December to April; the central and southern Pacific coasts from April to November; and the Caribbean coast's short big-wave season is December through March. Surf lessons, usually private or in a small group, will run from $20 to $40 per hour, including the board.

Whitewater Rafting & Kayaking

Whether you're a first-time rafter or a world-class kayaker, Costa Rica's got some fast water ready for you. Rivers rise and fall with the rain, but you can get wet here any time of year. Full-day rafting trips run between $75 and $110 per person.

The best whitewater rafting ride in Costa Rica is the **Pacuare River,** which some say is one of the best rafting rivers in the world. It's clean and scenic, and it has heart-jolting Class IV rapids. There is also excellent rafting on the **Savegre** and the **Sarapiquí,** while the **Reventazón** has fallen on hard times because of hydroclcctric dams. Somc of thc most challenging rafting in the country is at the **El Chorro** section of the Naranjo River, where Class V rapids rush through a narrow, steep canyon. Whitewater rafting operators can be found in almost every corner of Costa Rica, and they're worth looking up.

Ríos Tropicales ★★ (www.riostropicales.com; ✆ **866/722-8273** in the U.S. and Canada, or 2233-6455 in Costa Rica), founded in 1985, is perhaps the oldest and most reliable rafting operator in Costa Rica, with tours on most of the country's popular rivers. Accommodations options include a very comfortable lodge on the banks of the Río Pacuare for the 2-day trips.

Aventuras Naturales ★★ (✆ **888/680-9031** in the U.S., or 2224-0505 in Costa Rica) is a major rafting operator that runs daily trips on the most popular rivers in Costa Rica. Its **Pacuare Jungle Lodge** ★★★ is very plush and a great place to spend the night on one of its 2-day rafting trips.

Exploradores Outdoors ★ (www.exploradoresoutdoors.com; ✆ **646/205-0828** in the U.S. and Canada, or 2222-6262 in Costa Rica) is another good company run by a longtime and well-respected river guide. It has trips on the Pacuare and Reventazón rivers, and even combines a 1-day river trip with transportation to or from the Caribbean coast, or the Arenal Volcano area, for no extra cost.

Windsurfing & Kiteboarding

Windsurfing is not very popular on the high seas here, where winds are fickle and rental options are limited, even at beach hotels. However, **Lake Arenal** is considered one of the top spots in the world for high-wind boardsailing. During the winter months, many of the regulars from Washington's Columbia River Gorge take up residence around the nearby town of Tilarán. Small boards, water starts, and fancy gibes are the norm. The best time for windsurfing on Lake Arenal is between December and March. See "Along the Shores of Lake Arenal" in chapter 7 for details.

The same winds that buffet Lake Arenal make their way to **Bahía Salinas** (also known as Bolaños Bay), near La Cruz, Guanacaste, where you can get in some good windsurfing. Both spots also have operations offering lessons and equipment rentals for the high-action sport of kiteboarding. Board rentals run around $55 to $85 per day, while lessons can cost $50 to $100 for a half-day private lesson.

MEDICAL & DENTAL TOURISM

Costa Rica is an increasingly popular destination for dental and medical tourists. Facilities and care are excellent, and prices are quite low compared to the United States and other private care options in the developed world. Travelers are coming for everything from a simple dental checkup and cleaning to elective cosmetic surgery or a triple heart bypass operation. In virtually every case, visitors can save money on the overall cost of care. In some cases, the savings are quite substantial.

The country's two top hospitals have modern facilities and equipment, as well as excellent doctors and nurses, many of whom speak English. **Clínica Bíblica,** Avenida 14 between Calles Central and 1 (www.clinicabiblica.com; ✆ **2522-1000**), is conveniently close to downtown, while the **Hospital CIMA** (www.hospitalcima.com; ✆ **2208-1000**) is in Escazú on the Próspero Fernández Highway, which connects San José and the western suburb of Santa Ana. The latter has the most modern facilities in the country. An annex of the Hospital CIMA has also opened on the outskirts of Liberia, close to the beaches of Guanacaste.

STUDY & VOLUNTEER PROGRAMS

Language Immersion

As more people travel to Costa Rica with the intention of learning Spanish, the number of options for Spanish immersion vacations increases. You can find courses of varying lengths and degrees of intensiveness, and many that include cultural activities and day excursions. Many of these schools have reciprocal relationships with U.S. universities, so in some cases you can arrange for college credit.

Most Spanish schools can arrange for home stays with a middle-class local family for a total-immersion experience. Classes are often small, or even one-on-one, and can last anywhere from 2 to 8 hours a day. Listed below are some of the larger and more established Spanish-language schools, with approximate costs. Most are in San José, but there are schools in Monteverde, Manuel Antonio, Playa Flamingo, Malpaís, Playa Nosara, and Tamarindo. A 1-week class for 4 hours a day, including a home stay, tends to cost between $420 and $630.

Adventure Education Center (AEC) Spanish Institute ★ (www.adventurespanishschool.com; ✆ **800/237-2730** in the U.S. and Canada, or 2787-0023 in Costa Rica) has branches in Dominical and Turrialba, and specializes in combining language learning with adventure activities.

Centro Panamericano de Idiomas (CPI) ★ (www.cpi-edu.com; ✆ **877/373-3116** in the U.S., or 2265-6306 in Costa Rica) has three campuses: one in the quiet suburban town of Heredia, another in Monteverde, and one at the beach in Playa Flamingo.

Costa Rican Language Academy ★ in San José (www.spanishandmore.com; ✆ **866/230-6361** in the U.S., or 2280-1685 in Costa Rica) has intensive programs with classes held Monday to Thursday to give students a chance for longer weekend excursions. The academy also integrates Latin dance and Costa Rican cooking classes into the program.

Wayra Instituto de Español (www.spanish-wayra.co.cr; ✆ **2653-0359**) is a longstanding operation located in the beach town of Tamarindo.

Alternative Educational Travel

Adventures Under the Sun ★★ (www.adventuresunderthesun.com; ✆ **866/897-5578** in the U.S. and Canada, or 2289-0404 in Costa Rica) is a Costa Rican–based outfit specializing in adventure and volunteer-focused teen travel. Its strong suit is organizing custom group itineraries, but it also runs periodic "summer day camps" and set itineraries.

Costa Rica Rainforest Outward Bound School ★★ (www.crrobs.org; ✆ **800/676-2018** in the U.S., or 2278-6062 in Costa Rica) is the local branch of this international adventure-based, outdoor-education organization. Courses range from 2 weeks to a full semester, and they include surfing, kayaking, tree climbing, and learning Spanish.

The **Monteverde Institute** ★ (www.mvinstitute.org; ✆ **2645-5053**) has study programs in Monteverde along with a volunteer center that helps in placement and training of volunteers.

The **Organization for Tropical Studies** ★★ (www.threepaths.co.cr; ✆ **919/684-5774** in the U.S., or 2524-0607 in Costa Rica) represents several Costa Rican and U.S. universities. This organization's mission is to promote research, education, and the wise use of natural resources in the tropics. Research facilities include La Selva Biological Station in Sarapiquí and the Wilson Botanical Gardens near San Vito. It offers full-semester undergraduate programs, specific graduate courses, and tourist programs, among many others. Programs range in duration from 3 to 10 days, and costs vary greatly. Entrance requirements and competition for some of these courses can be demanding.

Sustainable Volunteer Projects

Below are some institutions and organizations that are working on ecology and sustainable development projects in Costa Rica.

Asociación de Voluntarios para el Servicio en Áreas Protegidas de Costa Rica (ASVO) ★ (www.asvocr.org; ✆ **2258-4430**) organizes volunteers to work in Costa Rican national parks. A 2-week minimum commitment is required, as is an ability to adapt to rustic conditions and remote locations and gain a basic ability to converse in Spanish. Housing is provided at a basic ranger station; a $245 weekly fee covers lodging, logistics, and food.

Sea Turtle Conservancy (www.cccturtle.org; ✆ **800/678-7853** in the U.S. and Canada, or 2278-6058 in Costa Rica) is a nonprofit organization dedicated to sea turtle research, protection, and advocacy. Formerly known as the **Caribbean Conservation Corporation,** its main operation in Costa Rica is headquartered in Tortuguero, where volunteers can aid in various scientific studies, as well as nightly patrols of the beach during nesting seasons to prevent poaching.

Vida (www.vida.org; ✆ **2221-8367**) is a local nongovernmental organization working on sustainable development and conservation issues; it can often place volunteers.

SPANISH TERMS & PHRASES

13

Ticos are pretty *tranquilo* about most things, and they tend to speak at a relaxed speed and enunciate clearly, especially when addressing a foreigner. Costa Ricans are known for saying "*Mae*," which means "Dude," but has become a form of verbal punctuation used in some circles in almost every sentence. A notable idiosyncracy here is creating diminutives with *"ico"* instead of *"ito"* (*"un poquitico"*)—hence the words *Tico* and *Tica* to describe Costa Rican men and women. *Ticos* are said to have an odd way of pronouncing the "R" at the beginning of a word, as in "Rica"—the "R" is never rolled or trilled. All in all, rest assured that if your *español* is not *buenísimo,* most Costa Ricans will speak slow, proper Spanish to you.

BASIC WORDS & PHRASES

English	Spanish	Pronunciation
Hello	Hola	***oh**-lah*
Good morning	Buenos días	***bweh**-nohss **dee**-ahss*
How are you?	¿Cómo está usted?	***koh**-moh ehss-**tah** oo-**stehd***
Very well	Muy bien	**mwee byehn**
Thank you	Gracias	***grah*-syahss**
Goodbye	Adiós	**ad-*dyohss***
Please	Por favor	**pohr fah-*vohr***
Yes	Sí	**see**
No	No	**no**
Excuse me (to get by someone)	Con permiso	**con per-*mee*-so**
Excuse me (to begin a question)	Disculpe	**dees-*kool*-peh**
Give me	Deme	***deh*-meh**
Where is . . . ?	¿Dónde está . . . ?	***dohn*-deh ehss-*tah***
the station	la estación	**la ehss-tah-*syohn***
the bus stop	la parada	**la pah-*rah*-dah**
the toilet	el servicio	**el ser-*vee*-syoh**
Where is there...?	Dónde hay...?	***dohn*-deh ai**
a hotel	un hotel	**oon oh-*tehl***
a restaurant	un restaurante	**oon res-tau-*rahn*-teh**

English	Spanish	Pronunciation
To the right	A la derecha	**ah lah deh-*reh*-chah**
To the left	A la izquierda	**ah lah ees-*kyehr*-dah**
Straight ahead	Adelante	**ah-deh-*lahn*-teh**
I would like . . .	Quiero . . .	***kyeh*-roh**
to eat	comer	**ko-*mehr***
a room	una habitación	**oo-nah ah-bee-tah-*syohn***
How much is it?	¿Cuánto es?	***kwahn*-toh es?**
When?	¿Cuándo?	***kwan*-doh**
What?	¿Qué?	**keh**
Yesterday	Ayer	**ah-*yehr***
Today	Hoy	**oy**
Tomorrow	Mañana	**mah-*nyah*-nah**
Breakfast	Desayuno	**deh-sah-*yoo*-noh**
Lunch	Almuerzo	**ahl-*mwehr*-soh**
Dinner	Cena	***seh*-nah**
Do you speak English?	¿Habla usted inglés?	***ah*-blah oo-*stehd* een-*glehss***
I don't understand Spanish very well.	No entiendo muy bien el español.	**Noh ehn-*tyehn*-do mwee byehn el ehss-pah-*nyohl***

Numbers

English	Spanish	Pronunciation
zero	cero	***ser*-oh**
one	uno	***oo*-noh**
two	dos	**dohss**
three	tres	**trehss**
four	cuatro	***kwah*-troh**
five	cinco	***seen*-koh**
six	seis	**sayss**
seven	siete	***syeh*-teh**
eight	ocho	***oh*-choh**
nine	nueve	***nweh*-beh**
ten	diez	**dyehss**
eleven	once	***ohn*-seh**
twelve	doce	***doh*-seh**
thirteen	trece	***treh*-seh**
fourteen	catorce	**kah-*tohr*-seh**
fifteen	quince	***keen*-seh**
sixteen	dieciséis	**dyeh-see-*sayss***
seventeen	diecisiete	**dyeh-see-*syeh*-teh**
eighteen	dieciocho	**dyeh-see-*oh*-choh**
nineteen	diecinueve	**dyeh-see-*nweh*-beh**
twenty	veinte	***bayn*-teh**
thirty	treinta	***trayn*-tah**

English	Spanish	Pronunciation
forty	cuarenta	**kwah-*rehn*-tah**
fifty	cincuenta	**seen-*kwehn*-tah**
sixty	sesenta	**seh-*sehn*-tah**
seventy	setenta	**seh-*tehn*-tah**
eighty	ochenta	**oh-*chehn*-tah**
ninety	noventa	**noh-*behn*-tah**
one hundred	cien	**syehn**
one thousand	mil	**meel**

Days of the Week

English	Spanish	Pronunciation
Monday	lunes	***loo*-nehs**
Tuesday	martes	***mahr*-tehs**
Wednesday	miércoles	***myehr*-koh-lehs**
Thursday	jueves	***wheh*-behs**
Friday	viernes	***byehr*-nehs**
Saturday	sábado	***sah*-bah-doh**
Sunday	domingo	**doh-*meen*-go**

TICO WORDS & PHRASES

Birra Beer
Boca Appetizer (literally "mouth")
Bomba Gas station (literally "pump")
Brete Job
Buena nota Right on
Casado Traditional lunch with meat, rice, beans, salad
Choza House, home; also called *chante*
Cien metros 100 meters, or one block
Con gusto/con mucho gusto You're welcome
Fría A cold beer—*una fría, por favor* (literally "cold")
Fut Short for *fútbol,* or soccer
Harina Money (literally "flour")
La sele La *Selección,* the Costa Rican national soccer team
Limpio Broke; out of money (literally "clean")
Mae "Man" or "Dude"
Mala nota Bummer
Mejenga Pickup soccer game
Ponga la maría, por favor How to ask a taxi driver to turn on the meter
Pulpería A small market or convenience store
Pura vida Literally, "pure life"; translates as "everything's great"
Qué torta What a mess; what a screw-up
Si Dios quiere God willing

Soda A casual diner-style restaurant serving cheap food
Tica, Tico Costa Rican
Tiquicia Costa Rica
Una teja 100 colones
Un rojo 1,000 colones
Un tucán 5,000 colones
Zarpe Last drink of the night; "one for the road"

MENU TERMS

BASICS

Aceite Oil
Ajo Garlic
Arreglado Small meat sandwich
Azúcar Sugar
Casado Plate of the day
Gallo Corn tortilla topped with meat or chicken
Gallo pinto Rice and beans
Hielo Ice
Mantequilla Butter
Miel Honey
Mostaza Mustard
Natilla Sour cream
Olla de carne Meat and vegetable soup
Pan Bread
Patacones Fried plantain chips
Picadillo Chopped vegetable side dish
Pimienta Pepper
Queso Cheese
Sal Salt
Tamal Filled cornmeal pastry
Tortilla Flat corn pancake

DRINKS

Agua con gas Sparkling water
Agua purificada Purified water
Agua sin gas Plain water
Bebida Drink
Café Coffee
Café con leche Coffee with milk
Cerveza Beer
Chocolate caliente Hot chocolate
Jugo Juice
Leche Milk
Natural Fruit juice
Natural con leche Milkshake
Refresco Soft drink
Ron Rum
Té Tea
Trago Alcoholic drink

OTHER RESTAURANT TERMS

Al grill Grilled
Al horno Oven-baked
Al vapor Steamed
Asado Roasted
Caliente Hot
Cambio or **vuelto** Change
Cocido Cooked
Comida Food
Congelado Frozen
Crudo Raw
El baño Toilet
Frío Cold
Frito Fried
Grande Big or large
La cuenta The check
Medio Medium
Medio rojo Medium rare
Muy cocido Well-done
Pequeño Small
Poco cocido or **rojo** Rare
Tres cuartos Medium-well-done

OTHER USEFUL TERMS

HOTEL TERMS

Aire acondicionado Air-conditioning
Abanico Fan
Almohada Pillow
Baño Bathroom
Baño privado Private bathroom
Caja de seguridad Safe
Calefacción Heating
Cama Bed
Cobija Blanket
Colchón Mattress
Cuarto or **Habitación** Room
Escritorio Desk
Habitación simple/sencilla Single room
Habitación doble Double room
Habitación triple Triple room
Llave Key
Mosquitero Mosquito net
Sábanas Sheets
Seguro de puerta Door lock
Silla Chair
Telecable Cable TV
Ventilador Fan

TRAVEL TERMS

Aduana Customs
Aeropuerto Airport
Avenida Avenue
Avión Airplane
Aviso Warning
Bus Bus
Cajero ATM, also called *cajero automático*
Calle Street
Cheques viajeros Traveler's checks
Correo Mail, or post office
Cuadra City block
Dinero or **plata** Money
Embajada Embassy
Embarque Boarding
Entrada Entrance
Equipaje Luggage
Este East
Frontera Border
Lancha or **bote** Boat
Norte North
Occidente West
Oeste West
Oriente East
Pasaporte Passport
Puerta de salida or **puerta de embarque** Boarding gate
Salida Exit
Sur South
Tarjeta de embarque Boarding pass
Vuelo Flight

EMERGENCY TERMS

¡Auxilio! Help!
Ambulancia Ambulance
Bomberos Fire brigade
Clínica Clinic or hospital
Doctor or **médico** Doctor
Emergencia Emergency
Enfermera Nurse
Enfermo/enferma Sick
Farmacia Pharmacy
Fuego or **incendio** Fire
Hospital Hospital
Ladrón Thief
Peligroso Dangerous
Policía Police
¡Váyase! Go away!

Index

See also Accommodations and Restaurant indexes, below.

General Index

A

B

C

D

E

S

T

U

V

W

X

Y

Z

Accommodations

Restaurants

NOTES

Before, During, or After your use of an EasyGuide... you'll want to consult

FROMMERS.COM

FROMMERS.COM IS KEPT UP-TO-DATE, WITH:

NEWS
The latest events (and deals) to affect your next vacation

BLOGS
Opinionated comments by our outspoken staff

FORUMS
Post your travel questions, get answers from other readers

SLIDESHOWS
On weekly-changing, practical but inspiring topics of travel

CONTESTS
Enabling you to win free trips

PODCASTS
Of our weekly, nationwide radio show

DESTINATIONS
Hundreds of cities, their hotels, restaurants and sights

TRIP IDEAS
Valuable, offbeat suggestions for your next vacation

***AND MUCH MORE!**

Smart travelers consult ***Frommers.com***